REFUGEES IN INTERN

Refugees in International Relations

Edited by

ALEXANDER BETTS AND GIL LOESCHER

UNIVERSITY PRESS

OXFORD
UNIVERSITY PRESS

Great Clarendon Street, Oxford OX2 6DP
United Kingdom

Oxford University Press is a department of the University of Oxford.
It furthers the University's objective of excellence in research, scholarship,
and education by publishing worldwide. Oxford is a registered trade mark of
Oxford University Press in the UK and in certain other countries

Reprinted 2013

British Library Cataloguing in Publication Data
Data available

Library of Congress Cataloging in Publication Data
Data available

ISBN 978-0-19-959562-4

To our students in Forced Migration Studies and International Relations

Foreword by Hedley Bull

Hedley Bull, the pre-eminent British scholar of international relations during the 1970s and early 1980s, wrote and lectured widely on international relations. His interests spanned practically the entire field of international politics at that time: nuclear strategy, development issues, ethics, justice and international affairs, the United Nations and international institutions, and world society, order, and authority.

While we were preparing the manuscript for this book, Claudena Skran, a former student of Bull's, brought to our attention a previously unpublished paper of his entitled 'Population and the Present World Structure' written some time in the early 1980s. She told us that during her time at Oxford, he showed an interest in the refugee issue in international relations and encouraged students to undertake research on the topic. For example, in 1983 he prepared a list of possible topics for graduate research students at Oxford. On that list was 'the refugee problem in world politics'. It seems he had become interested in refugees because of their connection to development topics and because of the African refugee issues at that time.

Claudena also recounted visiting Bull at his home in north Oxford in 1985 just a few weeks before he died. He was quite ill then, but was still seeing students and giving advice. Among the things he discussed with her was the conflict in Biafra. Claudena recounts that Bull told her that the Ibos had paid a very high price for order in that civil war. While she could not remember the rest of the conversation exactly, the meaning that she took away from their meeting was that refugees were connected to broader issues relating to order and justice and that forced migration was worthy of study and attention by both graduate students and advanced scholars in international relations.

Bull's paper 'Population and the Present World Structure' reflects his interest in development, injustice, and the inequality between the Global North and Global South.

The paper also discusses the significance of migration and refugee issues. In particular, Bull recognized the importance of strategic, political, and economic causes underlying most population movements. He lists as the primary causes: anti-colonial struggles, conflicts in newly independent states, ethnic cleansing, internal conflicts and foreign intervention, and human rights violations. Migration also occurs because of inequalities between the Global North and Global South with regard to economic conditions and opportunities, social well-being, and access to liberty and freedoms.

For those of us writing about refugees, migration, and international relations in the twenty-first century, Bull's analysis in this paper also remarkably foreshadows many pressing contemporary issues. He raises as concerns the mixing of refugee and migrant flows (today's so-called asylum–migration nexus), increasing state and popular concerns over sovereignty and control of borders, the growing fears and restrictionist attitudes and policies of the industrialized states, the growth and influence of diaspora networks, the importance of global information networks, and the spread of long-distance transport. These are among the key issues of concern to scholars, governments, and international organizations today.

We reproduce below a section of Hedley Bull's paper entitled 'Population and Migration' which we believe was written in the early 1980s, probably for presentation at a conference.

Alexander Betts and Gil Loescher

One way in which the pressure of population on the resources of poor countries may be relieved is through migration to places where resources are more plentiful. Some Third World governments seek to encourage migration of their surplus population to Western countries, or other areas of the Third World, such as the oil-producing states of the Middle East; some, like Mexico and Cuba, not merely demand entry into the United States for their surplus population, but speak as if entry were a moral right conferred by history or by present poverty. Such claims, moreover, do gain some recognition in those circles in the West in which there is sensitivity to global economic injustice.

From the point of view of poor sending countries, the benefits of this migration are clear enough. The migrants themselves escape from deprivation to a better standard of life, and, if they have gone voluntarily, show by their going at least that they themselves believe that they will benefit. Those that are left behind may benefit from remittances, from no longer having to provide sustenance for those that have departed, and from reduced burdens of welfare. The sending country as a whole will have lost actual or potential labour, and in the case of highly skilled migrants may suffer the effects of the 'brain-drain', but it may stand to gain from the export of unemployment, the acquisition of revenue and foreign exchange from remittances, and a safety-valve for the release of social tensions. The high growth rates following mass emigration from southern European countries in the postwar period and the advantages derived by South Asian countries from migration to the Gulf area in the 1970s provide illustrations of these benefits.

Emigration from Third World countries, which today has reached massive proportions, does not in itself necessarily contribute to the goal of a just geographical distribution of population in relation to available resources, nor imply any demand for it. The causes of emigration from Third World countries in the post-1945 era have been as much political as economic in nature: anti-colonial wars (as in Africa in the 1960s and 1970s), the oppression and sometimes expulsion of minorities by newly independent states dominated by particular ethnic groups (as of the Chinese in Indochina, Asians in east Africa, non-Amharic speaking peoples in Ethiopia), civil wars coinciding with foreign intervention (as in east Pakistan in 1971 or Afghanistan at present). The countries that have received the greater part of the migrants are not those of the West, nor indeed the oil-rich segment of the Third World, but other poor Third World countries (at present Sudan, Zaire, Somalia, Thailand, Pakistan, Jordan, Mexico). The mode of transport involved in much of this migration is by foot to a neighbouring state and is not a reflection of modern transport technology.

Nevertheless, the issues raised by these population movements almost invariably take us back to the perception that the present geographical distribution of population in relation to wealth, as between the West and the Third World, is an unjust one. First, there is in fact a great demand in Third World countries for migration into the rich Western countries, fed by the urge to escape from poverty, oppression, and instability in Third World countries, by the lure of economic opportunity, liberty, and security in the West, by the spread of information about the difference of conditions in different parts of the world, by the growth of social networks that facilitate the movement of migrants and their settlement in receiving countries, by the increasing ease and declining cost of long-distance transport, by the removal of barriers of racial and ethnic discrimination in the immigration and internal social policies of the receiving Western states, by the responsibilities recognized by Western countries towards migrants acknowledged to be 'refugees', by the bridgeheads established by those admitted as temporary migrants, and by the inability or unwillingness of Western governments to cope effectively with illegal migrants. The fact that the Western countries receive only a small proportion of total emigrants from the Third World reflects the barriers that exist to it, rather than lack of pressure for it.

Moreover, even where emigrants from Third World countries do not directly seek entry into them, the Western countries are often perceived—by themselves as well as others—to have special responsibilities in the matter, imposed by their wealth and resources. This is especially so when the migrants involved may be regarded as refugees. By long tradition, refugees are a privileged class of migrants (if in other respects under-privileged), in respect both of their claims of entry into receiving states (the so-called right of asylum) and of their claims to just treatment after entry. Where the concept of a refugee, as a person outside his or her homeland, and unable or unwilling to return to it because of persecution or well-founded fear of persecution, was once applied to small numbers of individuals, usually political activists, it has come in the twentieth century to be applied to millions of people, as in the mainly European upheavals of population brought about by the World Wars; today on some estimates there are as many as 16 million refugees in the world. Where earlier in this century the people involved were mainly European, today they are chiefly African and Asian. Where once the persecution in respect of which they were regarded as refugees was necessarily political in nature, today there is a tendency to speak also of economic persecution (meaning, moreover, not persecution by economic acts of state, but rather the mere existence of economic conditions that fail to satisfy standards of human rights). It has even been suggested that for a person to be regarded as a refugee it may be enough that in the sending country there was an absence of positive rights, and that no actual infringement of positive rights is presupposed.

The definition of a refugee (not only the legal definitions in the 1951 Refugee Convention and its 1967 Protocol, the 1969 Convention of the Organization of African Unity (OAU), or the U.S. Refugees Act of 1980, but more broadly what counts as a refugee in the public mind) has tended to expand. Along with refugees in the strict sense we have come to speak of *de facto* refugees, economic refugees, internal refugees, and crypto-refugees. The widening of the concept of the refugee reflects not only the extension of public sympathies in the rich countries to wider categories of Third World emigrants believed to have been denied rights of one kind or another, but also a certain artfulness on the part of the emigrants themselves: the availability of refugee services, it has been pointed out, tends itself to swell the number of refugees. The privileges enjoyed by designated refugees as recipients of special assistance, compared with other migrants in Third World countries and indeed with ordinary citizens of the latter, have sometimes generated resentment.

As the concept has expanded to embrace new categories of migrant, the responsibilities of the international community towards Third World emigrants are thought to have expanded also. The principal bearers of these responsibilities are the Western powers—the countries that have the strongest tradition of providing asylum to refugees, that have the most wealth in relation to their populations, that in some cases (the United States, Canada, Australia, New Zealand, South Africa) are accustomed to viewing themselves as countries of immigration, that harbour the chief international non-governmental organizations active in this field and provide the bulk of the funds for the intergovernmental organizations. The responsibilities they are thought to have, in particular, are to be generous themselves in providing asylum to refugees; to provide generous assistance to 'countries of first asylum', in cases where neither repatriation nor resettlement in third countries is an option; and to contribute *via* measures of development assistance or transfer of wealth to changing the conditions in the sending countries that have led to the exit of the refugees.

The response of the Western countries in accepting migrants from the Third World has not been such as to have made any great contribution to relieving the pressures of rapid population growth in poor countries. The number of migrants accepted by Western countries from the Third World in recent decades has constituted only a tiny proportion of world population growth in that period. While substantial numbers of 'refugees' have been accepted for resettlement, the most notable example being the million or so Indochinese refugees accepted in the United States, Canada, Australia, New Zealand, and European countries, the great majority of refugees in the world are in Third World countries. While the economic growth experienced by the European countries in the 1950s and 1960s was built in part on cheap immigrant labour from Third World (Commonwealth immigration in the United Kingdom, guest workers in West Germany and Switzerland), the advent of recession in the early 1970s led to the virtual cessation of legal immigration, apart from acceptance of refugees. In the United States, Canada, and Australia, the trend has also been towards restriction of entry. A new concern has developed with tougher measures to control illegal entry, 'interdiction of access', and measures to promote 'return migration'.

In the receiving countries, pressures to relax barriers to Third World immigration remain significant. There remains a demand for cheap labour, especially in relation to work which local labour is unwilling to perform, illustrated by employers lobbying for Hispanic immigration into the United States. Political or ideological factors still operate in favour of particular immigrant groups, for example, refugees from Cuba in the United States or from Vietnam in the United States and Australia. Campaigns are mounted by established ethnic groups, such as Indian and Pakistani communities in the United Kingdom, on behalf of particular individuals or families. In most Western countries, the diplomatic requirements of relationships with particular Third World countries operate to moderate what would otherwise be harsher policies (for Britain relations with Commonwealth countries, for Australia with ASEAN states, for the United States especially with Latin American countries).

But for the present, the pressures to keep the doors closed are stronger: recession and defence of jobs by organized labour; concern about the welfare burdens imposed by immigration; concern about the social consequences of large-scale immigration from Third World countries especially where (as in the case of Mexican immigration into the United States) the possibilities of successful integration are lessened by a 'temporary migrant mentality', historic anti-Americanism, linguistic separatism, and alienation resulting from repression of illegal immigration.

The flow of migration from poor to rich countries, and more generally, is impeded by the division of the world into sovereign states which claim the right and, by and large, possess the power to control the movement of persons across frontiers. The right of persons to exit from their own country, or indeed many countries, is asserted by liberal doctrine, proclaimed in the Universal Declaration of Human Rights and the 1975 Helsinki Final Act and is on the whole respected in practice by Western states, but in Communist states there is in practice no right of exit, and in many non-Communist states also exit is in practice a privilege rather than a right.

The right of entry into countries, by contrast, is universally denied as a legal right, even (indeed especially) by the Western democracies. It is generally recognized that a state has obligations to admit certain categories of persons, such as its own nationals, diplomatic agents, and representatives of international organizations (a special case is Israel's Law of Return, which confers a right of entry upon all Jews). There is widespread recognition, not only among Western but also among African and Latin American states of the rights of refugees to asylum, but this is not taken to entail a corresponding duty to admit them to one's own country, comparable with the positive duty that is generally recognized not to return refugees to the country from which they have fled (the duty of *non-refoulement*); and although some states are bound by regional treaties or by their own constitutions to grant rights of asylum, there is no general obligation in customary or treaty law requiring admission of refugees. The capacity to determine the entry of persons into one's territory, and thus the character of one's population, is a matter of the deepest sensitivity for most states: it touches not merely on the prosperity and security of a community, but also on its identity and control of its own destiny. For some peoples, like the Japanese, the price of preservation of social homogeneity is virtually to prohibit permanent immigration. Peoples which (like the Malays, the Fijians, or the Sinhalese under British rule) have lost control of their immigration policy have paid dearly for it, and it is among other things to control the entry of persons into their territory that peoples fight to gain or to defend their sovereign independence.

Migration is also impeded by failure of the sovereign state to accord equal treatment as between immigrants and established inhabitants or citizens, after they have gained entry. Again, liberal doctrine proclaims an ideal of the maximum interchangeability of civil rights as between one citizenship and another, and their conformity with wider standards of human rights. In practice, immigrants and other aliens are not accorded equality of rights with citizens, and indeed the rights of citizenship may vary between a core national group and peripheral groups, as in the British system of tiered gradations of nationality. Lying behind these distinctions in law in many countries there are social distinctions between natives or sons of the soil, and immigrant groups, even of long standing, and oppression of the latter by the former, which at its worst takes the form of mass expulsion or genocide.

It is sometimes suggested that the sovereign state's control of migration is breaking down in the face of a 'tidal wave' of pressure from poor countries. Perhaps the U.S.-Mexican or U.S.-Caribbean examples lend support to this idea, but these arise from special circumstances: the broad situation is that the Western countries, the most attractive targets of Third World immigration, and the countries most able to contribute to a global equilibrium between population and resources, have used their sovereign powers effectively to stem the flow.

Acknowledgements

This volume is based on a seminar series, 'Refugees in International Relations', that was hosted at the University of Oxford between October 2008 and March 2009. Like all seminar series, it represented a joint effort between convenors and the audiences and participants who provided critical and constructive feedback to contributors. The series was primarily run through the Global Migration Governance project. However, it was based upon collaboration with the Centre for International Studies (CIS), the Refugee Studies Centre (RSC), the Centre for Migration, Policy and Society (COMPAS), and the Global Economic Governance programme (GEG). The then directors of all of these centres—Andrew Hurrell, Roger Zetter, Nick Van Hear, and Ngaire Woods—offered important encouragement and advice relating to the conception and development of the project.

The audiences for the seminars were frequently diverse, drawing in participants from a range of disciplines and departments across Oxford. However, one important source of continuity was the class of the MSc in Forced Migration of 2008–9 who provided consistently probing questions and a wealth of feedback to authors. A range of our friends, students, and colleagues generously contributed their ideas and responses in ways that shaped the evolution of the project and the book's eventual content. Without being able to name everyone, we are grateful to Erik Abild, Matthew Albert, Oliver Bakewell, Richard Caplan, Erin Court, Sarah Cross, Sarah Deardorff, Jean-François Durieux, Matthew Gibney, Guy Goodwin-Gill, Jason Hart, Eva-Lotta Hedman, Wouter te Kloeze, Katy Long, Emanuela Paoletti, Dace Schlentz, Anna Schmidt, and Devi Sridhar. Claudena Skran played an important role, both in offering encouragement for the project and in locating and allowing us to use the piece by Hedley Bull which forms the basis of the foreword to the book. Mary Bull kindly provided permission to publish this piece.

The chapter by Patricia Owens is a revised version of an article which first appeared as 'Reclaiming "Bare Life"? Against Agamben on Refugees', International Relations, Vol. 23, no. 4 (2009), pp. 567–82. We are grateful to Sage for permission to reprint. The editors are indebted to Judith Benz-Schwartzburg, who generously designed and painted the striking and extremely appropriate image featured on the cover of the book. Esra Kaytaz worked tirelessly on organizational issues relating to the seminar series and the book. Miriam Bradley provided excellent research assistance in preparing the final manuscript for submission to OUP. We also gratefully acknowledge the financial support of the MacArthur Foundation which, through the Global Migration Governance project, provided financial support for the seminar series. Last, but not least, we are thankful to Dominic Byatt at OUP for nurturing this project from inception to publication.

Contents

About the Contributors

Michael Barnett is the Harold Stassen Chair of International Relations at the Humphrey Institute of Public Affairs and Professor of political science at the University of Minnesota. His books include *Security Communities* (co-edited with Emanuel Adler, Cambridge University Press, 1998); *Eyewitness to a Genocide: The United Nations and Rwanda* (Cornell University Press, 2002); *Rules for the World: International Organizations in World Politics* (with Martha Finnemore, Cornell University Press, 2004); and *Humanitarianism in Question: Politics, Power, and Ethics* (co-edited with Tom Weiss, Cornell University Press, 2008). His articles have appeared in *International Organization, International Studies Quarterly, European Journal of International Relations,* and *World Politics.*

Sophia Benz is a lecturer and doctoral student at the Institute of Political Science, Department of International Relations, Peace and Conflict Research at the University of Tübingen, Germany and a Visiting Research Scholar at the Department of International and Area Studies/Peace and Conflict Studies at the University of California at Berkeley, USA (2007–9). Her research focuses on the causes, duration, and consequences of non-state warfare (the concept of 'New Wars').

Alexander Betts is Hedley Bull Research Fellow in International Relations at the University of Oxford, where he is also Director of the MacArthur Foundation-funded Global Migration Governance Project. His research focuses on the international politics of migration and refugee protection, and his recent books include *Protection by Persuasion: International Cooperation in the Refugee Regime* (Cornell University Press, 2009), *Forced Migration and Global Politics* (Wiley-Blackwell, 2009), and *UNHCR: The Politics and Practice of Refugee Protection into the Twenty-First Century* (with Gil Loescher and James Milner, Routledge 2008).

Chris Brown is Professor of International Relations at the London School of Economics. He is the author of numerous articles in international political theory and of *Sovereignty, Rights and Justice* (2002), *International Relations Theory: New Normative Approaches* (1992), editor of *Political Restructuring in Europe: Ethical Perspectives* (1994), and co-editor of *International Relations in Political Thought: Texts from the Greeks to the First World War* (2002). His textbook *Understanding International Relations* (4th edition 2009) has been translated into Arabic, Turkish, and Chinese. A collection of his essays, *Practical Judgement and International Relations: Essays in International Political Theory* will appear in 2010.

Sarah Collinson is a Research Fellow with the Humanitarian Policy Group at the Overseas Development Institute. Her recent work encompasses humanitarian responses to internal displacement, livelihoods and the political economy of conflict, principles of humanitarian action, and the evolving international 'stabilization' agenda. She has previously taught at the Refugee Studies Centre, and has held senior research and policy positions at Chatham House and ActionAid. She has published widely, including co-authorship of UNHCR's *The State of the World's Refugees*, and co-authorship of a recent ODI HPG Report, *Realising Protection: the Uncertain Benefits of Civilian, Refugee and IDP Status* (2009).

Andreas Hasenclever is Professor of International Relations at the Eberhard Karls University of Tuebingen. His chief research interests are in the field of peace and conflict studies with particular reference to the analysis of democratic peace, regime analysis, and the impact of religious traditions on political conflicts. On these topics, he has authored numerous articles and books. His book *Macht der Moral in der internationalen Politik* (Campus 2001) was awarded the Helmuth-James-von-Moltke-Preis 2003 endowed by the German Society for Military Law and the Law of War.

Anne Hammerstad is Lecturer in International Relations at the University of Kent. Her DPhil on the UNHCR and the security dimensions of refugee movements won the 2003 BISA thesis prize. She is currently expanding her research in this field and is working on a book for Oxford University Press entitled *The Rise of a Global Security Actor: the UNHCR from Northern Iraq to Darfur.* Before moving to Kent she was a Senior Researcher at the South African Institute of International Affairs (SAIIA), based in Johannesburg, and a Research and Teaching Fellow at Royal Holloway, University of London. She was recently awarded a three year ESRC fellowship to study the securitization of refugees in South Africa and the United Kingdom.

Andrew Hurrell is Montague Burton Professor of International Relations at the University of Oxford. His research interests focus on the 'International Society' approach pioneered by Hedley Bull, and he has published on a range of international issues, including international institutions, authority, and legitimacy, and the role of emerging regional powers in world politics. His publications include *Inequality, Globalization and World Politics* (co-edited with Ngaire Woods, Oxford University Press, 1999), *Order and Justice in International Relations* (co-edited with Rosemary Foot and John Gaddis,

Oxford University Press, 2003), and *On Global Order: Power, Values and the Constitution of International Society* (Oxford University Press, 2007).

Jennifer Hyndman is Professor at the Centre for Refugee Studies at York University in Toronto, Canada. Her research spans the continuum of forced migration, from conflict zones to refugee resettlement in North America. Her work attends to issues of displacement, security, and the geopolitics of asylum. She is the author of the book *Managing Displacement: Refugees and the Politics of Humanitarianism* (University of Minnesota Press, 2000) and co-editor of *Sites of Violence: Gender and Conflict Zones* (University of California Press, 2004). A new monograph underway, *Dual Disasters*, explores the impact of the 2004 tsunami on extant conflicts in Sri Lanka and Aceh, Indonesia.

Gil Loescher is Visiting Professor at the Refugee Studies Centre, University of Oxford. He is Emeritus Professor of International Relations at the University of Notre Dame and has held visiting positions at Princeton University, LSE, and the Department of Humanitarian Affairs at the US State Department in Washington, DC. He has published numerous works on refugees, human rights, and conflict and security, including *UNHCR in World Politics: A Perilous Path* (Oxford University Press, 2001), *UNHCR: The Politics and Practice of Refugee Protection into the Twenty-First Century* (Routledge, 2008), and *Protracted Refugee Situations: Politics, Human Rights and Security Dimensions* (United Nations University Press, 2008).

James Milner is Assistant Professor of Political Science at Carleton University. He was previously an SSHRC Postdoctoral Fellow at the Munk Centre for International Studies, University of Toronto and has worked as a Consultant for the United Nations High Commissioner for Refugees (UNHCR) in India, Cameroon, Guinea, and its Geneva Headquarters. He is the author of *Refugees, the State and the Politics of Asylum in Africa* (Palgrave Macmillan, 2009, co-author of *UNHCR: The Politics and Practice of Refugee Protection into the Twenty-First Century* (Routledge, 2008), and co-editor of *Protracted Refugee Situations: Political, Human Rights and Security Implications* (United Nations University Press, 2008).

Patricia Owens is Senior Lecturer in the Department of Politics, Queen Mary, University of London and Senior Research Associate in the Leverhulme Programme on the Changing Character of War, University of Oxford. She is the author of *Between War and Politics: International Relations and the Thought of Hannah Arendt* (Oxford: Oxford University Press, 2007) and *War, Politics and Security* (Polity, forthcoming). She has held research positions at Princeton, Aberystwyth, UC-Berkeley, University of Southern California, and Oxford.

Sir Adam Roberts is President of the British Academy. He is also Senior Research Fellow, Department of Politics and International Relations, Oxford University, and Emeritus Fellow of Balliol College, Oxford. He was Montague Burton Professor of International Relations at Oxford University, 1986–2007. His books include (ed. with Vaughan Lowe, Jennifer Welsh, and Dominik Zaum) *The United Nations Security Council and War: The Evolution of Thought and Practice since 1945* (Oxford University Press, 2008) and (ed. with Timothy Garton Ash) *Civil Resistance and Power Politics: The Experience of Non-violent Action from Gandhi to the Present* (Oxford University Press, 2009).

Jack L. Snyder is the Robert and Renée Belfer Professor of International Relations in the political science department and the Saltzman Institute of War and Peace Studies at Columbia University. His books include *Electing to Fight: Why Emerging Democracies Go to War* (MIT Press, 2005), co-authored with Edward D. Mansfield; *From Voting to Violence: Democratization and Nationalist Conflict* (Norton Books, 2000) and *Myths of Empire: Domestic Politics and International Ambition* (Cornell University Press, 1991). His articles on such topics as democratization and war ('Prone to Violence: The Paradox of the Democratic Peace', *The National Interest*, winter 2005–6), imperial overstretch, war crimes tribunals versus amnesties as strategies for preventing atrocities, international relations theory after 11 September, and anarchy and culture have appeared in *Foreign Affairs*, *Foreign Policy*, and academic journals.

Dominik Zaum is Reader in International Relations at the University of Reading. He has written widely on post-conflict statebuilding and on the United Nations, most notably *The Sovereignty Paradox: The Norms and Politics of International Statebuilding* (Oxford University Press, 2007); *The United Nations Security Council and War: The Evolution of Thought and Practice since 1945* (Oxford University Press, 2008—co-edited with Vaughan Lowe, Adam Roberts, and Jennifer Welsh); and *Selective Security: War and the United Nations Security Council since 1945* (Routledge and the IISS, 2008).

List of Figures

List of Tables

List of Abbreviations

ANC	African National Congress
ASEAN	Association of Southeast Asian Nations
AU	African Union
CIREFCA	International Conference on Central American Refugees
CPA	Comprehensive Plan of Action
CRPC	Commission on Real Property Claims of Refugees and Displaced Persons (Bosnia)
DIDP	Development-Induced Displaced Person
DoC	Drivers of Change
DRC	Democratic Republic of Congo
EC	European Commission
ECOSOC	(United Nations) Economic and Social Council
EEC	European Economic Community
ExCom	(UNHCR) Executive Committee
GAD	Gender and Development
GCIM	Global Commission on International Migration
GFMD	Global Forum on Migration and Development
HPCC	Housing and Property Claims Commission (Kosovo)
HPD	Housing and Property Directorate (Kosovo)
IASC	Inter-Agency Standing Committee
ICARA	International Conference on Assistance to Refugees in Africa
ICRC	International Committee of the Red Cross
IDMC	Internal Displacement Monitoring Centre
IDP	Internally Displaced Person
ILO	International Labour Organization
IOM	International Organization for Migration
IPE	International Political Economy
IR	International Relations
ISM	Irregular Secondary Movements
KFOR	Kosovo Force
LICUS	Low-Income Countries Under Stress

LPDR	Lao People's Democratic Republic
MICIVH	(UN/OAS) International Civilian Mission in Haiti
MNF	Multinational Force
MPF	Multinational Protection Force
MSF	Médecins Sans Frontières
NATO	North Atlantic Treaty Organization
NGO	Non-governmental Organization
OAS	Organization of American States
OAU	Organization of African Unity
OCHA	Office for the Coordination of Humanitarian Affairs
OSCE	Organization for Security and Co-operation in Europe
PBC	(United Nations) Peacebuilding Commission
PBF	Peacebuilding Fund
PBSO	Peacebuilding Support Office
PCWG	Protection Cluster Working Group
PEC	Programme of Economic Cooperation
PLIP	Property Law Implementation Plan (Bosnia)
RAD	Refugee Aid and Development
RPF	Rwandan Patriotic Front
RRTF	Reconstruction and Returns Task Force (Bosnia)
SGBV	Sexual and Gender-Based Violence
SRV	Socialist Republic of Vietnam
TDA	Targeting Development Assistance
UN HABITAT	United Nations Human Settlements Programme
UN.GIFT	United Nations Global Initiative to Fight Human Trafficking
UNAMA	United Nations Assistance Mission to Afghanistan
UNAMIR	United Nations Assistance Mission for Rwanda
UNAMSIL	United Nations Mission in Sierra Leone
UNDP	United Nations Development Programme
UNESCO	United Nations Educational, Scientific and Cultural Organization
UNFPA	United Nations Population Fund
UNGA	United Nations General Assembly
UNGCI	United Nations Guards Contingent in Iraq
UNHCR	Office of the United Nations High Commissioner for Refugees

UNIFEM	United Nations Development Fund for Women
UNITAF	Unified Task Force (Somalia)
UNITAR	United Nations Institute for Training and Research
UNMIH	United Nations Mission in Haiti
UNMIK	United Nations Interim Administration Mission in Kosovo
UNODC	United Nations Office on Drugs and Crime
UNOSOM	UN Operation in Somalia
UNPROFOR	United Nations Protection Force (in the former Yugoslavia)
UNRWA	United Nations Relief and Works Agency for Palestine Refugees in the Near East
UNSG	United Nations Secretary-General
UNTAET	United Nations Transitional Administration in East Timor
WAD	Women and Development
WFP	World Food Programme
WID	Women in Development

1

Refugees in International Relations

Alexander Betts and Gil Loescher

Refugees are people who cross international borders in order to flee human rights abuses and conflict. Refugees are prima facie evidence of human rights violations and vulnerability. People who are persecuted and deprived of their homes and communities and means of livelihood are frequently forced to flee across the borders of their home countries and seek safety abroad. Historically, wherever states have persecuted their own populations or there have been wars, people have left their country of origin. From the Holocaust to the proxy conflicts of the Cold War, to the internal conflicts in the aftermath of the Cold War, to the occupations in Afghanistan and Iraq in the context of the 'War on Terror', refugees have emerged from just about every significant historical conflict or despotic regime. Because refugees find themselves in a situation in which their own government is unable or unwilling to ensure their physical safety and most fundamental human rights, they are forced to seek protection from the international community. Ensuring that refugees receive safety and access to their rights, livelihoods, and the possibility to be reintegrated into their country of origin or another state is therefore an important human rights issue.

However, refugees are more than simply a human rights issue. Refugee movements are also an inherent part of international politics. The 'figure of the refugee' is an integral part of the international system, symbolizing the failure of the state-citizen-territory relationship assumed by the state system to seamlessly ensure international order and justice (Haddad 2008). The causes, consequences, and responses to refugees are all closely intertwined with world politics. The causes of refugee movements are underpinned by conflict, state failure, and the inequalities of international political economy. The consequences of movements have been associated with security, the spread of conflict, terrorism, and transnationalism. Therefore, responding to refugees represents a challenge to world order and justice and to the facilitation of international cooperation.

At virtually every significant juncture in the evolution and development of the international system, the refugee has been a central figure. In Hannah Arendt's terms, refugees have been a 'vanguard of their peoples', not only witnessing but also being an integral aspect of the changing architecture of world politics. From the creation of the state system at the Peace of Westphalia in 1648, to the consolidation of the European state through the revolutions and state unifications of the nineteenth century, to the changing balance of power between the late nineteenth century and the two world wars, to the decolonization and the creation of the post-Second World War international society, to the bipolarity of the Cold War, to the post-Cold War era, to globalization, and to 9/11 and the emergence of new transnational threats linked to terrorism and the environment, refugees have been a central feature of world politics. Not only have refugees been a consequence of developments in the international system but they have also often had an important independent causal influence on the trajectory of world politics.

As world politics has changed so too the common understanding of who exactly is a 'refugee' has changed. Prior to the Peace of Westphalia of 1648 and in the early modern state system, refugees were seen in broad terms, implying people seeking sanctuary from political or religious persecution or conflict. In the formal refugee regime of the twentieth century, a legal definition of a refugee was defined in the 1951 Refugee Convention as someone who is outside his or her country of origin as a result of a well-founded fear of persecution. Since the early 1950s, however, the term 'refugee' has been widened in practice to include a variety of people in diverse situations who need protection and assistance. The most notable of these expansions occurred at the regional level, particularly in Africa in the 1960s and in Central America in the 1980s. Moreover, from the end of the twentieth century, the narrow, legal definition contained in the 1951 Refugee Convention has been challenged further and there has been an increasing focus on other groups of forced migrants in 'refugee-like' situations. Within policy circles, the Office of the United Nations High Commissioner for Refugees (UNHCR)'s mandate has expanded to address a broader range of 'people of concern'. This has involved a broadening to include people fleeing human rights violations not subsumed under persecution, notably survival migrants fleeing environmental disaster, environmental collapse, and state fragility. It has also involved a deepening, to include 'internally displaced people' (IDPs), who like refugees, flee conflict and persecution, but remain in their country of origin. There have also been changes in the way academia looks at refugee issues. For example, in recent years, Refugee Studies has expanded to become Forced Migration Studies.

Even if one expands from the narrow legal definition of a refugee, other aspects of forced migration—such as internal displacement, statelessness, and environmental displacement—also have an inextricable relationship to world politics. Whether the focus is on the narrow legal definition of a refugee or is broadened and deepened to include other categories of forced migration, the common conceptual feature that connects these areas remains the unwillingness or inability of the country of origin to ensure the protection of its own citizens, and hence the need for international protection. All forms of forced migration go to the core of questions relating to the nature of state sovereignty, and invite a host of other questions relating to international cooperation, security, and the international political economy.

Despite the political and international nature of forced migration, there has been surprisingly little work within International Relations (IR) on refugees. The discipline of IR has expanded its empirical focus beyond analysing war and peace and issues relating to state and military security to address a range of areas such as the global economy, environment, human rights, and international trade. However, it has paid comparatively little attention to the international politics of forced migration. Despite a strong tradition of looking at refugees within international political history, most work on refugees in world politics has been based on archival research and has not drawn fully upon the concepts offered by IR. Where conceptual and theoretical work has emerged, it has been in relatively isolated pockets, often marginalized from the mainstream of IR.

The pioneering work that has taken place that attempts to 'bridge the divide' between IR and forced migration suggests that the study of forced migration has enormous relevance for IR. It touches upon issues relating to international cooperation, globalization, human rights, international organizations, regime complexity, the role of non-state actors, regionalism, North–South relations, and security. Therefore, making the study of forced migration part of the mainstream study of IR has a potentially wide-ranging theoretical contribution to make to the discipline.

Furthermore, the discipline of Forced Migration Studies has rarely drawn upon the tools offered by International Relations to inform its analysis. Rather Forced Migration Studies has predominantly drawn upon other disciplines such as anthropology, sociology, geography, and law to analyse the causes and consequences of human displacement. It has generally offered a 'bottom-up' perspective which places displaced people at the centre of its analysis. Although exploring the perspective of forced migrants is crucial, and should not be neglected, there is also a need for a 'top-down' level of analysis in order to understand the macro-level structures that influence states' and other international actors' responses to forced migration. This is crucial because it is often the choices of states and other political actors that determine outcomes for the displaced. Bringing the tools of IR into the field of Forced Migration Studies therefore has an important contribution to make to the study and practice of forced migration.

Frustrated by the relative marginalization of refugees from the dominant scholarship within the discipline, the editors of this volume decided to invite some of the most high profile IR scholars in Europe and North America to consider the relevance of their wider scholarship for forced migration and to present their ideas as part of a lecture series. The series was held at the University of Oxford and jointly convened by the Department of Politics and IR and the Refugee Studies Centre between October 2008 and March 2009. The invited academics were drawn from a range of theoretical perspectives within IR—realism, liberal institutionalism, the English School, constructivism, critical theory, feminist theory, and normative and ethical approaches. Their work encompasses a range of conceptual areas, for example, power, international cooperation, security, international institutions, and international political economy. They also approach forced migration from a range of empirical angles, such as humanitarian assistance, intervention, peacebuilding, post-conflict reconstruction and state-building, conflict, durable solutions, and protection.

Some of the invited speakers in the lecture series had little background in refugees and forced migration, others had considerable expertise, and others fell somewhere in between having occasionally worked on related issues. The purpose of the lecture series was to demonstrate the value of the empirical area for testing and developing concepts in IR; to generate new ideas of potential benefit to both theory and practice; to influence and inspire future research on forced migration within IR; to highlight the value of IR's central concepts for Forced Migration Studies; and to make IR scholars aware of the myriad ways in which refugees and forced migration are intertwined with fundamental aspects of world politics. In other words, the series aimed to mainstream refugees *in* IR.

The outcome of the lecture series is this book. The book revisits an earlier edited Oxford University Press volume, *Refugees and International Relations*, edited by Gil Loescher and Laila Monahan in 1989. That volume mainly brought together authors within the field of refugee studies. Written twenty years ago, at the end of the Cold War, it addressed refugees in a very different international system and adopted an approach that was more historical and empirical, and less conceptual, than the approach adopted by this book. It nevertheless offers an important precedent on which this volume builds. The introduction to the current volume serves to contextualize the relationship between refugees and IR. The introduction draws heavily upon the textbook *Forced Migration and Global Politics* by Alexander Betts, published in 2009, which this edited volume is intended to complement.

REFUGEES IN WORLD POLITICS

The term 'refugee' means different things in different contexts. Its narrow legal definition is different from its vernacular use in everyday parlance. Under international law a refugee is a person who 'owing to a well-founded fear of persecution ... is outside of his or her country of nationality'. In that sense refugees are defined by a number of aspects—notably being outside the country of origin and fleeing persecution. In the vernacular, the term 'refugee' is often much broader. It is popularly seen by the media and the public as incorporating people fleeing a range of causes including authoritarian regimes; conflict; human rights violations; large-scale development projects; environmental disasters resulting from hurricanes, tsunamis, and climate change; and as including uprooted people who do not cross an international border but are instead displaced within their country of origin.

This volume recognizes the importance of preserving the narrow focus of the legal definition. However, within its focus on refugees in IR, it also includes analysis of other areas of forced migration that comprise the broader vernacular understanding of 'refugees'. The focus of both academic researchers and policy practitioners in forced migration now goes beyond those people who cross an international border fleeing individualized persecution to include those fleeing other significant human rights violations (civil, political, economic, social, and cultural) to which they have no domestic remedy. Meanwhile, the focus has been deepened to recognize that people need not necessarily cross an international border to be in a refugee-like situation, and that IDPs have particular protection needs.

The 2x2 matrix in Table 1 illustrates the way in which the legal definition of a refugee has been broadened and deepened, and highlights the labels that have been used to capture these broader categories of vernacular 'refugees'. The horizontal axis illustrates the breadth of forced migration. The heading 'narrow' refers to flight on the basis of persecution or conflict, while the heading 'broad' refers to flight on the basis of any significant threat to that person's fundamental rights such as basic subsistence, basic security, or basic liberty (Shacknove 1985; Shue 1980). The vertical axis illustrates whether the person has crossed an international border or not. Within each box are different categories. The top left designates the narrow legal definition of a

Table 1 Typology of the vernacular 'refugee'

	Narrow	Broad
Outside country	1951 Refugee Convention	Survival Migrant
Within country	Conflict-induced IDP	Guiding Principles IDP

refugee under the 1951 Refugee Convention. The top right highlights the notion of 'survival migration' as people who flee an existential threat to which they have no domestic remedy, whether as a result of conflict and persecution or other causes not covered by the 1951 Convention such as environmental disaster, livelihoods failure, or state collapse (Betts and Kaytaz 2009). The bottom left highlights the category of conflict-induced IDPs. The bottom right highlights the broader notion of IDPs enshrined within the UN Guiding Principles on Internal Displacement, which includes not only conflict-induced displacement but also, for example, people displaced by 'man-made or natural disaster' (Phuong 2004; Weiss and Korn 2006).

Conceptually, what connects these categories of people is that the assumed relationship between state and citizen is likely to have broken down. Implicit to IR's understanding of the normative basis of the state system is the idea that all people have a state that is responsible for ensuring their most basic rights and protection (Carr 1946; Hobbes 1914; Locke 1924; Morgenthau 1948). The most salient characteristic which connects different categories of the vernacular 'refugee' is not geographical movement *per se* but rather the inability or unwillingness of the country of origin to ensure a citizen's protection. In the absence of the ability or willingness of the country of origin to provide protection, the rights of those people are only likely to be met when another state or collection of states is willing to stand-in as the substitute provider of rights—whether temporarily or permanently.

Given these characteristics, refugees have a historically symbiotic relationship to the development and evolution of the international system (Haddad 2008). Although refuge and sanctuary have been provided by city states and religious groups throughout history, the basis of the refugee regime emerged alongside the creation and consolidation of the modern state system. The institution of refugee protection parallels the emergence and evolution of the international system. In many ways, changes in how states have collectively responded to refugees serve as a barometer of wider change in the state system.

The origins of the modern refugee regime can be found within the Peace of Westphalia, which is also widely recognized as the starting point of the modern European state system (Haddad 2008). The Peace incorporated the notion of *jus emigrandi*, the idea that with the creation of states citizens should have the right to leave as a means of becoming a member of another state. This idea was most notably applied when Louis VIV revoked the Edict of Nantes in 1685 and proclaimed Protestantism to be illegal, triggering the flight of the Huguenots (French Calvinists). After this, an estimated 200,000 to 1 million Huguenots fled to neighbouring Protestant countries such as England, the Netherlands, Switzerland, Norway, Denmark, and Prussia (Haddad 2008: 51–4; Orchard 2009).

During the eighteenth and the nineteenth centuries, refugee creation and protection was an integral part of the state-building process within Europe. Refugees were a product of processes of state consolidation, with émigrés fleeing revolutions in France between 1789 and 1815, and elsewhere in Europe such as in Italy and Poland in 1848. The creation of unified nation states in Italy, Germany, and France led to significant refugee populations leaving those newly created states (Haddad 2008: 55–6).

Furthermore, the provision of protection to refugees was an integral part of European state-building. As Haddad (2008) argues, the creation of the Alien Acts, establishing the state as the arbiter of the right of entry on to the territory of the state, alongside the discretionary provision of protection to certain groups of exiles, was part of the nation-building process. Providing protection offered a means to constitute the nation state by defining the 'citizen' in opposition to the foreign 'other', consolidating national identity and the authority of statist governance (Biersteker and Weber 1996).

Refugees were also an integral part of the changing balance of power in the context of the formation, consolidation, and expansion of the modern state system in the early part of the twentieth century. In Europe, the Hapsburg, Romanov, Ottoman, and Prussian empires all succumbed to the pressures and conflicts that accompanied the transition from imperial social and political orders to successor nation states. As the First World War accelerated the dismantling of these multi-ethnic empires into nation states, masses of people were excluded from citizenship in the new national states on the grounds of language, location, ethnicity, or religious affiliation. Consequently, there arose the need for an international institutional framework to restore international order and to ensure that the displaced would be reintegrated into the changed international system (Hobsbawm 1990).

The reconfiguration of the European balance of power in the aftermath of the First World War gave rise to the creation of an Inter-War refugee regime under the League of Nations between 1921 and 1939. With the collapse of empires and the creation of new states, Russians leaving the Russian Revolution, Armenians fleeing genocide, and Jews fleeing persecution across Europe, for example, left their countries of origin as refugees and stateless people

(Marrus 1985; Simpson 1938; Skran 1995). Although relatively informal and highly dependent on the ad hoc and discretionary contributions of individual states, the inter-war refugee regime nevertheless set out structured international rules to ensure the protection of refugees. Its most significant innovation was the Nansen Passports designed in 1922 which were internationally recognized identity cards entitling hundreds of thousands of stateless people and refugees to travel to a country that would allow them to integrate (Loescher et al. 2008).

Following the Second World War, the basis of the current international refugee regime was created in order to protect and find solution for those displaced in Europe by the War (Loescher 2001). The regime set out a more formally institutionalized and multilateral basis for international cooperation than its inter-war predecessor. It was based on two core elements: a treaty and an international organization. The 1951 Convention on the Status of Refugees set out the definition of a refugee and the rights to which refugees would be entitled. Meanwhile, the 1950 Statute of the Office of the UNHCR formally established the UNHCR, and gave it supervisory responsibility for states' implementation of the 1951 Convention (Loescher et al. 2008).

The *Travaux Preparatoires* for the 1951 Convention reveal that the negotiating states had a dual concern that guided their negotiation of the regime. On the one hand, they were concerned with international order. Ensuring that Europe's refugees were afforded protection and promptly reintegrated within states was seen as a means of contributing to stability and security in post-Second World War Europe. On the other hand, states were also concerned with justice. There was widespread acknowledgement of the significant and unprecedented human consequences of the Second World War and establishing a refugee regime was seen as a way of promoting values of human rights within the context of the emerging United Nations system. A refugee regime, it was believed, would ensure that all states made a collective contribution to overcoming what was a common humanitarian and political problem (Betts 2009).

The geographical scope of the refugee regime was initially confined to Europe. It was only in 1967, and with the liberation of former colonies in much of the developing world and the expansion of international society (Bull and Watson 1984; Keene 2002), that the scope of the refugee regime and UNHCR's work was expanded to the rest of the world. As had been the case during the process of state formation in Europe, new groups of refugees resulted from the creation and consolidation of new post-colonial states elsewhere in the world. The dissolution of European colonial rule in the Global South and the fragmentation of newly independent states led to significant refugee movements across the developing world, and hence the need for a global refugee regime.

Throughout the past half century, the major trends in the causes and consequences of, and responses to, refugee protection have continued to parallel, and been an integral part of, the main developments in the international system. During the Cold War, refugee protection became an instrument of East–West rivalry within the bipolar world. The United States, in particular, offered sanctuary and protection to anyone fleeing the Communist world, using their flight as a symbolic means to discredit the Soviet Union. The United States and the USSR also selectively supported different groups in exile and so-called refugee warriors as part of their strategy for contesting the proxy conflicts of the developing world. Refugees thereby became pawns in the superpower rivalry of the Cold War (Loescher 2001; Stedman and Tanner 2003; Zolberg et al. 1989).

While bipolarity led to generosity towards exiles from the Communist world, globalization and increasing opportunities for South–North spontaneous arrival asylum-seeking from the 1980s dramatically changed the nature of refugee protection. Where once there had been little opportunity for transcontinental movement by people from the developing world, globalization contributed to people from conflicts and human rights abusing regimes travelling to developed countries to seek asylum. In particular, movements between Africa and Europe, and Latin America and North America, overburdened and fundamentally changed the asylum policies of the North, leading to an emerging set of restrictive practices and border control measures (Crisp 2003).

The post-Cold War era—and the so-called new wars to which it has given rise—led to a range of complex emergencies and humanitarian crises during the 1990s (Duffield 2001; Kaldor 1999). Internal conflicts in the Balkans, the Caucuses, and Sub-Saharan Africa led to significant displacement of people both within their country of origin and across borders. The response by the international community was twofold. Firstly, it gave rise to the desire to prevent possible refugee flows being used as a justification for international intervention. In both the aftermath of the first Gulf War and in the break-up of the Former Yugoslavia, refugee flows were the basis on which two predominantly internal conflicts were identified as a 'threat to international peace and security' under Chapter VII of the UN Charter (Loescher 2001). Secondly, the international response to forced migration during this period contributed to a broadening of international attention from refugees to IDPs. In Iraq, Somalia, Bosnia, Kosovo, and Chechnya, for example, IDP protection was used as a means to ensure the protection of people before they needed to cross an international border (Dubernet 2001; Weiss and Korn 2006). This shift in attention, and the desire to contain 'potential refugees', culminated in the development of a new normative and institutional framework.

In 1998, the so-called Guiding Principles on Internal Displacement were developed as a 'soft law' consolidation of international human rights and international humanitarian law's application to the situation of IDPs. Subsequently, a significant proportion of the responsibility for IDP protection was devolved to UNHCR (Loescher et al. 2008).

As we embark on the twenty-first century, refugees are at the heart of many of the major contemporary developments in world politics. The new security agenda in the post 9/11 world has had a major focus on asylum and refugee protection. Concerned with the threat of transnational terrorism, states have developed strong border regimes to control and manage international migration. These measures have limited refugees' ability to seek asylum in both North and South. Furthermore, states have identified refugee camps—for Afghans, Palestinians, and Somalis, for example—as being located at the frontline of the so-called War on Terror. Those displaced by major conflicts and caught in protracted refugee situations are now recognized by many governments as potential sources of radicalization and recruitment by Islamic terrorist organizations (Juma and Kagwanja 2008). Refugees are also one part of the broader and increasingly challenging issue of international migration and the growing significance of transnationalism. The emergence of diaspora groups and a range of transnational networks, of which refugees comprise a part, challenge the state system and require us to expand our understanding of interstate relations.

Refugees are also a significant part of the emerging international focus on state fragility. Within the context of international occupation, and state-building in states such as Iraq and Afghanistan, and the discourse on 'fragile' and 'failed states' in countries like Somalia, refugees are being recognized by academics and policy-makers as an important element of successful post-conflict reconstruction and peace-building. The repatriation, reintegration, and rehabilitation of refugees and IDPs within countries of origin has been increasingly acknowledged by development agencies such as the World Bank to be an important aspect of how the international community engages with post-conflict settings (Milner 2009).

As climate change emerges as one of the most significant global issues of the twenty-first century, so states are beginning to broaden how they understand refugee protection. The threat of large-scale human displacement related to environmental change has led to an understanding that the international protection regime will need to go beyond the protection of those displaced by conflict and persecution (Boano et al. 2008; Myers 1997; Piguet 2008).

Attributing displacement directly to environmental change, let alone climate change, is extremely challenging except in the most extreme situations of rapid onset disasters or 'sinking islands'. Nevertheless, it is clear that environmental change will, in its interaction with livelihood failure and state fragility, contribute to human displacement within countries and across borders as 'survival migrants' (Betts and Kaytaz 2009). This trend, and the international institutional response that it will require, again serves to illustrate how refugees will remain at the core of the most salient issues in world politics for the foreseeable future.

REFUGEES IN INTERNATIONAL RELATIONS

The concepts that have emerged from IR have great relevance for understanding the relationship between refugees and world politics. They can shed light on the relationships that exist between broader global political trends, on the one hand, and the causes and consequences of forced migration, on the other hand. They can also contribute to explaining the behaviour of states and other actors towards forced migration and so offer insights into the conditions under which forced migration can be prevented and its most serious human consequences mitigated.

However, given the important relationship between forced migration and world politics, there has been little systematic attempt either from within IR or Forced Migration Studies to explore what the central concepts within IR might offer to the study of forced migration. Instead, only relatively isolated pockets of theoretically informed literature have emerged on the international politics of forced migration. Some have emerged from within Forced Migration; some from within IR. Depending on which side of this disciplinary fence they have emerged from, the work has had a different character and a different purpose. The work within Forced Migration Studies has used IR theory to get insights for the practice of forced migration; the work within IR has used the empirical area to develop IR theory. However, the two subdisciplines have not been systematically integrated to explore the relevance that integrating the concepts of IR theory with the empirical terrain of forced migration can offer both areas.

The most prominent body of academic work on the international politics of forced migration is within the area of international political history (Gordenker 1987; Loescher 2001; Skran 1995; Zolberg et al. 1989). For example, in the early 1990s, the University of Lund undertook an international history project to examine the emergence of the post-Second World War refugee regime. Recently, the Graduate Institute in Geneva initiated a new archive-based project on international refugee policy during the Cold War. This research lays the empirical groundwork for work on IR and refugees. It offers insights into the emergence and development of the international refugee regime and interaction with the changing international political context. The majority of this work has been archival and strongly empirical, and so has not generally applied the conceptual and theoretical developments of IR. There has also been some pioneering conceptual work on the politics of forced migration. However, it has not been systematic or coherent in examining either the potential of IR for Forced Migration Studies or the significance of the refugee issue for IR. Nor has the study of refugees and forced migration become a mainstream part of IR. In that sense the scope for conceptual and theoretical debates to draw upon and be shaped by the area of forced migration has yet to reach its full potential.

Nevertheless, the isolated pockets of pioneering work that have attempted to bridge the divide between Forced Migration Studies and IR offer ample evidence that it is an enterprise that can be immensely fruitful both for improving our understanding of the politics of forced migration and for refining and developing the concepts that IR uses to understand and explain world politics. The relationship between forced migration and IR can be conceptualized on three different levels: the *causes* of forced migration, the *consequences* of forced migration, and *responses* to forced migration. Each of these three levels of analysis is useful for highlighting, firstly, the empirical relationship between forced migration and world politics and, secondly, the conceptual relationship between IR theory and Forced Migration Studies.

Table 2 highlights many of the main topics and debates within IR that are relevant to examining the causes, consequences, and responses to forced migration. It shows how, for example, the study of International Political Economy (IPE), international order, and conflict and security is useful in understanding and explaining the causes of forced migration; how work on conflict, terrorism, and transnationalism is relevant in examining the consequences of forced migration; and how work on international cooperation, securitization, and normative approaches to IR has particular application in examining responses to forced migration. Within each of the three areas it exemplifies the contribution that research 'bridging the divide' has so far made, highlighting ways in which analysis of forced migration has enriched IR theory and ways in which drawing upon IR has enriched Forced Migration Studies. The table is explained in more detail below.

Causes

The underlying causes of forced migration are highly political. Analytically, if displacement is seen as a dependent variable, political factors represent important independent variables in explaining displacement. The causes of

Table 2 Typology of the relationship between IR and Forced Migration Studies

Level of Analysis	Topics of Relevance	Contribution to IR Theory	Contribution to Forced Migration
Causes	IPE	Critical IPE	Root Causes
	International order	Mutual Constitution of Westphalia	Historical emergence of the refugee
	Security and conflict	'New Wars'	Human security
Consequences	Conflict	'Spoilers'	Peace-building
	Terrorism	Conflict Diffusion	Impact of 9/11 on asylum
	Trans-nationalism	Diaspora mobilization	Remittances
Responses	International cooperation/ institutions	Issue-Linkage	The role of UNHCR
	Securitization	Biopower	Third World security predicament
	Normative	Arendt/Agamben	Normative and ethical analysis of asylum

human displacement are closely connected with trends in the international system, geopolitics, and the global political economy. These broader macro-level trends may in turn shape the country conditions that lead to human displacement. For example, wider interstate relationships between countries of origin and great powers or former colonizers may sustain oppressive, authoritarian governments that persecute their populations; environmental trends at the global level may mean people are compelled to leave their homes; an international demand for raw materials or commodities such as diamonds may fuel or mitigate conflicts that lead to displacement; and the role of multinational corporations may contribute to the type of development project that leads to displacement. In other words, in order to understand why forced migration occurs, it is likely to be insufficient to look only at trends within the country in which displacement takes place. Instead, there is a need to also look at global political trends.

Oppressive regimes may be supported or installed by major powers or former colonizers. Internal conflicts, which lead refugees to cross international borders or IDPs to move to other parts of the country, may be connected to wider international political issues. They may be triggered or exacerbated by military intervention, occupation, colonialism, or the global political economy. During the Cold War, the proxy conflicts of the 1970s, in which the superpower rivalry between the United States and the USSR was played out in the developing world, led to massive displacement in the Horn of Africa, Southern Africa, Indochina, South Asia, and Central America. Today, the involvement of large powers such as China in Sudan and the United States in Iraq and Afghanistan indirectly contributes to human displacement. Colonialism also has a relationship to displacement. The post-colonial regimes installed in countries like Rwanda, the Cote d'Ivoire, and Zimbabwe have contributed to social conflicts that underlie forced migration. Meanwhile, economic links between developing countries and developed countries have often contributed to creating the conditions for displacement. The diamond trade from Sierra Leone and oil in Angola have been factors underlying conflicts that have led to both internal displacement and refugee movements.

In order to understand these underlying causes, a number of debates in IR have great relevance: notably work on the IPE, international order and the international system, and security and conflict. Each of these areas offers concepts and ideas that are useful in understanding how issues such as system-level changes in the distribution of power in the international system, the allocation of resources within and between states, ethnicity, or religion and identity may affect conflict, oppression, and other sources of forced migration.

There is a critical IPE literature within Forced Migration Studies that attempts to examine the way in which the 'root causes' of displacement are underpinned by North–South relations and wider inequalities in the international system. Much of this work argues that an exclusive focus on humanitarian assistance or refugee protection sidelines critical engagement with the power relations that lead to forced migration in the first instance. The work highlights, for example, the roles of structural adjustment policies, Southern states' access to markets, and the international trade in commodities and raw materials as underlying forced migration (Castles 2003; Chimni 1998; Collinson 2003; Duffield 2001). Mark Duffield's *Global Governance and the New Wars* (2001), for example, makes extensive use of the refugee and broader humanitarian context in order to examine important aspects of the relationship between North–South relations and liberal global governance.

Related to this, analysis of forced migration has played an important role in the development of the concept of the 'new wars' during the 1990s. In both Duffield's work and that of authors like Mary Kaldor's *New and Old Wars* (1999), refugees and IDPs were an important feature of the new internal conflicts that took place in the Balkans and Sub-Saharan Africa following the end of the Cold War. The recognition of displacement as an outcome of the new conflicts was an important element of conceptualizing the so-called new wars. In many cases such as Bosnia and Kosovo, displacement was not only a form of collateral damage but also an instrument of war.

Within the same post-Cold War era, IR developed the concept of human security as a way of changing the dominant referent object of security from the nation state to the individual (Booth 2004; MacFarlane and Khong 2006; Paris 2001). This idea had significant resonance in the forced migration literature, allowing the refugee to be made the referent object of security and to critically examine the way in which state centric notions of security undermine the security of individual refugees and other forced migrants (Edwards and Ferstman 2009; Poku and Graham 2000). Through a series of case studies, Edward Newman's and Joanne Van Selm's *Refugees and Forced Displacement: International Security, Human Vulnerability, and the State* (2003) drew upon the human security literature to offer insights into the underlying causes of displacement.

On a more fundamental level, a literature has also emerged that examines the very notion of the 'refugee' as a constitutive element of the state system. Rather than being an aberration, Emma Haddad (2008) argues in *The Refugee in International Society*, that sovereignty and refugees are mutually constituted. Drawing upon and complementing work on the social construction of sovereignty (Biersteker and Weber 1996; Bull 1977; Krasner 1999), she argues that not only are refugees an inevitable consequence of the state system but that they have historically helped to reinforce and socially construct state sovereignty. The refugee has contributed to reinforcing and legitimating the sovereign state system by creating clear notions of insider and outsider and creating the refugee as an 'other', which can be offered a form of quasi-citizenship prior to being reintegrated within the 'normal' logic of the state system (Haddad 2008: 113–27). On the one hand, therefore, refugees represent an anomaly or failure of the state system, which the refugee regime was created to correct. On the other hand, the insider–outsider relationship created by refugees reinforces the social construction of the nation state. Haddad's work therefore usefully highlights the complex and mutually constitutive relationship between the concept of the refugee and the international state system.

Consequences

It is not just the case that scholars and policy-makers with an interest in forced migration should be concerned with understanding its relationship to global politics. Forced migration may also have an impact on other areas of international politics. In other words, human displacement may be an important independent variable in explaining other issues within global politics. It may, for example, be one factor amongst other variables, that has a significant effect on conflict, peace-building, state-building, terrorist recruitment, sources of foreign direct investment, transnational crime, or even interest group formation and voting patterns in domestic politics.

In particular, forced migration has an important and inextricable relationship with conflict. During the Cold War, refugees were often supported by the superpowers to fight or offer support to combatants in the proxy conflicts in the developing world. Similarly, the colonial liberation wars were often waged by nationalist groups in exile. For example, the Rwandan Patriotic Front (RPF) in Uganda from the 1970s until the early 1990s, the African National Congress (ANC) in other parts of Southern Africa in the 1970s and 1980s, and the Nicaraguan Contras in Honduras in the 1980s highlight the role that exile and refugees play in developing opposition movements that engage in fighting the government in the country of origin. In the Cold War context the phrase 'refugee warriors' was frequently used to describe the relationship between guerrilla movements and refugees in the regional proxy conflicts of that era. Refugee camps often serve as sanctuaries and bases for combatants. For example, following the Rwandan genocide, many of the Hutu *interahamwe* implicated in the genocide sought refuge in the camps of Eastern Democratic Republic of Congo (DRC). Furthermore, refugees have often been identified as potential 'spoilers' in peace deals. The repatriation of groups in exile, the existence of refugee camps that serve as rebel bases, and cross-border smuggling facilitated by refugee camps can all undermine the prospects for peace and post-conflict rehabilitation. In recent years, refugees and returnees have, for example, been regarded as 'spoilers' in attempted peace-building in West Africa and the Great Lakes region.

Furthermore, refugees and displaced people are frequently part of transnational networks in ways that have significant cross-border effects. Refugee camps and protracted refugee situations are potential sources of radicalization and terrorism. With few prospects for education, livelihood opportunities, or freedom of movement, young people in protracted refugee situations may represent a pool of potential recruits for terrorists. In recent years, Western governments have identified the refugee camps that host Palestinian refugees in the Middle East or Somali refugees in East Africa or Afghan refugees in Pakistan as sources of Islamic radicalization and sources of recruitment for terrorist cells.

In other areas, the transnational networks created by refugee movements, and their links with diaspora groups, may have significant political effects. For example, in many cases refugees represent a significant source of foreign direct investment. Refugees frequently engage in remittance sending, which, for countries under stress such as Somalia, represents one of the biggest sources of overseas income. Refugee flows are also associated with other trans-boundary movements such as organized crime and the demand for trafficking and smuggling networks. These types of transnational networks, whether positive or negative in their effects, can feed into domestic politics by defining voting behaviour, influencing the perception held by electorates of foreigners in general and introducing a focus on asylum, immigration, and transnationalism to the domestic political process.

A significant proportion of the literature on refugees and IR highlights that refugees are not only a consequence of insecurity and conflict but may also contribute to insecurity and conflict. In particular, a growing body of work from IR scholars examines the empirical relationship between refugee movements and conflict and tries to identify the conditions under which refugees exacerbate conflict (Lischer 2005; Loescher 1993; Salehyan and Gleditsch 2006; Stedman and Tanner 2003; Weiner 1995).

In *Refugee Manipulation*, Steve Stedman and Fred Tanner (2003) identify the way in which refugees, and the refugee regime, have been manipulated as resources of war by both states and non-state actors. They show how refugees have been instrumentally used in conflicts by great powers and by groups in exile in ways that have had significant implications for international security. Building on this argument, Sarah Kenyon Lischer (2005) explores, in *Dangerous Sanctuaries*, the conditions under which refugee crises represent a catalyst for the diffusion of conflict—both internal and interstate. She claims that variation in the relationship between refugee crises and the exacerbation of conflict can be found in political explanations, based on three principal factors: the origin of the refugee crisis, the policy of the receiving state, and the influence of external state and non-state actors.

This recognition that refugees can, under certain conditions, be a catalyst for conflict has contributed to the development of the concept of 'spoilers'. In other words, in post-conflict situations, in particular, refugees and IDPs, if they are not provided with adequate protection and durable solutions, may become a barrier to the development of peace-building initiatives (Milner 2009; Morris and Stedman 2008). They may disrupt post-conflict reconstruction and peace-building as returnees with property and rights-based claims, through remaining militarized groups in exile, by remaining outside of peace negotiations, postponing possibilities for repatriation, or refusing to renounce violence, for example. This recognition has been used to highlight the need to include a focus on refugees both in analysis of conflict and within policy initiatives relating to peace-building.

Work within both IR and Forced Migration Studies has recognized the significant role of refugees as transnational actors. Within IR, refugees have been highlighted as being one important part of diaspora mobilization, in ways that can have implications for conflict or forms of group mobilization (Adamson 2006; Salehyan 2008). Within Forced Migration Studies, significant empirical work has been done examining the role that people displaced by conflict play as transnational actors in their own right through processes of remittance transfer and through maintaining identity-based networks across international boundaries (Lindley 2010; Van Hear 2006).

Responses

Beyond seeing forced migration itself as either a dependent or independent variable in global politics, there is also a need to understand how states respond to forced migration. The way in which states respond to forced migrants—whether they have crossed borders as refugees or remain within their country of origin—is highly political. It involves a decision on how to weigh the rights of citizens versus non-citizens. Indeed, the decision of states to provide protection, contribute to durable solutions for refugees or IDPs, or to address the root causes of displacement through military intervention, diplomacy, development, post-conflict reconstruction, or peace-building are all determined by political as well as other factors. Understanding the conditions under which there is variation in states' (and other actors') responses to forced migration is a crucial part of understanding how to reduce the negative human consequences of displacement.

When states decide to provide assistance to refugees or IDPs from or within another state, they choose to allocate scarce resources to non-citizens. They may contribute to finding solutions for refugees by making financial contributions through humanitarian organizations. However, states' financial contributions have generally been highly selective and have rarely been motivated exclusively by humanitarian or altruistic concerns. There is therefore a need to understand the range of political motives that underlie states' selective contributions to supporting displaced people who are in need of international protection and assistance.

States respond to forced migration not only by offering financial assistance. They may also contribute to durable solutions for refugees or IDPs in terms of supporting resettlement, local integration, or repatriation. However, states have been increasingly reluctant to provide resettlement and local integration to refugees, and have instead promoted repatriation as 'the preferred durable solution'. In relation to IDPs, states are only just beginning to consider what 'durable solutions' might mean and how external contributions might go beyond humanitarian relief. Yet there is nevertheless a need to understand the conditions under which states have historically been willing to contribute to working towards sustainable solutions that allow forced migrants to end the cycle of displacement and rebuild their lives.

The same applies to understanding the conditions under which states are prepared to engage in addressing the root causes of displacement. Responding to the causes and consequences of forced migration requires engagement in wider issues related to prevention as well as refugee and IDP return and repatriation such as post-conflict reconstruction and peace-building. It is necessary, therefore, that researchers explore when and why states are prepared to contribute in different ways to post-conflict related initiatives within the country of origin.

A significant amount of the existing IR literature on responses to forced migration has examined the conditions under which international cooperation has taken place in the refugee regime (Betts 2009; Cronin 2003; Suhrke 1998; Thielemann 2003) or has examined the role of UNHCR as the main international organization working on refugee protection (Barnett and Finnemore 2004; Betts and Durieux 2007; Loescher 2001; Loescher et al. 2008; Whitaker 2008). Not only has the wider literature on regime theory, international institutions, and international organizations helped to shed light on the workings of the refugee regime and UNHCR but it has also contributed to IR's understanding of international institutions.

Gil Loescher's *The UNHCR in World Politics* (2001), for example, offers an in-depth analysis of an international organization and its struggle to define its autonomy in the context of an international system dominated by state power and interests. Loescher's work also demonstrates the important role that individuals play in world politics, notably the importance of the personality of different High Commissioners for Refugees in defining the personality and direction of the Office.

Michael Barnett and Martha Finnemore (2004) used UNHCR as one of their primary case studies in developing their understanding of international organizations. In *Rules for the World*, they examine the shift in UNHCR's mandate towards working on repatriation in the 1990s. They argue that rather than being passive automotive actors that respond in predictable ways to states, international organizations such as UNHCR have their own organizational sociologies and pathologies that define their behaviour and change in their mandates over time.

The refugee regime also has some unique features that make it of wider interest to scholars of international institutions. In particular, while states have a legal obligation to support refugees on their own territory, they have no legal obligation to support refugees on the territory of other states. This has meant that Northern support for the majority of the world's refugees in the South has been discretionary. In fact, the refugee regime has been characterized by a fundamental North–South power asymmetry that UNHCR has had to work to overcome. In this context, the politics of other issue-areas has been crucial for defining the interests that have shaped the engagement or disengagement of Northern states in the refugee problem in the Global South. Alexander Betts' *Protection by Persuasion* (2009) highlights how, in the absence of an altruistic commitment by Northern states to support refugees in the South, issue-linkage has been integral to achieving international cooperation on refugees. Furthermore, he develops the concept of cross-issue persuasion to demonstrate how UNHCR has sometimes been able to persuade states that refugees in the South are substantively linked to Northern interests in other issue-areas such as migration, security, and trade, and to use this as the basis of overcoming the North–South power asymmetry and achieving international cooperation within the refugee regime.

Aside from contributing to our understanding of international institutions, IR's focus on the politics of refugees has made a significant contribution to the emerging literature on biopower (Huysmans 2006; Nyers 2006). The concept of biopower introduces a post-structuralist perspective to the study of security and forced migration. It can be defined as the practice of modern states in exercising control over their population. Work on biopower focuses on analysing the techniques (beyond the use of violence) that are used by states in order to exercise power over the population. In *Rethinking Refugees*, Peter Nyers (2006) applies the concept of biopower to explore how states respond to refugees, the techniques that states use and the consequences they have for refugees, and the discourses of refugee policy.

In attempting to understand developing country states' responses to refugees, some authors have drawn upon the little IR work that addresses itself to the international politics of the developing world. For example, in *Refugees, the State and the Politics of Asylum in Africa* (2009), James Milner draws upon and develops the work on Ayoob's '*Third World Security Predicament*' (1995) and Jackson's notion of '*Quasi-States*' (1990) as a means to understand how the nature of the African state requires us to have a more nuanced view of asylum policy in Africa than would be offered by a purely Eurocentric and rationalist conception of the state. In that sense a focus on asylum and refugees in the developing world offers IR an empirical context in which to begin to critically interrogate the universality of mainstream concepts within IR that are seldom adapted to address the realities to international politics in other regions of the world such as Africa.

In addition to analytical attempts to understand and explain responses to refugees, forced migration has also offered opportunities to engage in normative analysis to examine how states' responses to refugees *should* look. A range of normative theorists have drawn upon the wider literature on normative approaches to IR to examine states' obligations towards refugees (Gibney 2004). However, analysis of the refugee issue has also brought new sources of normative theory to IR. In particular, the work of Hannah Arendt and Giorgio Agamben has been most notably developed in relation to discussions of 'bare life' and 'states of the exception' in discussions of the refugee in world politics (Haddad 2008; Levy 2009; Owens 2007). Yet, as Owens highlights, their work has far wider relevance and resonance for understanding contemporary world politics in an era characterized by state responses to terrorism, states of the exception, and an emerging biopolitics.

THE APPROACH OF THIS BOOK

This volume and the lecture series on which it is based were conceived with three principal aims in mind. First, it seeks to bridge the divide between IR and Forced Migration Studies. Although international political history has looked at refugees, it has not taken full advantage of the concepts that have developed within IR theory. Only selective conceptual work looking at refugees in world politics has emerged. These pockets of conceptual work have not been coherently integrated with one another nor have they generally been part of the dominant mainstream of IR scholarship. The volume therefore represents the first attempt to develop an edited volume that self-consciously draws upon the concepts and theories of IR to explore what they can offer the study of forced migration, and vice versa.

Secondly, the volume aspires to generate new ideas. It hopes to do so in three areas: to develop new ideas within IR; to develop new ideas for Forced Migration Studies; and to develop new ideas for practice, both through the chapters contained in the volume and through the future work inspired by the volume. Within IR, it attempts to show that through engagement with an under-explored empirical area, old concepts can be tested and reappraised and new concepts can emerge with wider relevance for understanding and explaining world politics. Within Forced Migration Studies, it attempts to import a set of ideas and concepts from IR that can enhance understanding of the international politics of forced migration. Within policy and practice, it aspires to develop ideas that can be of practical use in facilitating the prevention and mitigation of the negative human rights, security, and development consequences of forced migration.

Thirdly, the book aims to provide the basis of a future research agenda on 'refugees in IR'. Through exemplifying the way in which the concepts of IR and the empirical terrain of forced migration can be successfully combined, the book hopes to inspire a generation of new scholars to engage in rigorous, high quality political science research looking at various aspects of forced migration. Furthermore, by including work from some of the most established and successful scholars of IR in Europe and North America, the volume aspires to legitimate that scholarship so that it is no longer viewed as a marginal aspect of political science and IR. In doing so, the book seeks to inspire and legitimate work on politics of other areas of forced migration including human trafficking, environmental displacement, statelessness, and development-induced displacement, among other areas.

In choosing the authors and topics to solicit for this volume, the editors faced a dilemma: should the chapters begin from a 'theoretical' or an 'empirical' starting point? On the one hand, we wanted to explore what different theoretical approaches in IR could offer the study of forced migration. On the other hand, we did not want what emerged to be too rigidly shaped by pre-existing lenses or to miss opportunities for identifying unique empirical features of the politics of forced migration. The way in which we chose to reconcile that dilemma was by attempting to do both. All of the chapters are both theoretical and empirical. However, the chapters in the first section have a more theoretical starting point, beginning from within a given conceptual approach to IR. In contrast, the chapters in the second section set a more empirical starting point, beginning from within a given empirical issue in forced migration.

For the first set of chapters, we solicited contributions from authors who have worked within a given 'approach' to IR—realism, liberalism, international society, constructivism, critical theory, gender, normative. The purpose of this was not to have a rigid application of that approach but to ensure a full coverage of theoretical perspectives in order to highlight the relevance of the empirical area to scholars of different theoretical backgrounds. We did not invite those authors to apply a given 'approach' but rather we attempted to include authors who would provide a broad coverage of theoretical starting points. Our nominal 'realist' was Jack Snyder; our nominal 'liberal institutionalist' was Alexander Betts; our 'English School' author Andrew Hurrell; our 'constructivist', Michael Barnett; our 'critical theorist', Patricia Owens; our 'feminist', Jennifer Hyndman; our normative theorist, Chris Brown.

In practice, though, these authors do not focus on the theoretical approach per se but on sets of concepts that are predominantly addressed by those approaches. For example, Snyder examines the relationship between humanitarianism, on the one hand, and state power and interests, on the other hand. Betts explains the conditions under which international cooperation has taken place in the refugee regime. Hurrell examines the historical relationship between the refugee and international society. Barnett develops the concept of 'paternalism' by exploring the constitutive role of ideas and norms. Owens draws upon social theorists such as Arendt and Agamben in order to understand the position of the 'figure of the refugee' in the international system and issues relating to encampment. Hyndman uses post-structuralist work on gender and IR to look at protracted refugee situations. Brown critically engages in debate on the value of normative and ethical approaches to IR. Although the authors' starting point is to address these issues from a given approach, none is rigidly tied to a specific approach. For example, Snyder's work on humanitarianism is arguably heavily influenced by liberal ideas and Betts' work on cooperation is strongly influenced by constructivism.

For the second set of chapters, we solicited contributions from authors whose starting point was more explicitly empirical than theoretical. The purpose of this was to ensure coverage of a set of key and emerging issues within forced migration, and to examine what new concepts and ideas a more empirical starting point might offer. The chapters look at a range of important and cutting-edge empirical issues within forced migration. They cover global governance, military intervention, security, conflict and peace-building, post-conflict reconstruction, and an international political economy approach to the root causes of displacement. Of course, each of these chapters is also informed by concepts and theory but the 'cart and horse' of theory-empirics are somewhat reversed. For example, Andreas Hasenclever and Sophia Benz use regime theory. Anne Hammerstad draws upon securitization theory. James Milner uses theoretical literature relating to conflict and peace-building. Adam Roberts' approach to intervention is broadly within English School tradition. Dominik Zaum draws upon the growing theoretical literature on state-building and post-conflict reconstruction. Sarah Collinson couples a macro-level IPE approach with micro-level political economy analysis to examine the causes of displacement.

As a collection, the set of essays contained in this volume is not intended to be the definitive word on 'Refugees in IR'. Rather, it purports to be an important step forwards in 'bridging the divide' between IR and Forced Migration Studies and bringing refugees into the mainstream of IR. The book hopes to raise awareness about the multifaceted ways in which refugees and forced migration are a part of much broader issues on world politics. It hopes to inspire a new research agenda and the development of new ideas through insinuating the ways in which refugees and forced migration can offer a rich empirical terrain for IR scholarship. Finally, it hopes to demonstrate how the concepts of IR can be useful for policy and practice as a means of preventing and mitigating the most serious human rights consequences of forced migration.

The relationship between refugees and IR will remain important for policy-makers and scholars interested in either world politics or forced migration. As the nature of forced migration and world politics changes over time, new scholarship will be constantly needed. Refugees are not specific to one historical juncture in IR. Rather, they have played an evolving part of world politics and will continue to do so. As new issues take centre stage in world politics—climate change, state fragility, and terrorism—refugees will be a central feature of those issues. The causes of refugee movements will change. For example, survival migration—resulting from economic collapse, environmental disaster, and state failure—may become more common relative to displacement resulting from individualized persecution. However, the centrality of people displaced by or within states that are unable or unwilling to ensure their basic rights will remain an omnipresent feature of international relations. The causes, consequences, and responses to these people will be shaped by different configurations of power, interests, and ideas at different historical junctures, but refugees will nevertheless remain an inherent feature of world politics with important linkages to a host of other policy fields.

BIBLIOGRAPHY

Adamson, F. B. 2006. Crossing Borders: International Migration and National Security. *International Security* 31(1).

Ayoob, M. 1995. *The third world security predicament: state making, regional conflict and the international system*. London: Lynne Rienner Publishers.

Barnett, M. and Finnemore, M. 2004. *Rules for the world: international organizations in global politics*. New York: Cornell University Press.

Betts, A. 2009. *Protection by Persuasion: International Cooperation in the Refugee Regime*. Ithaca, NY: Cornell University Press.

——and Durieux, J.-F. 2007. Convention Plus as a Norm-Setting Exercise. *Journal of Refugee Studies* 20(3), 509–35.

——and Kaytaz, E. 2009. *National and international responses to the Zimbabwean exodus: implications for the refugee regime*. Geneva: UNHCR.

Biersteker, T. J. and Weber, C. eds. 1996. *State sovereignty as social construct*. Cambridge: Cambridge University Press.

Boano, C. et al. 2008. *Environmentally displaced people: understanding the linkages between environmental change, livelihoods and forced migration*. RSC Policy Brief No 1, Oxford: RSC.

Booth, K. ed. 2004. *Critical security studies and world politics*. Boulder, CO: Lynne Rienner Publishers.

Bull, H. 1977. *The anarchical society: a study of order in world politics*. London: Palgrave Macmillan.

——and Watson, A. 1984. *The expansion of international society.* Oxford: Clarendon Press.

Carr, E. H. 1946. *The twenty years' crisis, 1919–1939: An introduction to the study of international relations.* London: Macmillan.

Castles, S. 2003. The International Politics of Forced Migration. *Development* 46, 11–20.

Chimni, B. S. 1998. The Geopolitics of Refugee Studies: A View from the South. *Journal of Refugee Studies* 11(4), 350–74.

Collinson, S. 2003. *Power, livelihoods and conflict: case studies in political economy analysis for humanitarian action.* London: Overseas Development Institute.

Crisp, J. 2003. Refugees and the Global Politics of Asylum. *Political Quarterly* 74(s1), 75–87.

Cronin, B. 2003. *Institutions for the common good: international protection regimes in international society.* Cambridge: Cambridge University Press.

Dubernet, C. 2001. *The international containment of displaced persons: humanitarian spaces without exit.* Aldershot: Ashgate Publishing.

Duffield, M. 2001. *Global governance and the new wars.* London: Zed Books.

Edwards, A. and Ferstman, C. eds. 2009. *Human security and non-citizens: law, policy and international affairs.* Cambridge: Cambridge University Press.

Gibney, M. J. 2004. *The ethics and politics of asylum: liberal democracy and the response to refugees.* Cambridge: Cambridge University Press.

Gordenker, L. 1987. *Refugees in international politics.* New York: Columbia University Press.

Haddad, E. 2008. *The refugee in international society: between sovereigns.* Cambridge: Cambridge University Press.

Hobbes, T. 1914. *Leviathan.* London: J.M. Dent & Sons.

Hobsbawm, E. J. E. 1990. *Nations and nationalism since 1780: programme, myth, reality.* Cambridge: Cambridge University Press.

Huysmans, J. 2006. *The politics of protection: sites of insecurity and political agency.* Abingdon: Routledge.

Jackson, R. J. 1990. *Quasi-states: sovereignty, international relations and the third world.* Cambridge: Cambridge University Press.

Juma, M. K. and Kagwanja, P. M. 2008. In: Loescher, G. and Milner, J. eds. *The politics, human rights and security dimensions of protracted refugee situations.* Tokyo: United Nations University Press.

Kaldor, M. 1999. *New and old wars: organized violence in a global era.* Cambridge: Polity Press.

Keene, E. 2002. *Beyond the anarchical society: grotius, colonialism and order in world politics.* Cambridge: Cambridge University Press.

Krasner, S. D. 1999. *Sovereignty: organized hypocrisy.* New Jersey: Princeton University Press.

Levy, C. 2009. Into the Zone: EU Projects for the Extra-territorial Processing of Forced Migrants and the Limitations of Agamben. Oxford: Refugee Studies Centre Public Seminar (March).

Lindley, A. 2007. *The early morning phonecall: remittances from a refugee diaspora.* Oxford: Berghahn.

Lischer, S. K. 2005. *Dangerous sanctuaries: refugee camps, civil war, and the dilemmas of humanitarian aid.* Ithaca, NY: Cornell University Press.

Locke, J. 1924. *Two treatises of civil government.* London: Dent.

Loescher, G. 1993. *Beyond charity: international cooperation and the global refugee crisis.* Oxford: Oxford University Press.

——2001. *The UNHCR and world politics: a perilous path.* Oxford: OUP.

——et al. 2008. *UNHCR: The politics and practice of refugee protection into the twenty-first century.* Abingdon: Routledge.

MacFarlane, S. N. and Khong, Y. F. 2006. *Human security and the UN: a critical history.* Bloomington, IN: Indiana University Press.

Marrus, M. R. 1985. *The unwanted: European refugees in the twentieth century.* 1st edition. New York, Oxford: Oxford University Press, xii, 414.

Milner, J. 2009. *Refugees, the state and the politics of asylum in Africa.* Basingstoke: Palgrave Macmillan.

Morgenthau, H. 1948. *Politics among nations: the struggle for power and peace.* New York: Alfred A Knopf.

Morris, E. and Stedman, S. J. 2008. Protracted Refugee Situations, Conflict and Security: The Need for Better Diagnosis and Prescription. In: Loescher, G. et al. eds. *Protracted refugee situations: political, human rights and security implications.* Tokyo: United Nations University Press.

Myers, N. 1997. Environmental Refugees. *Population & Environment* 19(2), 167–82.

Newman, E. and van Selm, J. eds. 2003. *Refugees and forced displacement: international security, human vulnerability, and the state.* Tokyo: United Nations University Press.

Nyers, P. 2006. *Rethinking refugees: beyond states of emergency.* Abingdon: Routledge.

Orchard, P. 2009. Change, Transformation, and Replacement within the International Refugee Regime(s). In: *IASFM.* Nicosia, Cyprus.

Owens, P. 2007. *Between war and politics: international relations and the thought of hannah arendt.* Oxford: Oxford University Press.

Paris, R. 2001. Human Security: Paradigm Shift or Hot Air? *International Security* 26(2), 87–102.

Phuong, C. 2004. *The international protection of internally displaced persons.* Cambridge: Cambridge University Press.

Piguet, E. 2008. *Climate change and forced migration.* UNHCR Working Paper No 153, Geneva: UNHCR.

Poku, N. K. and Graham, D. eds. 2000. *Migration, globalisation and human security.* London: Routledge.

Salehyan, I. 2008. The Externalities of Civil Strife: Refugees as a Source of International Conflict. *American Journal of Political Science* 52(4)

——and Gleditsch, K. S. 2006. Refugees and the Spread of Civil War. *International Organization* 60(2), 335–66.

Shacknove, A. 1985. Who Is a Refugee? *Ethics.* 95(2), 274–84.

Shue, H. 1980. *Basic rights: subsistence, affluence, and u.s. foreign policy.* Princeton, NJ; Guildford: Princeton University Press, xiii, 231.

Simpson, J. H. 1938. *Refugees: preliminary report of a survey.* London: Royal Institute of International Affairs.

Skran, C. 1995. *Refugees in inter-war Europe: the emergence of a regime.* Oxford: Clarendon Press.

Stedman, S. J. and Tanner, F. 2003. *Refugee manipulation: war, politics, and the abuse of human suffering.* United Nations University Press.

Suhrke, A. 1998. Burden-Sharing During Refugee Emergencies: The Logic of Collective Action Versus National Action. *Journal of Refugee Studies* 11(4), 396–415.

Thielemann, E. 2003. Between Interests and Norms: Burden-Sharing in the European Union. *Journal of Refugee Studies* 16(3), 253–73.

Van Hear, N. 2006. Refugees in Diaspora: From Durable Solutions to Transnational Relations. *Refuge* 23(1), 9–14.

Weiner, M. 1995. *The global migration crisis: challenges to states and to human rights.* New York: Harper Collins Publishers.

Weiss, T. G. and Korn, D. A. 2006. *Internal displacement: conceptualization and its consequences.* Abingdon: Routledge.

Whitaker, B. E. 2008. Funding the International Refugee Regime: Implications for Protection. *Global Governance* 14(2), 241–58.

Zolberg, A. R. et al. 1989. *Escape from violence: conflict and the refugee crisis in the developing world.* Oxford: Oxford University Press.

2

Realism, Refugees, and Strategies of Humanitarianism

Jack Snyder

ABSTRACT

Although realism and humanitarianism may seem strange bedfellows, they have much to offer each other. Realism offers profound and lasting insights into strategic competition in settings that lack an overarching sovereign power to enforce rules and agreements. A crucial reason for humanitarians to adopt a strategic perspective is that perpetrators of forced migration themselves typically act strategically. They not only expel populations to seize their land and cut off rebels from popular support, but sometimes they also use the threat of a manufactured refugee disaster to intimidate neighbouring states into making concessions. Facing strategically ruthless opponents, humanitarians need to act strategically in order to accomplish their goals. In contrast to the apolitical doctrine that characterizes traditional humanitarian approaches, realists favour humanitarian strategies that are self-consciously political, pay close attention to the power and strategic interests of actors, and are consequentialist in their ethics. The chapter compares four humanitarian strategies in terms of these criteria: 'a bed for the night', tactical humanitarianism, 'back a decent winner', and comprehensive peacebuilding.

Realism, the paradigm of international relations that equates interest with power, seems ill-suited as a source of inspiration for strategies of humanitarian action on behalf of refugees. Indeed, John Mearsheimer's influential restatement (2001: 46–7) of realist theory dismisses humanitarianism with the remark that 'offensive realism certainly recognizes that great powers might pursue these non-security goals, but it has little to say about them, save for one important point: states can pursue them as long as the requisite behavior does not conflict with balance-of-power logic, which is often the case'. 'Despite claims that American foreign policy is infused with moralism,' he adds, 'Somalia (1992–93) is the only instance during the past one hundred years in which U.S. soldiers were killed in action on a humanitarian mission.'

Realists not only doubt the likelihood of costly altruism in international relations, but they are also wary of what they see as its dangerous pretensions. According to Hans Morgenthau (1951), the founder of modern realism, only communities bound together in a dense web of reciprocity are able to sustain altruism within the group without degenerating into two deformations: masking self-interest as the universal good and imposing local values as if they were universal values. When states claim that they are acting in the interests of others, they are either lying or fooling themselves, realists like Morgenthau and Reinhold Niebuhr (1932: 11, 17) believe.

Realism, however, is a big tent that encompasses scholars who look not only at the narrow logic of military power and state security interests, but also some who acknowledge that great powers have sometimes been willing to pay high costs to act on their humanitarian concerns. Chaim Kaufmann and Robert Pape (1999), for example, calculate that the British navy's effort to suppress the slave trade cost the United Kingdom an average of nearly two percent of GDP per year over sixty years and a cumulative total of 5,000 lives.[1] The reason, they say, is that morally motivated Dissenters, such as the Quakers, became a swing constituency in Parliament and so were able to extract slave trade suppression as their price for sustaining ruling coalitions in office. Their motivations were principled, but the principle of human rights protections abroad helped to solidify the Dissenters' own civil rights in Britain. This argument is not out of step with the eclecticism of many unquestionably realist scholars, such as Stephen Walt (1987), who added perception of threat to balance of power theory; Randall Schweller (1996), who allows for substantial variations in state goals; defensive realists (Snyder 1991; Van Evera 1999), who bring in ideology and domestic politics to explain anomalies that diverge from sound realist strategy; and neoclassical realists (Christensen 1996; Dueck 2006), who show how domestic political and ideological mobilization can make foreign policy deviate from the expectations of more parsimonious realist theory.

Although realism and humanitarianism may seem strange bedfellows, they have much to offer each other. Facing the criticism that aid to refugees has sometimes fuelled conflict, the field of humanitarian assistance to victims of emergencies has recently been undergoing a rethinking of its traditionally apolitical dogmas, moving instead towards pragmatism. At the same time, the stock of realism has risen in public discourse in the wake of the Bush Administration's neoconservative foreign policies that are widely perceived as having violated the paramount realist dictum of prudence. Presidential candidates John McCain and Barack Obama crossed swords in debate over whether arch realist Henry Kissinger had advocated talks with Iranian leaders without preconditions. And yet no one really wants a return to principle-free power politics. Rather, they want principled policies that are effective and take into account the world as it really is, not as ideologues would wish it to be. Realism in this sense can be a great ally of humanitarianism.

Realism offers profound and lasting insights into political competition in settings that lack an overarching sovereign power to enforce rules and agreements. Realists see a strand of continuity that goes back to Thucydides' account of the Peloponnesian Wars, which he says arose from the rising power of Athens and the fear this inspired in Sparta, a source of insight that continues to illuminate international relations in the era of unipolarity.[2] Staying relevant to new problems of interest to humanitarians, realists have expanded the scope of their theory to help understand violent conflicts within states. They have followed the lead of Barry Posen (1993) in noting that group competition in failed states and collapsed empires share a structural similarity with the struggle for security among states in international anarchy. Actors in such settings operate in a self-help system in which violence is an ever-present possibility, and even those who are motivated principally by the need to survive may face compelling incentives to attack others preventively.

A crucial reason for humanitarians to adopt a strategic perspective is that perpetrators of forced migration themselves typically act strategically. They not only expel populations to seize their land and cut off rebels from popular support but sometimes they also use the threat of a manufactured refugee disaster to intimidate neighbouring states into making concessions (Greenhill 2010. Ithaca: Cornell University Press). Facing strategically ruthless opponents, humanitarians need to act strategically in order to accomplish their goals.

For this reason, realist insights may help humanitarian organizations analyse the anarchic political dynamics in which they are often required to carry out relief tasks, including the establishment of refugee camps, which have not infrequently become military bases exacerbating an armed struggle (Terry 2002). In anarchic political arenas, where state authority is weak or absent, pursuit of any goal—even humanitarian relief—must take into account the role of coercive power. This includes the coercive power of those who help secure the humanitarian enterprise, such as peacekeepers, allied armed forces, and private security forces who 'ride shotgun' on humanitarian expeditions, as well as the power of armed groups who see humanitarian resources, including food, shelter, and vehicles, as potential war material to be exploited, and who see humanitarian organizations as powerful competitors for influence over society.

Because realists see the potential use of force as casting a shadow over all political decisions in anarchy, they typically join Morgenthau in defining interest in terms of power. Without coercive power (or a reputation for having coercive power at one's disposal, if needed) nothing can be accomplished in anarchy. It is a precondition for all other interests, including humanitarian ones.

Sometimes cavalier writers describe any policy that involves the use of armed force as 'realist'. The neoconservative journalist Charles Krauthammer (2004) talked about the forceful spread of democracy as 'realist' in this bogus sense. In fact, realists often reject the use of force on the grounds that it is imprudent, for example, because the available means are insufficient, because attacking may provoke the formation of an opposing coalition, or because threats and opportunities are illusory. Even the self-styled 'offensive realist' John Mearsheimer (2001) notes that smart realists often stay on the defensive, waiting for a better opportunity to fight or biding their time in the expectation that others will bear the costs of opposing aggression. The characteristic realist move is not necessarily to use force but to calculate the consequences of the possible use of force by one's own side and by the opponent.

Realists are often described as amoral, because they do not reduce morality to Kantian categorical imperatives. In fact, most realists are at least as concerned about peace as are non-realists, and many of them are also concerned about democracy, justice, and human rights. The difference is that they adhere to a consequentialist approach to ethics, in which 'ought' implies 'can', and in which good intentions count for nothing if an action fails to achieve good results. This consequentialist mentality, which goes hand in hand with an appreciation of the role of coercive power in anarchy, is not at odds with recent developments in humanitarian thinking, which could benefit from a familiarity with the ways in which realists have addressed such issues.

In the following sections, I will discuss realist insights on the question of, first, when do states intervene militarily in humanitarian crises, many of which involve forced migration, and, second, how should international actors intervene effectively using military or humanitarian tools.

MOTIVATIONS FOR INTERVENTION

Samantha Power (2002) has won countless prizes for her book on why powerful actors have done so little to stop genocide (let alone forced migration), even when the costs of acting would probably have been low. She is shocked to learn that state leaders have little inclination to take even the smallest political risks on behalf of people who are not their constituents. Michael Barnett's equally excellent, if not quite so famous book (2002) presents similar findings about the role of the UN in the Rwanda genocide. Some scholars who are closer to the realist camp are equally dismayed, though perhaps less surprised, at the lack of action to stop mass killing. Benjamin Valentino (2004), for example, finds that mass killing is normally perpetrated by a fairly small group of people aligned with a state that is acting for some strategic purpose. He concludes that intervention by more powerful outsiders could often have stopped these cabals. But all too often interveners have taken the view of George Herbert Walker Bush's realist Secretary of State James Baker during the atrocities that followed the breakup of Yugoslavia: 'we have no dog in this fight'.

Principled proponents of humanitarian intervention have generally offered three kinds of arguments: two of them realist and one non-realist. Like Valentino, they have argued that the perpetrators are often weak, so the costs and risks of intervening would be low. Like former Secretary of State Madeleine Albright, they have also argued that peace and security are indivisible, that violence and rights abuses tend to spill across boundaries, that violence unchecked anywhere undermines deterrence of violence elsewhere, and consequently that strong states have a generalized interest in suppressing such abuses as genocide and forced migration before they metastasize to vital areas. The third argument, a non-realist one, is that states, as a matter of law and morality, should (and sometimes do) act to prevent humanitarian disasters even when they have no self-interested reason to do so. These three arguments can be taken as possible explanations for humanitarian intervention. Let us see how well they fare in accounting for recent cases.

Altruistic or Self-interested Motives?

Taking the last of these first, political scientist Martha Finnemore (2003: 75–8) has attempted to trace the emergence of a norm of altruistic humanitarian intervention, but in fact her list of humanitarian interventions shows just the opposite. She discusses a few cases of unilateral humanitarian intervention in which a state's atrocities directed at its own citizens provoked military intervention by a neighboring state, which in every case had strong self-interested motives as well as humanitarian ones. India invaded East Pakistan in 1971 in order to repatriate refugees and to undermine its arch enemy Pakistan by creating the new state of Bangladesh. Tanzania intervened to topple the ruthless dictator Idi Amin in 1979 in response to Uganda's invasion of disputed border territory. Vietnam similarly intervened to topple the genocidal Khmer Rouge regime in 1979 in response to a series of border incursions.

Finnemore (2003: 78) then lists five multilateral interventions since 1989 that she argues illustrate the strengthened altruistic norm, but despite

Finnemore's protestations, these too all manifest a significant self-interested motivation. US, British, and French protection of Kurdish and Shiite populations inside Iraq after the 1991 Gulf War served the strategic goal of putting pressure on Saddam's regime and containing its ability to resurrect its offensive capacity. In encouraging Shiites to rebel and then failing to protect them, the strategically motivated allies helped to cause a humanitarian disaster. The UN's mission in Cambodia also had broad political motivations in attempting to create a democratic buffer state that would simultaneously limit Vietnamese influence while marginalizing the Khmer Rouge and containing threats to the stability of neighboring Thailand.

In Bosnia and Kosovo, the United States and NATO were motivated not only by humanitarian concerns, but also by the Clinton Administration's wish to demonstrate that the United States and NATO remained relevant to solving security problems in Europe. In both instances, humanitarian concerns took a back seat to the desire to keep the interveners' casualties low. The UN notoriously failed to protect civilians in 'save havens' in Bosnia, while the NATO intervention in Kosovo triggered rather than deterred Serbia's systematic expulsion of the Albanian population. The US interventions in both instances implicitly echoed Paul Wolfowitz's suppressed 1992 Defense Guidance memorandum written for Defense Secretary Richard Cheney, which argued that the United States should act preemptively to solve Europe's and Japan's security problems in order to head off decisions by Germany and Japan to take matters into their own hands, including nuclear proliferation (Pentagon 1992).

Finnemore's strongest case, which even Mearsheimer accepts, is the humanitarian military intervention by the UN and the United States to prevent starvation in warlord-torn Somalia. But even this seemingly purely altruistic case is not free of the taint of self-interest. Political scientist Jon Western (2002, 2005) has mounted considerable evidence to show that General Colin Powell, then Chairman of the Joint Chiefs of Staff, maneuvered the Bush Administration into the Somalia intervention in order to be able to argue that US forces could not simultaneously undertake an intervention in Bosnia, which he feared would be a quagmire.

Subsequent military interventions in humanitarian crises likewise included some form of self-interest, sometimes simultaneously serving humanitarian goals but sometimes undermining them. Australia took the lead in East Timor because of concerns about instability in its neighborhood and to head off refugee flows, just as the United States did in Haiti. Great Britain took the lead in Sierra Leone as the former colonial power. France played a key role in Francophone Rwanda, supporting the rights-abusing Hutu regime and then creating a safe zone that perhaps inadvertently had the effect of protecting

Hutu genocidaires from Tutsi invaders. Finally, the main objective of the United States in its military interventions in Iraq and Afghanistan was to topple regimes that threatened US security; correcting abuses of the local population was only an incidental goal.

In short, further scrutiny of Finnemore's own evidence suggests that states and even multilateral coalitions intervene with military force for humanitarian purposes only when the intervention also serves some perceived self-interest, typically the national interest of the intervening states. This is dismaying for those, like Finnemore, who place their hope in a rising norm of principled humanitarian intervention. However, a realist might be less discouraged by this finding. A number of these interventions accomplished humanitarian goals, so if selfish national interests helped motivate the intervention, then let us have two cheers for those interests. I hesitate to say three cheers, however, because partially selfish humanitarian interventions may be carried out in ways that severely compromise humanitarian outcomes. For example, the Clinton Administration's bargaining strategy of confronting Serbia with an obviously unacceptable ultimatum at Rambouillet, which stipulated NATO military access throughout Serbia, combined with Clinton's zero-casualty approach to military operations to trigger the mass expulsion of Albanians from Kosovo.

What then of the two realist-type arguments in favour of humanitarian military interventions, namely, low cost and the indivisibility of peace?

Low Cost

It is not accidental that humanitarian interventions have been on the rise since the collapse of the Soviet Union, not only because of alleged change in norms but especially because the costs and risks of interventions seem more calculable and controllable. During the Cold War, calculations of the cost of interventions, whether humanitarian or not, had to take into account the danger that the opposing superpower might escalate the conflict by supporting the other side, including gun-running to proxies who could tie down the interveners, as the United States did to the Soviet Union in Afghanistan. This danger disappeared in the 1990s, so humanitarian intervention seemed somewhat safer and perhaps worthwhile even in cases where other national interests were not significantly engaged.

However, it obviously did not make the cost of humanitarian intervention fully calculable. Even if Valentino is right that mass killing is usually perpetrated by small groups of rather lightly armed people who can be defeated by first-world armed forces, recent interveners have in almost every case learned the difficulty of imposing a non-violent order on a society with extremely weak political institutions. Counter-insurgency is a devilishly hard task, especially for actors that espouse humanitarian motives and consequently must be scrupulous in their rules of engagement with rebels and in minimizing harm to civilians. Indeed, one of the classic strategies of counter-insurgency purposefully causes refugees by removing populations from areas where they provide support to rebel fighters (Greenhill 2004, 2008). Another danger is that humanitarian interventions premised on low cost will run out of steam before creating the kind of lasting social peace that is needed to prevent atrocities from re-emerging as soon as the peacekeepers leave. Colin Dueck's survey (2006) of American foreign policy in the twentieth century argues that this pattern of 'limited liability internationalism' is endemic.

Indivisibility of Peace

The argument that peace is indivisible receives some support from social science research. The Political Instability Task Force finds that the presence of a civil war in a neighbouring state is one of the four main risk factors for civil war (Goldstone et al. 2005). Refugees themselves are one of the causal mechanisms that account for the geographical clustering of civil wars (Salehyan and Gleditsch 2006). They have this effect through the militarization of refugee camps, the transnational diffusion of arms and combatants, the dissemination of ethnic or religious ideologies that foment conflict, the alteration of ethnic demographic balances in host states, and the sharpening of ethnic economic competition (Muggah 2006; Salehyan and Gleditsch 2006). Examples include the spread of violence in connection with refugee flows from Israeli-occupied Jordan to Lebanon, from Afghanistan to Pakistan, from Rwanda to Eastern Congo, from Kosovo to Macedonia, from Morocco to Western Sahara, and from Darfur to Chad.

However, this falls short of a fully convincing realist argument for intervention, in part because the spillover of violence from one destitute, powerless state to another does not necessarily constitute an increase in the level of threat to more coherent and geopolitically significant states. Whereas refugees from violence in Rwanda and Burundi destabilized the weak state of Zaire/Congo, they did not disturb the political stability of the better institutionalized regime in Tanzania. In some cases, however, the spread of violence by refugees or other spillovers from humanitarian crises has roiled the domestic politics of states that are unquestionably of geopolitical significance, including the effect of Iraqi Kurdish strife on Turkey and Chechen instability on Russia. Another potentially convincing argument for the indivisibility of peace is the danger of terrorist bases in lawless states, though this does not necessarily depend on the mechanism of refugees or of spillover to direct neighbors.

Another problem with spillover arguments as realist justifications for humanitarian military intervention is that intervention sometimes makes the problem worse. Refugee camps may become militarized. Rebels have seized equipment of NGOs and of peacekeepers, using it to prosecute the war and carry out their pillaging. Finally, intervention may alienate local populations, offer tempting targets for attack, and fail to prevent further refugee flows.

In short, most military interventions for humanitarian purposes also have a self-interested and usually strategic motivation. This is not necessarily a bad thing, since it provides an added motivation that may outweigh the reluctance of most potential interveners to undertake costs and risks for purely humanitarian purposes. But strategic motivations are likely to be weak in the kind of cases where refugee crises are common, that is, where the state is poor, powerless, and remote. Moreover, intervention on the cheap for partially self-interested motives may lead to a pattern of military intervention that not only fails to solve humanitarian problems but can even exacerbate them. Realism may be a fairly good predictor of the pattern of humanitarian intervention, but it offers mixed blessings from the standpoint of the normative evaluation of those interventions.

Strategic Problems of Military Intervention in Humanitarian Crisis

A realist-inspired view of humanitarian intervention begins with the assumption that the perpetrator of the abuses is a strategic actor. The abuses—such as genocide, mass killing, forced migration, ethnic cleansing, targeted killing, torture, and even rape—are probably intended to achieve some result that improves the security, power, or resources of the perpetrator. The likelihood of further abuses is affected by the perpetrator's strategic motivation.

Even predators are motivated by fear or by the need to counteract threats from those whom they exploit. Atrocities usually occur in wartime, when actors face armed opposition that threatens their survival or control over territory. This was the case, for example, in the Kosovo insurgency, the rebellion in Darfur, and the Rwandan and Armenians genocides. Strategic motivations underlie the use of coercive tactics to separate rebels from populations that supply them, to intimidate opponents to deter them from resisting, to extract information about who is an opponent, and to eliminate potential opponents before they can improve their position by obtaining support from outsiders (Kalyvas 2006; Valentino 2004).

One irony of humanitarian military intervention is that actions to deter opportunistic atrocities typically threaten the relative power and security of the perpetrator and therefore increase his motivation to use atrocities to shore up his position. If the humanitarian force intervenes decisively with instantly overwhelming force, then the perpetrator's threat to use further atrocities to save its endangered fortunes is of no concern. However, if the intervention is slow in implementation or lacks the power to decisively disarm the perpetrator, the perpetrator of atrocities has a strong incentive to quickly use whatever tactics are available to decisively weaken or eliminate the people on whose behalf the intervention is being undertaken.

A further complication is that the threat of external intervention changes the balance of power in favour of the group that is being abused. In a situation of civil war, this makes the potential victims cocky about their prospects in a continued armed struggle. As in Bosnia and Kosovo, they now have the US Air Force on their side. Although the perpetrators may be compelled to reduce their demands, this may not lead to a settlement of the conflict if the victims increase their demands correspondingly. As a result, the intervener may have to deter both sides simultaneously, telling the victims that they will get support only if they conform to strict limitations on military action and negotiating position. Such conditional support is difficult to make credible in wartime, especially in a humanitarian intervention that the intervener has sold to its domestic constituency as a struggle on behalf of the weak and innocent against absolute evil (Crawford 2002; Kuperman and Crawford 2006).

Despite these complications, recent social science research supports the conclusion that peacekeeping tends to increase the chance the peace settlements will endure, taking into account that peacekeepers tend to be deployed in more difficult settings where a reversion to conflict is more likely (Fortna 2008). Peacekeeping works in part for reasons that correspond to realist theory. In particular, peacekeepers provide information that reduces each side's fear of cheating by the other side and thus mitigating the security dilemma that drives conflict in anarchy.

However, contemporary peacekeeping is typically embedded in a far more ambitious, multifaceted effort to achieve 'comprehensive peace-building'. This goes beyond simple realism, but is not inconsistent with it. As laid out by Michael Doyle and Nicholas Sambanis (2006: 339), peacebuilding entails a step-by-step program that starts with the provision of basic security, secures the state's international borders through cooperation with neighboring states, gains the goodwill of the population through a quick infusion of humanitarian aid, then turns to the work of building institutions of governance and rule of law, and finishes with reconciliation between the formerly fighting groups, which no longer face each other in an anarchical setting.

This raises the question of how to integrate a strategy of humanitarian intervention across its military, political, economic, and emergency aid dimensions. Humanitarians were long reluctant to think about such integration, preferring to adhere to their traditional doctrine of neutrality, independence, and impartiality. However, a realist approach to humanitarianism, insisting on an ethic of consequences and political feasibility, provides the right mindset for thinking about integrating humanitarian strategies within a broader political framework.

STRATEGIES OF HUMANITARIANISM

The variety of humanitarian strategies undertaken by states, international organizations, and non-governmental organizations has increased over the last several decades. In order to better conceptualize the kinds of humanitarian actions we have seen, I differentiate them along two dimensions.[3] The first dimension is whether they are apolitical or political. 'Apolitical' actions are those that are not intended to alter the governance arrangements that are hypothesized to be the cause of suffering, and political actions are those that are intended to do so. Humanitarian action can also be categorized according to whether its goals are modest or ambitious. Some try to change the incentives and constraints facing local actors in significant ways; others work largely within the parameters of the existing circumstances. These two dimensions produce a fourfold taxonomy of different kinds of humanitarianism: bed-for-the-night, tactical humanitarianism, back-a-decent-winner, and peacebuilding (see Figure 2.1).

Although this taxonomy can include both interventions that are provoked by natural and man-made events, I am particularly interested in using it to illuminate patterns in conflict settings. This taxonomy can be used to trace changes in the kinds of interventions that are most prevalent, to discriminate between strategies used in different phases of a humanitarian operation, to discern differences in the strategic preferences of different types of actors that are more likely to fall into one cell or another, and thus to identify where mismatched strategies might emerge and to assess their consequences. Realists will favour strategies that are self-consciously political, pay close attention to the power and strategic interests of actors, and are consequentialist in their ethics.

	Apolitical	Political
Accept constraints	**Bed for the night** Unqualified short-term emergency relief to those in life-threatening circumstances	**Back a decent winner** Deploy resources to achieve a stable political bargain that will halt gross violations of human rights
Change constraints	**Tactical humanitarianism** provide relief while minimizing the negative side effects	**Peacebuilding** Eliminate the root causes of conflict and help promote a more peaceful, stable, and legitimate political and economic system

Figure 2.1 Kinds of humanitarianism

Bed for the Night

This kind of intervention is so named for the title of the (in)famous book by David Rieff (2002), *A Bed for the* Night, where he asserts that aid agencies should limit themselves to the impartial, independent, and neutral provision of relief to victims of conflict and natural disasters. This strategy is modest in its ambitions because it is about relief and nothing but relief. It is apolitical because it cleaves to the principles of neutrality, impartiality, and independence, and therefore attempts to avoid any engagement with the political world (even as it recognizes that its interventions can have political consequences). Rieff and others who advocate this position argue that while providing relief is modest in its ambitions, it is its very modesty that makes it ethically appealing; while it cannot do a lot, what it does it can do very well; it can make a huge difference to those whose lives hang in the balance; and the attempt to do more might very well undermine the very essence of humanitarian action—saving lives. If there is a 'classical' approach to humanitarian action, this is it.

This classical approach has a lot of consequentialism in it. To be sure, aid agencies present impartiality, neutrality, and independence as non-negotiable values that are connected to their humanity, and while this might be true for impartiality, it is less so for neutrality and independence. Being perceived as neutral and independent can help create a 'humanitarian space' that protects aid workers in the field and facilitates their access to populations at risk on all sides of a conflict. Conversely, the moment that relief workers deviate from these principles they will be seen as 'political' and thus have difficulty delivering aid. The upshot, then, was that while many believed that such a classical approach rested on a non-instrumental logic, in fact their motives for adopting this approach had strong consequentialist elements.

Beginning in the 1990s, though, those favouring a bed-for-the-night humanitarianism found themselves increasingly on the defensive. The strategy of strict neutrality, impartiality, and independence makes sense in some contexts and for some issue areas: in natural disasters where those in charge seek outside assistance; in inspections to insure that parties are observing the rules with respect to prisoners of war; and in settings where taking sides is impractical, such as when aid workers lack military backup and there is no decent local ally to support. Yet a strategy that delivers aid first and asks questions later (if ever) might be so focused on the highly visible short term that it can cause more harm than good to the populations that it seeks to serve. This was the situation arguably faced by many aid workers in these complex humanitarian emergencies. Aid not only saved lives. It also fueled conflict and repression by supporting repressive governments, feeding warring factions through theft or gate-keeping access to aid, helping to militarize refugee camps, enabling warring groups to exercise social control over populations, legitimizing governments and rebels, and allowing outside states to appear to be doing something about a crisis without having to intervene in more effective ways. Aid, moreover, may increase distortions into the local economy, displacing or discouraging local economic activity, distorting local economic incentives, and creating a short-term, hot-house aid economy. Moreover, emergency aid can produce new kinds of dependencies and keep in place existing political and economic inequalities.

Although these negative externalities were always present, deliverers and observers of humanitarian assistance began to focus on them during the 1990s in part because of the nature of the humanitarian emergencies they encountered. Many of these emergencies were being produced by perverse political patterns in situations of war and repression. In these situations, powerful local actors sought to benefit from famine or from the commandeering of aid. They developed strategies that were designed to exploit to their benefit, and had the power to move outcomes in the direction that they wanted. Local political and economic elites developed fairly astute strategies for hijacking international benevolence for their own political, military, and economic agendas, and aid agencies that did not adjust found themselves unwitting accomplices. Furthermore, aid agencies sometimes found themselves following their existing principles into moral dead ends. Remaining neutral and independent can come at a high cost to those whose lives are at risk. In response to the Srebrenica report, UN Secretary General Kofi Annan (2004) wrote of 'an institutional ideology of impartiality even when confronted with attempted genocide'. Where an autocrat has the power to repress opposition and sees an incentive to exploit subjects in ways that create a humanitarian crisis, apolitical humanitarians face a Hobson's choice between providing aid that may prop up the regime and perhaps not even reach the needy, or doing nothing. The North Korean famine and the food crisis in Zimbabwe provide powerful examples.

The recognition of the limits of bed-for-the-night humanitarianism and of the need for humanitarian workers to acknowledge how their actions might be contributing to unsavoury outcomes led many to try and identify new tactics that might reduce negative side-effects. Mary Anderson's famous credo (1999) of 'do no harm', inspired by the Hippocratic oath, urged aid agencies to develop new policies that acknowledged the unintended consequences of aid. In response, Fiona Terry (2002) observed that all aid does some harm and will have some unforeseen consequences, and that the best that aid agencies can do is try and minimize the harmful effects of aid. Towards that end, she advised that aid agencies eschew the seduction of becoming more political and instead put into place monitoring mechanisms to reduce the siphoning of aid, and if political authorities would not comply, aid agencies should be prepared to suspend assistance (Lischer 2005; Terry 2002). A literature on moral dilemmas acknowledged that pursuing one highly desired goal might hurt the prospects of another (Moore 1998). These criticisms of bed-for-the-night led many donors and aid agencies to look for alternatives.

Tactical Humanitarianism

Tactical humanitarianism occurs when external actors have as their main goal the provision of relief to those in life-threatening circumstances but adjust their policies in order to minimize overly negative consequences. It shares with a bed-for-the-night the desire to remain apolitical to the extent possible. Yet it is slightly more ambitious than this strategy because of its explicit willingness to examine the effects of assistance and consider whether those outcomes require the deliverer of aid to manipulate the incentives and constraints facing local parties. Humanitarian practitioners have initiated a healthy debate about how to bargain more cleverly with warlords, which local intermediaries have to deal with, how to keep camps from falling into the hands of fighters that perpetrate atrocities, when to rely on military protection from one of the sides or from hired security forces, when and how to flood the market with aid, and how to create local environments where aid can work even if the overall problem is not resolved. In general, this strategy tries to maintain the principles of neutrality, impartiality, and independence to the fullest extent possible, but attempts to reduce negative consequences.

Those advocating a hard-headed, tactical humanitarianism confront three critical issues. The first is assessing whether, in fact, their aid is doing more harm than good. Following Fiona Terry's insight that all aid does some harm, the challenge is to identify how much harm is the result of aid. The second issue concerns the threshold for withdrawing aid if perverse incentives for local actors cannot be eliminated through tactical adjustments. Aid workers will draw the line in different places. Médecins Sans Frontières (MSF) withdrew from the militarized refugee camps following the Rwandan genocide on the grounds that aid was being used to embolden the genocidaires and thus to prolong the suffering, but it is less well known that several MSF chapters stayed behind in the camps and continued to provide relief. The third issue concerns whether or not to make aid conditional and if so, on what conditions. Many aid agencies are adamantly opposed to the very idea of making basic needs conditional on good behaviour, but tactical humanitarianism does just that—it makes the aid conditional on the good behaviour of those who are obstructing its delivery and thus holds the victims captive to others. Those who question the effectiveness of these tactical adjustments in the face of strong, predatory local actors are likely to be limited, and often wonder whether more ambitious policies might produce better results. In some cases, they requested international military protection or intervention, hoping that armed escorts would reduce the rate at which food supplies were stolen.

Comprehensive Peacebuilding

Although peacebuilding can have various definitions, former UN Secretary General Boutros Boutros-Ghali's original formulation has considerable staying power: 'action to identify and support structures which will tend to strengthen and solidify peace in order to avoid relapse into conflict'.[4] Peacebuilders aspire to remove the root causes of violence and create this pacific disposition by investing post-conflict societies with various qualities, including democracy in order to reduce the tendency towards arbitrary power and give voice to all segments of society; the rule of law in order to reduce human rights violations; a market economy free from corruption in order to discourage individuals from believing that the surest path to fortune is by capturing the state; conflict management tools; and a culture of tolerance and respect.

States, international organizations, and international aid agencies both have helped to make and jump on this ambitious peacebuilding agenda. Its attractions are many. It aspires to address not only symptoms but also causes. It is consistent with the existing interests of both international and domestic actors that want to try and help states emerging from civil wars, societal breakdowns, and a violent past.[5] International actors increasingly view peacebuilding as instrumental to the broader humanitarian and international peace and security agenda. Its comprehensiveness is presumably one of its attractions, allowing lots of existing actors to envision how their activities are contributing to something that is bigger than them.

This peacebuilding agenda became quickly linked to humanitarianism, and, indeed, helped to define a 'new humanitarianism' (Macrae 2002; Weiss 1999). Many aid agencies that were increasingly working in conflict and post-conflict settings were forced to think about both their relationship to multilateral organizations that were providing aid and protection and how their relief-oriented activities might be linked to the post-conflict setting and the broader goal of creating a stable peace. Claire Short, who served as Britain's Secretary of State for International Development, argued that strategically obtuse aid could do harm, that aid should be based on rights as well as need and should involve political advocacy, that humanitarianism should dovetail with conflict resolution and peacebuilding, and that neutrality should be abandoned in some circumstances (Macrae and Leader 2001). According to her, aid agencies should work with states and international organizations that are seeking to establish a democratic, law-abiding, rights-observing, market-oriented, economically rational state that provides improved conditions for all of its citizens.

The idea that relief and other forms of assistance to those in life-threatening circumstances must be treated as part of a broader strategy for removing the root causes of conflict gains support not only from practitioners but also from scholars. A systematic study of UN comprehensive peacebuilding efforts by Michael Doyle and Nicholas Sambanis (2006: 339) includes timely humanitarian assistance on their list of seven key steps to peace, taking second place only to military security. 'Quick "wins" will win support and time,' they say. 'Distributing food, medicine, turning the electricity back on, cleaning up the rubble: all send the message that a new order means a better life. It builds temporary support that is needed for longer term changes.'

This peacebuilding strategy has come under heavy criticism in recent years. Peacebuilding does not have an impressive track record; while outsiders have been able to help reduce the probability that states will return to war five years after a peace agreement, they have been less successful at creating a stable peace. Perhaps the simplest explanation is that peacebuilders are expected to achieve the impossible dream, attempting to engineer in years what took centuries for West European states and doing so under very unfavourable conditions. Peacebuilding operations, after all, confront highly difficult conditions, including a lack of local assets, high levels of destruction from the violence, continuing conflict, and minimal support from powerful donors and benefactors (Chesterman 2004; Doyle and Sambanis 2000, 2006; Orr 2004). Consequently, the goal of sweeping transformation to a stable democracy is too hard to reach for many of the states where humanitarian emergencies occur. In fact trying this kind of revolutionary transformation of society and failing to follow through in an effective way might be worse than keeping in place some of the existing stabilizing forces of society.

This leads to an additional criticism: the goal of transplanting liberal democracy in war-torn soil has allowed former combatants to aggressively pursue their existing interests to the point that it rekindles the conflict. In their effort to radically transform all aspects of state, society, and economy in a matter of months, peacebuilders are subjecting these fragile societies to tremendous stress. States emerging from war do not have the necessary institutional framework or civic culture to absorb the potential pressures associated with political and market competition. Consequently, as peacebuilders push for instant liberalization, they are sowing the seeds of conflict, encouraging rivals to wage their struggle for supremacy through markets and ballots (Paris 2004; Zakaria 2003). International pressures to democratize have gone hand-in-hand with rising ethnic and sectarian conflict in Burundi in 1993 and Iraq today. This is not accidental: statistical studies show that partial democracies and incomplete democratic transitions are more likely to break down into civil war than are autocratic states (Hegre et al. 2002). Shock therapy, peacebuilding style, undermines the construction of the very institutions that are instrumental in producing a stable peace.

International peacebuilders also are expected to accomplish the impossible without adequate time, resources, and international support. Yet even when international interveners are willing to pony up resources, they may lack the knowledge to transform crisis-prone countries into stable, liberal, free-market societies (Feldman 2004). At present, many peacebuilders escape their uncertainty by relying on general models that frequently are developed from their most recent experiences in the field. In a report on Liberia and Sierra Leone, for example, the International Crisis Group (ICG 2004: 21–2) writes that peacebuilders possess an 'operational checklist' that does not recognize the underlying political dynamics. Universal models can be a false sanctuary. Relatedly, peacebuilders, especially in post-conflict settings and transitional administrations, tend to protect their authority and power, thus arrogating for themselves what gets done when. Yet, historically, stable democracy has been most likely to emerge in those post-colonial settings where the colonial power allowed its subjects to play the largest possible role in self-administration; today, proconsuls chafe at giving the teenager the keys to the car.

State transformation seems most promising in 'easy' cases (countries that have been democracies before, have fairly high GNP and literacy, and where the spoilers have been decisively defeated) or tiny cases where an overwhelming and perhaps long-term international presence is feasible (Bosnia, Kosovo, East Timor). Since donors intervene—or limit their intervention—for reasons that are only partly humanitarian, their willingness to stay the course for purely humanitarian reasons is always in doubt. Even in little East Timor, for example, the departure of peacekeepers and the scaling back of aid turned out to be very premature. Where the scale of the challenge is larger, as in Zaire/Congo, the level of effort may fall far short of what is needed to provide security and meet basic needs, let alone establish democracy.[6]

But is full-bore peacebuilding-cum-neo-trusteeship really necessary to produce stable outcomes? Among fourteen post-Cold War cases where the peacekeepers eventually packed up and left the country, Fortna (2008: chapter 4) and Doyle and Sambanis (2006: 75–81, Table 3.1) find that seven are successes in establishing a 'participatory peace' with the state intact, no residual fighting, an end to massive rights abuses, and at least minimal political openness. An eighth case, Rwanda, is mysteriously coded as a success by Doyle and Sambanis, but as a failure by George Downs and Stephen John Stedman (2002: 59, Table 2.1). The UN undertook 'multidimensional peacekeeping operations' in four of the successes by these criteria (El Salvador, Guatemala, Mozambique, and Namibia), a successful 'peace enforcement' mission in Croatia, and a successful traditional 'observer' mission in Nicaragua (Doyle and Sambanis 2006, Table 3.1). Among these, the 2006 Freedom House democracy score remains at the level of fully 'free' for Croatia, El Salvador, and Namibia, and 'partially free' for Mozambique and Nicaragua. Multidimensional efforts failed in Haiti and East Timor (fighting broke out and peacekeepers had to come back) and led to an ambiguous result in the Central African Republic. Doyle and Sambanis (2006: 76) code Cambodia as a multidimensional 'participatory peace', but its 2006 score of 'not free' should demote it to what they call a 'sovereign peace'. Downs and Stedman code Cambodia not as a success but as a mixed outcome.

Notwithstanding the label 'multidimensional peacekeeping', it is noteworthy that none of the unambiguous successes where peacekeepers actually left the country were cases of international military occupation with a transformational agenda along the lines of Bosnia, Kosovo, East Timor, Sierra Leone, and Iraq. Rather, they were all cases in which the local parties to the conflict were exhausted by war, perceived incentives to settle it, and got some international help to facilitate a transition to a somewhat more open society where the belligerents could lay down their arms. In all these cases, including Cambodia, elites with blood on their hands and a questionable track record remained in power, but decided to behave better for practical reasons of their own. There was no internationally imposed social revolution—indeed no social revolution of any kind. The good news, therefore, is that less ambitious strategies of change have sometimes been successful in creating the basis for political stability that reduces the risk of future humanitarian disasters.

Back-a-Decent-Winner

The combination of these criticisms of peacebuilding, the growing recognition that a 'second-best' outcome of workable stability might in fact be better than the preferred but infeasible outcome of a fully liberal society, and the natural inclination of resource-sensitive states who want a 'cheap peace' have paved the way towards a strategy of back-a-decent-winner. The thrust of this strategy is to negotiate with those who are capable of ending the violence, creating a stable ceasefire, and improving the local conditions so that human rights abuses are reduced. It shares with peacebuilding the desire to stop the causes of suffering. It differs because it is modest in its goals; it aims to promote those who are willing to favour an enlightened stability but does not attempt to radically transform political, economic, and cultural structures.

There are two defining aspects of this strategy. To begin, international actors are willing to negotiate with and make deals with those who once held or who currently hold power: patrons of traditional patronage networks, defensive-minded regional leaders, authoritarian state leaders who want to defeat ruthless resource-dealing rebels, internationally oriented technocrats, holders of property in legitimate business enterprises, or any organized groups that have an interest in using pragmatic bargaining and limited use of force to maintain a stable social order. Second, in order to promote this outcome, they use various tools and resources: the occasional show of force; economic incentives; and the conferral of recognition on those elites that will make the bargain. Barnett and Zuercher (2009) call this the 'peacebuilder's contract', wherein peacebuilders achieve the cooperation of local elites for some of their agenda and local elites receive resources and promise protection in return.

This strategy is not without its controversies or its problems. How indecent can the winner be and still be considered a 'decent' outcome? According to some, the threshold for a decent winner does not have to be very high in order to succeed as long as the incentives are auspicious. In the Doyle and Sambanis success cases, international cooperation with 'decent' winners included a Communist dictator in Cambodia, a repressive agrarian oligarchy shifting to a neo-liberal export strategy in El Salvador, warlords whose source of foreign support dried up in Mozambique, heirs to a genocidal regime in Guatemala, and victorious, war-weary ethnic nationalists in Croatia. This low threshold will leave some aid agencies, states, and international organizations wondering whether they have completely compromised their values. Colombia's freely elected President Uribe runs another regime which is controversial for its light treatment of the criminal paramilitaries that the regime's predecessors had relied upon to wage a dirty war against the drug-dealing FARC rebels—while incidentally expropriating the land of innocent peasants and adding to the flow of internally displaced persons. The human rights community has denounced Uribe for his amnesty policy, yet this is a country that has huge humanitarian needs after years of violence and displacement, as well as a competent, elected government to work with. The effectiveness of international refugee strategies depends at least as much on the creation of compelling political incentives for such political opportunists as they depend on the ethical commitment of humanitarians to provide a 'bed for the night' for those who are suffering.

CONCLUSION: REALISM AND HUMANITARIAN STRATEGY

Most people think that realism and humanitarianism mix about as well as oil and water. In fact, the realist sensibility with its attention to power, strategy, and consequences is of great potential value in analysing the problem of providing humanitarian aid to refugees and other victims of political strife. Realism helps to explain why states and multilateral coalitions are sometimes motivated to undertake humanitarian intervention. It also helps to explain why those interventions sometimes fail to accomplish their humanitarian goals or occasionally even cause more suffering. Realist ways of thinking may also help focus attention on the political nature of humanitarian assistance. Realism provides a framework for understanding the limitations of some traditional apolitical humanitarian strategies, such as the one I have called 'a bed for the night'. A realist orientation also highlights the possible advantages of pragmatic humanitarian strategies that consciously integrate politics and relief work, such as the one I have called 'back a decent winner'. While the choice of an effective strategy for aiding refugees and other victims will depend on varying circumstances, realism provides a set of prudential criteria that has much to recommend it.

NOTES

1. Both authors are theoretically eclectic, but draw heavily on realist-style theory. Pape has written on the balance of power and offered strategic theories of terrorist behaviour; Kaufmann has explained ethnic conflict as a security dilemma.
2. See the special issue of *World Politics*, Vol. 61, No. 1 (January 2009) on unipolarity.
3. This section draws on Michael Barnett and Jack Snyder (2008).
4. Agenda for Peace, para. 21. In his *Supplement to an Agenda for Peace*, Boutros-Ghali expanded on the basic ideas behind peacebuilding and then defined its essential goal as 'the creation of structures for the institutionalization of peace.' 1995, para. 49. A few years later the Brahimi Report on Peace Operations further refined the definition of peacebuilding: 'activities undertaken on the far side of conflict to reassemble the foundations of peace and provide the tools for building on those foundations something that is more than just the absence of war.'
5. On the conditions under which local actors invite in peacekeepers, see Fortna (2008).
6. Against this scepticism, Doyle and Sambanis argue that the most spectacular failures of international peacekeeping, nation-building, and humanitarian intervention were the consequence of outmoded Cold War peacekeeping models in places like Somalia, Bosnia, and Rwanda during the early post-Cold War period. As a result of these trials and errors, they claim, multilateral peace operations have developed a more comprehensive and much more effective strategy, which includes humanitarian assistance among a whole set of mutually supportive tools.

BIBLIOGRAPHY

Anderson, M. B. 1999. *Do no harm: how aid can support peace—or war.* London: Lynne Rienner.

Annan, Kofi. 2004. 'Genocide is a threat to peace requiring strong united action, Secretary-General tells Stockholm International forum.' Press Release of office of United Nations Secretary-General, SE/SM/9126, 26 January 2004.

Barnett, M. and Zuercher, C. 2009. The peacebuilder's contract. In: Paris, R. and Sisk, T. D. eds. *The dilemmas of statebuilding: confronting the contradictions of postwar peace operations*. New York: Routledge.

Barnett, M. 2002. *Eyewitness to a genocide: the United Nations and Rwanda*. Ithaca, NY: Cornell University Press.

Chesterman, S. 2004. *You, the people: the United Nations, transitional administration, and state-building*. Oxford: Oxford University Press.

Christensen, T. J. 1996. *Useful adversaries: grand strategy, domestic mobilization, and Sino-American conflict, 1947–1958*. Princeton, NJ: Princeton University Press.

Crawford, T. W. 2002. Pivotal deterrence and the Kosovo war: why the Holbrooke agreement failed. *Political Science Quarterly* 116(4), 499–523.

Downs, G. and Stedman, S. J. 2002. Evaluation issues in peace implementation. In: Stedman, S. J. et al. eds. *Ending civil wars: the implementation of peace agreements*. Boulder, CO: Lynne Rienner.

Doyle, M. W. and Sambanis, N. 2000. International peacebuilding: a theoretical and quantitative analysis. *American Political Science Review* 94(4), 779–801.

———2006. *Making war and building peace: United Nations peace operations*. Princeton, NJ: Princeton University Press.

Dueck, C. 2006. *Reluctant crusaders: power, culture, and change in American grand strategy*. Princeton, NJ: Princeton University Press.

Feldman, N. 2004. *What we owe Iraq: war and the ethics of nation building*. Princeton, NJ: Princeton University Press.

Finnemore, M. 2003. *The purpose of intervention: changing beliefs about the use of force*. Ithaca, NY: Cornell University Press.

Fortna, V. P. 2008. *Does peacekeeping work? Shaping belligerents' choices after civil war*. Princeton, NJ: Princeton University Press.

Goldstone, J. A. et al. 2005. A global forecasting model of political instability. In: convention paper, *Annual Meeting of the American Political Science Association*. Philadelphia.

Greenhill, K. M. 2004. Draining the sea, or feeding the fire? Evaluating the role of population relocation in counterinsurgency operations.

——2008. Strategic engineered migration as a weapon of war. *Civil Wars* 10(1), 6–21.

——2010. *Weapons of massed migration: forced displacement, coercion, and foreign policy*. Ithaca, NY: Cornell University Press.

Hegre, H. et al. 2002. Toward a democratic civil peace? Democracy, political change, and civil war, 1816–1992. *American Political Science Review* 95(1), 33–48.

ICG 2004. *Liberia and Sierra Leone: rebuilding failed states*. Dakar/Brussels: ICG.

Kalyvas, S. N. 2006. *The logic of violence in civil war*. Cambridge: Cambridge University Press.

Kaufmann, C. D. and Pape, R. A. 1999. Explaining costly international moral action: Britain's sixty-year campaign against the Atlantic slave trade. *International Organization* 53(4), 631–68.

Krauthammer, C. 2004. In defense of democratic realism. *National Interest* Fall, 15–25.

Kuperman, A. J. and Crawford, T. W. eds. 2006. *Gambling on humanitarian intervention: moral hazard, rebellion and civil war.* London: Routledge.

Lischer, S. K. 2005. *Dangerous sanctuaries: refugee camps, civil war, and the dilemmas of humanitarian aid.* Ithaca, NY: Cornell University Press.

Macrae, J. ed. 2002. *The new humanitarianisms: a review of trends in global humanitarian action.* London: Overseas Development Institute.

——and Leader, N. 2001. Apples, pears and porridge: the origins and impact of the search for 'coherence' between humanitarian and political responses to chronic political emergencies. *Disasters* 25(4), 290–307.

Mearsheimer, J. J. 2001. *The tragedy of great power politics.* New York: W. W. Norton & Co.

Moore, J. 1998. *Hard choices: moral dilemmas in humanitarian intervention.* Lanham, MD: Rowman & Littlefield.

Morgenthau, H. J. 1951. *In defense of the national interest: a critical examination of American foreign policy.* 1st ed. New York: Knopf.

Muggah, R. 2006. *No refuge: the crisis of refugee militarization in Africa.* London: Zed Books.

Niebuhr, R. 1932. *Moral man and immoral society: a study in ethics and politics.* New York: Charles Scribner's Sons (reprinted Louisville: Westminster John Knox Press, 2001).

Orr, R. 2004. The United States as nation builder. In: Orr, R. ed. *Winning the peace: an American strategy for post-conflict reconstruction.* Washington, DC: CSIC Press.

Paris, R. 2004. *At war's end: building peace after civil conflict: building peace after civil conflict.* Cambridge: Cambridge University Press.

Pentagon 1992. Excerpts from Pentagon's plan: 'Prevent the re-emergence of a new rival'. *New York Times.* 8 March 1992.

Posen, B. 1993. The security dilemma and ethnic conflict. *Survival* 35(1), 27–47.

Power, S. 2002. *A problem from hell: America and the age of genocide.* New York: Basic Books.

Rieff, D. 2002. *A bed for the night: humanitarianism in crisis.* London: Vintage.

Salehyan, I. and Gleditsch, K. S. 2006. Refugees and the spread of civil war. *International Organization* 60(2), 335–366.

Schweller, R. L. 1996. Neorealism's status-quo bias: What security dilemma? *Security Studies* 5(3), 90–121.

Snyder, J. L. 1991. *Myths of empire: domestic politics and international ambition.* Ithaca, NY: Cornell University Press.

Terry, F. 2002. *Condemned to repeat? The paradox of humanitarian action.* Ithaca, NY: Cornell University Press.

Valentino, B. A. 2004. *Final solutions: mass killing and genocide in the twentieth century.* Ithaca, NY: Cornell University Press.

Van Evera, S. 1999. *Causes of war: power and the roots of conflict.* Ithaca, NY: Cornell University Press.

Walt, S. M. 1987. *The origins of alliances.* Ithaca, NY: Cornell University Press.

Weiss, T. G. 1999. The humanitarian identity crisis. *Ethics and International Affairs* 13, 1–42.

Western, J. 2002. Sources of humanitarian intervention: beliefs, information, and advocacy in the US decisions on Somalia and Bosnia. *International Security* 26(4), 112–42.

——2005. *Selling intervention and war: the presidency, the media, and the American public.* Baltimore, MD: Johns Hopkins University Press.

Zakaria, F. 2003. *The future of freedom: illiberal democracy at home and abroad.* 1st ed. New York: W. W. Norton & Co.

3

International Cooperation in the Refugee Regime[1]

Alexander Betts

ABSTRACT

This chapter examines the conditions under which international cooperation takes place in the refugee regime. It does so in two parts. First, it identifies the nature of the cooperation problem within the refugee regime. While the dominant conception of the refugee regime is as a Prisoner's Dilemma game, the chapter argues that this is misrepresentative because it fails to capture the asymmetric North–South power relations inherent to the regime. Given that the majority of the world's refugees are in the South and the regime sets out few norms obligating Northern states to contribute to the protection of refugees who are not on their territory, the regime is more appropriately characterized by the game theoretical analogy of a Suasion Game. Secondly, through archival research, the chapter explores the conditions under which that cooperation problem has historically been overcome. It examines the four main examples of *ad hoc* bargaining processes convened by the United Nations High Commissioner for Refugees (UNHCR) between 1980 and 2005 to facilitate North–South cooperation to address long-standing refugee situations. The chapter argues that variation in the success or failure of these initiatives is best explained by the role of issue-linkage. Rather than contributing to refugee protection in the South for its own sake, Northern states' willingness to contribute has depended upon a belief that there is a substantive causal relationship between refugees in the South and interests in other issue-areas affecting the North such as security, migration, and trade. However, because the material relationship between refugee protection in the South and other issue-areas in the North has been subject to uncertainty or ambiguity, UNHCR has played a significant role in influencing Northern states' beliefs about the causal relationship between issue-areas through a combination of information provision, argumentation, institutional design, and playing an epistemic role. The chapter has wider implications for IR insofar as it highlights the way in which substantive issue-linkages can be used by international organizations to overcome power asymmetries.

There has been a surge in interest in understanding the conditions under which international cooperation takes place in relation to international migration (Ghosh 1999; Hansen 2008; Hollifield 2008; Kessler 1996; Koslowski 2008; Martin et al. 2006). In contrast, there has been less work exploring the conditions under which international cooperation has historically taken place in the global refugee regime. Yet it is an important topic because understanding when and why states have been willing to contribute to refugee protection and durable solutions is integral to the work of anyone striving to improve the plight of refugees and displaced people. However, it also has significance because the refugee regime has a number of features that make the analysis of wider relevance to international relations (IR). In particular, although the regime places an obligation on states to protect refugees who reach their territory, it sets out few obligations on far away states to contribute to the protection of refugees who remain on the territory of another state. Given that the overwhelming majority of the world's refugees come from and remain in the global South, this means that the regime is characterized by a significant asymmetry in power between North and South. Southern states host the majority of the world's refugees and Northern contributions to addressing their plight are discretionary. Historically, as is the case in many other policy fields such as international migration, global health, or development assistance, one of the regime's greatest challenges has therefore been to overcome this power asymmetry. As this chapter demonstrates, analysing the refugee regime has the potential to offer important wider insights into the conditions under which North–South power asymmetries may be overcome.

The argument I make is a simple one, based on two main claims. First, I argue that, in contrast to the dominant literature within Refugee Studies, which characterizes the regime by the game theoretical analogy of Prisoner's Dilemma (Suhrke 1998), the cooperation problem can more appropriately be characterized by the analogy of a Suasion Game, which takes into account the inherent North–South power asymmetry within the regime (Betts 2009; Hasenclever et al. 1997; Martin 1993). The overwhelming majority of the world's refugees come from and are hosted in the South and the regime places no obligation on Northern states to engage in burden-sharing to support protection in the South. Secondly, I argue that this cooperation problem has historically been overcome through issue-linkage (Aggarwal 1998; Haas 1980, 1990; Keohane 1982; Martin 1993; McGinnis 1986; Mitchell and Keilbach 2004; Stein 1980; Young 2002). Northern states have not been concerned with refugee protection in the South for its own sake or for altruistic reasons but because they have perceived protection in the South to be linked to their interests in other issue-areas, notably security, immigration, and trade.

However, while most of the existing literature on issue-linkage within IR focuses on the role of tactical linkage—that is, the way in which issues are made explicitly or implicitly conditional upon one another within bargaining—the most important linkages within the refugee regime have been substantive linkages—that is, the real or perceived causal relationship between issue-areas. What has mattered for influencing Northern states' contribution to the South has not only been the way in which pay-offs in different issue-areas have been made formally conditional upon one another but also the underlying beliefs that actors have had about causal relationships between refugee protection in the South and security, immigration, and trade in the North. International cooperation in the refugee regime has relied upon there being a substantive linkage—whether material, ideational, or institutional—between refugee protection in the South, on the one hand, and security, immigration, or trade in the North, on the other hand.

Furthermore, the chapter argues that the UNHCR has played a significant role in creating, changing, or communicating substantive linkages. Given that substantive linkages are not simply material, and that even when there are material relationships they may be obscured by uncertainty, UNHCR has played a role in influencing Northern states' underlying beliefs about the causal relationships between issue-areas. In other words it has engaged in what might be described as *cross-issue persuasion*, which may be formally defined as when an actor A influences an actor B's beliefs about the relationship between issue-area X and issue-area Y as a means of inducing actor B to act in issue-area X on the basis of its interest in issue-area Y. In the empirical case studies examined by this chapter, UNHCR has been able to use cross-issue persuasion to shape Northern states' beliefs about the relationship between refugee protection in the South and security, immigration, and trade in the North through four main mechanisms: (*a*) the provision of information, (*b*) argumentation, (*c*) institutional design, and (*d*) playing an epistemic role.

In order to make this argument, the chapter explores two hypotheses. Firstly, in order for international cooperation to take place, there have needed to be *substantive linkages* between refugee protection and issue-areas in which Northern states have had an interest. Secondly, *UNHCR has played an important role in creating, changing, and communicating substantive linkages*. In order to demonstrate that these two claims about the conditions for international cooperation hold, the chapter explores and rejects two null hypotheses in relation to the four case studies. First, it rejects the null hypothesis (Ho1) that Northern states have contributed to in-region protection for altruistic reasons. Secondly, it rejects the null hypothesis (Ho2) that UNHCR has been irrelevant to the bargaining process. Each one of these serves to provide the counterfactual against which the two core conditions for cooperation are tested.

These hypotheses are explored through a qualitative analysis of four case studies of international conferences convened by UNHCR to address refugee crises between 1980 and 2005: the International Conferences on Assistance to Refugees in Africa (ICARA I and II) of 1981 and 1984; the International Conference on Central American Refugees (CIREFCA); the Indo-Chinese Comprehensive Plan of Action (CPA) of 1988–96; and the so-called Convention Plus initiative of 2003–5. All four cases represent initiatives convened by UNHCR in order to overcome long-standing refugee situations in the global South. In the absence of a clear normative and legal framework governing international burden-sharing on refugee protection, each of the initiatives was conceived as an *ad hoc* bargaining process with its own institutional design. Two of the case studies were successes in terms of leading to significant international cooperation, and two failures. The variation in their success and their institutional design makes them a useful empirical context in which to examine the conditions for international cooperation.

Reflecting the chapter's main contributions, it divides into two main sections. The first part briefly outlines the nature of the cooperation problem with the refugee regime. After briefly outlining the main analytical features of the global refugee regime, it demonstrates how the refugee regime can be appropriately characterized as a North–South impasse that can be represented by the game theoretical analogy of a Suasion Game. The second part develops the chapter's main theoretical argument and explains the conditions under which the cooperation problem has historically been overcome. It demonstrates the role of substantive issue-linkages in overcoming the North–South impasse, and the role that UNHCR has played in creating, communicating, or changing those linkages. The chapter concludes by outlining the main practical and theoretical implications of the analysis.

COOPERATION PROBLEM: NORTH–SOUTH IMPASSE

The global refugee regime represents the set of norms, rules, principles, and decision-making procedures that regulate states' responses to refugees (Hasenclever et al. 1997; Krasner 1983: 2). The aim of the regime is to facilitate cooperation to ensure that refugees receive access to protection and a durable solution to their situation. The contemporary regime is based mainly on, first, the 1951 Convention on the Status of Refugees, which defines who qualifies as a refugee and the rights to which refugees are entitled, and, secondly, UNHCR, which is the organization that was created to uphold and oversee implementation of the 1951 Convention (Loescher et al. 2008).

The refugee regime comprises two main norms: 'asylum' and 'burden-sharing'. Asylum can be considered to relate to the provision of protection to refugees who reach the territory of that state. Burden-sharing can be considered to be the provision of protection to refugees who are on the territory of another state—for example, through resettlement or financial contributions to UNHCR. The degree of institutionalized cooperation that exists in relation to these two norms contrasts markedly. Asylum is governed by a strong normative and legal framework, underpinned by the principle of *non-refoulement*, whereby states must refrain from sending a refugee back to a state in which he or she faces a well-founded fear of persecution (Allain 2001; Lauterpacht and Bethleham 2001). In contrast, burden-sharing is governed by a weak normative and legal framework (Milner 2009; Thielemann 2003). States' contributions to supporting refugees who are on the territory of another state are almost entirely discretionary.

Given their differing degrees of institutionalization, UNHCR's role in facilitating cooperation has therefore historically been different in relation to these two norms. In relation to asylum, its role has been one of surveillance and legal expertise in order to oversee states' compliance with legal norms. In relation to burden-sharing, on the other hand, it has needed to play a more proactive role of political facilitation, convening a range of ad hoc appeals, conferences, and other initiatives in order to persuade predominantly Northern donor and resettlement states to voluntarily contribute to supporting refugees' access to protection and durable solutions.

On an analytical level, the nature of the cooperation problem in relation to asylum and burden-sharing is also different. Understanding why states contribute to asylum is part of the broader question of 'why do states comply with international law?' (Koh 1997). Explaining cooperation on asylum relates to issues of reciprocity and legitimacy. States regard compliance with the strongly institutionalized norm of asylum as a means both to ensure other states' long-term compliance and as a means on which to be recognized as legitimate states and hence to exercise authority in the international system (Hurd 2007; Hurrell 2007). On the other hand, understanding why states contribute to burden-sharing is a different conceptual puzzle. In the absence of a strongly institutionalized basis to the norm, and significant scope for state discretion, cooperation on burden-sharing is much more dominated by power and interests than issues of reciprocity and legitimacy.

While understanding cooperation in relation to asylum and burden-sharing is important, they point in analytically different directions and so the focus of this chapter is exclusively on explaining cooperation in relation to burden-sharing.

The default explanation for the nature of the cooperation problem in relation to burden-sharing in the refugee regime can be found in Astri Suhrke's groundbreaking 1998 *Journal of Refugee Studies* article, in which she argues that the refugee regime has historically been characterized by collective action failure. This, she argues, is because the provision of refugee protection constitutes a global public good. As with the provision of street lighting at a domestic level or international action against climate change, all actors will benefit from one state providing refugee protection and so, in the absence of binding institutional mechanisms for burden-sharing, states will 'free ride' on the provision of other states.

Suhrke (1998) captures this situation with the game theoretical analogy of Prisoner's Dilemma, whereby there is a disjuncture between what is rational for an individual state acting in isolation and what *would be* a rational strategy for states acting collectively. Collectively, states recognize the value of refugee protection (both for security and humanitarian reasons); individually, states' optimum strategy is to 'free ride' on other states' contributions. Drawing upon neo-realist assumptions, she suggests that the only circumstances under which collective action failure has been overcome is when a global hegemon such as the United States has unilaterally underwritten the costs of refugee protection on the basis of its own interests.

However, the analogy of Prisoner's Dilemma partly misrepresents the reasons for collective action failure in the refugee regime. A core assumption of Prisoner's Dilemma is that states have symmetrical interests and power relations. While this assumption may hold at the regional level, on a global level the states in the refugee regime have different interests and power relations. Aside from their differential capabilities and bargaining power, Southern states also tend to have greater proximity to conflict and human rights abusing states and less ability to control their borders than Northern states. The radically different positions held by Northern and Southern states within the regime render the assumption of symmetrical interests and power relations untenable.

IR theory has identified alternative situation-structures, beyond Prisoner's Dilemma, which create different cooperation problems, which better capture North–South relations. One of these is the idea of a Suasion Game, which has been used to understand the power relations created by North–South relations. This situation will arise when, in a two-actor model, there is one player which is stronger and has little interest in cooperating, and one

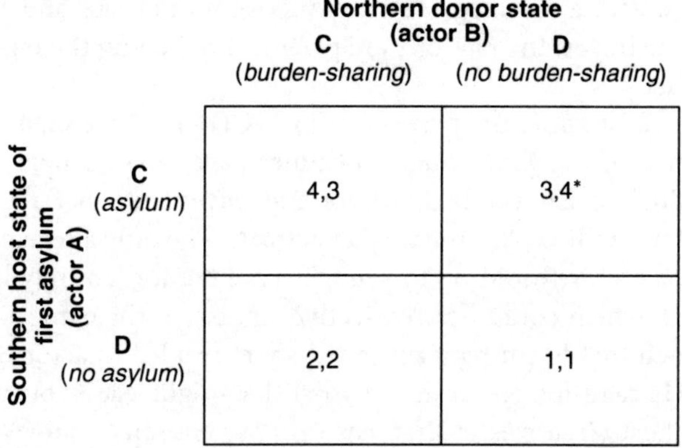

Figure 3.1 Suasion Game. Number left (right) of comma refers to A's (B's) preference ordering (1 = worst outcome; 4 = best outcome). * = equilibrium

actor who is weaker and has little choice but to cooperate. This situation structure has been applied, for example, to analyse North–South relations in relation to the international trade regime when a Northern state may have very little interest in cooperating by opening up its markets to a Southern state, while the Southern state will have very little choice but to accept the terms of trade offered by the Northern state as attempting to impose a retaliatory trade sanction would hurt the Southern state even more. The Suasion Game, then, leads to a situation in which the weaker actor either 'takes what is on offer', or hurts itself more by not cooperating at all (Hasenclever et al. 1997; Martin 1993).

The Suasion Game can be illustrated (Figure 3.1). It involves two actors—one weaker actor A (Southern host state of first asylum) and one stronger actor B (Northern donor state). Because of their different relative power, the two actors have different interests. The situation can be represented in game theory in one of two ways. *Either* one (weaker) actor, A, has a dominant strategy to cooperate, which the other (stronger) one, B, can exploit, *or* one actor, B, has a dominant strategy to defect (stronger), while the other must cooperate in order to avoid an even worse outcome (weaker). In either case, the weaker actor's preferred strategy is to cooperate—either because non-cooperation is not practically viable or because it would lead to even greater costs. However, the stronger actor is in a position to choose to defect and that is likely to be its preferred position. The Northern state's cooperative strategy (C) is burden-sharing; its defecting strategy (D) is limited or no burden-sharing. The Southern state's cooperative strategy (C) is to provide asylum; its defecting strategy (D) is to close its borders and not provide asylum. In the boxes, the pay-offs are given, with 4 being the biggest pay-off and 1 the least.

An instance of unrequited cooperation (CD) is consequently the most likely outcome of the game. Suasion Games have only a single equilibrium outcome, which satisfies only one actor and leaves the other aggrieved. The stronger actor B will exploit the weaker actor A. The only alternative strategy available to actor A would be to scupper cooperation entirely by choosing outcome DD, which could be an effective strategy if the game was repeated over time such that harming itself in the short run led to actor B enhancing its long-run bargaining power in a manner that might lead to outcome CC. In reality, few host countries of first asylum have chosen to move to box DD. However, examples of successful attempts by the weaker actor, A, to move to box DD in the short-run as a means to obtaining outcome CC are rare. One notable exception, when this was achieved, includes Macedonia closing its borders to Kosovar refugees in the late 1990s, which led to significant European burden-sharing (Burutciski and Suhrke 2001; Williams and Zeager 2004). Generally, though, Southern host states of first asylum avoid moving to DD in the short-run, fearful that it will leave them stranded in DD rather than inducing a move to CC.

As with all game theoretical representations, the Suasion Game merely provides an analogy to describe a real-world situation. It is not one that should be taken too literally. As with all game theoretical analogies it depends upon the highly stylized assumption of 'simultaneous play'. However, the analogy is useful because it highlights the inadequacies of the dominant conception that the cooperation problem in the global refugee regime can be represented by Prisoner's Dilemma. Furthermore, it is an analogy that highlights the centrality of North–South relations in explaining the under-provision of refugee protection. Moving beyond the game theoretical analogy of a Suasion Game, however, the source of collective action failure in the refugee regime might more generally be described as a North–South impasse situation.

North–South impasse situations may therefore be defined as occurring when a problem primarily originates in and remains relatively confined to the South, while the economic and political means to address the problem are largely held by the North. Consequently, in the absence of Northern states having either a binding legal or normative framework impelling cooperation or having a perceived interest in addressing the problem for its own sake, Southern states will have little bargaining power to induce Northern contributions. Southern states will then either have to 'take what is on offer' from Northern states or risk harming themselves more by scuppering negotiations entirely. Such situations are particularly important for understanding certain areas of global governance in which collective action failure arises on a global scale because of a combination of the 'problem' being mainly located in and confined to the South, on the one hand, and the differential power capabilities of North and South, on the other.

Many of these structural features apply in the case of the refugee regime. The refugee regime can therefore be characterized as a North–South impasse situation. The majority of refugees who come from Southern states remain in and are hosted by Southern states. In the absence of a clear, binding normative framework on burden-sharing, Northern states have few obligations or incentives to contribute to refugee protection in the South. Southern host states have only limited ability to control their border and little bargaining power in the international system. They are therefore left in a position in which they have few options other than either to take 'what is on offer' in terms of limited earmarked contributions of the North or to disengage from negotiations entirely.

Aside from its impact on international cooperation, this North–South impasse has had significant human consequences. In particular, it has contributed to the so-called 'protracted refugee situations' in which refugees often remain for several years in confined camps or settlements in insecure border locations in Southern states, without access to many of the rights to which the 1951 Convention entitles them and with little prospect of a durable solution to their plight (Loescher and Milner 2005). There are estimated to be around 12 million refugees in such situations—for example, Somalis in Kenya, Burundians in Tanzania, Afghans in Iran and Pakistan, Palestinians in Lebanon and Jordan, and Burmese in Thailand. Protracted refugee situations and the absence of effective protection represent a consequence of the North–South impasse insofar as the absence of burden-sharing economically constrains the opportunities for enhancing protection and durable solutions and politically constrains Southern host states in their ability to allocate scarce resources to supporting non-citizens. These human consequences mean that it is extremely important to understand the conditions under which the North–South impasse has been and can be overcome.

CONDITIONS FOR COOPERATION: CROSS-ISSUE PERSUASION

On certain, albeit rare, occasions this North–South impasse has been overcome, and international cooperation has taken place. Understanding the factors that lead Northern states to contribute to refugee protection in the South is important because it can shed light on the conditions under which the North–South impasse may be overcome in future. In order to explore the conditions under which cooperation has taken place, this section looks at the main four examples of attempts by UNHCR to facilitate international cooperation and burden-sharing to address long-standing refugee situations in the global South between 1980 and 2005. Each case study represents an *ad hoc* initiative intended to facilitate North–South cooperation to address protracted or mass influx situations in the South. The four case studies are analytically useful because, firstly, there is variation in their outcome—two being 'successes' and two 'failures' in terms of promoting international cooperation—and, secondly, because, in the absence of an overarching institutional framework governing burden-sharing, each initiative was conceived from scratch and had its own unique institutional design. These two factors make it methodologically possible to explore a range of questions relating to the relationship between institutional design and outcome.

Conceptual Framework

In order to explain the variation in outcome between the cases, I use a particular conceptual framework based on the concept of issue-linkage (Figure 3.2). Issue-linkage has been identified as a way of overcoming the Suasion Game. It refers to the way in which issues are grouped together in formal interstate bargaining (McGinnis 1986; Stein 1980). The literature on issue-linkage describes two ways in which issues come to be connected: tactical and substantive linkages. The former describes the way in which issues which may not necessarily have any substantive relationship to one another are made formally conditional on one another through horse-trading. The latter describes the way in which issues are grouped together on the basis of having some kind of structural relationship to one another (Aggarwal 1998; Haas 1980). Issue-linkage has been identified in the bargaining and international cooperation literature as a means to overcome collective action failure. By introducing additional issues to the negotiations, side-payments may create additional side-payments that incentivize cooperation (Aggarwal 1998; Axelrod 1984; Haas 1980; Keohane 1982).

Lisa Martin has argued that issue-linkage offers a means to overcome the Suasion Game, claiming that 'private linked benefits contribute to the supply of a public good in suasion games' (Martin 1993: 105). In a situation in which there are asymmetrical interests or power relations between actors—like North–South relations—and the stronger actor has little incentive to cooperate and the weaker actor has little means to induce or coerce action by the stronger actor, issue-linkage may have a role to play (Bhagwati 1984;

Type of linkage	Basis for linkage	Mechanism of influence
Tactical	Conditionality	Bargaining
Substantive	Perception	Persuasion

Figure 3.2 Typology of issue-linkage

Ravenhill 1990). This is because introducing additional issues may address the underlying causes of the Suasion Game. Firstly, it may provide the stronger actor with an incentive to cooperate. If its cooperation is linked to its derivation of side-payments in relation to another issue, this may create an interest that was previously absent. Secondly, this increased interest on the part of the stronger actor may, in turn, strengthen the weaker actor's bargaining position vis-à-vis the stronger actor. Put differently, issue-linkage may create an incentive for Northern states to have an interest in an issue in which they may not have an interest for its own sake and so facilitate North–South cooperation. The mechanism by which it would do so is through changing the pay-offs in the Suasion Game, such that the pay-offs in the top left-hand box might read '4,5' instead of '4,3' and the equilibrium outcome would be box CC rather than CD.

However, Martin's analysis explicitly relates to what the broader linkages literature calls 'tactical linkages'. Tactical linkage assumes that two issues need to be part of the same formal negotiations, and explicitly made conditional upon one another, in order for interests in relation to one issue to shape action related to the other issue (Aggarwal 1998; McGinnis 1986; Stein 1980). The basis of tactical linkage is horse-trading and tactical linkage can be used as a mechanism of influence through bargaining. In other words, an actor A can change the behaviour of another actor B through inducement or coercion based on a conditional relationship between two issues or issue-areas.

However, in the case of the refugee regime, the types of issue-linkage that have mattered for explaining cooperation have predominantly been substantive linkages. These relate to the real or perceived causal relationship between issues or issue-areas. Often the material relationship between two issue-areas may be ambiguous, uncertain, or contested. This ambiguity implies an important role for the way in which causal relationships are perceived. This opens up the possibility that substantive linkages can be created, changed, or communicated in order to influence the underlying beliefs of another actor. Substantive linkages can thereby be used as a mechanism of influence through what I call 'cross-issue persuasion'.

Cross-issue persuasion describes the conditions under which an actor A influences an actor B's beliefs about the relationship between issue-area X and issue-area Y as a means of inducing actor B to act in issue-area X on the basis of its interest in issue-area Y. It represents a form of persuasion insofar as it is a form of influence designed to change beliefs (Crawford 2002; Keohane 2003; Risse 2003). Within the refugee regime, UNHCR has sometimes been in a position to create, change, or communicate substantive linkages to influence the behaviour of Northern states and overcome the North–South impasse. Within the four initiatives looked at by this chapter, it has effectively engaged in cross-issue persuasion through four principal mechanisms: (*a*) *institutional design*, (*b*) *an epistemic role*, (*c*) *argumentation*, and (*d*) *information provision*.

Empirical Application

In order to substantiate the theoretical argument outlined above, this section tests two hypotheses in relation to the four case studies of UNHCR-convened conferences between 1980 and 2005. The first hypothesis (H1) is that *substantive linkages across issue-areas have been necessary for cooperation*. For Northern states to contribute to in-region refugee protection in the South, there has needed to be a substantive relationship between refugee protection in the South and immigration, security, or trade in the North. In order to provide evidence for this hypothesis, the article seeks to reject the null hypothesis (Ho1) that Northern state contributions to protection have been altruistic. The second hypothesis (H2) is that *UNHCR has been necessary for cooperation*. For Northern states to contribute to refugee protection in the South, they have needed to recognize the relationship between in-region protection and their interests. Where this has been complex and subject to uncertainty, UNHCR has had an important role to play in enabling states to recognize these interests. In order to provide evidence for this hypothesis, the chapter seeks to reject the null hypothesis (Ho2) that UNHCR has been irrelevant to the bargaining process.

Northern states have voluntarily contributed to burden-sharing insofar as they have believed that there has been a material, ideational, or institutional relationship between refugee protection in the South and their interests in security, trade, and immigration, for example. Without these interests, Northern states would not have contributed. In ICARA and Convention Plus there were very few Northern contributions. However, the very limited contributions that were made were based on a relationship to security and immigration respectively. In CIREFCA, European contributions were based on the belief in a relationship between protection, regional security, and development, and inter-regional trade. In the CPA, the important contribution of the United States was based on the relationship between protection, regional security, and ensuring global security at the end of the Cold War. The causal relationships on which Northern contributions were based are illustrated below.

Furthermore, UNHCR has played a crucial role in creating, changing, or simply communicating these substantive linkages. Although it has not been able to significantly influence the material relationship between issue-areas, it has nevertheless played a significant role in shaping states' beliefs about the causal relationship between issue-areas. In practice, there is a large degree of uncertainty and ambiguity about the relationship between refugee protection and other issue-areas. This ambiguity has allowed UNHCR (along with other actors) to influence states' perception of substantive linkages. The Office has played a role in providing information in order to address uncertainty and imperfect information on linkages. In an ideational context, it has played an important epistemic role in developing a common understanding of the 'nexus' between refugee protection and other issue-areas. For example, it has played an important role in developing the so-called 'migration-asylum nexus' and the 'refugee aid and development' discourse. It has often reinforced a certain set of beliefs about linkages through argumentation. Given the absence of a clearly defined normative and legal framework on burden-sharing, UNHCR has been able to play an important role in the institutional design of its ad hoc conferences and so shape the contractual relationship between issue-areas.

ICARA

The International Conferences on Assistance to Refugees in Africa of 1981 and 1984 (ICARA I and II) represent African state-initiated conferences to seek compensation from Northern donor states for the infrastructural costs of having hosted large rural refugee populations throughout much of the 1970s. The 'ICARA process' was based on two one-off Geneva-based pledging conferences convened in 1981 and 1984, at which the African states solicited financial contributions to support a range of development projects that would be jointly implemented by UNHCR and UNDP. These projects were intended to simultaneously benefit local populations and to promote the self-sufficiency and local integration of refugees (Betts 2004; Gorman 1986, 1987, 1993).

UNHCR's assumption was that Northern states would altruistically fund the projects and programmes, providing money for the sake of supporting Africa's refugees. However, there were few financial contributions.[2] The only significant contributions that were made were by the United States and were mainly earmarked to support refugee groups who were on the 'right' side of proxy conflicts in strategically significant parts of the Horn of Africa and Southern Africa.[3] Although a second conference—ICARA II—was convened, which sought to highlight that both Northern donors and African states could simultaneously gain from burden-sharing, neither ICARA I nor ICARA II ultimately led to significant Northern contributions to support in-region protection.[4]

One of the core problems with ICARA was that there was very little structural interdependence between refugee protection in Africa and Northern interests. At the time, there was very little South–North movement between Africa and Europe through asylum or migration channels. The only causal link that connected in-region protection to Northern security related to the proxy conflicts of the Cold War (refugee protection → support for anti-communist guerrillas → US strategic interests). Only the United States' interests in supporting anti-Communist 'refugee warriors' in Africa led to significant donor pledging. Consequently, there were few substantive linkages connecting refugee protection to other issue-areas. The only substantive linkages that existed related to the side-payments to the United States emerging from their earmarked support for anti-Communist refugees in the Horn of Africa and Southern Africa.

UNHCR's role in the bargaining process was extremely limited. It took a largely technocratic and apolitical role, compiling the projects and programmes for donors and then assuming that altruistic giving would take place. In ICARA II, it tried to convince Northern states that they could benefit from solutions for refugees in Africa as a way of reducing the long-term need for humanitarian assistance. In order to do this it tried to play an epistemic role through developing a discourse on 'Refugee Aid and Development', which purported to show how donor development assistance might be used to facilitate refugee self-sufficiency and local integration and hence reduce the long-term humanitarian assistance budget (Betts 2004; Gorman 1986; Stein 1987). However, in the absence of an African state commitment to provide local integration or self-sufficiency opportunities for refugees, there was very little substantive basis on which to claim that there would be a relationship between increased support in the present and a reduction in humanitarian needs in the future.[5]

ICARA I and II were therefore a failure in terms of overcoming the Suasion Game and facilitating international cooperation. Northern states had little interest in cooperating and Southern states had little choice but to cooperate and accept the little that was offered by donor states. In the absence of significant interdependence between Northern interests and in-region protection in Africa, there was little substantive linkage connecting in-region protection to Northern interests. The ICARA experience provides evidence to support rejecting Ho1 insofar as its institutional design was premised on altruistic giving and yet the only Northern contributions were correlated with US strategic interests in the Cold War context. However, ICARA does not provide evidence to reject Ho2 because, in the absence of structural interdependence, UNHCR had little basis on which to create, change, or communicate substantive linkages. The limited earmarked contributions that did take place would have done so even in the absence of UNHCR.

CIREFCA

The International Conference on Refugees in Central America (CIREFCA),[6] agreed at a Guatemala City conference in 1989, attempted to address the situation of refugees and other displaced people in the aftermath of Central America's Cold War civil conflicts. Based on the financial commitment of mainly European states, it developed a series of integrated development projects that facilitated access to sustainable repatriation, local integration, and self-sufficiency for refugees (Betts 2008). Ultimately, CIREFCA was a great success which led to significant international cooperation. Around 90 per cent of CIREFCA's projects received full-funding and CIREFCA attracted over US$400m in new financial commitments.

By far the biggest donors were European states, both individually and through the then European Economic Community (EEC).[7] One of the most important differences between CIREFCA and ICARA was the degree of interdependence that existed between in-region protection in Central America and the European states' interests in international trade. Refugee protection in Central America was structurally related to trade insofar as solutions for refugees was a necessary condition for peace and security, and peace and security was a necessary condition for economic reconstruction and development (refugee protection → regional peace and security→ reconstruction and development → European–Central American inter-regional trade).

Indeed, European countries' contributions to CIREFCA were mainly motivated by the goal of improving regional security to facilitate improved trade relations. Towards the end of the Cold War, the EEC was trying to expand its global influence and international trade relationships. The 1984 San José Declaration had established an annual forum for economic cooperation between the EEC and Central American States. The annual San José Summits created a basis for sustained dialogue between the regions' Foreign Ministers throughout the CIREFCA process.[8] The EEC had a particular concern to support the conditions which would facilitate Central America emerging as a viable European trade partner. Twenty percent of the region's trade was with the EEC countries and Europe therefore had a significant stake in ensuring that there was sufficient regional security to allow economic stability, growth, and development (Garoz and MacDonald 1996: 5). Insofar as refugee protection could be regarded as an important part of regional security and development, it too would therefore be strongly in Europe's interests.

During CIREFCA, UNHCR played a crucial role in creating, changing, and communicating the substantive linkage between refugee protection and other issue-areas. While the relationship between regional security, economic development, and inter-regional trade may have been obvious to states, how refugees fitted into this picture was more ambiguous. UNHCR's role in the institutional design of CIREFCA contributed to highlighting interdependence between refugee protection and these broader areas. As High Commissioner Sadako Ogata argued towards the end of the process, 'CIREFCA has been a key formative experience in many respects, breaking new ground in…demonstrating the important linkages between solutions, the consolidation of peace and development.'[9]

UNHCR played an important epistemic role in fostering the 'Refugee Aid and Development' (RAD) discourse, in which, alongside academics with Refugee Studies, it developed the argument that development assistance might play a role in refugee protection and that refugee protection might also contribute to the development of the host country (Betts 2009; Gorman 1993). Where RAD had failed in ICARA, the contribution of refugee self-sufficiency and local integration in Mexico's Yucatan Peninsula, for example, began to demonstrate to states that development and durable solutions for refugees could be mutually reinforcing.

UNHCR conceived CIREFCA to be institutionally nested within the broader post-conflict reconstruction and development initiative for the region and the Esquipulas II peace deal. The peace deal for the region, Esquipulas II, had been concluded in 1987 and Article 8 focused on displacement, presaging an opportunity for CIREFCA to be identified as a part of the peace deal. Furthermore, CIREFCA plugged into and became Chapter X of the UN's post-conflict reconstruction initiative for the region, the Programme of Economic Cooperation (PEC). These references created an opportunity for UNHCR to make CIREFCA a part of these wider initiatives and so channel the interests of states in these other areas into CIREFCA.[10]

The impact of these linkages on donor states' behaviour can be inferred from a number of comments at the time about states' motivations for contributing to CIREFCA. An in-house UNHCR reflection piece noted:

> The most important aspect of CIREFCA is its intimate link to the concerted search by the Central American Presidents, with the support of the Secretary-General of the UN, for a negotiated peace...A careful reading of the CIREFCA documents leads to the conclusion that Esquipulas II is the philosophical underpinning of the Conference. An analysis of the CIREFCA Declaration highlights the interrelationship of efforts in favour of refugees, returnees and displaced persons and those in favour of peace, democracy and development taking place in the regions. This interrelationship is more explicitly reaffirmed in the sections entitled Fundamentals of the Plan of Action where the affected countries link the proposals for solutions in favour of the affected groups with efforts towards regional peace and development; frame these proposals within Esquipulas II; and tie the success of the Plan of Action to economic and social development in the region.[11]

Specifically in relation to the motives of the EEC, UNHCR noted at the time that 'the Community has regarded CIREFCA as an integral part of efforts towards peace, development, and democracy in Central America'.[12] Meanwhile a joint UNDP-UNHCR document also noted that the main European commitment, which led the EEC and a number of European states to fund 90 per cent of the CIREFCA projects, was precisely its relationship to Esquipulas II.[13] The Government of Sweden explicitly stated at a CIREFCA meeting that 'the support of Sweden for CIREFCA was inextricably linked to its support for the Central American peace process'.[14] Indeed, UNHCR's Juridical Committee of CIREFCA noted the logic underpinning states' perception of an association between the peace process and population displacement:

> Massive flows of refugees might not only affect the domestic order and stability of receiving states, but may also jeopardize the political and social stability and economic development of entire regions, and thus endanger international peace and security. The solution to the problems of displacement is therefore a necessary part of the peace process in the region and it is not conceivable to achieve peace while ignoring the problems of refugees and other displaced persons.[15]

Analysis of CIREFCA provides evidence for rejecting Ho1 on the basis that European states' contributions were not motivated purely by concern with refugee protection. Rather, they were based on broader concerns with regional security and development as the basis for inter-regional trade. Only insofar as refugee protection was substantively linked to these other issues were European states prepared to contribute. CIREFCA also provides evidence for rejecting Ho2 on the basis that it is unlikely that European states would have recognized the substantive linkage between their broader interests in other issue-areas and refugee protection in Central America without UNHCR institutionally designing CIREFCA in such a way as to highlight the complex interdependence across issue-areas.

Indo-Chinese CPA

Like CIREFCA, the Indo-Chinese Comprehensive Plan of Action (CPA) focused on an international conference convened by UNHCR in 1989. The CPA led to successful international cooperation in order to address the long-standing plight of the so-called 'boat people' who fled Communist Indo-China in large numbers in the aftermath of the Vietnam War. It serves as an example of a situation in which states were prepared to cooperate to address the problem on the basis of interests that had little to do with altruistic concern for refugees, and in which UNHCR played a key role in facilitating cooperation.[16]

Soon after the United States evacuated Saigon in 1975, the Socialist Republic of Vietnam (SRV) was formed. Many people began to flee the SRV and the other Communist states in the region in order to escape a mixture of persecution and economic deprivation. Many fled on small, unstable boats and arrived on the shores of other South-East Asian states or in Hong Kong. However, many of the Association of Southeast Asian Nations (ASEAN) states and Hong Kong refused to admit the asylum seekers and pushed the boats back into the water. In order to address this problem, an initial agreement was made in 1979, whereby the United States and a number of other Northern states agreed to resettle all the Indo-Chinese boat people, provided the countries in the region did not close their borders. By the late 1980s, however, this agreement had broken down; resettlement numbers were dwindling, the detention and reception centres in the region were full, and the ASEAN states and Hong Kong were again pushing boats back into the water (Sutter 1990).

The end of the Cold War and the collapse of the USSR created a new opportunity for cooperation. By the end of the 1980s, without the USSR to rely upon as an ally, the SRV was isolated in the international community. It therefore began to seek a means to rehabilitate itself in the eyes of the international community and attract new sources of overseas development assistance. This change created the opportunity for a new international agreement to address the situation of the Indo-Chinese boat people. UNHCR led a series of negotiations that culminated in the 1989 CPA being agreed at an international meeting in Geneva. The CPA led to an interlocking three-way agreement between the country of origin (the SRV), the first countries of asylum (the ASEAN states and Hong Kong), and the resettlement countries (the

United States and a number of other Northern states). The first countries of asylum agreed to refrain from 'push backs' and to host an asylum screening process to determine who were genuine and non-genuine refugees. In return, the resettlement countries agreed to resettle all of those boat people recognized as refugees and the main country of origin agreed to accept the 'voluntary' return of all those who were not recognized as refugees in the screening process.

The CPA was criticized on human rights grounds for the conditions of return to Vietnam (Helton 1993: 544–58; Towle 2006: 539). However, on the level of international cooperation, the CPA was a success that led to the complete resolution of the 'boat people' situation by 1996. One of the key elements of the CPA's success was the willingness of the United States to underwrite the initiative by committing to resettle a significant proportion of the Vietnamese refugees and to convince European states and Australia to also resettle refugees. The US commitment to voluntarily contribute to resettle an enormous number of refugees was therefore essential to facilitating international cooperation and ensuring that the mass influx came to an end.[17]

The US willingness to contribute was underpinned by structural interdependence between the refugee crisis and its strategic interests in the region (refugee protection → regional security → global security). In the aftermath of the Vietnam War, the promotion of regional security had been a major priority for the United States. Insofar as the long-standing Indo-Chinese refugee crisis represented a threat to that stability, it was materially intertwined with US interests. Indeed, the mass exodus was related to regional security on two levels: US-ASEAN relations and US-Vietnamese relations.

Firstly, the US's commitment to resettlement was part of its wider relationship with ASEAN and it used the 'refugee issue' as a means to enhance its relationship with ASEAN in other areas of strategic importance. As Sutter claimed of the period before 1988, '[US] admission levels for refugees are related to ASEAN-US relations' (Sutter 1990: 85). By 1984, the region was the US's 5th biggest trading partner (in terms of the value of exports and imports); the United States had military bases in Philippines and Thailand, and relied upon Indonesia for a reliable oil supply outside of the Middle East. During the Cold War, ASEAN had served as an important buffer against Communism and the ASEAN states continued to be seen as important for US regional interests after the Cold War. The US's resettlement of refugees contributed to facilitating intra-ASEAN cooperation, and reduced the potentially destabilizing consequences of the mass exodus. For Malaysia and, to a lesser extent, Indonesia, the principal security threat of hosting refugees came from their precarious demographic and ethnic make-ups and their precarious relationship with the People's Republic of China. The exodus of Hoa Chinese from the SRV was seen as something that could rapidly destabilize the states' demographic equilibria. As Sutter explained in relation to Malaysia, 'the refugees pose a serious security threat related to the larger context of Sino-Malaysian relations' (Ibid: 135).

Secondly, the CPA was a means to ensure transition and stability within Vietnam. The US position on return was directly related to the SRV's progress with the *Doi Moi* (progressive and gradual economic liberalization) reform process and emerged only from the end of alignment with the USSR, the planned withdrawal from Cambodia, and the reform announcements of the 6th Congress in 1986. The return and reintegration of people screened out during the CPA process, allowed a starting point for the normalization of relations with Vietnam. The Report to Congress on the CPA noted, 'It is time to take some concrete steps towards normalizing relations—of talking more directly and frequently with Hanoi... There is ample precedence for establishing American "interests" sections in other countries where we do not have diplomatic relations, but with which we desire more regular diplomatic contact' (Ibid). The Director of the Indochinese Policy Forum argued that the US national interest in the CPA lay in fostering regional stability:

> The long-term policy goal of the United States is to help bring about a peaceful and stable Vietnam that is fully integrated into the international community and is not threatening to its neighbours. As this process occurs, we shall encourage Vietnam to move increasingly towards establishing democratic institutions... The United States should encourage conditions to help Vietnam reduce its reliance upon the Soviet Union, particularly by improving its relationship with ASEAN.[18]

UNHCR played a significant leadership role in enabling the United States to recognize its interests in supporting the CPA. Return to Vietnam for 'screened out' asylum seekers was central to the CPA. However, the US Government was initially reluctant to allow the return of people to a Socialist country. UNHCR played a significant role in persuading the United States that it could best meet its interests through compromising on this principle. When the process of negotiating the CPA began with an interstate meeting in Bangkok in October 1988, it was the first time since 1979 that the SRV or the Lao People's Democratic Republic (LPDR) had been involved in talks on refugees from their countries.[19] By December, the SRV had agreed a Memorandum of Understanding with UNHCR.[20] However, between 1989 and 1990, the main divisions in the negotiations focused on the position of the SRV.[21] In particular, the ASEAN states needed to be certain that return would take place for those who were screened out but the United States insisted that return be voluntary. The British Foreign Minister, Douglas Hurd, wrote to the High

Commissioner, stating, 'My own discussions with Secretary of State Baker and President Bush in Washington on 29 January give me little hope that the United States will be willing to join in the consensus which was acceptable to all other participants in the Geneva meeting except Vietnam.'[22] This reluctance led to significant disappointment from the ASEAN states at the slow rate of return. For example, the Malaysian Foreign Minister stated:

> The United States, which opposes involuntary repatriation for its own reasons, has not been helpful either. In fact the United States' position provides comfort and protection to the Vietnamese intransigence... It is the United States' insistence on treating the Vietnamese economic migrants differently that is putting the very principle of first asylum in peril.[23]

The impasse between the United States and the ASEAN countries on return led to crisis talks in Manila in mid-1990. Here, UNHCR played a crucial leadership role in persuading the United States to compromise by reminding the United States of their overarching interests in the success of the CPA. Vieira de Mello, as coordinator of the CPA, suggested that 'Seldom... have we been so close to a breakdown of this otherwise exemplary process.'[24] Interviews with participants to the process highlight the key role that Sergio Vieira de Mello played in reminding states, including the United States of their own interests and finding a compromise.[25] In the words of Dennis McNamara, 'the consensus [on return] was not to call it forced and not to call it voluntary; just to say that those who were found to be refugees could not be sent back'.[26] While the basis of the compromise was semantic, underlying it was a renewed willingness of the United States to allow the return of non-refugees to Vietnam.

The CPA therefore provides evidence for rejecting Ho1 on the basis that US commitment to resettlement was not motivated purely by concern with refugee protection. Rather, it was based on broader concerns with regional security in the aftermath of the Vietnam War. Only insofar as refugee protection was substantively linked to these other issues was the United States prepared to contribute. The CPA also provides evidence for rejecting Ho2 on the basis that it is unlikely that the United States would have compromised on its initial unwillingness to allow the return of 'screened out' asylum seekers to Vietnam unless UNHCR had used argumentation to highlight that compromise on this aspect was necessary for the success of the overall initiative.

Convention Plus

UNHCR's so-called Convention Plus initiative of 2003–5 is different from the previous three cases addressed above. Where the other cases examined in the chapter focused on addressing specific regional refugee situations,

Convention Plus tried to develop international agreements at the global level that could then be applied to address specific regional refugee situations. Its aim was to address areas of refugee protection not adequately dealt with by the existing 1951 Convention. In particular, its aim was to develop a normative framework on international burden-sharing through interstate bargaining. Convention Plus divided into three sets of interstate bargaining: on resettlement, targeting development assistance (TDA), and irregular secondary movements (ISM). These three areas had in common that they all related to the international division of responsibility for refugee protection. The first two (resettlement and TDA) related to Northern support for in-region protection in the South; the last one (ISM) related to the Southern commitment to provide sufficient protection to refugees to avoid the need for refugees to move onwards and seek protection in the North (Durieux and Kelley 2004).

The initiative was premised upon the idea that Southern states wanted greater burden-sharing, whether in terms of resettlement or development assistance, and Northern states wanted to reduce the movement of asylum seekers from South to North, and that these two sets of interests could lead to mutually beneficial cooperation. The intention was to apply these abstract agreements to address the long-standing refugee situations of Afghan and Somali refugees. Ultimately, however, Convention Plus was characterized by North–South polarization. No agreement of any substance was reached and the abstract negotiations were never applied to address specific regional situations in the way that had been envisaged.

The failure of Convention Plus presents an interesting paradox. The type of interdependence that one would expect to give Northern states an interest in supporting in-region protection was arguably stronger than ever. Since the 1990s, there had been a massive increase in South–North asylum movements. Structurally, refugee protection in the South appeared to have a material relationship to migration management and border security in the North (refugee protection → reduce need for onward movement of asylum seekers → reduce irregular migration → security). Yet, despite this apparent interdependence, there was little new cooperation, and Northern states were reluctant to voluntarily commit new resources to strengthen refugee protection 'in regions of origin'.

Initial funding for the activities of Convention Plus was provided by Denmark, Netherlands, United Kingdom, and the European Commission (EC). They were prepared to support the process because they recognized it as a means to develop the concept of 'protection in the region of origin' as a substitute for the onward movement of spontaneous arrival asylum seekers, primarily from Africa and the Middle East to Europe. These three countries and the EC were especially concerned about the increasingly politicized nature of asylum in Europe (Schuster 2005). However, aside from this initial and small-scale funding for the secretariat of the initiative, there were very few further Northern commitments made to support in-region protection within the framework of Convention Plus.

In many ways the lack of substantive linkages within bargaining can be attributed to UNHCR's role in the process. It did very little to highlight the complex interdependence that connected Northern states' interests to refugee protection in the South and, if anything, it played a counterproductive role in highlighting how Northern states interests could be met through additional burden-sharing. To take an example, UNHCR's institutional design of the initiative did little to highlight the interdependence of Northern interests and refugee protection. The three strands of the initiative were negotiated in isolation from one another. The resettlement negotiations were chaired by Canada; the ISM negotiations were convened by South Africa and Switzerland; and the development debates were organized by Denmark and Japan. The debates within the strands therefore involved different actors and took place in different locations. Yet the very basis of cooperation would have been the linkages that existed across the three areas of debate—*between* burden-sharing and onward migration. UNHCR's institutional design of the initiative therefore hindered recognition of interdependence and substantive linkages across issue-areas.

To take another example of UNHCR's role in hindering rather than helping substantive issue-linkage, UNHCR commissioned a survey by the Swiss Forum for Migration to investigate the empirical relationship between in-region protection for Somali refugees in East Africa and the onward movement of Somali asylum seekers to Europe.[27] While the empirical survey purported to provide evidence of the relationship, many states were sceptical of the validity of the survey findings and questioned whether it provided a credible basis on which to commit resources to refugee protection.[28] Meanwhile, those states that did accept the basis of the relationship chose to bypass UNHCR channels in order to develop North–South cooperation and instead developed bilateral or inter-regional forms of cooperation.[29]

Convention Plus is therefore interesting because it highlights a situation in which there was structural interdependence between refugee protection in the South and Northern interests, and yet there was very little international cooperation within the framework of the initiative. It provides some evidence for rejecting Ho1 because it once again shows how Northern states were uninterested in contributing to refugee protection in the South except where there was a clear correlation with wider interests. It also provides some evidence for rejecting Ho2, albeit on different grounds than in the previous case studies.

Indeed, it demonstrates that UNHCR's failure to provide leadership or an institutional design that makes complex interdependencies transparent can undermine the prospects for cooperation even when the structural basis for issue-linkage and cooperation—North–South interdependence—exists.

Overview of Case Studies

In the successful cases, Northern states did not contribute to refugee protection in the South for altruistic reasons. They contributed only insofar as they had linked interests in other issue-areas. In both CIREFCA and the CPA, substantive linkage between refugees in the South and wider consequences for Northern interests in security and trade were the basis of cooperation. In ICARA, there was an assumption that Northern states would contribute to refugee protection for altruistic reasons. However, in the absence of structural interdependence, Northern states' contributions were very limited. In Convention Plus, there was structural interdependence but it largely went unrecognized by Northern states.

Furthermore, UNHCR has played a significant role in determining whether cooperation has taken place by its role in creating, changing, or communicating substantive linkages through a combination of information provision, institutional design, argumentation, and playing an epistemic role. CIREFCA's institutional design, along with the Office's epistemic role, helped demonstrate to European states the causal relationship between refugee protection, regional security and development, and trade. In the CPA, UNHCR's leadership and argumentation role through individuals like Sergio Vieira de Mello helped to highlight to the United States the importance of the CPA for its wider interests. On the other hand, in Convention Plus, UNHCR's institutional design, lack of leadership, and failed epistemic role meant it failed to credibly highlight substantive issue-linkages. In ICARA, UNHCR had little interdependence to highlight and so was largely unable to use substantive issue-linkage to influence Northern state behaviour.

CONCLUSION

International cooperation in the global refugee regime is a substantively important and neglected topic in International Relations. This chapter has attempted to highlight the nature of the cooperation problem within the regime and the conditions under which that problem has historically been overcome. It has demonstrated that the dominant characterization of the refugee regime as a Prisoner's Dilemma game is misrepresentative because it fails to capture the importance of asymmetric power relations within the regime. Instead, the chapter has suggested that a more appropriate game theoretical analogy for the cooperation problem is that of a Suasion Game, which captures the important North–South dynamics within the refugee regime. The chapter has argued that, following the work of Lisa Martin, the Suasion Game logic has been overcome through the role of issue-linkage. Where Northern states have had linked interests in other issue-areas—notably in migration, security, and trade—they have sometimes been prepared to voluntarily contribute to refugee protection in the South. Where such interests have been absent, the Suasion Game logic has prevailed.

However, the most relevant linkages in the refugee regime have not been tactical linkages, on which Martin focuses, but substantive linkages. The existence of a structural relationship between issue-areas—on a material, ideational, or institutional level—has led Northern states to voluntarily contribute to protection in the South. Furthermore, given the ambiguity and uncertainty of the material relationship between refugee protection and other issue-areas, UNHCR has played a significant role in creating, changing, and communicating substantive linkages (Figure 3.3). It has been able to engage in cross-issue persuasion, which the chapter has defined as when an actor A influences an actor B's beliefs about the relationship between issue-area X and issue-area Y as a means of inducing actor B to act in issue-area X on the basis of its interest in issue-area Y. The mechanisms through which the Office has been able to use cross-issue persuasion to influence states have included institutional design, information provision, playing an epistemic role, and argumentation.

In terms of policy, the analysis has important implications for the role of UNHCR. The Office has often been assumed to be a 'non-political' actor insofar as it purports to uphold humanitarian principles such as impartiality, neutrality, and independence. Yet, given the findings of this chapter, it is likely to be at its most effective in facilitating international cooperation on refugee protection when it engages with, recognizes, and understands states' interests. The two hypotheses, for which there is supporting evidence, have implications for UNHCR's work. The first—that Northern states contribute to refugee protection on the basis of linked interests in other issue-areas—implies that UNHCR should not assume that states will altruistically contribute to refugee protection for its own sake. Rather, UNHCR needs to be aware of the broader political context of its work and recognize and channel states' interests into a commitment to protection. The second—that UNHCR has been relevant for how states' understand substantive linkages—implies

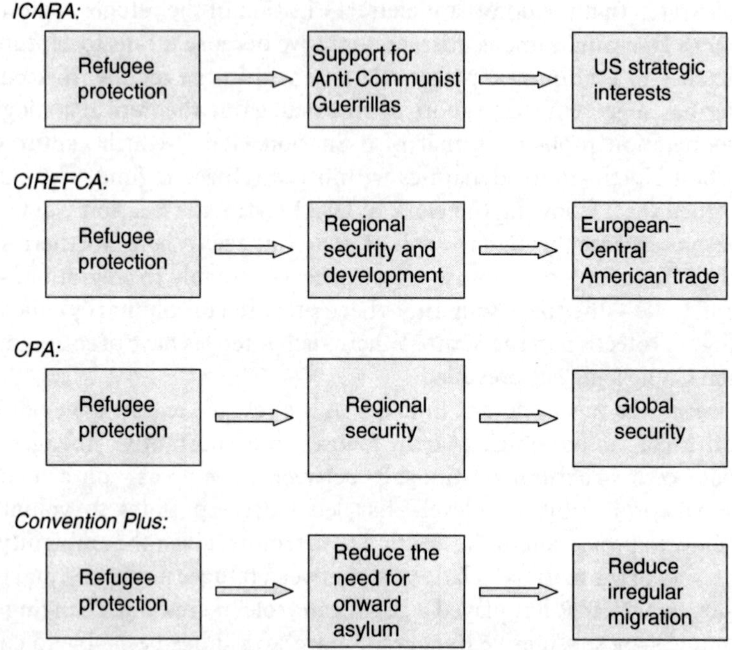

Figure 3.3 Diagram illustrating the substantive linkages between refugee protection in the South and other issue-areas in which the North has an interest

the need for the Office to enhance its analytical and political capacity in order to engage in information provision, institutional design, argumentation, and playing an epistemic role in ways that are favourable to cooperation.

In terms of theory, the analysis highlights the role of substantive issue-linkage as a resource of power. The concept of cross-issue persuasion illustrates how actor A can create, change, or communicate substantive linkages as a means to influence the behaviour of actor B. Where material relationships between issue-areas are uncertain, as is often the case in the social realm, the causal relationship between action in one issue-area and outcomes in another issue-area may be ambiguous. This creates significant opportunities for actors to use cross-issue persuasion to change other actors' beliefs about the relationship between two issue-areas. The chapter has identified four mechanisms through which an actor can engage in cross-issue persuasion in order to influence the behaviour of another actor: information provision, institutional design, argumentation, and playing an epistemic role. Cross-issue persuasion represents an important means through which International Organizations (IOs) and other actors with relatively limited military or economic resources may nevertheless influence states with far greater military or economic power. The potential of cross-issue persuasion to enable weaker actors to offset power asymmetries and overcome Suasion game situations implies that it merits further research in relation to the politics of other issue-areas. In health, development, and the environment, for example, substantive linkages to other issue-areas play a defining role in shaping the politics of those issue-areas. The concept of cross-issue persuasion may shed light on the actual and potential use of those linkages as a means to influence other actors.

NOTES

1. This chapter builds upon drafts previously presented at the International Studies Association annual conventions in San Francisco on 27 March 2008 and New York City on 17 February 2009, at a lecture at Georgetown University on 15 September 2008, and at the London Migration Research Seminar at SOAS on 14 October 2008. The author would like to thank Fiona Adamson, Karen Alter, B.S. Chimni, Sarah Cross, James Hollifield, Andrew Hurrell, Robert Keohane, Susan Kneebone, Rey Koslowski, Gil Loescher, Susan Martin, Neil MacFarlane, Walter Mattli, Kalypso Nicolaides, Joseph Nye, Eiko Thielemann, Nick Van Hear, and Ngaire Woods for comments on earlier drafts. The chapter is based on the book *Protection by Persuasion: International Cooperation in the Refugee Regime*, published by Cornell University Press in October 2009.
2. $560m in conference pledges. By September 1981, the Steering Committee in charge of post-ICARA Coordination noted that further specifications by donors left only $144m not earmarked, leaving UNHCR with an estimated $40m available for the high-priority projects that did not fall into its regular or specific programmes. Consequently, a ceiling of $2m per country was fixed and this was focused on humanitarian assistance needs such as food, water, shelter, and the delivery of medical services (UNHCR Archives 1981).
3. In Loescher's words, 'almost all of the $560m offered by donor states was earmarked for projects and allocated to most favoured nations. Very few funds went to especially hard hit nations like Ethiopia and other countries in the Horn of Africa' (Loescher 2001: 227).
4. When the conference met in July 1984, it aimed to raise $392m to meet 128 aid schemes in the fourteen African states over a period of three years. However, only $81m was pledged at the conference (UNHCR Archives 1984).
5. Most African states preferred voluntary repatriation, which was consequently highlighted as the 'ideal durable solution' throughout the conference. Later UNHCR evaluation revealed that 'the African countries tried to win funds for development projects under the guise of refugee emergency relief. They were more interested in being compensated for the burden of hosting refugees than they were in using these funds to promote local integration' (Loescher 2001: 228; UNHCR 1994*a*).

6. CIREFCA represents the acronym for the Spanish title of the conference, *La Conferencica Internacional Sobre Los Refugiados Centroamericanos.*
7. In total, CIREFCA is estimated to have channelled US$422.3 million in additional resources to the region and the process has been widely credited with helping to consolidate peace in Central America. This financial support emerged gradually as the process evolved. US$245m was pledged by the First International Follow-Up Meeting in New York in June 1990 and a further US$81m was pledged at the Second Follow-Up in El Salvador in April 1992 (UNHCR Archives 1993*a*, 1994*a*).
8. UNHCR Archives (1993*b*).
9. UNHCR Archives (1994*b*).
10. *Ibid.*
11. UNHCR Archives (1992).
12. UNHCR Archives (1993*c*).
13. UNDP and UNHCR (1995).
14. UNHCR (1994*b*).
15. UNHCR Archives (1990*a*).
16. For an overview of the CPA, see Robinson (1997) and Towle (2006).
17. It is widely acknowledged (e.g. by Suhrke 1998 and Towle 2006) that US hegemony played a crucial role in facilitating the CPA. However, this still leaves open the question of what interests underlay the commitment of the hegemon.
18. The Aspen Institute (1988).
19. UNHCR Archives (1988*a*).
20. UNHCR Archives (1988*b*).
21. UNHCR Archives (1989*a*).
22. UNHCR Archives (1989*b*).
23. UNHCR Archives (1990*b*).
24. UNHCR Archives (1990*c*).
25. For an analysis of Sergio Vieira de Mello's important role in influencing states' behaviour on behalf of UNHCR, see Power (2008).
26. Interview with Dennis McNamara.
27. Swiss Forum for Migration (2005).
28. Interviews with states' permanent missions to the UN in Geneva, November–December 2005.
29. A range of new bilateral and inter-regional partnerships have emerged in the context of asylum and migration. See, for example, Haddad (2008: 165–91).

BIBLIOGRAPHY

Aggarwal, V (ed). 1998. *Institutional designs for a complex world.* Ithaca, NY: Cornell University Press.

Allain, J. 2001. The *jus cogens* nature of *non-refoulement. International Journal of Refugee Law,* 13: 533–58.

Axelrod, R. 1984. *The evolution of cooperation*. New York: Basic Books.

Betts, A. 2004. International cooperation and targeting development assistance for refugee solutions: lessons from the 1980s. *New Issues in Refugee Research*. Working Paper No. 107, UNHCR, Geneva.

——. 2008. Historical lessons for overcoming protracted refugee situations. In: Loescher et al. eds. *The politics, human rights and security implications of protracted refugee situations*. Tokyo: UNU Press.

——. 2009. *Protection by persuasion: international cooperation in the refugee regime*. Ithaca, NY: Cornell University Press.

Bhagwati, J. 1984. Introduction. In: J. Bhagwati and J. Ruggie, eds., *Power, passions and purpose: prospects for North-South negotiations*. MIT: Cambridge.

Burutciski, M. and Suhrke, A. 2001. Lessons from the Kosovo refugee crisis: innovatons in protection and burden-sharing. *Journal of Refugee Studies*, 14(2): 95–134.

Crawford, N. 2002. *Argument and change in world politics*. Cambridge: Cambridge.

Durieux, J-F. and Kelley, N. 2004. UNHCR and current challenges in international refugee protection. *Refuge*, 22(1).

Garoz, B. and Macdonald, M. 1996. *La politica de cooperacion de la Union Europa hacia Guatemala*. Estudio elaborado para Asamblea de la Sociedad Civil (ASC), Guatemala.

Ghosh, B. 1999. *Managing migration: time for a new international regime?* Oxford: Oxford.

Gorman, R. 1986. Beyond ICARA II: implementing refugee-related development assistance. *International Migration Review*, 8(3): 283–98.

——. 1987. *Coping with Africa's refugee burden: a time for solutions*. Martinus Nijhoff: Hague.

Gorman, R. 1993. Linking refugee aid and development in Africa. In: R. Gorman, ed., *Refugee aid and development: theory and practice*. London: Greenwood Press.

Haas, E. 1980. Why collaborate? Issue-linkage and international regimes. In: F. Kratochwil and E. Mansfield, eds., *International organization: a reader*. New York: Harper Collins, 1994, pp. 364–84.

——. 1990. *When knowledge is power: three models of change in international organizations*. Berkeley, CA: University of California Press.

Haddad, E. 2008. *The refugee in international society: between sovereigns*. Cambridge: Cambridge University Press.

Hansen, R. 2008. Making cooperation work: interests, incentives and action. Paper presented at workshop on Migration and International Cooperation: South-South Perspectives, IOM Headquarters, Geneva, 7–8 August 2008.

Hasenclever, A., Mayer, P. and Rittberger, V. 1997. *Theories of international regimes*. Cambridge: Cambridge University Press.

Helton, A. 1993. Refugee determinations under the Comprehensive Plan of Action: overview and assessment. *International Journal of Refugee Law*, 5(4): 544–58.

Hollifield, J. 2008. Migration as a global public good. Paper read at International Studies Association, March, 25–28, 2008, San Francisco.

Hurd, I. 2007. *After anarchy: legitimacy and power at the UN Security Council*. Princeton, NJ: Princeton University Press.

Hurrell, A. 2007. On global order: power, values and the constitution of international society. Oxford: Oxford University Press.

Interview with Dennis McNamara, Deputy Director of the Department of Refugee Law and Doctrine at the time of the CPA, Geneva, 28 November 2005.

Keohane, R. 1982. The demand for international regimes. *International Organization*, 36(2): 325–55.

——. 2003. The causal pathways of persuasion, unpublished memo written following the conference, 'Arguing and persuasion in international relations and European affairs', European University Institute, Florence, 8–10 April 2002.

Kessler, A. 1996. International migration, cooperation, and policy-making in post-War Europe. Paper Presented at ISA Annual Convention, San Diego.

Koh, H. 1997. Why do states obey international law? *Yale Law Journal*. 106: 2615–34.

Koslowski, R. 2008. Global mobility regimes. Unpublished paper.

Krasner, S. D. (ed.) 1983. *International regimes*. Ithaca, NY: Cornell University Press.

Lauterpacht, E. and Bethlehem, D. 2001. The scope and content of the principle of non-refoulement. In: E. Feller, V. Türk, and F. Nicholson, eds., *Refugee protection in international law*. Cambridge: Cambridge University Press.

Loescher, G. 2001. *The UNHCR and world politics*. Oxford: Oxford University Press.

—— and Milner, J. 2005. *Protracted refugee situations: domestic and international security implications*. Adelphi Paper 375. London: Routledge.

——, Betts, A. and Milner, J. 2008. *UNHCR: The politics and practice of refugee protection into the twenty-first century*. London: Routledge.

Martin, L. 1993. The rational state choice of multilateralism. In: J. Ruggie, ed., *Multilateralism matters: the theory and praxis of an institutional form*. New York: Columbia University Press, pp. 91–121.

Martin, P., Martin, S., and Weil, P. 2006. *Managing migration: the promise of cooperation*. Lanham, MD: Rowman and Littlefield.

McGinnis, M. 1986. Issue-linkage and the evolution of international cooperation. *Journal of Conflict Resolution*, 30(1): 141–70.

Milner, J. 2009. *Refugees, the state and the politics of asylum in Africa*. Basingstoke: Palgrave.

Mitchell, R. and Keilback, M. 2004. Situation structures and institutional design: reciprocity, coercion and exchange. In: B. Koremenos, C. Lipson, and D. Snidal, eds., *The rational design of institutions*. Cambridge: Cambridge.

Power, S. 2008. *Chasing the flame: Sergio Vieira de Mello and the fight to save the world*. London: Penguin.

Ravenhill, J. 1990. The North-South balance of power. *International Affairs*, 66(4): 744–8.

Risse, T. 2003. Let's argue!: Communicative action in world politics. *International Organization*, 54(1): 1–39.

Robinson, C. 1997. *Terms of refuge: the Indochinese exodus and the international response*. London: Zed.

Schuster, L. 2005. *The realities of a new asylum paradigm*. COMPAS Working Paper No. 20, Oxford University, COMPAS.

Stein, A. 1980. The politics of linkage. *World Politics*, 33(1): 62–81.

Stein, B. 1987. ICARA II: burden-sharing and durable solutions. In: R. Rogge, ed., *Refugees: a Third World dilemma*. Lanham: Rowman and Littlefield.

Suhrke, A. 1998. Burden-sharing during refugee emergencies: the logic of collective action versus national action. *Journal of Refugee Studies*, 11(4): 396–415.

Sutter, V. 1990. *The Indo-Chinese refugee dilemma*. Louisiana: Baton Rouge.

Swiss Forum for Migration. 2005. Movements of Somali refugees and asylum seekers and states' responses thereto. SFM: Neuchatel.

The Aspen Institute. 1988. Recommendations for the new administration on United States policy towards Indochina. By Dick Clark, Director of the Indochina Policy Forum, November 1988.

Thielemann, E. 2003. Between interests and norms: burden-sharing in the European Union. *Journal of Refugee Studies*, 16(3): 253–73.

Towle, R. 2006. Processes and critiques of the Indo-Chinese Comprehenive Plan of Action: an instrument of international burden-sharing? *International Journal of Refugee Law*, 18(4): 537–70.

UNDP and UNHCR. 1995. CIREFCA: an opportunity and challenge for inter-agency collaboration. May 1995. On file with the author.

UNHCR Archives. 1981. 3rd Draft of steering committee of post-ICARA coordination meeting. Held 15/9/81, New York, HCR/NY/572. Fonds UNHCR 11, 391.62/460.

——. 1984. Press clippings on ICARA II, 26/7/84. Fonds UNHCR 11, 391.78/1019C.

——. 1988*a*. UNHCR informal consultations on Indochinese asylum-seekers in South-East Asia, Bangkok, 27–28 October 1988. 10/11/88. UNHCR Fonds 11, Series 3, 391.89 100.Ich.gen.

——. 1988*b*. Memorandem of Understanding Between the SRV and UNHCR. 13/12/88. UNHCR Fonds 11, Series 3, 391.89.

——. 1989*a*. Note for the file: informal consultations of the IGC in Kuala Lumpur. 5/3/89. UNHCR Fonds 11, Series 3, 391.89.

——. 1989*b*. Letter, Douglas Hurd to HC Thorvald Stoltenberg. 2/2/90. UNHCR Fonds 11, Series 3, 391.89.

——. 1990*a*. Principles and criteria for the protection and assistance of refugees, repatriation and displaced persons. Prepared by the Juridical Committee of CIREFCA. UNHCR Fonds 11, Series 3, 391.86.3 HCR/Mex/0890.

——. 1990*b*. Statement by Malaysian Minister of Foreign Affairs, 23rd ASEAN Ministerial Meeting, Jakarta, 24–5 July 1990. UNHCR Fonds 11, Series 3, 391.89.

——. 1990*c*. Introductory remarks by Sergio Vieira de Mello at informal steering committee meeting, Manila. 17/5/90. UNHCR Fonds 11, Series 3, 391.89.

——. 1992. From conflict to peace and development: note on implementation of the Concerted Plan of Action of CIREFCA, Pablo Mateu (JSU) to K. Asomani (RBLAC). 17/3/92. UNHCR Fonds 11, Series 3, 361.86.5.

UNHCR Archives. 1993*a*. Questions and answers about CIREFCA. Prepared for seminar on the implementation of a human development approach for areas affected by conflict in Central America and related strategies for the post-CIREFCA process, June 1993. UNHCR Fonds 11, Series 3, 391.85.5

——. 1993*b*. Memo, Ruprecht Von Arnim, Representative to Brussels, to Jenifer Otsea, Headquarters. The Ninth San José Summit of Foreign Ministers of the EC and Countries of Central America. 3/3/93. UNHCR Fonds 11, Series 3, 391.86/381.

——. 1993*c*. Jenifer Otsea, CIREFCA JSU, to UNHCR Brussels. CIREFCA: A Strategy for Solutions. 8/2/93. UNHCR Fonds 11, Series 3, 391.86.5.

——. 1994*a*. Memo, Chefeke, D to all SMC members. CIREFCA Process: External Evaluation. 21/9/94. UNHCR Fonds 11, Series 3, 391.86.5.

——. 1994*b*. Introductory Statement by Mrs Sadako Ogata', Informal Meeting of ExCom, Geneva. 28/1/94. UNHCR Fonds 11, Series 3, 391.86.5.

UNHCR. 1994*a*. *Returnee aid and development*. UNHCR: Geneva.

——. 1994*b*. Reunion tecnica informal sobre CIREFCA. San José, 15–16 February 1994. On file with the author.

Williams, J. and Zeager, L. 2004. Macedonian border closings in the Kosovo refugee crisis: a game theoretic perspective. *Conflict Management and Peace Studies*, 21: 233–254.

Young, O. 2002. Institutional linkages in international society: polar perspectives. *Global Governance*, 2(1): 1–24.

4

Refugees, International Society, and Global Order

Andrew Hurrell

ABSTRACT

This chapter explores what the study of international society (sometimes labelled an English School approach) can contribute to our understanding of refugees, and considers how a focus on refugees can help us to identify some of the core challenges facing international society. Refugees surely provide one of the clearest examples of the political importance of constitutive norms and practices and of the ways in which such norms can be embedded in politically consequential institutions. Moreover it is certainly the case that one of the contributions of international society thinking is precisely that it places the 'problem of the refugee' in relation to the historically contingent ways in which political life and forms of political community have been imagined and practised. At the same time, it is important to avoid an overly teleological account and to understand the crucial ways in which the changing character of international society has impacted on the ways in which the problem of the refugee has been manifest. In terms of the recent evolution in international society, refugees provide a sobering reminder of the limits of liberal solidarist change within international society. In part this has to do with the intrinsic tensions within the liberal solidarist conception of international society and in part with a broader set of forces pressing international society back towards 'Westphalia'. The final section considers the normative agenda and examines the challenges to the English School's notion of embedded ethics posed by the phenomenon of refugees.

It is often said that the nature of any society is exposed at its margins. Sometimes, following Foucault (1991), those living at the margins or in the interstices of social life—in prisons, in mental hospitals—expose the macro or deep structures of power and governmentality. For others, such as Diego Gambetta (2009), it is by looking at those who live and operate at the margins of society—mafiosi, prisoners, terrorists—that we can better understand the micro-mechanisms of social life (e.g. how trust develops or the role of codes and signals in social behaviour).

To what extent can both the politics of refugees as a general problem and the particularly tragic predicament of the individual refugee help us to understand the nature of international society? This chapter explores what the study of international society (sometimes labelled an English School approach) can contribute to our understanding of refugees, and considers how a focus on refugees can help us to identify some of the core challenges facing international society. It suggests that refugees can tell us a great deal about international society at both the macro- or structural level, but also at the more micro-level. Indeed, many of the most important intellectual challenges have to do with the ways in which the micro- and the macro-levels can be related to each other. This is especially relevant given the extent to which so much of the study of Forced Migration Studies has been 'bottom-up' and concerned with particular situations of forced migration whilst so much of International Relations theory is 'top-down'—or, to put it less kindly, often prone to excessive abstraction and generality.

The chapter addresses four questions:

1. What has been the place of refugees in the historical evolution of international society?
2. Where do refugees fit within liberal solidarist accounts of the changing character of international society?
3. What can refugees tell us about the evolving challenges of global order?
4. How does international society writing address the ethical dilemmas posed by refugees?

WHAT HAS BEEN THE PLACE OF REFUGEES IN INTERNATIONAL SOCIETY?

The central concern of international society writers has been with the nature and possibilities of international order. What kinds of ordered and cooperative relations have states and their governments established amongst themselves? What kinds of shared purposes and values (if any) can be discerned in the norms, rules, and institutions by which states and other actors have sought to structure and regulate their interaction?

The dominant way of proceeding has been to explore and to analyse the common framework of rules and institutions that developed within the anarchical society of the classical European state system. This society was anarchical in that there was no common power to enforce law or to underwrite cooperation; but it was a society insofar as states were conscious of common rules and values, cooperated in the working of common institutions, and perceived common interests in observing these rules and working through these institutions. It involved the creation of certain minimalist rules, understandings, and institutions designed to limit the inevitable conflict that was to be expected within such a pluralist and fragmented political system. The normative structure of this society was built around the mutual recognition of states as independent and legally equal members of international society, on their freedom to promote their own ends subject to minimal constraints, and on the unavoidable reliance on self-preservation and self-help. The core goals of international social order were survival and coexistence and the political framework was composed of the institutions of a pluralist international society of states—international law, Great Powers, the balance of power, diplomacy, and war. And the core problem was threefold: the management of unequal power, the capturing of common interests, and the mediation of value diversity (Bull 2002: 3–21).

In thinking about the problem of order in international relations, this approach involved three elements. There is an *analytical* move (what are the minimum conditions that would have to exist before any society could be meaningfully so described?); a *historical* move (how far can one isolate and identify an acceptance of these conditions in the evolving practices of states?); and a *normative* move (on what minimum conditions of coexistence might the holders of sharply conflicting values be able to agree?) (Alderson and Hurrell 2000, chs 1–3). The subsequent task has been to map and explain the changing normative constitution of international society—in particular the move from a limited pluralist society of states built around coexistence to a liberal solidarist society of states united by denser institutional forms and by stronger moral and legal ties and also to the growth of different forms of complex governance beyond the state (Hurrell 2007).

One of the most distinctive features of international society writing is the importance attached to norms and institutions. Central to the 'international system' is a historically created, and evolving, structure of common understandings, rules, norms, and mutual expectations. The concepts of state sovereignty, international law, or war are not given by the game of power politics. Rather, shared and historically grounded understandings of war or sovereignty shape what the nature of the game is, how it is to be played and, very critically, how it has changed and evolved. International society approaches stress the multiple roles played by norms, rules, and institutions in international life. These may well serve as regulatory rules designed to constrain choices or as the parameters within which individual agents pursue their own preferences. This is the view of rules that lies behind the common claim that international law in relation to, say, the use of force, is not able to 'control' what states do. Whilst this may very often be true, the critical point is that norms and rules have many other roles and do much more than this. In particular norms and rules help explain how actors are constituted, who can act, and through what forms of social and political action.

Refugees surely provide one of the clearest examples of the political importance of constitutive norms and practices and of the ways in which such norms can be embedded in politically consequential institutions. A great deal of the struggle of refugee politics has been about notions of definition and of labelling. Think of the political and life-or-death impact in terms of the entitlements that derive from being able to enter into the legal category of 'refugee'. Think of the way in which understandings of refugee status have been connected to broader social norms, as for instance in the way in which orthodox distinctions between the public and private spheres have shaped understandings and evaluation of gender-related persecution. Or think of the political importance for an organization such as UNHCR of the gradual expansion of the accepted categories of forced migration that are deemed the subject of international concern.

The emphasis on norms in international society writing is sometimes associated with a cosy liberal or 'Grotian' view of international life concerned with order and cooperation. But norms are just as central to understanding the nature of conflict and the operation of social power, especially the creation of stable and legitimate forms of power. Refugees provide a very clear example of the role of normative claims in mobilizing political power and justifying political action. It is very difficult to explain either the circumstances that generate refugees or the reasons why the acceptance of refugees is so often viewed as problematic without reference to the clash of norms and values. Equally, the attempt to legitimate power has increasingly involved claims to be protecting or promoting particular normative claims or sets of rights.

At the specific or micro-level it is clear that the politics of refugees simply cannot be understood outside of the institutional and normative categories of international law and society. But what about the macro-level? To what extent is the problem of refugees bound up with the very existence of international society?

This view has been powerfully put forward by Emma Haddad. Refugees, on this view, are intimately and inescapably bound up with the historically constructed concept of 'Westphalian sovereignty' and with the very existence of an international society of states. Understanding this, for Haddad, is the most crucial contribution that the English School can make to the study of refugees. 'Refugees are not the consequence of a breakdown in the system of separate states, rather they are an inevitable if unanticipated part of international society. As long as there are political borders constructing separate states and creating clear definitions of insiders and outsiders, there will be refugees' (Haddad 2008: 7). Or again: 'In other words, much of the literature fails to examine the relationship of the refugee with the very workings of international society. But without an international states system there would be no refugees; thus the one cannot be divorced from the other' (Haddad 2008: 4). Refugees are created when the link between state, citizen, and territory is broken: 'The (modern) refugee is only fully intelligible within the context of a pluralist system of states in which individual political communities fail to guarantee the content of substantive sovereignty' (Haddad 2008: 63).

It is indeed the case that one of the contributions of international society thinking is precisely that it places the 'problem of the refugee' in relation to the historically contingent ways in which political life and forms of political community have been imagined and practised (Haddad 2008). At the same time, it is important to avoid an overly teleological account and to understand the various ways in which the changing character of international society has impacted on the ways in which the problem of the refugee has been manifest.[1]

In the first place, we need to recognize the importance and variability of state strength and of state capacity. One of the stranger claims about 'Westphalia' is that it was a system characterized by tightly patrolled borders and by limited economic interdependence. This is strange because the high-point of the sovereignty-based order in the nineteenth century coincided with an era of globalization, with high levels of cross-border exchange, and with sustained demographic openness, which on many dimensions was more extensive and more far-reaching than that of the late twentieth century. In part this disjuncture between the formal claims to exclusive sovereignty and an economically and demographically open world society was the result of particular political choices. But it also followed from the limited coercive capacity of states to exercise effective control over their boundaries. It was only towards the end of the nineteenth century that states gained the effective administrative and financial resources effectively to police their boundaries and to develop the panopoly of controls over the entry of aliens and over their presence within the state.

But if increasing state strength helps understand one side of the emergence of refugees as a political problem, the other side concerns state weakness. This problem is not new: think of the link between the successive rounds of imperial dissolution, the formation of new and weak states, and massive population displacements. But state weakness has become a major theme of international politics in the post-Cold War period. In many parts of the world, the old dichotomy between domestic 'order' and international 'anarchy' has been recast; an increasing number of states are perceived to be 'failing'. The international community has faced increasing calls to act in order to prevent domestic problems from spilling over borders; to uphold humanitarian norms in the midst of widespread civil conflict; and to ensure the effective local implementation of policies that affect outsiders.

Second, seeking a link between sovereignty as a formal claim and refugees is clearly not enough and we need to give particular emphasis to changes in the character of political community. One important—and mostly problematic—part of that story has to be related to the growth of different forms of political nationalism. If states and state sovereignty provide the basic institutional framework of international society, it is some notion of political community and a belief in the moral value of self-determination—most commonly national but often shading into cultural and religious—that has come ever more to provide the political power and the moral meaning to the idea of living in a world made up of separate nation-states. National self-determination has added powerful justification for the existence of separate nation-states and for obligations owed to them rather than to humankind in general. States, now nation-states in aspiration and in the ideology of the system, are deemed legitimate because they embody the exercise of political self-determination; because they allow groups of individuals to give expression to their values, their culture, their sense of themselves; and because they offer protection to groups who would otherwise be extremely vulnerable. Hence state boundaries become both politically and morally far more important. They are, after all, the lines that demarcate not just abstract units of administration but communities that are supposed to share both an identity and a legitimate political purpose.

National self-determination is fundamental to the modern understanding of political community and therefore to the creation of the categories of refugees, minorities, stateless peoples, unwanted aliens, and displaced populations. Nationalism and claims to national self-determination have been intimately connected with many of the conflicts that have generated the greatest number of refugees—the wars of nation building, of nation breaking, and of imperial dissolution. It was of course precisely against this background that Arendt developed her argument about the loss of the 'right to have rights', not just through direct persecution and expulsion from one's homeland but through being deprived of the very right to belong to some kind of organized political community—'not the loss of specific rights, then, but the loss of a community willing and able to guarantee any rights whatsoever' (Arendt 1951/1968: 297).

Finally, and most importantly, any story about the link between international society and refugees has to relate changing notions of citizenship and political community on the one hand to the broader transformation in the role of the state on the other. Historically, the role and character of the state underwent a profound transformation that gathered pace from the later part of the nineteenth century—away from a narrow concern with the wealth and power of the sovereign and towards ever deeper involvement in an increasing number of aspects of social, economic, and political life. In this process the legitimacy of governments (democratic and authoritarian) came to depend on their capacity to meet a vastly increased range of needs, claims, and demands. In part this involved increased expectations of the role of the state in economic management and social welfare (thereby sharpening questions of what is owed to citizens and to outsiders). In part it was driven by war and conflict and the increasingly pressing idea of the nation-state as a shared community of fate. And in part it reflected changed notions of political legitimacy and broadened understandings of self determination, of human rights, and of citizenship rights. The different ways in which these developments come together help explain why the politics of refugees have assumed particular forms and also why population movement becomes such a very different political problem in the second half of the twentieth century—compared to, say, the massive movements of peoples and refugees in the latter part of the nineteenth century.

The changing nature of political community raises some doubt as to whether and how far the problem of refugees can be associated exclusively with the international society of states as the dominant form of global political order. There are many varieties of the claim that particular communities are morally significant and that differences between members and non-members can be morally justified. Communitarians, liberal nationalists, and modern-day civic republicans each have particular answers and arguments. For example, membership may be normatively special not only because it may embody some notion of cultural or other community but because special ties are owed to fellow citizens. The borders of political society are morally significant because principles of social justice are developed in order to regulate and then justify the relations of citizens engaged in shared systems of collective self-governance.

But the crucial point here is that *any* strong notion of political community will create some form of distinction between members and non-members, and insiders and outsiders. As Benhabib (2004*a*, 2004*b*) notes, even in the case of liberal democratic states, there is a deep tension between universal values and particular forms of civic community. 'The tension between universal human rights claims and particularistic cultural and national identities is constitutive of democratic legitimacy. Modern democracies act in the name of universal principles that are then circumscribed within a particular civic community. This is the 'Janus face of the modern nation' in the words of Jürgen Habermas'(Benhabib 2004*b*: 44).

Equally, territoriality is not only important within a territorially based system of nation-states. In justifying why a particular political community is worthwhile, many might wish to argue that a sense of place and a commitment to a particular location are crucial elements of the identity of both individuals and of groups. Indeed it is the loss of this attachment to place that lies at the heart of the tragedy of refugees. Finally, although it is undoubtedly the case that many of the particular pathologies of the international system are important drivers of refugee flows (above all interstate war), the causes of forced migration are broader, including forms of violence not related to the interstate system, to displacement caused by development, and to environmental factors (Betts 2009: 4–10). All of these would continue to exist within different forms of global political organization.

In other words, then, there are very important macro-linkages between the problem of refugees and the existence of international society. But the problem of how to treat those driven out of their own political community who arrive at the borders of a different political community is one that would not automatically go away with the abolition or transformation of international society. Indeed it is interesting to note that the projects for a better world developed by many cosmopolitan theorists have laid much greater emphasis on possible changes in the vertical distribution of power and authority than on the horizontal relationship of the different units that would continue to characterize global politics and on the character of the borders that would still remain.[2]

WHERE DO REFUGEES FIT WITHIN LIBERAL SOLIDARIST ACCOUNTS OF THE CHANGING CHARACTER OF INTERNATIONAL SOCIETY?

One of the dominant concerns of international society writers has been to track the changes in the constitution of international society and in its dominant norms and practices. The second half of the twentieth century witnessed a transformation in ideas about the nature and possibilities of international order. At the level of practice, there were important changes in patterns of institutionalization; a dramatic increase in the scope, density, and intrusiveness of international rules; far-reaching developments in both the making of international law and the basis on which legal, moral, and political norms were to be justified; and increasing efforts to move towards the more effective implementation of international norms. At the level of normative ambition the changes were still more far-reaching and led inexorably to the belief—at least within western liberal societies—that international order had to be re-conceived and re-conceptualized. A minimally acceptable order came increasingly to be seen as involving both limits on the freedom of states to resort to war and the creation of international rules that affected the domestic structures and organization of states; that invested individuals and groups within states with rights and duties; and that sought to embody some notion of a general common good.

The hugely increased normative ambition of international society is nowhere more visible than in the field of human rights: in the idea that the relationship between the ruler and ruled, the state and citizen, should be a subject of legitimate international concern; that the ill treatment of citizens should trigger international action; and that the external legitimacy of states and their position within international society should depend in some way on their domestic political arrangements. This normative expansion has taken many forms: the expansion in the scope of rights encompassing civil and political rights, social and economic rights, as well as more recent claims to so-called 'third generation' or 'solidarity rights' (rights to development, peace, clean environment, cultural identity); the coming together of human rights with the notion of democratic rule as an international norm; the moves to apply the laws of war and humanitarian law to 'internal' conflicts and civil wars, and to revived ideas of internationally recognized and protected minority rights; and the growth of norms and practices concerned with humanitarian intervention.

But where are the refuges in all of this? Of course they have not been wholly absent, as we shall see below. The crucial point, however, is to underscore the limits. When it comes to refugees and to people movement in general we remain much closer to a pluralist world of Westphalian sovereignty, even at the level of proclaimed normative ambition.

We can start by noting the obvious discrepancy between the openness associated with liberal globalization and the closure of borders in relation to the movement of labour. There has been very little erosion of the state's political or legal authority to control borders and to exclude. Beyond law and politics, and as noted above, many of the most prominent moral and political theorists in the West argue strongly for a world of closed political communities in which control of membership is a legitimate right of the self-constituted members. More striking still is the degree to which migration policy has not been subject to any international oversight. In all other areas of human rights, minimal progress has involved the idea that what a state does at home should be the legitimate subject of international concern and that states should at least have to justify their policies to the international community. But in the area of people movement no such progress has been visible and state policies can run in the face of other accepted international norms. There is, for example, no external constraint on a race-based migration policy. Finally, of all the treaties and agreements concerned with human rights, those relating to migrants' rights and labour rights have by far the lowest levels of ratification, especially amongst labour-receiving states.

Asylum is, of course, supposed to at least qualify this unfettered exercise of state power through the process of refugee-seeking and the granting of asylum status until either possible resettlement or naturalization. In addition, the increased concern with internally displaced persons; the expansion of the role of UNHCR in many conflict zones (as in its involvement in 'safe return', in the administration of camps, and in assistance during conflict); and the increasingly central role of refugees in both understanding of security and in the practice of humanitarian intervention could all be added to this picture. But, as is often noted, although there is a right to seek asylum and although the legal order has moved some way towards the acceptance of the idea of entitlement provided certain criteria are met, there is no corresponding duty on states to admit. States have continued to exercise close political control over the process of the determination of refugee status and there has been great variation in the willingness of states to accept refugees. Moreover, if we think that one of the great gains of the human rights system has been the gradual increase in the pressure on states to justify their actions—whether political or through formal reporting—there is astonishingly little pressure on states to justify what they do in relation to refugee protection.

Even in the 1990s when liberal solidarists were celebrating the emergence of 'post-Westphalian world', the picture in relation to refugees looked rather different: the erosion of the core idea of non-voluntary return; the very limited progress towards the provision of material assistance towards those societies in the South most burdened by refugees (in 2001 around 75 per cent of the world's 20 million refugees were in developing countries); political blindness and institutional failures in terms of the protection of human rights of the estimated 6 million refugees living in camps; and even growing calls for the revision or replacement of the core of the international refugee regime, namely, the 1951 Convention. The increased salience of national security concerns and the growth of racism and xenophobia in many developed states have pressed further in this direction with further moves to undermine the formal right to asylum. These include sanctions on carriers, off-shore processing, the use of 'safe third country' concepts, the denial of benefits or imprisonment of those seeking asylum, and limited access to appeals. If we add to all of this the structural capacity of the rich to set the terms of global burden-sharing on refugee protection and at least some of the links between global economic inequality and the generation of refugees, then the progress of liberal solidarism appears limited, not just in terms of implementation but also in terms of normative ambition and even the visibility given to the issue by major human rights groups.

Liberal solidarists and cosmopolitan liberals often look to Kant as the inspiration for so much of their thinking. Kant, as is well known, laid out three levels of right—the national, the international, and the cosmopolitan. His view of the cosmopolitan is often described as limited. But it is still worth noting that he was clear, first, that what he described as universal hospitality was not a matter of charity or benevolence but of right ('As in the foregoing articles, we are here concerned not with philanthropy, but with *right*'); and second, that strangers should, as a matter of duty, never be turned away if this would result in their death (Kant 1991: 105–6). Even such moral minimalism sits very uncomfortably with the conclusion of one of the leading international lawyers concerned with refugees: 'Notwithstanding decades of practice, there seems now to be little clear sense of the refugee as an individual *entitled* to international protection' (Goodwin-Gill 2008: 22).

Before we look at some of the reasons for this situation, it is important to highlight the tensions within liberal solidarism itself. On one side of course, liberal solidarism is centrally concerned with the rights of the individual. It involves a crucial conceptual change in the nature of sovereignty—away from the idea of the state as sovereign to the idea of the state as agent—an agent acting both in the interests of its own citizens and on behalf of an international community that is increasingly supposed to embody and reflect shared interests and shared values. Sovereignty in the sense of power of the state over its nationals has been eroded by human rights law and by the increased availability to groups and individuals of a range of national courts and international tribunals.

But it is also important to recognize the extent to which international human rights regimes in the post-1945 period have continued to be marked by statism and sovereignty—not just in terms of the capacity of states to resist the transfer of effective authority but also in terms of how the system itself was conceived (Haddad 2008: 47–69). States may be part of the problem, but they remain an essential part of the solution (Haddad 2008: 94–5). They are the source of the system, the locus of responsibility, and the focus of pressure for change. The road to a common humanity, on this account, lies through national sovereignty. Indeed within the solidarist image there is a consolidation and hardening of the boundary that separates political communities from each other and citizens from non-citizens. There may be a degree of greater space for other arrangements (protectorates, confederations, condominia, not-quite federal unions), but territorial states remain central. The statism of this model also narrows the range of options through which self-determination can be pursued—if not through one's own state then through the structure of rights and institutions created by, and around, states. In relation to refugees the solution to the problem is therefore seen in terms of repatriation, resettlement, or naturalization. Finally, if solidarism remains essentially statist in its conception, then the implementation of solidarist norms in the post-Cold War period has had a still more paradoxical character because of its dependence on powerful states for effective action whether through economic sanctions or military intervention.

WHAT CAN REFUGEES TELL US ABOUT THE EVOLVING CHALLENGES OF GLOBAL ORDER?

The all too evident limits of liberal solidarist progress in relation to refugees appear to vindicate the more realist, sceptical side of the international society tradition. But, as a mode of analysis, it is important to differentiate international society writing from realism and to recognize that, just because international relations may be conflict-prone, this does not mean that realism and neo-realism can provide an adequate account as to why this may be so. From an international society perspective, realists make their lives too easy by concentrating on material power and hard notions of state interest. Of course such factors are important. But they are insufficient. It is, after all, the very clash of meanings, ideologies, and claims to justice, interacting with patterns of unequal power, which makes stable cooperation so problematic. Realists take the importance of states and obviousness of state interests entirely as given rather than see it as historically constructed and reinforced by powerful and conflicting sets of values.

If one kind of political analysis is concerned with explanations of particular instances of conflict or cooperation, another seeks to identify broader historical trends within the international system as a whole. To what extent can the limits of liberal solidarism be associated with some bigger historical story? And to what extent does that bigger macro-story vindicate the claims of a more realist image of international relations? Here we might certainly note the depressingly long list of factors that seem to point towards a 'return of Westphalia'—either in terms of the decentralized power-political order emphasized by neo-realism or of a more classical pluralist form of international society, dominated by the twin problems of managing power and mediating value conflict.

The first, and most obvious, concerns the renewed salience of security. As with previous critiques of liberal claims concerning change and transformation, this lies at the heart of the realist view that international politics is naturally dominated by logics of power and insecurity and by the centrality of military force. Hence, at the national level, we have witnessed the reassertion of claims about the centrality of national security and the apparent obviousness of Schmittian arguments that it is 'our' security that matters most; that leaders have a duty to protect national security even at the cost of liberty and the protection of human rights; and that state control should be reasserted over borders, over citizens and, of course, over aliens. Hence, at the international level, there is a parallel set of Schmittian arguments, namely, that, in seeking to constitutionalize international politics, liberal solidarists had detached law from effective power. Again, on this view, security is a prior value and all international political orders depend ultimately on a strong state or group of states willing and able to provide a minimal degree of security which will necessarily involve the threat and use of coercive force, including in terms of the renewed salience of nuclear weapons. Finally, and related, there is the renewed centrality of war in its classic and Clausewitzian sense—as a reciprocal, dynamic, and unpredictable form of conflict in which there is a constant tension between the internal logic of violence and the political objectives that this violence is supposed to help achieve.

Second, there is the continued or renewed power of nationalism, no longer potentially containable politically or analytically in a box marked 'ethnic conflict' but manifest in the identity politics and foreign policy actions of the major states in the system. On this view, nationalism as a force and as a powerfully felt community of fate shows little sign of declining in many of the largest states of the world (and has been powerfully reasserted in Russia, in China, and in the United States); and demands for national self-determination, the exploitation of such claims by outside states, and newer forms of resistance to alien rule continue to underlie a very great number of violent conflicts in the world, including many associated with the growth of terrorism.

Third, there are the various ways in which economic globalization has fed back into the structures and dynamics of a Westphalian state system rather than pointing towards its transcendence. Hence, as in previous rounds of debate, analysts have noted the resilience of the state as an economic actor in seeking to control economic flows and to police borders and in seeking to exploit and develop state-based and mercantilist modes of managing economic problems, especially in relation to resource competition and financial instability. Still more important is the need to recognize that the most important effect of liberal economic globalization has been on the distribution of interstate political power. If the debate over power shifts in the 1990s concentrated on the shift of power from states to firms and non-state actors, the 'power shift' of the past decade has focused on rising and emerging powers, on state-directed economic activity, and on the mismatch between existing global economic governance arrangements and the distribution of power amongst those with the actual power of effective economic decision. In this respect the global economic crisis is significant because of the challenge that it represents to the idea of a stable Western-led liberal global order and because of the reinforcement that it is giving to the forces and factors outlined above, especially economic nationalism.

And fourth there is the renewed centrality of the balance of power as both a motivation for state policy and as a core element of international political order. The relevance and utility of balance-of-power theory is not limited to those cases where unbalanced power poses a 'direct security challenge to other states', and needs to include 'soft' as well as 'hard' balancing strategies. But, however understood, this quintessential institution of classic international society has very clearly not faded from the scene.

In the light of these factors there does indeed appear to be a systemic pattern to many of the individual aspects of the politics of refugees. This macro-narrative seems to fit well with, for example, the increased state control over borders, the intensification of xenophobic nationalism, or the claim that humanitarian intervention has to take second place to the demands of national as opposed to human security. Other linkages might well reappear in the future, for example, the increased politicization of refugee populations as part of a return of major power rivalries or intensified resource conflicts.

It is possible to see these developments simply as international relations returning once more to its 'Westphalian norm'—the return of history and the end of dreams, as Robert Kagan (2008) would have it. However, it is more accurate and intellectually honest to face up to the complex, hybrid, and contested character of contemporary global order. International society faces a series of classic Westphalian problems, especially to do with the rise of new powers and the re-emergence of nationalism and economic statism and resource mercantilism. But it faces these problems within a context that is clearly post-Westphalian. The politics of refugees provide one illustration of why this is the case.

Global order is post-Westphalian, first, because the complexity of governance challenges necessarily involves external intervention and deep engagement. If states are to develop effective policies on economic development, environmental protection, human rights, the resolution of refugee crises, the fight against drugs, or the struggle against terrorism, then they need to engage with a wide range of international and transnational actors and to interact not just with central governments but with a much wider range of domestic political, economic, and social players. This tendency has been increased by the erosion of states and of state capacity and by the inability of states in many parts of the world to play their allotted role as the provider of local order. This does not make everything global. But, however difficult it may be to measure and assess particular linkages, it is highly implausible to believe that the 20 per cent of the world's population living in the high-income countries can insulate itself from the instability and insecurity of the rest and from the revisionist demands for change. The limits of rich state responses to refugee flows and the costs entailed in current policies provide a good illustration of such interconnections.

Second, the structural logic at play in the generation of demands for governance is also reflected in the ever-more complex ways in which different issues are linked together. As always, it is important to ask critical questions about such linkages and not to assume that such linkages are somehow natural. The link between migration and security—the so-called 'migration-security nexus'—is a good example of how Western states have sought to shape the migration and asylum agenda in ways that reflect their own interests and concerns. But, even allowing for the operation of power and even remaining persistently sceptical, there are important structural connections between different areas and domains of global governance—between the environment and development (as in the idea of sustainable development); between trade regulation and health, labour standards, and the environment; or between democracy, state-building, and post-conflict resolution. One of the features of these changes is the erosion of the legal and conceptual categories. The complex linkages between different categories of people movement are therefore emblematic of a more general pattern.

Finally, there is the question of identity politics and the struggle for recognition. The massive movement of peoples, the intensification of contacts and interconnections between societies, and the multiple dislocations of established ways of thinking and of doing have intensified identity politics and have given a sharper and often destructive twist to struggles for cultural recognition. But these same developments undermine the view of states as empirically or morally viable containers of cultural pluralism. The globalization and the de-territorialization of identity politics is one of the most important reasons why a neat pluralist global order has been rendered obsolete.

HOW DOES INTERNATIONAL SOCIETY WRITING ADDRESS THE ETHICAL DILEMMAS POSED BY REFUGEES?

The global justice agenda has expanded hugely in recent years. Discussions of global justice are often structured around debates between those who seek to justify a pluralist system of sovereign states with only minimal duties beyond their borders and those who press for more expansive cosmopolitan conceptions and practices of justice (Brown, this volume, chapter 7). And yet it is striking to note how rarely these debates have been directly concerned with refugees, forced migration, and people movement (Benhabib 2004*b*: 2).[3] And, when these issues have been addressed, that engagement has been distinctly uncomfortable.

On one side, communitarians, republicans, and liberal nationalists have produced extensive and elaborate arguments justifying why obligations to particular communities matter and why the right to decide upon membership should not be constrained by external rules or institutions. It is important to note that such accounts rarely suggest that no obligations are owed to non-members. Michael Walzer, for example, is clear that coercive intervention is fully justified in cases of the serious and sustained violation of human rights (Walzer 1995). But, for Walzer and others, the distant oppressed stranger seems to attract greater attention than the stranger at the gates. Indeed communitarians have rarely faced up to the human costs of exclusion and to the daily violence that occurs at the borders of the nation-state as governments seek to exclude unwanted migrants and to check the flow of those seeking asylum. Between 1999 and 2004, for example, there were 2411 deaths of migrants on the outer borders of the European Union, plus a further 760 people counted as missing (Kiza 2008: 214). Around 400 to 500 people die each year trying to cross the US-Mexican border.[4]

Cosmopolitans, on the other side, have been relentless in their critiques of communitarian and nationalist positions. But they too have tended to focus on the macro-level injustices of the global system rather than on injustices closer to home. In particular they have often sought to mitigate the moral dilemmas posed by people movement by arguing for distributive justice on a global scale. From this perspective, such reforms will work to undercut the factors that produce both forced migration and economic migrants. Moreover, as noted earlier, in their visions for a better world, cosmopolitan theorists have laid far greater emphasis on the importance of unpacking sovereignty and creating systems of multi-level governance and dispersed sovereignty than on the character of the borders that would continue to separate political communities, on the degree of porosity of those borders, and on the principles that should continue to govern membership.

But if forced migration raises problematic questions for both cosmopolitan and communitarian theorists, the same is no less true for those who adopt an international society perspective to ethics. There are three particularly acute challenges.

In the first place, the ethics of international society is grounded on those norms and normative ideas that exist within international society or at least that might be immanent within existing practices. At the minimal level the limited interstate order underpinned by the society of states is seen by international society theorists as providing a morally significant means of promoting coexistence and limiting conflict in a world in which consensus on more elaborate forms of cooperation does not exist and in which more elaborate international institutions are always liable to be captured by the special interests and particular values of the most powerful. But, more positively, international society has the potential not just to help manage international conduct in a restrained way but also to create the conditions for a more legitimate and morally more ambitious political community to emerge: by providing a stable institutional framework within which substantive norms can be negotiated; by developing a common language in which claims and counterclaims can be made and debated with some degree of accessibility and authority; and by embedding a set of formal rules that embody at least elements of equality and at least some restraints on the power and ambitions of the strong.

The problem, however, is precisely the gulf between what states do in relation to refugees and what even the most minimal notions of justice require. As Cochran puts it in her discussion of Bull: 'Bull had the problem, at once both practical and moral, of how to get his ethic to bite on deeply unjust practices that lacked a sufficient consensus among international actors on the need to address them' (Cochran 2009: 220). If we stay within the confines of state practice or even the proclaimed normative goals of international society, it appears extremely difficult to find a secure foundation on which to argue why the treatment of refugees in international society is so morally problematic. The all too evident absence of solidarist progress in relation to refugees makes it very difficult to bridge the gulf between the empirical and the normative.

The second ethical challenge for international society theorists concerns the importance of agency at the micro-level. Given the problems of managing unequal power and mediating between deep value conflicts, international society writers have long been sceptical of the claims made by the powerful to speak in the name of universal principles of global justice. Instead the focus has been increasingly on the political institutions through which negotiation over moral claims might take place and on the need for dialogue and deliberation (Hurrell 2007, ch 12; Linklater 1998). But any claim about the importance of dialogue raises the issue of who is to participate and how: in particular how are those whose rights are violated to be given voice? Increasing attention has been given to ways in which human rights politics can work to empower the powerful, to create dependency, and to institutionalize paternalism (Kennedy 2004). But the position of the refugee is particularly problematic. After all refugees are precisely those who cannot find either voice or protection within their own states and who have been deprived of the capacity to engage in political action. Even compared with others whose rights have been violated, the ability of those seeking refuge to assume any form of individual or collective agency is extremely circumscribed—by the legal and political constraints placed on all those seeking asylum and by the imperatives of invisibility on the part of those living illegally. In his Arendtian analysis, James Ingram may well be correct to identify 'human rights politics first and foremost with the activity of rights claimants' and to argue that 'Rights are only secure and effective when they are an expression of the autonomy, the creation and possession of their bearers' (Ingram 2008: 413, 414). But the degree to which this can find 'direct political expression' on the part of the refugees and those seeking asylum must be open to some considerable doubt.

The final challenge again focuses on the question of agency but this time at the macro or systemic level. International society writing is wedded to the state, both empirically and normatively: not in the simplistic sense that states are the only important actors, but rather in the claim that a state-anchored set of governance norms and institutions can provide both a stable order and a degree of justice in a global society undergoing the multiple changes and challenges often captured in short-hand by the term globalization. The implicit norm is of membership within relatively closed political communities and of a world in which people movement is limited or where the movements of people are caused by factors that are at least potentially subject to improvement or rectification.

The question is whether this implicit picture of the world can deal with a situation in which the movement of peoples is not just an aberration; in which migration is not a straightforward once-only event but rather involves the creation of complex transnational social spaces; and in which refugees will continue to exist in large numbers driven by a broad range of factors and circumstances. As we have seen, even a liberal solidarist international society struggles to provide a political or legal framework in which the refugee's 'right to have rights' can be secured. Many potential avenues for future reform have been suggested. These include the meshing of non-exclusive constitutionalism within states with the transnationalization of a culture of human rights that includes the rights of groups and different sorts of transnational constituencies, the importance of residence and settlement in the acquisition of citizenship rights, the strengthening of labour rights, and, perhaps above all, avoiding the stark and unbridgeable divide between the full member of a community and the distant and needy 'other'.

But if international society writing has one single message it is that all sets of legal and moral norms have to be related to the agency of those who possess power and to the particular values of the power-holders. The macro-challenge is to find a means of reconciling the continuing centrality of the old pluralist interstate order with the structural changes and normative challenges of a patently post-Westphalian world. The fate of many groups depends on the success of such mediation—and none more so than the refugee.

NOTES

1. Haddad (2008: 13–14) criticizes the English School for too often assuming a static and uniform international society and correctly notes that concepts such as sovereignty and the state are ambiguous and dynamic concepts. At the same time, her own view somewhat underplays the very different forms of international society and is sometimes a little teleological—for example, in talking of the modern notions of nationality and citizenship as 'the natural extension of what was set in motion in 1648 and 1789 ...' (Haddad 2008: 58).
2. A small minority of liberal cosmopolitans argue for open borders, most notably Joseph Carens (1987). Onora O'Neill is unusual in emphasizing the crucial need to focus on the character of borders within cosmopolitan political visions. See O'Neill (2000, especially pp. 189–90).
3. For exceptions, see Benhabib (2004*b*) and Gibney (2004). In addition there are other aspects of contemporary normative theory whose implications for refugees and people movement have been under-explored, for example, duties that are owed by virtue of historic and uncompensated injustice.
4. Stephen Macedo (2007) does consider the issue: 'Creating the apparatus of a police state at the border is too high a price to pay, even for social justice at home'; but then underplays the ease of avoiding the structural violence created by state borders: 'But of course there are policy options that could curtail illegal immigration without militarizing the border and imposing the burdens of compliance on poor immigrants seeking a better life.'

BIBLIOGRAPHY

Alderson, K. and Hurrell, A. eds. 2000. *Hedley Bull on international society.* Basingstoke: Palgrave Macmillan.

Arendt, H. 1951/1968. *The origins of totalitarianism.* London: Deutsch.

Benhabib, S. 2004*a*. Reclaiming universalism: negotiating republican self-determination and cosmopolitan norms. In: *The Tanner lectures on human values*. University of California, Berkeley, 15–19 March 2004.

——. 2004*b*. *The rights of others: aliens, residents and citizens*. Cambridge: Cambridge University Press.

Betts, A. 2009. *Forced migration and global politics*. Oxford: Wiley-Blackwell.

Bull, H. 2002. *The anarchical society: a study of order in world politics*. 3rd ed. Basingstoke: Palgrave.

Carens, J. 1987. Aliens and citizens. The case of open borders. *Review of Politics* 49(2), 251–73.

Cochran, M. 2009. Charting the ethics of the English School: what good is there in a middle-ground ethics? *International studies quarterly* 53(1), 203–25.

Foucault, M. 1991. *Discipline and punish: the birth of the prison*. Harmondsworth: Penguin Books.

Gambetta, D. 2009. *Codes of the underworld: how criminals communicate*. Princeton, NJ: Princeton University Press.

Gibney, M. J. 2004. *The ethics and politics of asylum: liberal democracy and the response to refugees*. Cambridge: Cambridge University Press.

Goodwin-Gill, G. S. 2008. The politics of refugee protection. *Refugee Survey Quarterly* 27(1), 8–23.

Haddad, E. 2008. *The refugee: the individual between sovereigns*. Cambridge: Cambridge University Press.

Hurrell, A. 2007. *On global order: power, values and the constitution of international society*. Oxford: Oxford University Press.

Ingram, J. D. 2008. What is a 'right to have rights'? Three images of the politics of human rights. *American Political Science Review* 102(4), 401–16.

Kagan, R. 2008. *The return of history and the end of dreams*. London: Atlantic.

Kant, I. 1991. Perpetual peace. In: Reiss, H. ed. *Kant. Political Writings*. Cambridge: Cambridge University Press.

Kennedy, D. 2004. *The dark side of virtue: humanitarianism reassessed*. Princeton, NJ: Princeton University Press.

Kiza, E. 2008. *Tödliche Grenzen: Die fatalen Auswirkungen europäischer Zuwanderungspolitik*. Berlin: Lit Verlag.

Linklater, A. 1998. *The transformation of political community: ethical foundations of the post-Westphalian era*. Cambridge: Polity Press.

Macedo, Stephen. 2007. The Moral Dilemma of US Immigration Policy: Open Borders vs. Social Justice? In: Swain, C. ed. *Debating immigration*. Cambridge: Cambridge University Press.

O'Neill, O. 2000. *Bounds of justice*. Cambridge: Cambridge University Press.

Walzer, M. 1995. The politics of rescue. *Social Research* 62(1), 53–66.

5

Humanitarianism, Paternalism, and the UNHCR

Michael Barnett

ABSTRACT

This chapter explores how the discourse of humanitarianism contains elements of both emancipation and domination, argues that such seemingly contradictory impulses are best understood through the concept of paternalism, and illustrates these possibilities in the case of the United Nations High Commissioner for Refugees (UNHCR)'s repatriation policies. Section I provides the conceptual inventory that informs this argument. It begins by outlining the different forms of power, focusing on productive power both because it is overlooked by scholars of international relations and because it provides the clearest conceptual link to paternalism. Paternalism, the interference with a person's liberty on the grounds that it is in his or her best interests, partly constitutes humanitarianism and helps to account for the latter's fusing of care and control. While paternalism has a sordid reputation, overlooked is that there are defensible reasons for paternalism, and humanitarian action is often justified by them. Consequently, the conceptual and practical challenge is to reconcile our general repugnance with paternalism with the recognition that some paternalistic practices are justified some of the time. Section II then uses the UNHCR to explore these themes in the power and paternalism of the international humanitarian order. The UNHCR is a humanitarian organization, and as a humanitarian organization it has considerable moral and expert authority. It has used that authority to expand its protection and assistance activities to more populations around the world over the decades. This same authority not only gave UNHCR the opportunity to provide more relief to more displaced populations, but it also conferred on it the role of spokesperson for and guardian of refugees. The underlying assumption, in other words, is that UNHCR knows what is in the best interests of refugees—a population that is often assumed to be too uninformed to know what is in its best interests or too weak to act on them. This is paternalism by any other name, and UNHCR's assistance and protection practices illustrate how compassion and care exist alongside command and control. The conclusion reflects on international paternalism in practice and in theory.

Individuals have been forced to flee their homes ever since God exiled Adam and Eve from Eden. Yet the legal and political category of refugees is only a century old. Prior to the twentieth century, decisions by governments to grant asylum were usually ad hoc and based on their attitude towards those seeking refuge. There were no international mechanisms for considering or handling refugees. Private voluntary agencies sometimes mobilized to assist specific ethnic, national, or religious groups, and sometimes states cooperated with these groups. But for the most part those who were on the move were forced to survive on their wiles, their connections, their luck, and the kindness of strangers.

Yet over the last century we have witnessed the evolution of an international refugee regime, a structure of laws, rules, and principles and a network of states, international organizations, and non-governmental organizations to govern those who are forced to flee their homes because of a fear for their lives (Betts 2009*a*, 2009*b*; Loescher et al. 2008). These political, legal, and institutional developments are a reflection not simply of the objective reality of the existence of displaced peoples but rather of the evolving category of 'refugee' to construct and a new social reality. Some cynics dismiss changes in language as little more than rhetoric, wordplay, or empty victories at some conference centre in Geneva, all of which have no practical effects. But in this instance, at least, the cynics got it wrong. The evolving international refugee regime, and this includes the evolving meaning of the concept of refugees, translates into assistance and protection activities for those who are unable to seek safety from their home government (Haddad 2008). Refugees are not the only class of 'protected' populations. Over the last century we have witnessed an explosion of various kinds of interventions that are intended to assist and protect all kinds of populations that are fighting for their lives and their futures. Much recent attention has been heaped on the contested concept of a 'responsibility to protect', but the much less publicized, celebrated, and coronated 'right to relief' has real teeth. The rise of the international refugee regime in particular, and the international humanitarian order more generally, is evidence of the evolution, if not sheer revolution, in international ethics (Barnett 2009: Introduction).

Revolutions, even those carried out in the name of progress, can elicit worry, and increasingly over the last several years humanitarianism has created a fair number of in-house critics who worry about a 'dark side' (de Waal 1997; Kennedy 2004; Rieff 2002; Terry 2002). Although there are various explanations for why humanitarianism has begun to draw unfavourable attention, perhaps most important for my purposes is the belief that with the end of the Cold War humanitarianism left its ethical sanctuary for the world of politics and power. In this view, humanitarianism was at its best when it stuck to the independent, neutral, and impartial provision of relief to victims of conflict and natural disasters, and began to lose its way and fall on hard times when it began to work alongside and with states, when it ventured away from symptoms to tackle the 'root causes' of suffering, and became involved in basic matters of governance (Barnett 2005). If so, then the obvious remedy is for humanitarianism to recover its ethical bearings and return to its pre-Cold War practices. While I agree that post-Cold War global developments have heightened the dilemmas, tensions, and quandaries confronted by humanitarianism, the diagnosis and thus the prescription does not dig deep enough. What if the very discourse of humanitarianism simultaneously radiates light and dark?

This chapter explores how the discourse of humanitarianism contains elements of both emancipation and domination, argues that such seemingly contradictory impulses are best understood through the concept of paternalism, and illustrates these possibilities in the case of the United Nations High Commissioner for Refugees (UNHCR)'s repatriation policies. Section I provides the conceptual inventory that informs this argument. It begins by outlining the different forms of power, focusing on productive power both because it is overlooked by scholars of international relations and because it provides the clearest conceptual link to paternalism. Paternalism, the interference with a person's liberty on the grounds that it is in his or her best interests, partly constitutes humanitarianism and helps account for the latter's fusing of care and control. While paternalism has a sordid reputation, the fact that there are defensible reasons for paternalism has been overlooked, and humanitarian action is often justified by them. Consequently, the conceptual and practical challenge is to reconcile our general repugnance with paternalism with the recognition that some paternalistic practices are justified some of the time (Feinberg 1986: 25).[1]

Section II then uses the UNHCR to explore these themes in the power and paternalism of the international humanitarian order. The UNHCR is a humanitarian organization, and as a humanitarian organization it has considerable moral and expert authority. It used that authority to expand its protection and assistance activities to more populations around the world over the decades. This same authority not only gave UNHCR the opportunity to provide more relief to more displaced populations, it also conferred on it the role of spokesperson for and guardian of refugees. The underlying assumption, in other words, is that UNHCR knows what is in the best interests of refugees—a population that is often assumed to be too uninformed to know what is in its best interests or too weak to act on them. This is paternalism by any other name, and UNHCR's assistance and protection practices illustrate how compassion and care exist alongside command and control. The conclusion reflects on international paternalism in practice and in theory.

SECTION I: POWER AND PATERNALISM

International relations scholars have done themselves incredible harm assuming that power comes in a single form and failing to appreciate the multiple ways in which global social relations shape the ability of actors to influence their lives. In an attempt to alert scholars to the diversity of possibilities, Raymond Duvall and I offered a conceptual framework for thinking about power in international relations. We defined power as the production, in and through social relations, of effects that shape the capacities of actors to determine their circumstances and fate. To best understand the various ways social relations have such effects, we argued that scholars should be attentive to two dimensions: the kinds of social relations through which power works and the specificity of relations through which effects on actors' capacities are produced (Barnett and Duvall 2005). 'Kinds' refers to the polar positions of social relations of interaction and social relations of constitution. Accordingly, power is either an attribute of particular actors and their interactions or a social process of constituting what actors are as social beings, that is, their social identities and capacities. It can operate, for example, by pointing a gun and forcibly repatriating refugees over the border and back to a place that remains a threat to their safety, or by assuming that a 'refugee' is not only vulnerable but also probably does not have enough education, experience, or knowledge to make good decisions. Specificity concerns the degree to which the social relations through which power works are direct and socially specific or indirect and socially diffuse. It can operate, for example, at the very instant when refugees are forced over the border at gunpoint or through diffuse processes embedded in international institutions that shape who is entitled to be categorized as a refugee.

These two dimensions produce a taxonomy of four different types of power. Compulsory power concerns the relations of interaction of direct control by one actor over another. Institutional power is the control actors exercise indirectly over others through diffuse relations of interaction. Structural power is the constitution of subjects' capacities in direct structural relation to one another. And productive power is the socially diffuse production of subjectivity in systems of meaning and signification. These different conceptualizations provide distinct answers to the fundamental question: in what respects are actors able to determine their fate, and how is that ability limited or enhanced through social relations with others?

The international governance of refugees illustrates these multiple possibilities and the need to see power in its multiple dimensions. There are plenty of instances of compulsory power. Forced migration is perhaps the clearest and most horrific example of the ability of one actor, in most cases the state, to force others, often through either the threat or use of violence, to leave their homes. While international relations scholars are typically focused on violence and force, compulsory power can also work through symbolic instruments. For instance, non-governmental organizations use various kinds of symbolic tools to advocate for their cause and 'name and shame' states into changing their behaviour. Examples of institutional power include when the United States imposed a narrow mandate on the UNHCR in 1951, thus shaping whether and how the agency could assist populations outside of Europe; and when UNHCR staff use its agenda-setting power to influence what is discussed at the annual Executive Committee meetings. There are fewer obvious instances of structural power, but arguably the structure of sovereignty generates the distinction between citizen and non-citizen, thus making possible the (contingent) category of refugee.

I want to highlight instances of productive power both because there is a gap between its significance in international affairs and its recognition by international relations scholars and because it is central to my argument regarding the conceptual link between humanitarianism and paternalism. Productive power, to repeat, concerns how systems of signification and meaning highlight how diffuse processes of social constitution shape the ability of actors to shape their fates and circumstances. Although this sounds like a mouthful, in fact it concerns how our everyday practices and what we take for granted can have a potent effect on what we know, what we think we know, what we want to know, who we think we are, and what we believe we should be doing and are capable of doing (Hayward 2000). There are several features of productive power that are particularly prominent in the international governance of refugees. One, it draws our attention to what counts as a 'problem'. Not everything in the world is a problem. For most of history displaced peoples were not a 'global' problem. At what point did actors come to 'see' refugees as a 'global' problem that required international action, what happened in the world that made possible this category, and why were refugees made into a 'problem' at this time and not another? (Finnemore et al. 2009)

Two, it alerts us to the importance of authority in world affairs. Although authority is related to power, it is not the same thing. Authority can be broadly understood as the ability of one actor to deploy discursive and institutional resources in order to get other actors to defer judgement to them (Barnett and Finnemore 2004). There are at least four kinds of authority.[2] First, there is rational–legal authority, made famous by Weber, which claims that in modern society those organizations, like bureaucracies, that are organized around impersonal rules and objective decision-making procedures are conferred authority. These kinds of organizations are valued because they are perceived as efficient, objective, and rule-governed. Delegated authority exists when one actor hires another actor to act on its behalf. The authority, in this respect, is borrowed. Expert authority exists when an actor's voice is given credibility because of his or her specialized training, knowledge, or experience. Moral authority exists when an actor is perceived to be speaking and acting on behalf of the community's values and interests and defending the lives of the weak and vulnerable. As we will see, UNHCR depends heavily on its moral and expert authority to justify its interventions in global affairs.

One reason why actors covet being conferred the status of authority is because authorities get to define 'reality', and whoever gets to define 'reality' has considerable influence over future action. In other words, discourses distribute social capacities, thus giving some actors the ability to influence outcomes and others less so. What is a humanitarian emergency? (Keen 2008: chapters 4–7). Not just anyone can claim that there is an 'emergency'. Instead, those who have moral and expert authority frequently have the ability to name, label, and define how we should understand a set of processes, events, and outcomes. When Médecins Sans Frontièrs speaks about the 'emergency' in Niger, people listen. Certainly not all recognized authorities in a particular domain will agree on what is the proper name or label. There is considerable debate among non-governmental organizations regarding whether Darfur should be classified as 'genocide', underscoring the contested nature of all authority relationships and the social and political processes involved in giving meaning to a constructed reality. Authorities not only get naming rights, but they also are frequently the ones who are called upon to intervene to improve the situation. When Médecins Sans Frontièrs claims that there is an emergency in Niger, it also is appropriating the right to intervene. At the very moment that UNHCR declares the existence of a refugee crisis it is also authorizing itself to act. In general, the process of who gets to define what is a problem; who should be responsible for solving that problem; and the very categorization of an event, object, or action is central to productive power.

Critically, then, productive power, discourse, and knowledge are conceptually intertwined. Knowledge can be generically understood as the construction of information in ways that gives it meaning.[3] As Peter Berger and Thomas Luckmann (Berger and Luckmann 1967: 3) famously put it, 'the social construction of knowledge is concerned with the social construction of reality'. Conceptualization, classification, and categorization are central to meaning-making activity. There are lots of ways to classify killings but only some of these killings become defined as genocide; once an event becomes defined as genocide, instead of tribal hatreds or ethnic conflict, it takes on an entirely different meaning and demands a very different set of responses. Bureaucracies are a particularly good place to see the labour of classification—they could not exist without them. Bureaucracies map social reality as they collect and store files and data; create divisions-of-labour and specialized units; and construct rules that define, categorize, and classify the world. In this way, bureaucratic knowledge not only reflects the social reality as defined by the bureaucracy but also constructs that reality. The world is filled with individuals that have either been forced or chosen to flee their homes, and the UNHCR operates with a classification scheme that distinguishes between refugees, migrants, internally displaced peoples, and other sorts of displaced peoples or those who cannot return home. The act of classification, labeling, naming, and sorting is an essential feature of power because it 'moves persons among social categories or by inventing and applying such categories' and, therefore, constitutes a way of 'making, ordering, and knowing social worlds' (Bowker and Star 1999; Handelman 1995: 280; Schneider and Ingram 1993; Starr 1992; Wright 1994). Anyone casually familiar with an asylum hearing understands the power of classification.

Lastly, productive power considers how discursive processes and practices produce social identities and capacities as they give meaning to them. In Michel Foucault's archetypical formulation, humans are not only power's intended targets but also its effects (Foucault 1970: 170). To be labeled a refugee can increase one's sense of marginalization, powerlessness, incompetence, and social exclusion; therefore, the identity of a refugee often comes with various kinds of self-identified stigmata. Yet there are instances in which refugees attach positive significance to the label and try to preserve it (Andrews 2003; Malkki 1995; Zetter 1991). Moreover, refugees themselves are knowledgeable actors who might not only understand the socially situated signification and meaning of 'refugees' but use that label to their advantage—to engage in performative practices, for instance, that convey weakness and vulnerability in order to generate more resources from aid agencies (Hammond 2008). Being labeled a victim has its advantages (Fassin and Rechtman 2009).

Humanitarianism exhibits these elements of productive power. Throughout history there have been acts of kindness to distant strangers, but the discourse of humanitarianism emerged in the early nineteenth century as a consequence of urbanization and industrialization, changes in religious discourse and practice, and the development of a modern state with an ideology that increasingly accepted that it had responsibilities to its most vulnerable citizens and subjects. Like all discourses, humanitarianism's practices and meanings have been contingent on historical context, but three enduring elements help us to understand its productive power. Humanitarianism is linked to the broader discourse of humanity, which both is reflective of a presumed shared belonging and is a project that is supposed to help create a sense of oneness. The discourse of humanity is tied to a disinterested care. Humanitarianism, in other words, suggests a deeply felt belief in the need to help others because of their circumstances and not because of who they are. In this way, humanity is tied to humanitarianism's principle of impartiality. Second, the discourse of humanitarianism also has a depoliticizing quality. Humanitarianism and politics are binaries—to be humanitarian is to act outside of the realm of politics and power. To help others based on their needs and not on their histories or identities is the antithesis of politics. Thirdly, and relatedly, humanitarianism radiates a purity of motives and an ethics of care. Precisely how ethics should be practiced is a source of lively debate among humanitarians, but there is little disagreement that humanitarianism operates within the world of ethics (Barnett and Weiss 2008; Fassin and Rechtman 2009: chapters 7–8; Malkki 1995).

Those who are recognized as humanitarians are generally accorded moral authority precisely because their statements and actions are connected to a disinterested concern for the suffering of distant strangers. Accordingly, humanitarians are recognized as having the authority to speak on behalf of suffering strangers, a claim that has several roots. It comes from a longstanding claim that they are 'witnesses' to suffering, and that even when they cannot directly relieve the pain and anguish they can at least record and publicize that suffering to others. As witnesses who have had proximity, they can speak with the authority of an eyewitness. This act of representation also gives humanitarians their ability to influence whether and how those in political power decide to provide aid to the needy. Humanitarians, in other words, not only aspire to do more than provide an account of tragedy but also hope to mobilize international action for them. Therefore, by appropriating the pain of others humanitarians enhance their own power. Moreover, humanitarianism gives those who are recognized as 'humanitarians' the right to speak on the behalf of the suffering and to intervene to address their suffering on the grounds that they are unable to act in their own interests. In this respect, the contemporary discourse of humanitarianism produces two kinds of actors: those who are subjects, who are good, who are expected to prevent human suffering, and who have the tools of emancipation; and those who are objects, whose humanity is to be secured or restored, and who are judged incapable of helping themselves (Moulin and Nyers 2007).

MSF's témoignage includes a range of practices, including dramatic reporting about what it sees not only to bring more international action to a cause and medical relief to the underserved but also to call for new kinds of outside intervention. Their moral authority emanates from the perception that they express humankind's highest ideals, are value rather than interest-driven, and act not for themselves but rather for vulnerable populations.

In addition to their moral authority, humanitarian organizations also rely on expert authority. From where does their expertise derive? Many claim an expertise founded on experience, on having spent decades in the field working with displaced peoples around the world and thus have accumulated considerable insight based on years of trial-and-error. Many aid organizations also claim expertise based on their presence on the ground, that is, their ability to provide first-hand accounts. Over the last decade, moreover, the humanitarian sector has become increasingly professionalized, with various kinds of degree programmes that presumably give those in the field greater knowledge than those who have not been through such training. Many aid organizations also have invested considerable resources in developing their own research units, an investment they justify in part on the grounds that it gives them more credibility.

The discourse of humanitarianism has both empowering and disempowering effects and these simultaneously present tendencies which can be causally connected through the concept of paternalism. Among the many existing definitions of paternalism (Archard 1990; Dworkin 1972, 2000; Garren 2006, 2007; Gert and Culver 1976; Husak 2003; Mead 1997; Sartorius 1983; VanDeVeer 1986; Young 2008), Gerald Dworkin's classic definition (1972: 70–6) works well: 'the interference with a person's liberty of action justified by reasons referring exclusively to the welfare, good, happiness, needs, interests or values of the person being coerced.' Paternalism has two critical features. One, it is an act of imposition. Because paternalism involves an actor claiming the right to make a decision for another, it is an act of power and domination. At times the exercise of power includes coercion; for instance, during natural disasters states will physically and forcibly remove individuals from their homes if they believe that they are in danger if they remain. Yet exercises of power need not always involve force. Formal institutions are designed to limit choice, and their choice-constraining properties are justified on the grounds that they will improve individual and collective welfare (Sunstein and Thaler 2003; Thaler and Sunstein 2003, 2008).

A critical issue in any discussion of paternalism is what counts as an act of unwanted or unjustified interference. Crucial, and especially for the purposes of humanitarian action, is the matter of consent. There are times when those who intervene without explicit consent are doing so in ways that probably do not count as unjustified interference—and thus probably do not count as instances of paternalism. Individuals often defer judgement to others on the grounds that they know what is best for them, a point captured by principal–agent analysis. In these contexts, consent is given a priori to agents to use their discretion in designated areas. Actors can rationally delegate authority to another. The danger, of course, is when these delegated actors begin wandering past their zones of authority on the grounds that they know what is best for others. In addition to situations of ex ante delegation, an actor might act without the other's consent but consent can be assumed. Emergency room doctors must frequently act first and get patient consent later, and their actions would hardly be labeled paternalistic (assuming, for the moment, that the patient wants to be saved). However, most medical interventions take place outside an emergency context and thus typically require consent of the patient, which depends not on a signature on a release form but rather a doctor that has carefully informed the patient of all available options and consequences before being asked to make a decision; a doctor that failed to do so, and thus made a decision without informed consent, would be acting paternalistically. Humanitarian agencies that are providing life-saving relief without stopping to ask whether populations really want clean drinking water are probably not acting paternalistically; those agencies that continue into the post-conflict phase and make various decisions without the consent of the affected populations are. In general, to count as an act of paternalism there must be evidence of some form of involuntary interference and acting without consent, on the grounds that it helps the person or group being intervened upon. In short, we should be mindful of any and all social relations that might consciously and unconsciously limit the ability of an actor to exercise autonomous choice and to give consent to actions taken on its behalf.[4]

Second, interference is defended on the grounds that it is in the best interests of another (Applbaum 2007; Grill 2007; Kelman 1981). We are right to be suspicious of any and all claims by one actor that he is acting in someone else's interest. Individuals frequently present their private interests as in the public interest and self-interested states routinely suggest that they are acting in the name of the international community. Ideology also can convince individuals that they truly know what is in the best interest of others. Those who are assumed to be acting on behalf of the welfare of others, including, most famously, aid workers, can be 'selfish altruists' (Vaux 2001). Still, at a minimum, paternalism must include reasons that refer explicitly to the welfare of another. In this respect, paternalism is based on a consequentialist ethic. Although many who oppose paternalism do so on Kantian grounds—it is never right to interfere in the liberty of another—the ultimate defence of paternalism is the claim that the action will improve the welfare of another relative to a decision made without that interference. In general, not just any interference counts as paternalism—it must be interference that is justified explicitly in relationship to the best interests of others.

Yet how do we know what is best for others? Following on my earlier claims regarding authority, arguably most justification (and especially when associated with humanitarianism) revolves around expert and moral claims. Expert paternalism exists when the subject refers to a body of knowledge—some claim superior knowledge because they have lived longer and experienced more, others because of credentials, education, and other institutionally accredited forms of learning, and still others because of bureaucratic rules that are deemed to be in the best interests of society (even if not always in the best interests of the individual). Experts almost always claim to know more than anyone else especially those who appear to be illiterate, poor, and backward (White 2000: 5). Moral paternalism depends on transcendental discourses. Religious figures will often claim divine knowledge that gives them the right to interfere in the lives of their religious compatriots. Liberal humanitarians will often refer to a secularized humanity and natural law to defend their right to interfere.

The flip side of the claim that some know what is best is the belief that others do not know what is in their best interests, and most arguments revolve around limited capacity and competence. In other words, the actor is cognitively, emotionally, or intellectually unable to make the right decision. Sometimes an actor might not know what is in her best interest—individuals might not be aware of how individual rationality might lead to collective irrationality. At other times we might insist that the actor does not have the right priorities—children want to have fun and have difficulty delaying gratification; many parents insist that their children complete their homework before going on Facebook. And, lastly, there are times when an individual might not know how to achieve what she wants; others might have a better idea regarding what path is most efficient and efficacious. The parent–child relationship is the classic instance of paternalism because parents are best positioned to make decisions for them because they are most likely to best know their children, know what is best for them, and are likely to act with their interests in mind; and children are not competent to make informed decisions.

There are strong arguments against paternalism, most passionately voiced by liberal political theorists. John Stuart Mill (1975: 10–11), the patron saint of the anti-paternalism camp, famously wrote that

> The sole end for which mankind are warranted, individually or collectively, in interfering with the liberty of action of any of their number, is self-protection. That the only purpose for which power can rightfully be exercised over any member of a

civilized community, against his will, is to prevent harm to others. His own good, either physical or moral, is not a sufficient warrant.

Autonomy and liberty are central to human dignity. No one can know better than us what we want and we can never know what is best for another. Even if individuals act in ways that appear to be irrational or demonstrating poor judgement, to stop them from acting on their perceived interests violates their autonomy and dignity. It denies them an opportunity to learn from their mistakes. Nor can paternalism be defended on the grounds that the interference improves the welfare of the individual—ends do not justify ends. Paternalism presumes that an individual is incompetent or inferior (Smiley 2001: 31). Although an actor might give reasons of benevolence, the powerful are always deluded by the belief that they know what is best for everyone. We should be worried whenever actors become convinced of their benevolence. Modern international history demonstrates the violence and suffering that has been leveled by those who think that they know best for others. The nineteenth-century European powers were so enlightened and cared so much about the colonial peoples that they convinced themselves that colonialism was a good thing (Narayan 1995).

For many legal theorists, philosophers, and bioethicists the principle of non-interference is not a categorical imperative and exceptions can be made, exceptions that generally depend on an assessment of whether the individual's decision puts him at unnecessary risk or leads to unacceptable societal consequences. Speed limits, mandatory safety belts, and rules requiring motorcyclists and bicyclists to wear helmets are examples where the state defends its right to interfere in a person's liberty on the grounds of collective welfare (and others note that such laws, when passed in democratic settings, are not paternalistic because they were decided through an inclusive, representative, decision-making process). More controversial cases concern whether one person can or should intervene to stop another from harming herself, and frequently the argument turns on whether the person is competent to make an informed decision; suicide and elective amputations are good examples where we question whether people truly know what is best for them (Shafer-Landau 2005). In general, the anti-paternalist argument begins with the assumption that one actor should never interfere in the liberty and voluntary choice of another and then proceeds to look for exceptions that test the boundaries of voluntary choice.

Building on these exceptions, a critical issue is whether individuals have the competence to know either what is in their best interests or how to further them. The very same John Stuart Mill who wrote against nearly all forms of intervention on the grounds that it violated a person's liberty also recognized two categories of people who were exceptions to this rule—children and 'barbarians'—because neither possesses the necessary moral and cognitive skills to act in their own best interests. Children do not have the moral or intellectual intelligence to make decisions until they reach a certain age, at which point they are assumed to be competent unless proven otherwise. Barbarians lack civilization. For Mill, the level of a society's development has great moral implications, providing justification for the various kinds of civilizing missions nineteenth-century European colonialists were famous for (Habibi 1999). Although today's enlightened thinkers condemn such civilizing discourse and the racism that often accompanied it, the core of the claim regarding competence remains in various guises. Many argue that democratic societies have a right to intervene to help those who suffer under tyrannical regimes—a position advanced by John Rawls's Law of the Peoples (Rawls 2001). There is considerable support for the claim that the haves should help the have-nots, but helping the have-nots means not transferring wealth but rather educating them so that they can make informed decisions (and making decisions on their behalf in the meantime).

You say 'humanitarianism', I say 'paternalism'. The discourse of humanitarianism contains the ingredients for paternalism. It lives an ethic of care and compassion. It insists that we should be concerned about the needs of everyone, not just those we like, we happen to know, or who belong to the same religion. This ethic gives humanitarianism considerable authority, an authority it can use to stand up to the Goliaths of the world and generate greater attention and assistance for populations in need. Humanitarian actors are also notorious for believing that they not only care enough to act but that they also know what is probably best for others. This disposition, I want to stress, comes not only from a racism or elitism but also from a humanitarianism that generates two kinds of actors: those who are in jeopardy and who are too weak to help themselves and those who have the character and the capacity to act in ways that are consistent with their needs. In any event, the discourse of humanitarianism provides a justification for intervening in the lives of others. Such justifications should not be dismissed. There are many times when we believe that there are some who either know best or who are privileged enough to act on their knowledge who should use their positions to aid others, even if these peoples do not always consent or are not sure what they are consenting to. Those who work with refugee populations, especially during a humanitarian emergency, quite often act paternalistically and are probably justified in doing so.

Yet there is always a danger whenever someone has a position of power and believes that he is acting in someone else's best interests. The practice of humanitarian action and any sort of charitable activity often generates feelings of superiority on the part of the giver. The aid worker is best positioned to make decisions on the behalf of the illiterate, uneducated, and ill-informed refugee. Humanitarianism concerns the desire to help distant strangers, which means that those giving aid are crossing moral, political, social, and cultural boundaries. The problem of translation, of trying to interpret the wishes, needs, and experiences of other populations, especially those experiencing tremendous hardship, is always demanding, to say the least. And because motives are almost always mixed, it is sometimes difficult for the humanitarian to disentangle his interests from those of the objects of their compassion.

UNHCR

The discourse of humanitarianism generates UNHCR's moral authority, enabling it to compel states to create more assistance activities to more displaced populations, and its paternalistic tendencies to claim that it knows what is in the best interests of refugee populations. This section begins by noting how states created a highly confined UNHCR, and observing how UNHCR used humanitarianism's moral authority and its growing expert authority to expand assistance and programmes for a broader understanding of refugees and other populations in need. In this way, UNHCR's paternalism, if it was that, was justified in various ways. The discourse of humanitarianism and moral and expert authority, however, also contributed to UNHCR's willingness to act without the consent of refugees and in ways that directly affected their lives, as we will see in the case of voluntary repatriation.

The power of authority

The United States strongly influenced the design of the UNHCR, and it imagined not a ramshackle, bare-bones, makeshift agency. The two years of debate that led to the establishment of the UNHCR in late 1950 largely centred around two different visions of the future international refugee agency. The Americans had in mind an agency that would aspire to do very little and then slowly fade away, while the Europeans imagined a more permanent, muscular, and multidimensional agency (Holborn 1975: chapter 3; Lawyers Committee for Human Rights 1991: 25–6). The US vision largely carried the day, as the

UNHCR was given relatively little to do (at least when compared to what it might do) and there seemed to be little prospect that it might slip the noose placed around its neck by the United States.

States gave UNHCR a very limited mandate. A critical issue was the category of refugee. Their debate occurred against the backdrop of mass movements of populations in South Asia, the Middle East, and elsewhere, because of the effects of decolonization and state-making; arguably most of these displaced were fleeing because they wanted to escape the violence and find a safe ground. Taking note of these developments, the European states took the lead in arguing that refugees were a permanent problem in world politics that would require an international solution, and thus sought to establish a definition to serve that end. The United States saw it differently. The United States won. A refugee was defined as someone who, owing to events that occurred prior to January 1951, fled his or her homeland because of a fear of persecution. This definition's central feature is its narrowness, a reflection of states' desire to limit their responsibilities. A refugee had to have crossed an international border. States recognized that there are many displaced peoples, but only those who have managed to fall on the other side of the territorial divide could be legally classified as a refugee. Refugees, moreover, were defined as those persecuted by their national governments. Persecution further narrowed the definition of a refugee, for it omitted large numbers of peoples who might be forced to leave their country because of economic hardship, political events such as international and internal wars, famines, and authoritarian practices by their government. And, most importantly, even though refugees were well understood to be a permanent feature of global politics, especially a world undergoing decolonization, only those who were refugees before 1951 could expect assistance from the UNHCR.

Nor was UNHCR expected to do much to help those refugees it could. Because refugees were in a transnational limbo, UNHCR would offer refugees an 'international legal bridge between periods of national sovereign assimilation' (Kennedy 1986: 4). Towards that end, it would assist them by 'identifying them, issuing travel documents, assisting in obtaining recognition of their various legal statuses, and advocating ever more precise guidelines for handling recognized refugees' (Kennedy 1986: 5). But it was not delegated the authority to provide material assistance.

Even UNHCR's designation as a humanitarian organization was designed to limit its activities. As a humanitarian and apolitical organization, states created UNHCR to help coordinate the operations of states and NGOs and to provide legal assistance to refugees.[5] Stated negatively, states prohibited UNHCR from exploring the causes of refugee flight, which, by definition, were matters of sovereignty and politics (Holborn 1975: 89–90; Kennedy

1986: 14–15). If there remained any doubt that as a humanitarian organization UNHCR was to be resolutely apolitical, one only needed to glance at paragraph two of its statute: 'the work of the High Commissioner shall be of an entirely non-political character; it shall by humanitarian and social.' These restrictions did not necessarily bother UNHCR staff, who were content to stay out of politics, which would only have created trouble for them with states and complicated their ability to protect refugees.

States usually fear that international organizations, especially those that operate in highly sensitive matters, will want to act in ways that are contrary to their interests, and so they typically place various kinds of control mechanisms on them to limit this possibility. The United States and the Europeans differed in terms of how much control they needed to possess, and, once again, the United States won the debate as UNHCR was given very little autonomy. The High Commissioner would be vetted by the UN Security Council and then report to the General Assembly. An advisory committee of governments (which became the Executive Committee in 1957) would closely monitor the agency's activities. On the grounds that its job was to help the remaining refugees from World War II, UNHCR had a temporary mandate of three years. Its meagre budget came from the UN's general operating budget and it was explicitly prohibited from raising or spending money without prior approval of the UN General Assembly.

UNHCR was able to escape the hangman's noose in part because of permission granted by states in order to help them deal with international crises that involved refugee flows and in part because the discourse of humanitarianism and its growing expert and moral authority allowed it to tunnel into new regions and activities. Although states might have slapped the humanitarian label on UNHCR in order to keep it penned in, UNHCR was able to use the discourse of humanitarianism, and its role as representative of refugees, to increase its influence. In short, humanitarianism gave UNHCR a moral authority. It was a humanitarian organization that was protecting the weak, vulnerable, and displaced and thus was carrying out the highest values of the international community (Chimni 1998). It had a mandate to spread international refugee law, encourage states to comply with existing statutes, and promote the development of refugee law to 'meet the demands of contemporary refugee situations' (UNHCR 1985). UNHCR officials used their position of authority to extend general humanitarian principles to 'refugee-like' situations in places outside of Europe and to refugees created by events that occurred after 1951. Over time, moreover, UNHCR began to play the role of refugee expert with more credibility and authority, and states and others treated UNHCR as a leading expert on refugee matters—expertise that derived not only from its formal position in

the international system but also from its experience on the ground (Loescher 2001). Although limited, the UNHCR was using its authority to regulate how states treated refugees and to create new categories of action and practices that provided more assistance and protections to more populations than ever before.

UNHCR's expansion took a great leap forward with the end of the Cold War. The collapse of empires and the rise of ethnonationalist wars meant that the world was experiencing wave after wave of mass flight, and the agency became a major player. No one thought to ask whether these populations in flight were bona fide refugees or not. Additionally, many displaced were unable to cross an international border either because it was out of reach of the neighbouring country that refused them entry. In these new circumstances, states encouraged UNHCR to bring assistance to refugees rather than waiting until refugees crossed the border to safety. Lastly, UNHCR was becoming one of the world's 'lead' humanitarian agencies, handed operational control in new conflict zones and expected to help coordinate the delivery of relief efforts on an unprecedented scale. In most cases UNHCR could hardly be accused of paternalism because it was delivering assistance (and sometimes protection) to those who had no other sanctuary. And, at those times when it simply acted without asking the refugees what were their preferences, it might have had good reason, either because there were no good choices or because it would have been logistically and practically impossible to assess what the refugees wanted.

Yet, clearly, there is a fine line between care and control, where governing moves from simply providing public goods that refugees want to deciding what kinds of public goods they should want and what kinds of interventions are in their best interest. These possibilities were particularly evident in the area of protection. As UNHCR moved from its protection to its assistance mission, and as it began to redefine, on its own, what protection meant, it began to act in ways that were not only paternalistic but also potentially placed refugees in jeopardy—even though, according to UNHCR, it was in their long-term interests.

Repatriation, voluntary or not?

One of the UNHCR's goals is to try and find permanent solutions to refugee problems, and its founding documents identified three possibilities: asylum, third-country resettlement, and repatriation.[6] How would UNHCR know what was an acceptable solution or what refugees wanted? During the early days of the Cold War it was fairly obvious what most refugees wanted and what refugees wanted lined up nicely with what potential host governments were prepared to do. Refugees were coming from the Soviet bloc, did not want to return, and were immediately seeking asylum in the West. Because it would have been ideologically impossible for the West to send freedom-seeking peoples back to communist lands, the only issue was where they would resettle, not if they would (Coles 1985).

The context changed by the late 1970s, however, as the profile of the typical refugee began to change and Western and Third-World states became increasingly resentful of the heavy demands placed on them. The 'typical' refugee was no longer a man fleeing political persecution from the Soviet bloc and seeking freedom in the West but instead was a woman or child who was located in the Third World and was fleeing the effects of war. In many cases, these individuals did not want to resettle but rather hoped to return home as soon as possible, particularly evident as many began 'spontaneously repatriating' (Warner 1994). Even if refugees wanted to resettle outside their homeland it was increasingly the case that states were closing off this option. Indeed, states were hoping that UNHCR would keep refugees at home and follow a policy of containment or deterrence. Although many staff at UNHCR worried about this pressure to repatriate, they also watched these semi-permanent cities become a financial drain on the agency (Pitterman 1985: 51–4). States, refugees, and UNHCR were in general agreement that refugees should go home.

Yet when should refugees repatriate? Perhaps the most fundamental right granted refugees is non-refoulement: refugees cannot be returned to a country where they risk physical harm or persecution. This principle gives individuals the right to flee their homeland and to find sanctuary in another country, thus prohibiting both rejection at the frontier and expulsion after entry (Goodwin-Gill 1989). While states had rights to control their own borders, they had to do so in accord with the principle of non-refoulement. Non-refoulement thus was responsible for the later practice and concept of voluntary repatriation. Although never mentioned in the treaty, voluntary repatriation became a logical way of returning refugees while respecting non-refoulement. Its presumption is that refugees cannot be returned to a situation which refugees believe still represents a danger. Thus, what matters is not only that the situation at home has changed but that refugees have voluntarily consented to return.

But when could refugees return home and how would they know it was safe enough? UNHCR began looking into the conditions of refugee-producing countries, which represented an important shift in the optics of the agency. Whereas during the Cold War it avoided 'politics', which, for all intents and purposes meant the domestic affairs of states, now UNHCR was actively looking into the political conditions at home. UNHCR's repatriation practices included a commitment that refugees return home with 'safety and dignity', which invariably necessitated examining the political and human rights climate that would affect their reintegration. UNHCR also began to consider the relationship between refugee repatriation and economic assistance. Soon thereafter UNHCR began proposing concepts such as 'state responsibility' and 'root causes', stating that refugee flows are caused by 'violations of human rights and, increasingly, by military or armed activities', and exploring how these factors prevented the successful repatriation of refugees (Hocke 1986).[7] UNHCR's eyes got bigger over the course of the 1990s.

But, precisely, when should UNHCR authorize a repatriation exercise? A decades-long debate in refugee protection concerns how to balance the impulse for repatriation with refugee rights, voluntary repatriation, and protection (Lawyers Committee for Human Rights 1991: 3). This debate began in earnest in the 1980s, but became more pressing during the 1990s when UNHCR had to consider refugee repatriation to 'post-conflict' situations that were far from the 'ideal conditions' usually prescribed. Should the UNHCR follow a legalistic approach that stuck to long-accepted principles? Or should it adopt a more expedient, political, and pragmatic view of refugee law in the face of systemic pressures and new opportunities?

Steadily and ultimately UNHCR became much more favourably disposed toward repatriation, that return will and should happen under less than ideal circumstances, and that UNHCR must and should actively promote repatriation as soon as possible (Barnett 2001; Takahashi 1997: 594, 602; Zieck 1997: 438, 439). Repatriation was no longer a permanent solution but was now the durable solution. Repatriation now became tantamount to 'protection'. UNHCR developed new norms and rules that made desirable and proper repatriating under less demanding conditions, and introduced new terminology and categories of 'safe' return that clearly differentiated repatriation under 'ideal' conditions from repatriation under 'less than ideal' conditions. But UNHCR was not necessarily a neutral party in this move towards repatriation because over the 1990s it became increasingly interested in facilitating the return of refugees as quickly as possible (Crisp 2001: 9). Accordingly, UNHCR began to consider not only whether the conditions had changed but whether it might work to produce the right conditions. UNHCR might claim that it was simply acting in ways that were consistent with the preferences of refugees, but it was also the case that the organization's definition of 'success' was now measured in terms of repatriation—a measure, not coincidentally, that states favoured.

Most important, what 'voluntary' meant in 'voluntary repatriation' began to alter. Voluntary repatriation demanded that the refugee consent to return to a country that in her view no longer represented a threat to her safety. But UNHCR officials began introducing new concepts like 'voluntariness' that meant that refugee consent was no longer necessary and that the home situation need only have appreciably improved or held out the promise of improving. This development was partially driven by pressing circumstances as UNHCR officials increasingly found that it was nearly impossible to ascertain consent from thousands of people, and that post-conflict situations provided the possibility for 'safe' repatriation under 'less than ideal conditions'.

However understandable, the emergence of 'voluntariness' meant that refugee assessment of the situation or consent to repatriation was no longer necessary, leading to the possibility that UNHCR officials might violate traditional refugee rights in two important respects. First, there was no longer the requirement that the home situation had improved appreciably and no longer represented a threat to the safety of refugees. 'Less than ideal conditions' can be a euphemism for the simple fact that refugees are being asked to return to a situation that remains highly volatile and the pathogens of threat remain in the environment. There is any number of reasons to justify return under less fortunate circumstances. In a world where ultimate 'protection' is bound up with the preferred durable solution of repatriation, repatriation and protection become kissing cousins. Such discursive coupling is facilitated by the stark recognition that exile and camp life represents no safe haven. Camp life is almost always unstable and insecure and contains no hope for the future; repatriation is almost by definition a more desirable outcome assuming that the situation at home has marginally and steadily improved. Also, knowing that the other durable solutions are unavailable and that the only solution is to return, UNHCR officials were poised to think about the minimal conditions that are required before repatriation can proceed, and encouraged to create those conditions if they do not presently exist. The result was that repatriation can occur under less exacting standards, and refugees can be encouraged to return to a situation that resembles the one that triggered their flight.

Second, refugees were no longer required to provide informed consent before UNHCR authorizes a repatriation exercise. As UNHCR officials concede, its determination to promote repatriation is based not only on the refugees' preference but more fundamentally on UNHCR's objective assessment of whether life was better at home relative to life in the camps. Refugees, in this view, cannot objectively assess the situation, that is, taking into account, first, the short- and long-term prospects of the situation at home relative to the situation in the camps, and, second, for how long UNHCR officials might be present and able to maintain some necessary safety features (Chimni 1999).

But where 'protection' increasingly becomes tantamount to repatriation, UNHCR officials are increasingly of the view that getting refugees home, even to highly unstable situations, is preferred and legitimate. UNHCR might be tempted to oversell its capacity to monitor the return and the overall political situation at home in order to encourage repatriation under 'less than ideal conditions'. The moral benchmark is no longer whether the totality of rights available to refugees are defended and honored but rather whether one course of action is more likely to provide better protection to refugees—according to UNHCR's assessment.

UNHCR might well be correct that refugees should repatriate under less than ideal conditions because their circumstances will become even less ideal if they remain in exile. But the issue at hand is whose voice counts and what calculations are used to determine the efficacy of repatriation. The shift away from absolute standards regarding the desire by refugees to repatriate given their assessment of the situation in the home country towards a comparative evaluation by agency officials regarding whether refugees would be more secure at home or in the camps has the direct implication of privileging the agency's knowledge claims over those offered by refugees. UNHCR had the moral and expert authority to make decisions on behalf of refugees on the grounds that it knew what was in their best interests and had their best interests at heart. UNHCR demonstrated the ever-present dangers of paternalism.

CONCLUSION

UNHCR, like all humanitarian agencies, is paternalistic. This is not just an occupational hazard or a vestige of the nineteenth century. Instead, it is part of humanitarianism and the international humanitarian order. The institutions that comprise the international humanitarian order are paternalistic. They aspire to relieve suffering and improve the welfare of others and generally claim to do so on the grounds that they know best and that those who need help are unable to help themselves. Frequently, as I have emphasized, there are defensible grounds for paternalism.[8] There are times when humanitarian actors cannot be expected to get consent or where statements of consent (or denial) are difficult to interpret.

The issues evoked by paternalism are not limited to humanitarian action narrowly conceived but to all kinds of global practices that are defined and defended as being in the best interests of others. The international humanitarian order is partly shaped by paternalistic principles and all practices associated with that order show its colours. Consider, for instance, post-conflict reconstruction and peacebuilding. Although Mill's defence of colonialism in the lands of 'barbarians' offends our modern sensibilities, his substantive argument—that some populations are not competent to rule themselves—underlies the justification for modern-day trusteeships, transitional administrations, and other forms of international governance. The international community justifies intervention on the grounds that some populations are not quite ready, willing, and able to govern themselves, and that the international community has a responsibility to undertake such activities. Indeed, we are now informed that the international community not only has a responsibility to protect but it also has a responsibility to rebuild. But all rebuilding efforts in post-conflict zones do not aspire only to repair roads and communication lines, they imagine transforming political, economic, social, and cultural structures to promote what is broadly understood to be a more progressive, peaceful, and prosperous country. Sometimes such projects can be undertaken with local consent. But frequently there will be those who will object to what external interveners want to do because it is a direct threat to their immediate interests; indeed, they commonly insist on 'local ownership' because it provides an ideological fig leaf for them to sound like a democrat while continuing to accumulate power. And frequently it is difficult to bring about change because people either might not be able to imagine an alternative or prefer to minimize losses than maximize gains. In these and other instances external interveners will justify a need to act even in the absence of consent (Ashdown 2007; Evans 2009; Gheciu and Welsh 2009; Recchia 2009; Zaum 2009). Still, they can always challenge themselves by asking: on what grounds do they claim to know better? On what grounds do they claim to be able to articulate the general will and even a general will that cannot even be articulated by the public?

Humanitarian organizations are deeply aware that they are increasingly perceived by local populations as being paternalistic because they fail to listen to or involve them in the very activities that are being undertaken in their name. Indeed, over the last several years this issue has received considerable attention, especially as international agencies are forced to wrestle with the relationship between their lack of accountability and the ineffectiveness of aid, charges of exploitation and criminal activity, and dereliction of their moral and professional responsibilities (Chesterman 2004; Feldman 2004: 66–8). One broad response has been to improve their bureaucracies, become more professional, and adopt modern rational principles of action. Ironically, though, these same developments that were intended to increase local participation might be doing just the opposite. Over the last decade there has been a surge in new systems of accountability, but so far aid agencies appear to be more attentive to their donors than those who are in need. The humanitarian sector has introduced new kinds of methodologies that are intended to increase the voice of those in need, but there are lots of examples of aid workers dismissing these opinions on the grounds that refugees and other marginal populations do not understand what is in their best interests, what has worked or not worked in other settings, and the overall constraints on the possible. This dynamic has arguably increased with the growing professionalism of the sector, that is, the growing weight placed on expert knowledge. It might very well be that the expert authority is crowding out the moral authority.

So, what should humanitarians do? They could get serious about doing needs assessments and participatory methodologies, which is always easier said than done given the complexity of trying to gauge the needs of a community that is defined by patterns of exclusion. They could continue to develop methodologies for assessing impact, with a particular eye towards including not only 'measurables' such as mortality rates but also intangibles such as creating conditions that might help restore the liberty and dignity of individuals. But these new measures must be both context sensitive and meaningful to local populations. Following Marion Smiley's argument (1989) regarding the welfare state, humanitarians could constantly ask themselves, 'how can we regulate our activities so that we do not treat mature adults as if they were mentally incompetent children?' Lastly, for humanitarians to fully recognize that humanitarianism is a paternalistic enterprise would require them to acknowledge that they have power over the very people they want to help, which is a notorious blind spot for most aid agencies.

Recognizing the virtues and the vices of paternalism offers a direct challenge to practitioners and scholars: when and in what forms are we prepared to defend paternalism?

It is neither possible nor necessarily desirable to remove paternalism from the international humanitarian order. Paternalism is a latent or manifest feature of all relations of compassion.[9] Accordingly, to end paternalism in our lifetime would mean to cleanse humanity of these other highly desirable human traits. Said otherwise, if paternalism cannot be avoided in most instances, then are we prepared to conclude that paternalism is a greater sin than not doing anything at all? Are we ready to watch others suffer and transform indifference into a moral virtue? Do we really believe that moral progress can be delivered with strong condemnations of any sort of activity that potentially undermines some dehistoricized notion of sovereignty and the principle of non-interference? And, while most of us prefer romantic notions of justice, in which the impoverished and the downtrodden storm the gates at Versailles, moral progress often depends on a revolution from above and on 'condescension at the top' (Rorty 1999: 183). Paternalism, then, can be instrumental for progressive change. Such possibilities obviously connect to the more basic claim that there are times when some actors should interfere in the lives of others because it will be for their own good. Yet for institutions of care and compassion, the ethics of care is not an unambiguous good and contains its own dangers. But when are those times, and what do our observations tell us about how we understand the international community and ourselves in relationship to distant strangers?

NOTES

1. Cited from Peter de Marnefee, 'Avoiding Paternalism', *Philosophy and Public Affairs*, 34, 1, 69–94.
2. This argument draws from Barnett and Finnemore (2004).
3. Burkhart Holzner (1968: 20) summarized, Knowledge can only mean the 'mapping' of experienced reality by some observer. It cannot mean the 'grasping' of reality itself... More strictly speaking, we are compelled to define 'knowledge' as the 'communicable mapping of some aspect of experienced reality by an observer in symbolic terms'. Cited in Holzner and Marx (1973: 92).
4. Such claims, of course, open up the Pandora's box regarding how we know the exercise of free will and autonomous choice when we see it, whether there are objective preferences, and whether there is false consciousness; I will keep the box closed for the time being.
5. On the differentiation between the political and the humanitarian in UNHCR's mandate, see Sugino (1998).
6. An additional development was the growing number of attacks by home governments against militarized refugee camps on their border (Sugino 1998: 49, 52–3).
7. Cited in Sugino (1998: 55).
8. There is the obvious question of whether paternalism can exist without one actor *acting* paternalistically toward another.
9. There are obvious connections to the feminist literature on the ethics of care. For an application to international relations, see Robinson (1999). For statements regarding the ethics of care, see Deveax (1995), Tronto (1995), and Engster (2001).

BIBLIOGRAPHY

Andrews, B. L. 2003. *When is a refugee not a refugee? Flexible social categories and host/refugee relations in Guinea*. Geneva: UNHCR.

Applbaum, A. I. 2007. Forcing a people to be free. *Philosophy and Public Affairs* 35(4), 359–400.

Archard, D. 1990. Paternalism defined. *Analysis* 50(1), 36–42.
Ashdown, P. 2007. *Swords and ploughshares: bringing peace to the 21st century.* London: Weidenfeld & Nicolson.
Barnett, M. 2001. Humanitarianism with a Sovereign Face: UNHCR in the Global Undertow. *International Migration Review* 35(1), 244–77.
——. 2005. Humanitarianism transformed. *Perspectives on Politics* 3(4), 723–40.
——. 2009. *The international humanitarian order.* New York: Routledge.
——and Finnemore, M. 2004. *Rules for the world: international organizations in global politics.* Ithaca, NY: Cornell University Press.
——and Duvall, R. 2005. Power in international politics. *International Organization* 59(1), 39–75.
——and Weiss, T. G. 2008. Humanitarianism: a brief history of the present. In: Barnett, M. and Weiss, T. G. eds. *Humanitarianism in question: politics, power, ethics.* Ithaca, NY: Cornell University Press, 1–48.
Berger, P. L. and Luckmann, T. 1967. *The social construction of reality: a treatise in the sociology of knowledge.* Boston, MA: Anchor.
Betts, A. 2009*a*. Institutional proliferation and the global refugee regime. *Perspectives on politics* 7(1), 53–8.
——. 2009*b*. *Protection by persuasion: international cooperation in the refugee regime.* Ithaca, NY: Cornell University Press.
Bowker, G. C. and Star, S. L. 1999. *Sorting things out: classification and its consequences.* Cambridge, MA: MIT Press.
Chesterman, S. 2004. *You, the people: the United Nations, transitional administration, and state-building.* Oxford: Oxford University Press.
Chimni, B. S. 1998. The geopolitics of refugee studies: a view from the South. *Journal of Refugee Studies* 11(4), 350–74.
——. 1999. *From resettlement to repatriation: towards a critical history of durable solutions to refugee problems.* Geneva: UNHCR.
Coles, G. 1985. Voluntary Repatriation. Geneva: UNHCR.
Crisp, J. 2001. Mind the gap! UNHCR, humanitarian assistance and the development process. *New Issues in Refugee Research* 43. Geneva: UNHCR.
de Waal, A. 1997. *Famine crimes: politics and the disaster relief industry in Africa.* Oxford: Currey.
Dworkin, G. 1972. Paternalism. *The Monist* 56, 64–84.
Dworkin, R. 2000. *Sovereign virtue: the theory and practice of equality.* Cambridge, MA: Harvard University Press.
Engster, D. 2002. Mary Wollstonecraft's nurturing liberalism: between an ethic of justice and care. *American Political Science Review* 95(3), 577–88.
Evans, M. 2009. Moral responsibilities and the conflicting demands of jus post bellum. *Ethics & International Affairs* 23(2), 147–64.
Fassin, D. and Rechtman, R. 2009. *The empire of trauma: an inquiry into the condition of victimhood.* Princeton, NJ: Princeton University Press.
Feinberg, J. 1986. *Harm to self.* New York: Oxford University Press.
Feldman, N. 2004. *What we owe Iraq: war and the ethics of nation building.* Princeton, NJ: Princeton University Press.

Finnemore, M. et al. eds. 2009. *Who governs the globe?* New York: Cambridge University Press.

Foucault, M. 1970. *The order of things: an archeology of the human sciences.* New York: Pantheon.

Garren, D. J. 2006. Paternalism, part I. *Philosophical Books* 47(4), 334–41.

——. 2007. Paternalism, part II. *Philosophical Books* 48(1), 50–9.

Gert, B. and Culver, C. M. 1976. Paternalistic Behavior. *Philosophy and Public Affairs* 6(1), 45–57.

Gheciu, A. and Welsh, J. M. 2009. The imperative to rebuild: assessing the normative case for postconflict reconstruction. *Ethics & International Affairs* 23(2), 121–46.

Goodwin-Gill, G. S. 1989. Voluntary repatriation: legal and policy issues. In: Loescher, G. and Monahan, L. eds. *Refugees and International Relations.* Oxford: Clarendon Press, 255–91.

Grill, K. 2007. The normative core of paternalism. *Res Publica* 13(4), 441–58.

Habibi, D. 1999. The moral dimensions of JS Mill's colonialism. *Journal of Social Philosophy* 30(1), 125–46.

Haddad, E. 2008. *The Refugee in International Society: between sovereigns.* Cambridge: Cambridge University Press.

Hammond, L. 2008. The power of holding humanitarianism hostage and the myth of protective principles. In: Barnett, M. and Weiss, T. eds. *Humanitarianism in question: politics, power, ethics.* Ithaca, NY: Cornell University Press, 172–95.

Handelman, D. 1995. Commentary on Heyman. *Current Anthropology* 36(2), 279–81.

Hayward, C. R. 2000. *De-facing power.* Cambridge: Cambridge University Press.

Hocke, J.-P. 1986. Beyond humanitarianism and the need for political will to resolve today's refuge problem. In: *Joyce Pearce Memorial Lecture.* Oxford University, 29 October 29.

Holborn, L. W. 1975. *Refugees, a problem of our time: the work of the United Nations High Commissioner for Refugees, 1951–1972.* Metuchen, NJ: Scarecrow Press.

Holzner, B. 1968. *Reality construction in society.* Cambridge, MA: Schenkman Publishing Company.

——and Marx, J. 1972. *Knowledge application: the knowledge system in society.* Boston, MA: Allyn and Bacon.

Husak, D. N. 2003. Legal paternalism. In: LaFollette, H. ed. *The Oxford handbook of practical ethics.* New York: Oxford University Press, 387–412.

Keen, D. 2008. *Complex emergencies.* Cambridge: Polity Press.

Kelman, S. 1981. Regulation and paternalism. *Public Policy* 29(2), 219–54.

Kennedy, D. 1986. International refugee protection. *Human Rights Quarterly* 8(1), 1–69.

——. 2004. *The dark side of virtue: humanitarianism reassessed.* Princeton, NJ: Princeton University Press.

Lawyers Committee for Human Rights 1991. *UNHCR at 40: refugee protection at the Crossroads.* New York: LCHR.

Loescher, G. 2001. *The UNHCR and world politics: a perilous path*. Oxford: Oxford University Press.

——et al. 2008. *UNHCR: the politics and practice of refugee protection into the twenty-first century*. Abingdon: Routledge.

Malkki, L. H. 1995. *Purity and exile: violence, memory and national cosmology among Hutu refugees in Tanzania*. Chicago, IL: University of Chicago Press.

Mead, L. 1997. The Rise of Paternalism. In: Mead, L. ed. *The new paternalism: supervisory approaches to poverty*. Washington, DC: Brookings Institution, 1–38.

Mill, J. S. 1975. *On liberty*. New York: W.W. Norton.

Moulin, C. and Nyers, P. 2007. 'We live in a country of UNHCR': refugee protests and global political society. *International Political Sociology* 1(4), 356–72.

Narayan, U. 1995. Colonialism and its others: considerations on rights and care discourses. *Hypatia* 10(2), 133–40.

Pitterman, S. 1985. International responses to refugee situations: the United Nations High Commissioner for Refugees. In: Ferris, E.G. ed. *Refugees in world politics*. New York: Praeger.

Rawls, J. 2001. *The law of peoples*. Cambridge, MA: Harvard University Press, viii, 199.

Recchia, S. 2009. Just and unjust postwar reconstruction: how much external interference can be justified? *Ethics & International Affairs* 23(2), 165–87.

Rieff, D. 2002. *A bed for the night: humanitarianism in crisis*. London: Vintage.

Robinson, F. 1999. Globalizing care: ethics, feminist theory, and international relations. Boulder, CO: Westview Press.

Rorty, R. 1999. Human rights, rationality and sentimentality. In: Circle, T. B. ed. *The politics of human rights*. London: Verso, 67–83.

Sartorius, R. E. ed. 1983. *Paternalism*. Minneapolis: University of Minnesota Press, xii, 287.

Schneider, A. and Ingram, H. 1993. Social construction of target populations: implications for politics and policy. *American Political Science Review* 87(2), 334–47.

Shafer-Landau, R. 2005. Liberalism and paternalism. *Legal Theory* 11(3), 169–91.

Smiley, M. 1989. Paternalism and democracy. *Journal of Value Inquiry* 23(4), 299–318.

——. 2001. 'Welfare dependence': the power of a concept. *Thesis Eleven* 64(1), 21–38.

Starr, P. 1992. Social categories and claims in the liberal state. In: Douglas, M. and Hull, D. eds. *How classification works: Nelson Goodman among the social sciences*. Edinburgh: Edinburgh University Press.

Sugino, K. 1998. The 'non-political and humanitarian' clause in UNHCR's statute. Refugee Survey Quarterly 17(1), 33–59.

Sunstein, C. R. and Thaler, R. H. 2003. Libertarian paternalism is not an oxymoron. *The University of Chicago Law Review* 70(4), 1159–202.

Takahashi, S. 1997. The UNHCR handbook on voluntary repatriation: The emphasis of return over protection. *International Journal of Refugee Law* 9(4), 593–612.

Terry, F. 2002. *Condemned to repeat? The paradox of humanitarian action*. Ithaca, NY: Cornell University Press.

Thaler, R. H. and Sunstein, C. R. 2003. Libertarian paternalism. *The American Economic Review* 93(2), 175–9.

——and Sunstein, C. R. 2008. *Nudge: improving decisions about health, wealth, and happiness*. New Haven, CT: Yale University Press.

Tronto, J. C. 1995. Care as a basis for radical political judgments. *Hypatia* 10(2), 141–9.

UNHCR 1985. Note on International Protection, July 23, 1985. In: UNHCR ed.

VanDeVeer, D. 1986. *Paternalistic intervention: the moral bounds on benevolence*. Princeton, NJ: Princeton University Press.

Vaux, T. 2001. *The selfish altruist: relief work in famine and war*. London: Earthscan Publications.

Warner, D. 1994. Voluntary repatriation and the meaning of return to home: a critique of liberal mathematics. *Journal of Refugee Studies* 7(2–3), 160–74.

White, J. 2000. *Democracy, justice, and the welfare state: reconstructing public care*. University Park, PA: Penn State Press.

Wright, S. 1994. 'Culture' in Anthropology and Organizational Studies. In: Wright, S. ed. *Anthropology of organizations*. New York: Routledge, 1–31.

Young, R. 2008. John Stuart Mill, Ronald Dworkin and paternalism. In: Ten, C. L. ed. *Mill's 'On Liberty': a critical guide*. Cambridge: Cambridge University Press.

Zaum, D. 2009. The norms and politics of exit: ending postconflict transitional administrations. *Ethics & International Affairs* 23(2), 189–208.

Zetter, R. 1991. Labelling refugees: forming and transforming a bureaucratic identity. *Journal of Refugee Studies* 4(1), 39–62.

Zieck, M. 1997. *UNHCR and voluntary repatriation of refugees: a legal analysis*. The Hague, Boston, London: Martinus Nijhoff Publishers.

6

Beyond 'Bare Life': Refugees and the 'Right to Have Rights'

Patricia Owens[1]

ABSTRACT

This chapter critically assesses Giorgio Agamben's claims regarding the significance of refugees for international political thought. Agamben argues that refugees are the ultimate 'biopolitical' subjects, those who can be regulated and governed at the level of population in a permanent 'state of exception'. Refugees are reduced to 'bare life', humans as animals in nature without political freedom. While a welcome alternative to the flawed rationalist and weak constructivism of much international theory, it will nonetheless be argued here that Agamben's 'figure of the refugee' falls short. While much of the literature on so-called 'biopolitics' is illuminating and productive, we need not accept all aspects of Agamben's view of what happens when 'life' is placed at the centre of politics. The first part of the chapter sets out in more detail Agamben's claims regarding sovereignty and the political significance of 'naked' or 'bare life' for refugees. The second section suggests that while the breakdown of the distinction between human and citizen is at the heart of the problem faced by refugees (and potentially all bearers of 'human rights'), the 'abstract nakedness' of human beings is *politically* irrelevant. The argument is made by returning to Hannah Arendt whose writing has been enormously influential for Agamben but whose effort to rethink the 'right to have rights' he implicitly rejects. Arendt warned that there is no such thing as an inborn human dignity. If refugee populations are not to face some inexorable trend towards a rule of 'exception', then it will not be through reclaiming 'bare life'. It will be wholly dependent on the ability to forge a public realm grounded on the appropriate distinction between nature and political artifice, between human life and the political world.

The concept of human rights can... never be dependent upon some inborn human dignity which *de facto*, aside from its guarantee by fellow-men... does not exist.

(Hannah Arendt, *The Burden of Our Time*, p. 439)

Preoccupied with the sovereign nation-state, the discipline of International Relations (IR) tends to present refugees as exceptions to—rather than exemplars of—modern interstate politics in which citizenship and meaningful rights are codependent. In its starkest formulation, those forced to flee from one territory to another are either cared for or ignored at the whim of sovereign states or their surrogates based on a determination of how dangerous their movement is to global or Western security (Posen 1996). More focused analysis usually also becomes a question of territorial sovereignty, which, after all, is the very institution that produces the legal and territorial category of the refugee (Haddad 2008). Innumerable treaties regulate the movements of populations across state borders giving certain status to some and not others (Hyndman 2000). There has been an unparalleled proliferation of norms and regulations concerning refugees and the internally displaced as if to compensate for the declining legitimacy of the political order of the nation-state. Refugees are important to international studies because they represent the limits of the society of states in which populations are 'segmented, ordered, and governed' (Dillon 1999; Lui 2004: 121).

Some of the most innovative theoretical work on refugees has occurred outside or at the margins of IR. A relatively small but growing body of scholarship has emerged that takes sovereignty seriously but which theorizes the relationship between sovereign power and refugees in a radically different way. Most notably, Italian philosopher Giorgio Agamben presents the so-called 'figure of the refugee' as exemplary, *the* symbolic representation of social and political reality. It is no exaggeration to say that in the past decade, Agamben has challenged Hannah Arendt's place as *the* 'charismatic legitimator' (Jay 1993: 168) within critical refugee studies as well as provided the framework for some important international political theory discussions of refugees (Edkins 2000; Jenkins 2004; Edkins and Pin-Fat 2005; Puggioni 2005; Nyers 2006). Agamben's claims regarding refugees are made in a short essay written in 1993, 'We Refugees', which borrows its title from a 1943 essay by Arendt (1978) (Agamben's essay is printed as 'Beyond Human Rights' in *Means Without End* (2000)); in the book *Homo Sacer* (1998), one of the most influential works of recent political theory; and in *State of Exception*, which appeared in English in 2005.

Both Agamben and Arendt (1966) see refugees as the clue to a new politics and model of international relations. They both offer reasons to reject the liberal (and unsophisticated realist) effort to assimilate refugees to the old model of nation-state-territory. But what is so special about refugees, according to Agamben? First, 'the one and only figure of the refugee' (Agamben 2000: 16) is said to more deeply expose the 'fiction' of national sovereignty and all associated legal and political categories such as 'people', 'public', 'human rights', and 'citizen'. Second, he argues, 'the refugee' can be represented as the paradigmatic site—and victim—of modern techniques of what Michel Foucault (2007: 108) called 'governmentality', the organized practices and techniques used to produce, care for, and/or dominate individual subjects. Third, and perhaps most originally, Agamben argues that refugees can be seen as the ultimate 'biopolitical' subjects, those who can be regulated and governed at the level of population in a permanent 'state of exception' outside the normal legal framework: the camp. There they are reduced to 'bare life', humans as animals in nature without political freedom. Finally, it is suggested that by fully comprehending the significance of refugees we may countenance new ways of political belonging and the limits and possibilities of political community in the future. After the nation-state and its associated legal and political categories have been assigned to history, the refugee will remain as 'perhaps the only thinkable figure' (Agamben 2000: 16; also see Diken 2004, Diken and Lausten 2005).

This chapter critically assesses Agamben's claims regarding the significance of refugees for international political thought. How seriously should international theory take his construct? Certainly Agamben's critical and interpretive approach to history and theory joins others as a welcome alternative to the flawed rationalist and weak constructivism of much international theory. The empirical evidence in support of studies into the disciplining and biopolitical management of refugees is compelling as is the general criticism of the self-understanding of much international thought in which liberal-democratic states are understood simply as a form of limited government that checks the worst excesses of sovereign power. The field should take the 'corporeal turn' in political and social thought seriously, that is, analysis of the distinction and blurring of the distinction between our biological and political lives. This subject of analysis is routine in the humanities and other social sciences but it has only belatedly received attention by scholars in IR (for an excellent account see Elbe 2005). Agamben's work joins others in making it harder to accept liberal and conventional realist theory on their own terms; they do not provide sufficient analytical and normative understanding of the real and symbolic violence administered to refugees, including by liberal democracies (Gibney 2004). With forced migration reaching record figures it no longer makes sense, if it ever did, to represent political subjectivity in terms of nation-state-territory.

Nonetheless, it will be argued here that Agamben's 'figure of the refugee' falls short. This construction takes the reduction of refugees to the level of 'bare life' too far. While much of the literature on so-called 'biopolitics' is illuminating and productive, we need not accept all aspects of Agamben's view of what happens when 'life' is placed at the centre of politics. The first part sets out in more detail Agamben's claims regarding sovereignty and the political significance of 'naked' or 'bare life' for refugees. The second section suggests that while the breakdown of the distinction between human and citizen is at the heart of the problem faced by refugees (and potentially all bearers of 'human rights'), the 'abstract nakedness' of human beings is *politically* irrelevant (Arendt 1958: 8). The argument is made by returning to Hannah Arendt whose writing has been enormously influential for Agamben's thinking but whose effort to rethink the 'right to have rights' he implicitly rejects as outdated. Arendt warned that there is no such thing as an inborn human dignity. If refugee populations are not to face some inexorable trend towards a rule of 'exception', then it will not be through reclaiming 'bare life'. It will be wholly dependent on the ability to forge a public realm grounded on the appropriate distinction between nature and political artifice, between human life and the political world.

AGAMBEN ON SOVEREIGN POWER AND THE REFUGEE

Aristotle famously distinguished between two forms of life. There is *zoē*, life as it is rooted in nature and which we have in common with all living creatures, and *bios* or the 'good life', which since the time of ancient Greece has been understood as the political way of life. What was thought to distinguish humans from other animals is our capacity to speak and engage in political praxis. At the root of the most important political binaries in Western thought—between private and public, subject and citizen—is the seeming fact that political existence is different from the simple fact of living. Politics and the human body, free action and labour, and *homo politicus* and *animal laborans* have been distinguished from each other, placed in different spatial locations, and in the hierarchical ordering of human activities.

The greatest modern theorist of these distinctions was Hannah Arendt, from whom Giorgio Agamben extensively borrows. In *The Human Condition*, she reported that the demands of biological life, 'the cyclical movement of the body's life process' (1958: 144), were secured by women and slaves so that 'free' men could engage in politics in the ancient city-states. Tasks related to sustaining life processes—reproductive labour such as washing, cooking, cleaning, tending to the young—were located in the 'private' household and domestic sphere. Unburdened by the repetitive tasks of *zoē*, free citizens debated their political affairs and built a 'world', an artificial space for politics (as distinct from the natural 'earth'). In *Origins of Totalitarianism*, Arendt gave a concrete illustration of what happens when human beings have nothing to fall back on except their status as *zoē*. The classical concept of human rights, formulated as the 'Rights of Man and Citizen', presupposed the existence of a natural 'human being as such'. Arendt was one of the first to identify the central and still unresolved problems with this formulation. Those most in need of so-called 'inalienable' rights—stateless persons and refugees, those without a right to citizenship—are in no position to claim them. 'The paradox involved in the loss of human rights', she wrote, 'is that such loss coincides with the instant when a person becomes a human being in general' (1966: 302).

Refugees reveal the limits of any assumed continuity between 'man' and 'citizen' in the system of nation-states and in the related concept of human rights. The function of modern international organizations is to manage refugee populations in a manner that does not radically undermine the framework on which the nation-state rests. The three principle solutions to refugees, repatriation, integration into the society to which they have fled or resettlement in a third country, all affirm the classical trinity of nation-state-territory with its ideas of citizenship and rights. Eventually refugees must either return 'home' or be naturalized somewhere else. In Agamben's terminology (2000: 20), the bearer of human rights is 'the originary figure for the inscription of natural naked life in the political-juridical order of the nation-state'. By definition, a nation-state is one 'that makes nativity or birth (that is, naked human life) the foundation of its sovereignty' (2000: 21). The refugee camp is significant here because it supplements, but ultimately destroys the classical trinity; 'by breaking the identity between the human and the citizen and that between nativity and nationality, [the refugee] brings the originary fiction of sovereignty to crisis' (2000: 21).

For Agamben, the entire tradition of Western political thought and practice is founded on a constitutive exclusion (and therefore inclusion) of *zoē*, of biological life, from politics. There are several conceptual and historical paths to making this claim. For example, since Thomas Hobbes, much modern political theory has understood the central function of government to be one of protecting and fostering the life of its citizens (see Deudney 2007). Hobbes famously argued that in the state of nature fear of violent death was so great that the sovereign could claim obedience from its subjects in exchange for protection against violent death. This was a qualified protection. The state retained the monopoly on legitimate killing, including of its own subjects. Yet in giving up unfettered liberty subjects could expect certain rewards. The protection and sustenance of the 'life process' became the primary rationale of government; the so-called 'public' realm was reinterpreted as the administration of the commonwealth. In the nation-state, Arendt (1958: 28) reported, 'we see the body of peoples and political communities in the image of a family whose everyday affairs have to be taken care of by a gigantic, nation-wide administration of housekeeping'. In other words, where the ancients excluded *zoē* from what they considered to be properly political, modern nation-states have actively made 'life' central to politics. The distinction between *zoē* and *bios* was blurred with the emergence of the nation-state.

Equally important to Agamben's framework, as well as critical refugee studies, is Foucault's account of what he took to be an inexorable trend towards the incorporation of life into more and more spheres of state practice. In a series of studies that should shatter complacency about the extent of power's interference into the so-called 'private' sphere, Foucault showed how individual bodies and populations are regulated by those who represent 'sovereignty' in everyday life—the military, the Church, and schools. 'The old power of death that symbolized sovereign power', he wrote, 'was now carefully supplanted by the administration of bodies and the calculated management of life' (1978: 139–40). The biological existence of human beings becomes the primary subject of politics incorporating such matters as life expectancy, disease control, food, and water supply. Unlike sovereignty, this form of 'disciplinary' power is not, in essence, repressive. It is productive. It works across a variety of fields, such as mental and physical health, education, sexual activity, policing, and parenting to 'produce' functioning individuals. 'For millennia', Foucault (1978: 143) has claimed, 'man remained what he was for Aristotle: a living animal with the additional capacity for political existence; modern man is an animal whose politics places his existence as a living being in question'.

It has not been very difficult for critical refugee studies to present their subjects as vehicles for the circulation of disciplinary and biopolitical power (Lui 2004; Doná 2007). If the state manages the 'normal' population through tending to the needs of 'life', then the pastoral care of the international humanitarian regime performs this function for refugees, but without the consoling fictions of citizenship (Lippert 1998, 1999; Hardy 2003; Muller 2004). Scholars have traced the variety of 'discursive and institutional domains' that produce the 'figure of the refugee'. As L. H. Malkki (1995: 498) has put it,

> The segregation of nationalities; the orderly organization of repatriation or third-country resettlement; medical and hygienic programs and quarantining; 'perpetual screening' and the accumulation of documentation on the inhabitants of the camps; the control of movement and black-marketing; law enforcement and public discipline; and schooling and rehabilitation were some of the operations that the spatial concentration and ordering of people enabled or facilitated. Through these processes, the modern, postwar refugee emerged as a knowable, nameable figure.

Refugee populations are produced and governed as subjects amenable to public and private management techniques, the techniques closely linked to the rationalities of economic globalization (Soguk 1999; Puparec 2008). The increasingly comprehensive and diverse rules and practices that govern their lives thrive on breaking down older divisions between public and private, state and non-state, and security and development (Bigo 2002; Duffield 2007).

Investigation into the disciplinary and 'biopolitical' management of refugees has become routine and much of this work is persuasive. Agamben takes theory (and the representation of refugees) in a new direction with his claim that what is most significant about sovereignty is not the distinctly modern 'sovereign/subject relationship' found in Foucault (2003: 35). Rather Agamben builds on the most important non-Weberian definition of sovereignty by German jurist Carl Schmitt. Instead of a territorially defined entity successfully claiming the monopoly on the legitimate use of violence, 'sovereign' is 'he who decides the exception' (Schmitt 2005: 5). At issue in the concept of exception is the place of law and transgressions of the law within political order (Huysmans 2006). For Agamben, following Schmitt, legal and political order is defined by what is deemed exceptional to it. Only the 'sovereign' can decide when the law can be suspended because the sovereign is already the lawgiver, deciding the space in which the rule of law has validity. In other words, suspensions of the law, declarations of emergency, or the establishment of asylum seeker detention camps, where 'opt outs' from various human rights legislation is normal, are not rare or marginal phenomenon. They reveal the fundamental structure of the rule of law and the real character of juridical and political order.

Agamben is interested in the threshold, what he calls the zone of indistinction, between norm and exception. His originality resides in the claim that *zoē*, humans as animals without speech and political freedom, is *re-included* in politics when the state of exception is declared and materialized in the form of camps. This evocative term 'camp' is used to describe those places in which biological and political life, private and public, cannot be distinguished from each other. This exceptional spatial arrangement, for example, a detention centre for asylum seekers, a 'black' rendition site, or a Nazi death camp, continues to function outside the normal juridical (and often territorial) order. Agamben notes, for example, that the legal basis of the Nazi camps was not criminal or penal law, but an older Prussian martial law from 1851 related to the state of siege, which authorized the state to take any person into custody even if they had broken no law. Arendt (1966: 447) too noted that the first stage of total domination, killing the juridical person, was achieved 'by placing the concentration camps outside the normal penal system'. These zones of indistinction are created when the exception to the normal functioning of the law becomes the rule, when the state of exception is materialized and becomes permanent.

When a human (a refugee, an unlawful combatant) is excluded from the protection of the law, Agamben argues, it is tantamount to including naked life within it. We might say that the so-called 'state of nature' returns to the conceptualization of law, which according to classical political theory was supposed to be excluded by the establishment of law and civil society. Naked life is revealed as the ultimate foundation of sovereignty. 'The same bare life that…in the classical world was (at least apparently) clearly distinguished as *zoē* from political life (*bios*) now fully enters into the structure of the state and even becomes the earthly foundation of the state's legitimacy and sovereignty' (Agamben 1998: 127). In relation to refugees, sovereignty does not work simply through the ability to exclude them from a given territory (as in narrow versions of realism). Refugees remain subject to law. But this is not merely in the regulative sense of constraining their civil and political freedoms (as in liberalism or 'thin' constructivism). Sovereignty and law are productive. Refugees are included in the legal order through their constitutive exclusion.

One way to illustrate this, and one of the most distinctive and evocative elements of Agamben's notion of sovereign power (1998: 83), relates to the sovereign's capacity to decide on the 'human victim that may be killed and not sacrificed'. This victim is named '*homo sacer*' (sacred man) who in Roman law was a person who may be killed with impunity but not 'sacrificed' in a religious ritual (for a discussion of the accuracy of Agamben's account of Roman legal history, see Fitzpatrick 2005). Agamben argues that growing numbers of people are vulnerable to this specific form of violence. The suspension of the law, the creation of emergency conditions that legitimize torture, open-ended incarceration, and/or killing without punishment leads to death that is not honoured, mourned, or memorialized (Butler 2004). The refugee camp is an exemplary zone of indistinction where individuals can be subject to various forms of violence without legal consequence on territory that is outside the normal juridical order. Refugees are produced as (or reduced to) 'bare life' literally and metaphorically in camps. Even forms of resistance to sovereign power such as hunger strikes or when refugees sew together their eyes and lips (Leach 2003) are reduced to expressions of 'bare life'. Such acts, write Jenny Edkins and Véronique Pin-Fat (2005: 20), 'viscerally reveal and draw attention to the refugees' own person as the bare life produced by sovereign power: it is a re-enactment of sovereign power's production of bare life on the body of the refugee' (for a critique of this way of conceiving refugee lip-sewing, see Owens 2009*a*).

Agamben is certainly not the only thinker to declare the epistemological significance of refugees for political philosophy. But his efforts go beyond the project pursued by others such as Seyla Benhabib (2004) whose critical cosmopolitanism and normative theory of global justice—at least in light of Agamben's claims—would appear rather quaint. Benhabib argues that political membership and democratic attachments should be redefined to include more asylum rights, porous borders, and the right of all humans to be recognized as legal subjects. For Agamben and his followers, such efforts are beside the point. The production and management of refugees cannot be adequately grasped in any such Kantian model, which falls back on the workings of institutions that are understood to be more or less legitimate. These institutions and laws, it is argued, actually facilitate an infinite expansion of disciplinary coercion and 'biopolitical' control. Merely updating and expanding the classical discourse and reach of rights fails to grasp how power actually works in global politics (Larner and Walters 2004). Reform of existing institutions can only entrench rather than overcome the worst aspects of sovereign power and the system of nation-states that produces refugees.

Sovereign power, for Agamben, is not founded on the collective political will of individual subjects (as in Hobbes and John Locke). It is founded on the submission of naked life to the protection of the sovereign. The old republican and Marxist divisions—between subjects and citizens, between classes—are superseded. The more fundamental political distinction is between 'naked life' and the variety of different forms or modes of life, such as 'worker', 'voter', or 'consumer', which modern individuals are able to sustain as a supplement to their condition as a biological being. Hannah Arendt's account of the political realm as constituted 'in-between' people as they act in concert and Carl Schmitt's understanding of politics as defined by the distinction between friend and enemy are similarly replaced. Jürgen Habermas's quasi-liberal effort (2001) to theorize a cosmopolitan law of world citizenship is beside the point. In the face of the camps, Agamben claims, we need to throw out the entire tradition of classical (and much 'critical') political (and international) thought. Modern citizens exist on a continuum with refugees; they are a better-tended herd but are increasingly indistinguishable from *homo sacer*. We must abandon the classical concept of human rights 'and the rights of asylum... must no longer be considered as the conceptual category' around which we organize the political struggles of refugees (Agamben 2000: 22).

ARENDT CONTRA AGAMBEN

If we take seriously Agamben's claims then it is difficult to imagine a global political order less free than the one we inhabit today. The disciplining of individuals and the management of populations by states and their international organizations occur to such an extent that the liberal constitutional state and the totalitarian regime seem like two sides of the same coin. The liberties and freedoms achieved against state power in the constitutional democracies appear 'double-sided'. In Agamben's words(1998: 121), they 'simultaneously prepared a tacit but increasing inscription of individuals' lives within the state order, thus offering a new and more dreadful foundation for the very sovereign power from which they wanted to liberate themselves'. This is evident nowhere more than in what Agamben describes as the affiliation between the internment camps established in the interwar period, which housed, among others, Jews, Armenians, Spanish republicans, and Russians (Marrus 1985), and the Nazi concentration camps of World War II. The first camps in Europe were built to house refugees. The subsequent 'succession of internment camps—concentration camps—extermination camps', he argues, 'represents a perfectly real filiation' (2000: 22).

This argument is made through a reversal of the relationship Hannah Arendt identified between the Nazi-run death camps and the structure of totalitarian rule. According to Agamben, it was the triumph of naked life that produced total domination, not the other way around. Since modern politics is already a space of 'indistinction' between biological and political life the concentration camps easily followed. The re-inclusion of bare life in modern politics was fully realized in the totalitarian camps of the twentieth century. They were 'the most absolute biopolitical space that has ever been realized—a space in which power confronts nothing other than pure biological life without any mediation' (2000: 40; 1998: 120). The Nazi regime was just the most extreme, and for Agamben (2000: 36) it would appear inevitable, form of 'the political space in which we still live'. We were already living in a world of camps—both metaphorically and literally—by the time the gas chambers were built. There is a continuum, not a fundamental disjuncture, between camps, Agamben argues, because there is a continuum between constitutional democracies and the Nazi regime; both reduce populations to 'bare life', one to govern and manage people on grounds of nationality, the other to exterminate on grounds of race (Duarte 2007).

No doubt, for many, such claims are unconscionable. Nonetheless it is worth contrasting Agamben's ideas on the unidirectional logic of sovereign power with Arendt's writing on the historical and political origins of various forms of camps, a distinction which Agamben refuses. The Nazi concentration camps, Arendt maintained, were necessary instruments of total domination but they were also incomprehensible in terms of normal categories of thought and conventional forms of control. Detention and concentration camps, such as those used by the British in Africa, had long been used 'for "suspects" whose offences could not be proved and who could not be sentenced by ordinary process of law' (1966: 440). These camps can be comprehended as part of an *imperial* power arrangement and the principle behind them, their underlying justification in the eyes of their creators, is that 'everything is permitted'. Everything is permitted in the name of national security, the right of territorial sovereignty, and to protect the way of life of 'normal' citizens. Everything is permitted including the elimination and degradation of individuals and groups. However much they conflict with humanitarian law, imperial camps are defended with appeals to instrumentality.

In contrast, Arendt argued, Nazi camps were unprecedented, different in kind not just intensity to imperialism's camps. The totalitarian camps were entirely 'anti-utilitarian' from the perspective of the German state in total war. They were made to function as 'normal' even in the face of total military defeat. The underlying principle justifying this was not that 'everything is permitted', but that 'everything is possible'. Their purpose was not 'merely' to degrade human beings by treating them as a means to an end, but to destroy the concept of human beings as such, to make humans superfluous as human beings (1992: 69). Their purpose was to eradicate not just the Jews but human dignity itself; they came as close as we have seen to transforming humans into mere things (on the relevance for the debate about Guantanamo Bay, see Kinsella 2008 and Owens 2008).

While emphasizing the horrible originality of the extermination camps, Arendt (1994: 403) took great pains to uncover the *specific configuration* of large-scale historical processes that 'crystallized into totalitarianism'. These included the nineteenth- and early twentieth-century explosions of statelessness, rightlessness, mob violence, imperialism, and anti-Semitism. The outcome was not the inevitable product of some metaphysical properties of 'sovereign power', as argued by Agamben. It was wholly contingent on the particular way modern processes transformed what was politically and technologically possible. Crucially, for our discussion here, Arendt showed how the laboratories for altering human nature began with the creation of more and more rightless and stateless persons. During the nineteenth century, imperial regimes were imposed on populations 'without the foundation of a body politic' (1966: 135). The stabilizing forces of laws and territorial boundaries were swept away; no authentic political action was possible, only ideological expansion and the all-powerful stream of exploitative economic processes. By the early twentieth century, the ideological claims of Europe's pan-nationalisms emerged as similarly hostile to existing political structures and borders, a dangerous form of identity-politics without limits. Gravely flawed, but nonetheless relatively stable civic–political boundaries and associations disappeared across Europe in the name of expansion and ethnic and racial self-assertion.

Arendt had been a stateless Jewish refugee during World War II and was detained at a camp in France before she escaped and fled to the United States. She was what might be called a 'stateless non-person' for eighteen years. As Richard Bernstein (2005: 54) has put it, her 'experience of, and reflection upon, statelessness taught her what politics means, and why it is so essential to be a citizen in a polity to live a fully human life' (for discussion of Arendt on refugees see Benhabib 2004, Heuer 2007, and Hayden 2008; for Arendt and international politics more broadly see Owens 2007). But Arendt was no straightforward defender of the concept of 'human rights' and certainly not in its classical formulation of the 'Rights of Man and Citizen' or Universal Declaration of Human Rights. Agamben is largely following Arendt when he argues that human rights should not be viewed in such terms, that is, as representing some sort of ever-present pre-political, pre-legal human attribute meant to regulate and constrain state power. It was Arendt who first argued that the problem with the classical formulation is the assumed existence of a biological being with some inborn human dignity which, she argued, simply does not exist. Arendt was scathing of all abstract and individualist conceptions of rights. The problem, she wrote, is that

> they presume that rights spring immediately from the 'nature' of man.... The decisive factor is that these rights and the human dignity they bestow should remain valid and real even if only a single human being existed on earth; they are independent of human plurality and should remain valid even if a human being is expelled from the human community (1966: 297–8).

It was Arendt's consistent position that no coherent legal or political structure can emerge from 'man' in the singular. Politics is based on plurality, that there are many and not one of us; in her gendered terminology 'the fact that men, not Man, live on the earth and inhabit the world' (1958: 7). The human being *qua* human being in which our 'nature and essence is the same for all' is *politically* irrelevant (1958: 8). Where Agamben (2000: 20) laments that there is no 'autonomous space in the political order of the nation-state for something like the pure human in itself', Arendt argued that no properly political order can—or should—centre itself on the notion of a 'pure human'. 'Strictly speaking', she maintained, 'politics is not so much about human beings as it is about the world that comes into being between them and endures beyond them' (2005: 175). To engage in political action is to participate in founding and sustaining a common, political world that lasts longer than a natural human life. While there can be little doubt that the founding principles of the modern international system need to be transformed, it is less clear that normative political theory should be seeking, as Agamben (2000: 19) suggests, a 'stable statute for the human in itself'.

While Arendt never criticized the idea of human rights with the same vehemence as during her writing of the 1940s, she never dissociated herself from the claim that there is no such thing as inborn human dignity. 'Arendt's idea', as Etienne Balibar has written, 'is not that only institutions create rights, whereas, apart from institutions, humans do not have specific rights, only natural qualities. Her idea is that, apart from the institution of the community (...in the sense of the reciprocity of actions), *there simply are no humans*' (2007: 733). She went so far as to unfavourably compare the condition of statelessness to that of slaves in the ancient world. At least the latter, she remarked, 'still belonged to some sort of human community' (1966: 296–7; for a critique of the comparison see Tuitt (2004)). In other words, after imperialism and totalitarianism, 'human dignity needs a new guarantee which can be found only in a new political principle, in a new law on earth, whose validity this time must comprehend the whole of humanity while its power must remain strictly limited, rooted in and controlled by newly defined territorial entities' (1966: ix).

Arendt (1966: 296–7) reformulated the problem in terms of the 'rights to have rights', 'to live in a framework where one is judged by one's actions and opinions' and not some inborn human dignity. The first 'right' implies a claim to membership of a political world and associated right to speak and act with plural equals in that political space. It 'means to live in a framework where one is judged by one's actions and opinions and a right to belong to some kind of organized community' (Arendt 1966: 296–7). This right is universal but is nonetheless a huge departure from Kant's belief in the metaphysical properties of humanity and where 'the present state of each species [is] the *telos* inherent in all previous development' (1968: 92). Arendt's alternative is politically and historically grounded. That is to say, the political is always limited by a concrete political space and yet, inspired by Karl Jaspers' philosophy of mankind, 'it forever remains in reference to the world and the people in it, not because it is bound to any existing space. In fact, the opposite is the case, because [Jaspers'] deepest aim is to "create a space" in which the *humanitas* of man can appear' (1968: 79). The only thing that could guarantee human rights and a 'home in the world' were contingent political conditions. Each of us has a right to be treated as a member of humanity and our humanity is most fully realized through caring for the public world. The second reference to 'rights' (in 'the right to have rights') is to those already possessed by members of a distinct political community. By definition, these are the non-universal rights necessary for democratic self-determination. This is not, as Arendt (1968: 92) explicitly states, in the Hegelian sense in which 'to be a member of historical mankind meant to be a Greek and not a barbarian in the fifth century B.C., a Roman citizen and not a Greek in the first centuries of our era, to be a Christian and not a Jew in the Middle Ages', or, we might add, a citizen of the European Union and not an undocumented immigrant today.

CONCLUSION

There should be little doubt that one of the political problems of our time is the collapsing of *bios* into *zoē*. As Hannah Arendt (1965: 58) put it long before Agamben and Foucault, the 'politically most pernicious doctrine of the modern age' is 'that life is the highest good, and that the life process of society is the very center of human endeavor'. Agamben is even right to suggest that the inclusion of 'bare life' in modern politics was fully realized in the totalitarian camps of the twentieth century. However, largely under the influence of Schmitt and Foucault, he takes the critique of political distinctions too far. Ultimately, we can refuse the way so-called 'biopolitics' is presented by Agamben and others—as marking the limit of all public–private distinctions and the priority and autonomy of the public realm. But the refusal must be based on an explicit account of the problems with the merging of *zoē* and *bios* and a defence of some form of reinstatement of the distinction. Centring her thought on a defence of what totalitarianism and imperialism seek to wipe out, Arendt is the thinker who has done most to establish such a theoretical and empirical agenda.

As this discussion of refugees has sought to highlight, there is a great deal at stake for both classical and critical international theory in the so-called 'corporeal turn' in social and political thought, that is, discussion of the distinction (and in-distinction) between *zoē* and *bios*. We ought not to lose sight of Arendt's admonition (2005: 145) that political rights are dependent on a distinction between nature and artifice, and that 'the linkage of politics and life results in an inner contradiction that cancels and destroys what is specifically political about politics'. To the extent that we heed Arendt's warning, the implications are potentially grave for how we understand the conditions under which rights make sense, that is, the kinds of institutions that ought to be built by those currently without a political community willing or able to guarantee the 'right to have rights'. There are obvious political risks in Agamben's claim that refugee struggles for secular citizenship rights are somehow anachronistic. In contrast, Arendt (2007: 724, emphasis added) never abandoned the possibility of a democratic-republican model of interlinked polities that might enable both the free movement of populations in anarchy *and* the stability of worldliness, a framework of laws 'within which people *move* and act' (for an elaboration see Owens (2009*b*)). She even went so far as to correlate legal and political forms and identities with different modes of territorial movements with obvious implications for the status of refugees (see Herzog 2004). Nowhere did she set out a blueprint for how to design this political order, but some sort of newly conceived potentially world-wide republican political arrangement is closest to what she had in mind. In light of the 'calamity of the rightless', Arendt (1966: ix, 295) formulated new *political* grounds for human dignity. This is why Arendt remains a central figure in the history of political thought regarding refugees. Refugee Studies replaces her with Agamben at its peril.

NOTE

1. Thanks to Bille Eltringham, Alex Betts, Gil Loescher, and Ken Booth for comments and advice on earlier drafts. The material was also presented at the International Studies Association Annual Meeting in New York, February 2009; the International Conference on 'Concentrationary Memories: the Politics of Representation, 1945–1985', School of Fine Arts, University of Leeds, March 2009; and a workshop on 'The Prescience of Hannah Arendt' at the School of Humanities, University of Southampton, May 2009.

BIBLIOGRAPHY

Agamben, G. 1998. *Homo Sacer: sovereign power and bare life* (trans. Daniel Heller-Roazen). Stanford, CA: Stanford University Press.

——. 2000. *Means without end: notes on politics* (trans. Vincenzo Binetti and Casare Casarino). Minneapolis, MN: University of Minnesota Press.

——. 2005. *State of exception* (trans. Kevin Attell). Chicago, IL: Chicago University Press.

Arendt, H. 1951. *The burden of our time*. London: Secker and Warburg.

——. 1958. *The human condition*. Chicago, IL: University of Chicago Press.

——. 1965. *On revolution*. New York: Viking.

——. 1966. *The origins of totalitarianism* (new edition with added prefaces). New York: Harcourt Brace Jovanovich.

——. 1968. *Men in dark times*. New York: Harcourt Brace.

——. 1978. *The Jew as pariah: Jewish identity and politics in the modern age* (edited and introduction by Ron H. Feldman). New York: Grove Press.

——. 1994. *Essays in understanding, 1930–1954*. New York: Harcourt Brace.

——. 2005. *The promise of politics* (edited and introduction by Jerome Kohn). New York: Schocken.

Arendt, H. 2007. The great tradition I. Law and power. *Social Research*. Vol. 74, no. 3, 713–26.

——and Jaspers, K. 1992. *Correspondence, 1926–1969* (edited by Lotte Kohler and Hans Saner) (trans. by Robert and Rita Kimber). New York: Harcourt Brace Jovanovich.

Balibar, E. 2007. (De)Constructing the human as human institution: a reflection on the coherence of Hannah Arendt's practical philosophy. *Social Research*. Vol. 74, no. 3, 727–38.

Benhabib, S. 2004. *The rights of others: aliens, residents and citizens*. Cambridge: Cambridge University Press.

Bernstein, R. 2005. Hannah Arendt on the stateless. *Parallax*. Vol. 11, no. 1, 46–60.

Bigo, D. 2002. Security and immigration: towards a critique of the governmentality of unease. *Alternatives*. Vol. 24, 63–92.

Butler, J. 2004. *Precarious life: the powers of mourning and violence*. London: Verso.

Diken, B. 2004. From refugee camps to gated communities: biopolitics and the end of the city. *Citizenship Studies*. Vol. 8, no. 1, 83–106.

Diken, B. and Lausten, C. B. 2005. *The culture of exception: sociology facing the camp*. London: Routledge.

Dillon, M. 1999. The scandal of the refugee: some reflections on the 'inter' of international relations and continental thought. In: Campbell, D. and Shapiro, M. J. (eds.). *Moral spaces: rethinking ethics and world politics*. Minneapolis, MN: University of Minnesota Press, 92–124.

Doná, G. 2007. The microphysics of participation in refugee research. *Journal of Refugee Studies*. Vol. 20, no. 2, 210–29.

Deudney, D. 2007. *Bounding power: Republican security theory from the polis to the global village*. Princeton University Press.

Duffield, M. 2007. *Development, security and unending war*. Cambridge: Polity.

Edkins, J. 2000. Sovereign power, zones of indistinction, and the camp. *Alternatives: Global, Local, Political*. Vol. 25, no. 1, 3–25.

——and Pin-Fat, V. 2005. Through the wire: relations of power and relations of violence. *Millennium: Journal of International Studies*. Vol. 34 no. 1, 1–24.

Elbe, S. 2005. AIDS, security, biopolitics. *International Relations*. Vol. 19, no. 4, 403–19.

Fitzpatrick, P. 2005. Bare sovereignty: *Homo Sacer* and the insistence of the law. In: Norris, A. (ed.). *Politics, metaphysics, death: essays on Giorgio Agamben's* Homo Sacer. Durham, NC: Duke University Press, 49–73.

Foucault, M. 1978. *The history of sexuality, an introduction: volume one*. New York: Vintage.

——. 2003. *Society must be defended*. New York: Picador

——. 2007. *Security, territory, population*. London: Palgrave.

Gibney, M. 2004. *The ethics and politics of asylum: liberal democracy and the response to refugees*. Cambridge: Cambridge University Press.

Habermas, J. 2001. *The post-national constellation: political essays*. Cambridge: Polity Press.

Haddad, E. 2008. *The refugee in international society: between sovereigns.* Cambridge: Cambridge University Press.

Hardy, C. 2003. Refugee determination: power and resistance in systems of Foucauldian power. *Administration & Society.* Vol. 35, no. 4, 462–88.

Hayden, P. 2008. From exclusion to containment: Arendt, sovereign power, and statelessness. *Societies Without Borders.* Vol. 3, no. 2, 272–93.

Heuer, W. 2007. Europe and its refugees: Arendt on the politicization of minorities. *Social Research.* Vol. 74, no. 4, 1159–72.

Herzog, A. 2004. Political itineraries and anarchic cosmopolitanism in the thought of Hannah Arendt. *Inquiry.* Vol. 47, no. 1, 20–41.

Huysmans, J. 2006. International politics of exception: competing visions of international political order between law and politics. *Alternatives: Global, Local, Political.* Vol. 31, 135–65.

Hyndman, J. 2000. *Managing displacement: refugees and the politics of humanitarianism.* Minneapolis, MN: University of Minnesota Press.

Jay, M. 1993. *Force field: between intellectual history and cultural critique.* New York: Routledge.

Jenkins, F. 2004. Bare life: asylum-seekers, Australian politics and Agamben's critique of violence. *Australian Journal of Human Rights.* Vol. 10, no. 1, available at http://www.austlii.edu.au/au/journals/AJHR/2004/18.html.

Kinsella, H. 2008. Arendt and analogies. *International Politics.* Vol. 45, no. 4, 497–505.

Larner, W. and Walters, W. (eds.). 2004. *Global governmentality: governing international spaces.* London: Routledge.

Leach, M. 2003. 'Disturbing practices': dehumanizing asylum seekers in the refugee crisis in Australia, 2001–2002. *Refuge.* Vol. 21, no. 3, 25–33.

Lippert, R. 1998. Rationalities and refugee resettlement. *Economy and Society.* Vol. 27, no. 4, 380–406, available at http://www.informaworld.com/smpp/title~content=t713685159~db=all~tab=issueslist~branches=27—v27.

——. 1999. Governing refugees: the relevance of governmentality to understanding the international refugee regime. *Alternatives.* Vol. 24, no. 3, 295–328.

Lui, R. 2004. The international government of refugees. In: Larner, W. and Walters, W. (eds.). *Global governmentality: governing international spaces.* London: Routledge. 116–35.

Malkki, L.H. 1995. Refugees and exile: from 'Refugee Studies' to the national order of things. *Annual Review of Anthropology.* Vol. 24, 495–523.

Marrus, M. R. 1985. *The unwanted: European refugees in the twentieth century.* Oxford: Oxford University Press.

Muller, B. 2004. Globalization, security, paradox: towards a refugee biopolitics. *Refuge.* Vol. 22, no. 1, 49–57.

Nyers, P. 2006. *Rethinking refugees: beyond states of emergency.* London: Routledge.

Owens, P. 2007. *Between war and politics: International Relations and the thought of Hannah Arendt.* Oxford: Oxford University Press.

Owens, P. 2008. Humanity, sovereignty and the camps. *International Politics.* Vol. 45, no. 4, 522–30.

Owens, P. 2009*a*. Reclaiming 'Bare Life'? Against Agamben on refugees. *International Relations*. Vol. 23, no. 4, 567–82.

——. 2009*b*. Walking corpses: Arendt on the limits and possibilities of cosmopolitan politics. In: Moore, C. and Farrands, C. (eds.). *International Relations theory and philosophy: interpretive dialogues*. London: Routledge, 72–82.

Posen, B. R. 1996. Military responses to refugee disasters. *International Security*. Vol. 21, no. 1, 72–111.

Puggioni, R. 2005. Resisting sovereign power: camps in-between exception and dissent. In: Huysmans, J., Dobson, A., and Prokhovnik, R. (eds.). *The politics of protection: sites of insecurity and political agency*. London: Routledge, 68–83.

Pupavac, V. 2008. Refugee advocacy, traumatic representations and political disenchantment. *Government and Opposition*. Vol. 43, no. 2, 270–92.

Schmitt, C. 2005. *Political theology: four chapters on the concept of sovereignty* (trans and with intro by George Schwab; new forward by Tracy B. Strong). Chicago, IL: Chicago University Press.

Soguk, N. 1999. *States and strangers: refugees and displacements of statecraft*. Minneapolis, MN: University of Minnesota Press.

Tuitt, P. 2004. Refugees, nations, laws and the territorialization of violence. In: Fitzpatrick, P. and Tuitt, P. (eds.). *Critical beings: law, nation, and the global subject*. Surrey: Ashgate, 37–57.

7

The Only Thinkable Figure? Ethical and Normative Approaches to Refugees in International Relations

Chris Brown

ABSTRACT

The figure of the refugee poses a problem for normative/ethical thinking in international relations. Much normative thinking in this area is based on a contrast between cosmopolitan (impartialist) and communitarian (partial) theories, but this classification is unhelpful; both sets of theories agree that refugees who meet the criteria of the 1951 Convention should be acknowledged and assisted, but neither has much to say about the much larger group of individuals who are not technically fleeing a well-founded fear of persecution and are described by terms such as 'bogus asylum-seeker', but who are equally worthy of our concern. Theories of global and international justice which look at the supply side of refugee problems, (that is, the poverty and oppression that creates refugees) rather than focusing on the moral duties that should govern the behaviour of potential host countries, are valuable in their own terms, but equally unhelpful in guiding action. A feature of all these theories is that they effectively deny agency to the refugee and writers such as Agamben attempt to correct this by casting the figure of the refugee as the protagonist of contemporary political dramas, but this comes close to insulting the aspirations of refugees, who generally have no wish to take on this luminous role, hoping only to become citizens of a state that does not persecute them. It may be that finding a generally acceptable moral basis for action with respect to refugees is effectively impossible and a more overtly political, less moralizing approach to the subject is required—in other words, theory-centred moral thinking based on absolutes may need to give way to practically minded reasoning, based on bargaining and compromise.

> [the] most symptomatic group in contemporary politics
> (Hannah Arendt 1951: 277)

> [the] refugee is perhaps the only thinkable figure for the people of our time, and the only category in which one may see today... [the] forms and limits of a coming political community.
>
> (Giorgio Agamben 2000: 15)

INTRODUCTION

It is more or less compulsory for political theorists to begin a discussion of refugees with a quote from Arendt, especially if, like myself, one has not previously engaged in any depth with the issue of refugees, and is looking for a way into a complex subject where the usual pointers provided by the theory of the state or of the international look less than helpful.[1] A refugee herself, she saw the figure of the refugee as symptomatic of the changes in the nature of the state that had accompanied the rise of totalitarianism, a side-effect of the desire to standardize populations and define and exclude minorities, and she recognized that the emerging international human rights regime was unlikely in and of itself to 'solve' the problem of the refugee—the post-1948 human rights regime was established by states and purported to protect the rights of those who were already members of a political community, which, by definition, refugees were not. Although she saw refugees as figures uniquely qualified to understand their times, a kind of 'vanguard of their peoples' (Arendt 1943: 7 cited from Agamben 2000), she herself was someone for whom membership of a functioning political community was central to the living of a good life, and so she experienced statelessness as a loss which went beyond the material insecurity this status involved, a loss the only remedy for which was to find a new political community.

Fifty years later, the Italian theorist Giorgio Agamben, with characteristic hyperbole, reverses many of Arendt's assumptions, while still paying homage to the way in which she identified the importance of the figure of the refugee. From his perspective, to be a member today of the kind of political community that Arendt regrets losing is a practical and theoretical impossibility. Those of us who still think we inhabit such a role are obviously deluded—in the current era, there is no way in which we can make sense of the notion of membership of a territorially defined political community. Such communities are dying or dead, and—at least until they disappear altogether and a new concept of the political emerges—such representative figures as the 'citizen' and the 'sovereign people' or the 'worker' and the 'working-class' must give way to the only figure upon whom a new political philosophy can possibly be built, the only figure not implicated in the current collapse, the refugee.

One suspects that refugees do not quite see things that way, but for all his willingness to push an argument to the extremes of silliness, Agamben presents an interesting contrast to Arendt, not least because it is patently not the case that the kind of 'refugee problem' we (and they) face today is similar to that of the post-war years. Those refugees from Nazi Germany or Stalin's empire became refugees because of the 'well-founded fear of persecution' they experienced as individuals or as members of a targeted group, the fear that came to form the basis of the legal definition of their situation (Goodwin-Gill and McAdam 2007); today, many refugees are fleeing radically unsafe conflict zones but without being specifically targeted, or they are attempting to better their lives by gravitating away from the poor areas of the world to the rich (which may not fit the legal definition and thus leads them to acquire the unwanted status of 'bogus asylum seeker' but which is a flight from fearful conditions nonetheless). With a few exceptions amongst the moneyed-classes, most of Arendt's refugees struggled to escape persecution in trains and trucks or on foot, and collapsed into camps created for them more or less as soon as they had crossed the relevant borders—today's refugees will often target specific desired locations and, because of the reluctance of the developed world to act as hosts, will generally be forced to employ illegal means of entry in order to get to the point where they can actually make a claim for asylum.

Without, of course, intending to do so, Arendt and Agamben have between them mapped out many of the options available for a study of the normative dimension of the problem. There is surprisingly little explicit work on this dimension—Matthew Gibney's (2004) book being a recent, outstanding, exception to that generalization—and what there is tends to set the problem up in terms of a contrast between approaches that stress 'partiality' and 'impartiality', to use Gibney's terms. Communitarian accounts of duties to fellow-nationals are contrasted with cosmopolitan accounts of duties to humanity as a whole, but Agamben's admittedly way over the top rhetoric allows us to see that actually both partialist and impartialist accounts presume the existence of a stable political world-order composed of states and citizens into which refugees have to be fitted. This may not actually be the best way of thinking through the ethical dilemmas posed by the figure of the refugee, even though we may wish to insist against Agamben that the old categories are, in fact, thinkable and indeed offer the best entry point for a discussion of the issues.

COMMUNITARIAN AND COSMOPOLITAN APPROACHES

As many scholars have pointed out, the idea that normative thinkers on international topics can be divided into communitarian and cosmopolitan camps grossly oversimplifies complex arguments, and can mislead as much as it illuminates (Cochran 2000; Erskine 2008). Still, we have to start somewhere, and as long as this binary division is not taken too seriously it can help us to make sense of the ethical dilemmas which problems such as the appropriate ethical response to refugees pose. This division has the added advantage that, unlike, say, a classification into liberal and conservative thought, it allows us to draw on the history of political and moral thought, but is not based on the problems of domestic society. As we will see, one of the most interesting features of international normative thought is precisely that it does not map onto the categories we usually use to describe the moral dilemmas thrown up by contemporary domestic politics, most of which are shaped by the problems of property ownership in industrial societies.

The cosmopolitan–communitarian divide relates to the most central question of any normative international theory, namely, the moral value to be attributed to particularistic political collectivities as against humanity taken as a whole, or the claims of individual human beings. The term 'cosmopolitan' has its origins in the period immediately after the collapse of the classical Greek *polis*; theorists of the latter took their centrality in moral life for granted and needed no particular word to highlight this fact, so the term 'communitarian' had to wait for the 1980s to enter modern political philosophy, but the opposition between these two putative camps has been a constant feature of political thought since its beginnings. In spite of this long history, it should be said immediately that these camps have until recently had virtually nothing to say directly about the issue of refugees as that issue presents itself today. It is certainly true that notions such as 'guest-friendship' played a big role in Greek thought, and that Kant writes on the duties of hospitality, but these instances have little contemporary relevance—modern methods of transportation combined with changes in the nature of the state mean that virtually nothing written directly on the issues of refugees before the last few decades has much purchase on the problem. Rather, what thinkers such as Kant and Hegel do have to offer us is a set of attitudes, frames of mind, moral categories, and so on, which we can hope to apply to contemporary problems. In the Kantian case, it is the categorical imperative to treat others as ends and never solely as means that acts as the guiding principle for thinking about refugees, while for Hegelians it is the distinction between ethics of a community ('sitten') and absolute morality, and the refusal to prioritize the latter over the former, that shapes the way we see the problem. In other words, Hegel offers us ethical reasons to prioritize the interests of our fellow citizens as a matter of principle, while Kant requires us to acknowledge the moral claims of strangers (although this does not exclude the possibility of giving extra weight to the claims of co-nationals) (Brown 1992).

That at least is the bumper-sticker version of their thought; in reality, predictably, things are not really that simple and Kant's position in particular is more nuanced than this would suggest—but in any event rather than approach the problem via these figures it makes more sense to talk about some of the modern scholars who actually have addressed the issue of borders and refugees. Here thinkers such as Michael Walzer (1983) and David Miller (1995, 2007) on one side, and cosmopolitan theorists such as Charles Beitz (1979/2000), Thomas Pogge (2002), and Simon Caney (2006) on the other, provide the key reference points, and the central issue is the right to control membership of the community, or, to be more precise, the nature of the community itself, which determines whether and how it can be right to control its membership.

Identifying these authors as central is, of course, to restrict the way the issue is discussed by excluding certain positions. Thus, for some conservative communitarians the state is Burke's compact between the living, the dead, and the yet-to-be-born, and there is a kind of mystical relationship between a people and a territory, blood and soil—from this perspective membership can only be gifted to strangers, there can be no sense in which it could possibly be seen as an entitlement or the product of a duty (e.g. Scruton 2006). At the other extreme, libertarians believe that the right to move from one place to another on the earth's surface should be unconstrained by any factor other than the ability of the incomer to sustain him or herself—in such a world there are no benefits to membership of a political system, if such exists, therefore restricting membership is a non-issue (Steiner 1992). The first of these positions certainly still has quite a lot of political leverage, and the second gains some purchase as the *reductio ad absurdum* of a world where politics is increasingly seen in neo-liberal, consumerist terms, but neither position is easy to engage with. Moreover, from my perspective, neither pose the really interesting questions in the way that Walzer et al. do. The point is that both liberal communitarians and liberal cosmopolitans are, first and foremost, liberals—and liberals in the American, social-democratic, sense of the word. As liberals in this sense, both groups are committed to welfarist politics and both are committed to an essentially moralized vision of politics—they are not content to argue that issues of inclusion and exclusion from the political community can be settled simply by the exercise of power or on the basis of a friend-enemy distinction on Schmittian lines—and yet they draw different conclusions from these shared beliefs. This, I think, is interesting.

Walzer (1983, 1993, 2008) is a key figure here both in his own terms and in the reactions of others to his work. His fundamental point is that political communities have the right to control their own membership, and that membership is, as it were, a single, non-negotiable status—he opposes the kind of *Gastarbeiter* status that gives individuals certain legal and/or economic rights while denying them political rights. People are either in or out, members or non-members, and the decision as to whether they are 'in' rests with the existing membership. Why? As I read him, he gives two answers to this question, answers that are quite different and separable (although they can be related one to the other). First, most explicitly and at greatest length, he refers to the 'shared understandings' that constitute a political community; these understandings have developed over time and have come to define the political values of the community, its moral compass, and the way it sees the world. The community is entitled to protect these understandings by excluding those who would subvert them either deliberately—thus, no Western liberal democracy should be under the obligation to extend citizenship to those who have no respect for its basic principles (even though those principles will, and should, evolve over time)—or inadvertently, by sheer weight of numbers. This position has some points of contact with the conservative communitarian position outlined above, but with no connection to 'blood and soil'; it is consistent with a community composed of successive waves of immigrants who accept (and influence) its shared understandings, and it is based on values and the commitment to a way of life rather than to a particular territory.

Cosmopolitan liberals have little difficulty picking holes in this position. There may be some political communities based on such shared understandings but even where they exist the 'fit' between community and actually existing state is not good; more generally, the argument Walzer uses for describing a 'vanished Westphalian world', to borrow Allen Buchanan's dismissal of John Rawls's not dissimilar position in *The Law of Peoples*, is compelling (Rawls 1999; Buchanan 2000). Even in long-established states which can plausibly be seen as containers for political community, shared understandings may change very quickly. Walzer's vision looks to be exactly that, a vision, a picture based on an idealized image of a community that bears little relationship to really existing liberal societies.

Walzer's second argument, on the other hand, is less easily trashed. Walzer is, if nothing else, a democratic socialist, with a deep commitment to the creation of just social institutions and a vision of citizenship that goes beyond the political to the economic and social. He is an advocate of a full-blown welfare state, whose citizens would have extensive and valuable entitlements. There are two respects in which this impinges on membership. In the first place, there clearly has to be a way of determining who is entitled to the benefits of citizenship and who is not; it is perfectly clear that not all these benefits can be made available to all the peoples of the world simply on the basis that they are capable of reaching the territory of the welfare state in question.

Thus, for example, most welfare schemes provide some emergency medical cover to visitors but none are capable of providing long-term care to everyone who wants or needs it, irrespective of citizenship. Establishing with some clarity the membership criteria of a welfare scheme is a central task, and, more or less by definition, this means determining rules for inclusion and exclusion. Second, it is clear that any kind of effective welfare scheme will have redistributive features, and the more effective it is the more redistributive it will be, that is, the more it will rely upon those who have to support those who have not—and not as a matter of charity, but as a moral obligation. Walzer's argument (and that of David Miller) is that the wealthier members of the community will be more likely to accept their obligations in such a scheme if they have the sense of being members of the same community as their poorer co-citizens—here we touch base with, and give substantive content to, the 'shared understandings' argument outlined above.

Adding the two arguments together, welfare states can be expected to be more effective when membership is controlled and when all members have the sense of taking part in a common project validated by the generally shared sense of belonging to the same community. And Walzer can point here to the European Scandinavian model in support of both points. Scandinavian welfare states are based on a strong sense of community and, historically, they have been 'good international citizens', supporting the UN, aid-giving, and willing to provide peacekeepers and high-level UN bureaucrats, but they are not cosmopolitan in disposition. They maintain strict border controls and have resisted the more supranational elements of EU membership. Sadly, Scandinavia also provides negative examples; the current crisis of the Scandinavian welfare state is accompanied by a decline in community cohesiveness. Which is cause here, and which is effect is much debated, but that the two go together is less debatable (Einhorn & Logue 2003).

How do liberal cosmopolitans, most of whom are as committed to the welfare state as Walzer, handle this argument? Not very well, I judge. As liberals/social democrats they can hardly in good faith be indifferent to the strain on the welfare state simply because they, as members of the professional middle classes, rely less on its services than the ordinary citizen. Moreover, although an influx of foreign workers may have a positive impact on overall prosperity it will also hold down the wages of the least skilled and poorest part of the workforce, and again, most cosmopolitans will be reluctant to endorse such an outcome. Instead, what we see exhibited is usually the deployment of diversionary tactics, designed to dodge the difficult questions. Some doubt Walzer's commitment to democratic socialist values, making fun of his account of the 'spheres of justice'—but this is little more than Freud's narcissism of small differences. Others slide over the democratic socialist side of Walzer's argument rather quickly, preferring to focus on the more abstract, and more easily attacked, notion of 'shared understandings' rather than the very practical points about the organization of the welfare state and the political conditions for its survival. Or the point may be conceded that some controls are needed in an imperfect world, but this is generally followed by the accurate, but irrelevant, observation that not *everyone* is likely to want to move to those countries that have strong welfare states—irrelevant because clearly it would not need everyone to move to destroy all currently existing welfare systems. These are rhetorical tricks, designed to draw attention away from the embarrassing fact that Walzer is certainly correct to argue that no welfare state could survive a policy of open borders.

In fact, when we move to the specific case of refugees, as that category is legally defined, Walzer's position is much the same as that of many of his critics. He does not deny that we have obligations to take in those who, with a well-founded fear of persecution, turn up at our borders, on our shores, or at our international airports. Such 'classic' refugees will, in any event, most likely be loyal citizens, willing to adopt our shared understandings—after all, they have come to us presumably because they value freedoms we value. The fact that Walzer takes this position illustrates a rather important and surprising point. In effect, liberals on both sides of the communitarian vs. cosmopolitan argument converge on support for the right to membership of such refugees—but then many conservative communitarians would also agree and even libertarian communitarians would probably agree that such refugees could be given loans to allow them to start a new life (at the governing rate of interest of course).

The problem with this striking convergence is, of course, that nowadays many actual refugees do not fit this model, although they may be obliged to claim that they do if they wish to avoid being seen as 'bogus asylum seekers'. And, to complicate the picture still further, many refugees who are indeed fleeing a well-founded fear of persecution, and so do fit the classical model, may have absolutely no commitment to liberal values; for example, *jihadists* in London understandably will not wish to be returned to countries such as Egypt or Algeria, but this betokens no liking for the political orders that they believe will protect them from this fate—indeed they may regard our willingness to abide by the *non-refoulement* principle as a sign of weakness rather than an indication of virtue. Even if such figures do not actually intend to do us harm while under our protection—and this cannot be guaranteed—it is difficult to see them as welcome guests.

It is, I think, fair to say that neither Walzer nor his cosmopolitan critics has a convincing normative position to offer on the correct response to claims for refugee status from such individuals or from people who are pretty clearly 'economic' migrants, even if they pretend not to be. In effect we have a double convergence here—not only do cosmopolitans and communitarians actually agree on the position of refugees as classically defined, they are both impotent in the face of the new problems posed by those who are actually likely to turn up at our doorstep or (actually statistically rather more likely) at the doorstep of non-Western countries throughout the world.

This last point will feature more largely in the next section of this paper but deserves a little attention here. The point is that the paradigmatic exploration of refugee dilemmas in terms of impartialist vs. partialist accounts of membership and obligation is to all intents and purposes irrelevant to the refugee problems that most of the world faces. It is striking that the four case studies in Matthew Gibney's book focus on the United Kingdom, Germany, the United States, and Australia, while well over two-thirds of all 'people of concern to the UNHCR' (the widest definition of the groups affected) are in Asia, Africa, or Latin America. To take one striking statistic from the *The State of The World's Refugees, 2006*, as of 1 January 2005, there were at least 2 million refugees from Afghanistan, and probably nearer 4 million, of whom perhaps only around 100,000 were seeking refuge in Western Europe or elsewhere outside of the region, with the vast majority of the rest in Iran and Pakistan (Office of the UNHCR 2006).

To summarize, setting up the problem in terms of the divide between cosmopolitan and communitarian thought is to focus on what is actually pretty much of a non-debate; positions which in theory are miles apart, in practice come together—no cosmopolitan advocate of open borders actually wants to abolish all border controls under current conditions, and the way most communitarians wish to exercise the right they claim to control membership is actually consistent with what most cosmopolitans would like to see happen in the case of refugees who meet the standard legal definition of the term. Moreover, setting up the debate in this way is to focus on that aspect of the problem that most concerns us, the inhabitants of the rich liberal democracies—and to draw attention away from what is, in terms of numbers affected, the real issue.

CHANGING THE QUESTION

The partialist vs. impartialist debate is about what we in the liberal democracies should do when strangers arrive at our national points of entry demanding admission. This situation is indeed common, and poses serious moral questions about our obligations towards our fellow citizens as opposed to those towards these strangers; unfortunately it is difficult to see how these questions can be answered in a satisfactory way within the terms under which they are usually posed, even though theorists may actually agree on what would constitute good practice when confronted with specific cases. This theoretical aporia is one good reason for changing those terms; another, and better, reason is that to see refugee problems in this light is to miss what, from a global perspective, has to be seen as the real problem of refugees, which manifests itself in giant camps in the Great Lakes region of Africa, or in Pakistan, rather than at Heathrow or the Pas de Calais. But what alternative terms are available?

An easy—I will suggest ultimately too easy—answer here would focus on the reasons why people become refugees in the first place, to approach the problem from the supply side, as it were. A sensible working assumption is that no one actually wants to be a refugee (which is why although it makes some sense not to distinguish between 'political' and 'economic' refugees, it certainly is necessary to distinguish between refugees as a whole, and 'travellers' of one kind or another, that is, those who take to the road as a lifestyle choice rather than from necessity); this is a status that is forced on people either by grinding poverty or by intolerable oppression, or, sadly quite often, both at once. Sometimes, of course, the oppressors themselves will actually wish to create refugees in the name of ethnic cleansing, or to get rid of political opponents, but the individuals concerned do not desire this status. In an ideal world, where there were no oppressive regimes, and where all the citizens of every country were able to sustain themselves materially, there would be no refugees—it might still be the case that some people would wish, for one reason or another, to change their domicile, and this might present some practical problems, but there would be no refugee issue as such; and, in a world where no one is forced to leave their home, a general right of hospitality would not pose onerous duties on host populations. This is, I think, the context in which Kant's Third Definitive Article of a Perpetual Peace—that 'Cosmopolitan Right shall be limited to Conditions of Universal Hospitality'—should be read (Reiss 1970: 106). This is a Definitive Article (as opposed to the six Preliminary Articles) and the assumption is that a Federation of Free States has been established; in such a world there would be no need to make a general provision to provide sanctuary for citizens of such free states.

From this perspective, the task of establishing an ethical approach to the problem of refugees becomes subsumed into two wider issues of global justice and of the 'responsibility to protect'. Instead of asking 'what should we do about refugees?' we should be asking 'what should we do to prevent people being made refugees in the first place?' If, as Arendt suggested, refugees are to be seen as symptoms, the goal of normative theory should be to address the features of the world that produce these symptoms. Of course, shifting the focus in this way does not make the task of defining an appropriate normative position any easier than it was before. It will be apparent from even a cursory examination of the literature that there are a great many different conceptions of what constitutes global/international justice (Brown 2008). From some points of view, achieving a just world is a matter of establishing new global institutions which would have some of the attributes of a loose global federal government—this seems to be what Thomas Pogge (2002) envisages in his account of the interaction of human rights and global poverty. Such institutions would address the problem of global poverty, and, he suggests, act to prevent oppressive, dictatorial regimes from gaining access to the resources they need to establish themselves. John Rawls, on the other hand, argues that while a just world order may require liberal and 'decent' well-ordered states to give assistance to 'burdened societies' (who are, as it stands, incapable of being well-ordered), such assistance need not be material—what is crucial is the development of just institutions rather than the transfer of wealth (although in some cases, he acknowledges, the latter may be necessary) (Rawls 1999). He envisages peaceful 'democracy promotion' but he also suggests, rather hesitantly, that there are some societies ('outlaw states') where this may not be possible, and here some form of violent intervention may be called for.

This last point chimes with the idea that, if national governments are unable or unwilling to look after their own citizens, the international community has a kind of 'responsibility to protect'; some such idea is, I think, unavoidable in any complete account of the requirements of global or international justice—and this applies to redistributive quasi-federal schemes such as those of Pogge or Beitz as well as Rawls's anti-cosmopolitan vision of a society of peoples—and is clearly necessary if the aim is to prevent the creation of refugees. Interestingly, this is one area where theory and practice come together—as Nicholas Wheeler (2000) has shown, the argument that international intervention in domestic oppression can be legitimate because the refugee problems generated by oppression constitute a 'threat to international peace and security' has come up quite frequently in recent decades, and the notion of a Responsibility to Protect was formally adopted in the UN's World Summit Outcome document in 2005 (Evans 2008).

There are clearly lots of avenues to be explored if one were to take this approach, and explored they should be and have been—but they take us quite a way away from the original problem. It is almost certainly true that the ethical problems posed by refugees could be solved by establishing a generally just world order, and there is no compelling reason in principle why such an order could not be established—but the kind of political breakthrough which would allow this to happen seems some way off, while the problem of refugee protection exists in the here and now. Any complete account of the ethics of refugee protection is going to have to include a narrative about the supply side and any satisfactory solution to the normative dilemmas posed by refugees is going to have to include an account of the measures that need to be taken to prevent the creation of refugees, but such thinking cannot be a substitute for a focus on the problem as it actually exists today, rather than as it might be prevented in a better future.

To put the matter differently, a macro approach focusing on global justice shares with a more micro approach that looks to the politics and policies of particular rich states the same characterization of refugees as 'symptoms', with the (implicit or explicit) assumption that the location of the real problem is somewhere else, and that once that location is identified, the real problem can addressed, and, if we are very clever, solved. How to think about the moral dilemmas posed by refugees becomes a wholly secondary problem, the solution to which depends on the way in which we think about either the national or the international community. At this point perhaps we need Agamben to remind us that to see refugees simply as symptoms is to miss a very important trick.

THINKABLE SUBJECTS?

Why does Agamben attach such importance to refugees? Here it is necessary to give a brief account of his general approach to politics which is a heady blend of Foucaldian notions of biopower, his own thought on the significance of the Shoah and the death camps, and Schmittian conceptions of sovereignty and the nature of the 'exception' (Agamben 2005; Odysseos and Petito 2007; Foucault 2008). A key notion is 'bare life'—the human in itself, biological human existence, the unmediated physical being; on his account, bare life in this basic sense is transformed into something else in the *polis* (Agamben 1998). The purely biological human becomes the 'citizen' who is defined by the political and social relations of the community—'man' becomes Aristotle's political animal (*zoon politikon*). The absolute antithesis of the political animal is the inhabitant of the death camps, and particularly the so-called *Musselmanner* who become inert and fatalistic in the face of the horror around them. In the camps, the link between the human and the citizen is broken, and subsequent history, especially the recent history of terrorism and counter-terrorism, suggests to Agamben that it cannot be reconstituted. An extended quote relates this situation to the status of refugee and purports to show how the latter reveals things otherwise hidden:

> If the refugee represents such a disquieting element in the order of the nation-state, this is so primarily because, by breaking the identity between the human and the citizen, and that between nativity and nationality, it brings the originary fiction of sovereignty to crisis. Single exceptions to such a principle, of course, have always existed. What is new in our time is that growing sections of humankind are no longer representable inside the nation-state—and this novelty threatens the very foundations of the latter. Inasmuch as the refugee, an apparently marginal figure, unhinges the old trinity of state-nation-territory—it deserves instead to be recognised as the central figure of our political history. (Agamben, 2000: 19–21)

To tell refugees that they have this luminous status comes dangerously close to insulting their own aspirations—as noted above, most refugees want nothing more than to be the kind of citizens that Agamben argues no longer exist—but for all its faults, this way of setting out the issue does have the merit of questioning the value of the state-centric lens through which the figure of the refugee is usually viewed. It also invites us to reverse the assumptions upon which contemporary liberal normative theory is constructed.

As to the latter, modern liberal moral philosophy is generally seen as a debate between some version of consequentialism (the view that moral behaviour is to be judged in terms of its consequences) and some version of deontology (the view that some actions are required, or forbidden, regardless of consequences)—the two dominant theories here are utilitarianism in its various forms (e.g. act-utilitarianism, rule-utilitarianism) and Kantian thought, including neo-Kantianism. Consequentialist and deontological approaches are usually thought of as opposites and as occupying the space available for normative discourse, but in one important respect they are actually quite similar—although giving different answers, they both pose essentially the same question when faced with a morally problematic situation, which is 'what should we do'? or, perhaps more precisely, 'how should we go about deciding what we should do'?

As the advocates of a revival of classical moral philosophy and virtue ethics have insisted, this is actually not the only interesting normative question– the Greeks, for example, preferred to ask what kind of people they should be, how they should live, rather than what they should do, believing that the answer to this latter question would follow from the former (Anscombe 1958; Foot 1978; Williams 1985; Crisp 1996). In the context of this essay, the interesting question is 'who are the "we" in the question what should *we* do'? and the answer seems to be everyone except the actual refugee. 'We'—government authorities, private citizens of the liberal democracies, academics, NGOs, etc—possess agency; 'we' decide whether X, the refugee, is genuinely fleeing persecution or is a bogus asylum seeker; 'we' balance the claims of X against the interests of our existing fellow citizens and decide whether or not to admit X; and 'we' donate money to the various charities that maintain camps for refugees and internally displaced persons, people like X. X does not act, does not possess agency—X's role is to wait for someone else to act and decide his or her fate. Of course, X originally possessed a kind of agency, manifested either by the act of fleeing persecution or by scraping enough money together to make a desperate bid to improve his or her life, but once that crucial step is taken—or forced upon him or her—the capacity to act is lost; he or she enters the system and awaits the decisions of those who now possess agency. Communitarians and cosmopolitans argue about what X's fate should be, governments decide what it will be; X is now out of the power equation, acted upon but not acting, denied a voice in the proceedings except on terms decided elsewhere. Only rarely is the refugee's own voice heard (Moorehead 2006).

Of course, Agamben's recasting of the refugee as the protagonist of our contemporary political drama does not change this situation; it does not involve empowerment, nor does it take away from the fact that 'we' do actually have decisions to make about refugees. Threatened the nation-state may be, but it still exists and membership of a functioning nation-state is still a necessary, if not a sufficient, condition for human flourishing. The terms under which individuals gain membership of political communities are still of crucial importance and no refugee is likely to think otherwise. The liberal question 'what should we do' is still well worth posing—but it does no harm to be reminded that setting up the normative dilemmas of refugee policy by asking this question does involve marginalizing the actual figure of the refugee. Equally, it is important that when we talk of these issues we remember how fragile the notion of citizenship is, and how easily the relationship between the sovereign and the citizen can collapse. The notion that we live in a political world where Schmitt's exception has become the norm is the kind of rhetorical exaggeration that causes people not to take thinkers like Agamben too seriously—but the dangers posed to civil liberties by terrorism and the measures required to combat terrorism ought to make us wary of using ethical categories that presume the existence of stable communities.

Awareness of the fragility of citizenship may also stimulate consideration of new and different sorts of relationships between nationality, territory, and citizenship (Benhabib 2004; Sassen 2006). If refugees are an anomaly in a world where the identity of man and citizen is still asserted, they share this status with many other groups. In a world city such as London there are a great many groups who do not fit within the standard model—EU citizens, Commonwealth citizens, non-Commonwealth resident aliens with permission to work, undocumented aliens, students, certified refugees, non-refugees with leave to remain, and those awaiting decisions on their cases and those awaiting deportation. Some of these figures can work legally, others cannot; some can vote in some elections, others cannot; some get some welfare benefits, some do not. Meanwhile, in the other direction, several million Britons live or are travelling abroad, working, on gap years, or retired. Add all these anomalies together, and citizenship starts to look like a bundle of rights and benefits, all of which are possessed by the favoured few, but others of which are distributed very widely; although much contemporary theorizing (e.g. Walzer 1983) assumes one is either a citizen or not, in practice there seem to be all sorts of intermediate statuses. Crossing the Atlantic we can see similar sorts of anomalies—the illegal immigrants who are needed to keep American agriculture functioning in California and the South-West are undocumented and often do not receive the minimum wage or anything like it, but their children often attend school and may indeed be entitled to citizenship if born in the United States.

Again, we need to be careful not to compare like with unlike; as with the difference between refugees and travellers, there is a very big difference between foreign students in London who are most likely destined for elite careers in the global economy and the largely foreign work-force who clean the university's classrooms and refectories every night, and an even bigger difference between a British retiree in Spain and a Liberian inhabitant of a refugee camp in Guinea. Still the general point holds—a great deal of conventional thought on refugees relies on a model of how national politics works that is increasingly difficult to maintain—moreover, the contradictions here are likely to become even more apparent in the light of the current economic difficulties. Morally this may be an undesirable state of affairs leading to first and second-class citizenships, but it seems to be how contemporary capitalism works.

CONCLUSION

Stephen White (1991) refers to two kinds of political theory—'world-revealing' and 'action-guiding'—and clearly the kind of insights offered by Agamben involve the former rather than the latter. Partialist and impartialist theorists—and theorists of global justice—clearly want to be action-guiding, but, it is suggested above, they find themselves at an impasse when the subject changes from the theoretical basis of refugee policy to the actual problems posed by refugees. Even Caroline Moorehead's book which is filled with justifiable anger and induces the same emotion in its readers, is short on solutions; the governments of the West clearly ought to behave with greater humanity but greater humanity is not going to solve the dilemmas her subjects articulate with such force. In short, determining 'what is to be done?' may not be the only way of defining the task of normative theory, but it is an important question nonetheless, and one that international political theory appears to be unable to answer—the problem is not just the unwillingness of political actors to act ethically, but the apparent inability of normative theorists to work out what acting ethically might involve.

This would be a good point to pull a rabbit from out of the hat, and offer some kind of reassuring conclusion. Unfortunately there is no rabbit, and it is not even clear that we know what the hat looks like. In fact, what is required is precisely to stop looking for rabbits and hats—the right answers and the right questions—and to recognize that often normative theorizing can only generate negatives. The search for some kind of morally satisfying general theory which will delineate our duties to and responsibilities for refugees is almost certainly a waste of time, and too much emphasis on trying to determine the shape of a morally just world order, valuable though such theorizing is in principle, leaves things as they are in the here and now. Rather than a general moral theory, it may make sense to put the emphasis on the political and the local. Rather than seeing the outcome of clashes of interest between refugees and locals as to be determined by moral criteria, it may make more sense to acknowledge that such clashes are inherently political. Rather than trying to produce a compelling moral argument why refugees should be treated more favourably, it makes more sense to try to address directly the fears that key existing groups in society express and to try to meet those fears without compromising the interests of the newcomers. Instead of accusing the former of racism or xenophobia and trying to shame them into abandoning their opposition, a less moralized, more political approach would recognize that there is a genuine clash of interests here, which needs to be resolved in the way that such clashes are resolved in liberal democracies, by bargaining and compromise. Similar shifts of emphasis are needed at the international level; rather than looking for a general scheme of global social justice, or a set of general principles on responsibility and protection, it makes more sense to focus on doing something about *this* problem *here*. One of the reasons governments are so unwilling to address specific problems, so slow to act on complex emergencies even when they can see them coming is precisely because they fear they will be unable to limit their future commitments because precedents will be set.

Such relatively minor changes of direction may seem inadequate given the scale of the problem, and indeed they *are* inadequate, but the role of international political theory is not, or at least ought not to be, to pretend that answers exist when actually they do not. There is a role for 'theory-centred' moral thinking which maps possible morally just worlds, but there is also a role for 'practically-minded' moral reasoning which looks at problems as they are not as they might be (Toulmin 1990:14). This may involve a lowering of sights, but if the rabbit is not there, we have to acknowledge this fact and do what we can do, not what we would like to be able to do.

NOTE

1. I am grateful to Toni Erskine, to participants in the Staff Research Seminar at LSE, and to members of the Oxford Refugees in International Relations Seminar Series for comments on an early version of this essay; the usual disclaimers apply.

BIBLIOGRAPHY

Agamben, G. 1998. *Homo Sacer: sovereign power and bare life.* Stanford, CA: Stanford University Press.

——2000. *Means without end: notes on politics.* Minneapolis, MN: University of Minnesota Press.

——2005. *State of exception.* Chicago, IL: Chicago University Press.

Anscombe, G. E. M. 1958. Modern moral philosophy. *Philosophy,* 33(124), 1–19.

Arendt, H. 1943. We refugees. *Menorah Journal,* No. 1, New York City, NY: Menorah Association.

——1951/86. *The origins of totalitarianism.* London: Andre Deutsch.

Beitz, C. 1979/2000. *Political theory and international relations.* Princeton, NJ: Princeton University Press.

Benhabib, S. 2004. *The rights of others: aliens, residents and citizens.* Cambridge: Cambridge University Press.

Brown, C. 1992. *International relations theory: new normative approaches.* Hemel Hempstead: Harvester Wheatsheaf.

——2008. From international to global justice. In: Dryzek, J., Phillips, A. and Honig, B. eds. *The Oxford handbook of political theory.* Oxford: Oxford University Press.

Buchanan, A. 2000. Rawls's *Law of Peoples*: rules for a vanished Westphalian world. *Ethics,* 110(4), 697–721.

Caney, S. 2006. *Justice beyond borders.* Oxford: Oxford University Press.

Cochran, M. 2000. *Normative theory in International Relations.* Cambridge: Cambridge University Press.

Crisp, R. ed. 1996. *How should one live: essays on the virtues*. Oxford: Oxford University Press.

Einhorn E. and Logue, J. 2003. *Modern welfare states: Scandinavian politics and policy in the global age*. New York: Praeger.

Erskine, T. 2008. *Embedded cosmopolitanism: duties to strangers and enemies in a world of 'dislocated communities'*. Oxford: Oxford University Press.

Evans, G. 2008. *The responsibility to protect: ending mass atrocity crimes once and for all*. Washington, DC: Brookings Institute.

Foot, P. 1978. *Virtues and vices*. Oxford: Oxford University Press.

Foucault, M. 2008. *The birth of biopolitics*. Basingstoke: Palgrave Macmillan.

Gibney, M. 2004. *The ethics and politics of asylum: liberal democracy and the response to refugees*. Cambridge: Cambridge University Press.

Goodwin-Gill, G. and McAdam, J. 2007. *The refugee in international law*. 3rd ed. Oxford: Oxford University Press.

Miller, D. 1995. *On nationality*. Oxford: Oxford University Press.

——2007. *National responsibility and global justice*. Oxford: Oxford University Press.

Moorehead, C. 2006. *Human cargo: a journey among refugees*. London: Vintage Books.

Odysseos, L. and Petito, F. eds. 2007 *The international political thought of Carl Schmitt*. London: Routledge.

Office of the UN High Commissioner for Refugees. 2006. *State of the world's refugees 2006*. Oxford: Oxford University Press.

Pogge, T. 2002. *World poverty and human rights*. Cambridge: Polity Press.

Rawls, J. 1999. *The law of peoples*. Cambridge, MA: Harvard University.

Reiss, H. ed. 1970. 'Perpetual Peace' *Kant's political writings*. Cambridge: Cambridge University Press.

Sassen, S. 2006. The repositioning of citizenship and alienage: emergent subjects and spaces for politics. In: Tunstall, K. ed. *Displacement, asylum and migration*. Oxford: Oxford University Press.

Scruton, R. 2006. *England: an elegy*. London: Continuum.

Steiner, H. 1992. Libertarianism and the transmigration of people. In: Barry, B. and Goodin, R. eds. *Free movement*. Hemel Hempstead: Harvester Press.

Toulmin, S. 1990. *Cosmopolis: the hidden agenda of modernity*. Chicago, IL: University of Chicago Press.

Walzer, M. 1983. *Spheres of justice*. Oxford: Martin Robertson.

——1993. *Interpretation and social criticism*. Cambridge, MA: Harvard University Press.

——2008. *Thinking politically*. New Haven, CT: Yale University Press.

Wheeler, N. 2000. *Saving strangers*. Oxford: Oxford University Press.

White, S. 1991. *Political theory and postmodernism*. Cambridge: Cambridge University Press.

Williams, B. 1985. *Ethics and the limits of philosophy*. London: Fontana.

8

Feminist Geopolitics Meets Refugee Studies

Jennifer Hyndman

ABSTRACT

International relations and refugee studies represent 'two solitudes', a situation this collection aims to remedy. The same can be said for the relationship between gender and feminist approaches and IR, and between feminist thinking and refugee studies. This chapter aims to fill in some of these gaps by outlining salient gender-related approaches in humanitarian operations. In reviewing the development of gender and feminist thought in IR, an argument for 'feminist geopolitics' is made. This refers to an approach, or analytic, that combines post-structuralist critique in geopolitics and IR with material feminist theory to foreground refugees and humanitarianism in international relations. Using examples from fieldwork, feminist geopolitics is grounded in the 'everyday' life-worlds of refugees. By focusing on refugees, the unit of analysis shifts. Feminist geopolitics decentres the state, though does not ignore it, and insists upon multiple scales of security, from the state to the refugee household.

Why have the international politics of forced migration been largely ignored by mainstream international relations (IR)? What might a feminist analysis of displacement and asylum across international borders look like? The chapter begins by addressing these questions and discussing the salient gender-related approaches in humanitarian operations concerning refugees. It then traces the development of gender and feminist thought in IR, and moves on to make an argument for 'feminist geopolitics', an approach that combines poststructuralist critique in geopolitics and IR with material feminist theory to foreground refugees and humanitarianism in international relations. Finally, a feminist geopolitical approach is brought to bear on the gendered, racialized, and highly situated violence of war that results in human displacement and on the politics of refugee camps which demand a feminist approach. A feminist geopolitics, or feminist IR, has greater potential to be attentive to the protection of refugees because it decentres the state and insists upon multiple scales of security, from the state to the refugee household.

I begin by outlining gender-based approaches adopted first by development organizations and then by their humanitarian counterparts. Development agendas tend to focus on the alleviation of poverty, and yet their gender-based approaches have been uncritically adopted and adapted by humanitarian organizations to manage forced migration and refugees in temporary settlements. Neither sector has developed a comprehensive *feminist* analysis and practice.

WOMEN, GENDER, OR FEMINIST? WID, WAD, GAD . . . FAD?

While 'Third World development' has always been a part of international relations, especially during the Cold War when superpowers used development 'carrots' to woo potential allies, development studies and the more applied efforts to reduce poverty and enhance social indicators have not been central to IR theory. Gender-based approaches have largely been the domain of development studies steeped in world systems theory and other distributive justice approaches to poverty alleviation. However, I argue that such an approach elides issues of security at many scales.

The adaptation of development principles and programming for humanitarian purposes may seem commonsense. And the contexts in which they are applied differ vastly. Development work tends to involve long-term planning and change, and takes place in locations with stable governance structures and relative peace. Humanitarian activity to assist refugees, in contrast, occurs in a context of crisis where securing the 'right to life' is the first principle of response. Programming is temporary, at least in theory, until the emergency subsides and refugees can return home. History tells us, of course, that many refugees do not get to return home for years, if at all. So, the transposition of development concepts into humanitarian responses to refugees is fraught from the outset. Nonetheless, tracing its development is important to understanding how this occurred.

The introduction of 'women in development' (WID) in the early 1970s was largely a result of liberal feminist demands that women be *included* in the development project. Since then, several permutations of this formulation have been proposed, reformed, and challenged. These can be most clearly traced through the conceptual shifts delineated by now familiar acronyms: from WID, to WAD (women and development), to GAD (gender and development). As Eva Rathgeber (1990: 489) has noted, the WID approach is linked closely with modernization theory and 'is understood to mean the integration of women into global processes of economic, political, and social growth and change'. This approach became the dominant paradigm for understanding women's roles in development in the early 1970s, but by the end of the decade, another approach emerged, namely, women and development (Moser 1993; Lind 2005). This latter approach focused on the 'relationship between women and development processes' rather than purely on strategies to integrate women into development (Rathgeber 1990: 492). WAD approaches view the integration of women into a masculinist project of development as insufficient, and advocated separate projects for women designed by them.

Gender and development, or GAD, approaches were shaped by socialist feminist critiques of the modernization paradigm, emerging in the 1980s as an alternative to the WID and WAD approaches. Instead of focusing on women per se, the central concern of GAD approaches was the 'social construction of gender and the assignment of specific roles, responsibilities, and expectations to women and to men' (Rathgeber 1990: 494). Gender was relational and required reworking categories of gender identity, so that 'what it means to be a man' can change. GAD not only goes further in questioning the underlying assumptions of social, economic, and political relations but in fact 'demands a degree of commitment to structural change and power shifts that is unlikely to be found either in national or international agencies' (ibid.: 495). This commitment to structural and relational change is lost when agencies simply invoke the categories of 'women' or 'gender' in an effort to include gender programming in their projects. GAD attempts to probe the implications of gender identities and examines the division of labour *between* men and women.

The transformative potential of GAD thinking is often diluted by organizations that maintain it is impractical, especially in emergency situations where logistical challenges are acute and survival is deemed the goal (Hyndman and de Alwis 2003). Hence many non-governmental organizations (NGOs), humanitarian NGOs in particular, have sought to compromise an analysis of *power* by following policies of 'gender sensitizing' and 'gender mainstreaming'. Such strategies may take into account the social construction of gender and its iterative intersections with other bases of identity, but most often they reduce gender to an exercise in 'adding' women as beneficiaries or including women's perspectives to their larger frameworks of intervention which remain unchanged and unproblematized (Parpart 2000). In one sense, then, there is an unwillingness to face and name power differentials along lines of class, caste, race, and nation in humanitarian work. More analysis of 'the political', not less, is needed.

The United Nations High Commissioner for Refugees (UNHCR) introduced its Policy on Refugee Women in 1990 and guidelines the following year (UNHCR 1990, 1991). This was very much an expression of 'women in development' thinking. Women were to be included as a group that has unique needs and vulnerabilities rendered invisible by blanket, 'gender-blind' refugee policy.[1] By the 2000s, 'gender' had entered the lexicon of UNHCR, and a GAD approach was adopted. Sexual violence—which had been flagged as an issue in a note in 1993 (UNHCR 1993*a*)—also gained currency across the UN system and 'sexual and gender-based violence' (SGBV) was coined. As early as 1993, UNHCR had developed programmes to address violence against Somalian refugee women in Kenyan camps (UNHCR 1993*b*), but such programming was situated at the regional headquarters level and was not yet part of the culture of the organization.

The gender-based policies of humanitarian organizations like UNHCR provide a *grid of intelligibility* for field officers and other staff working with displaced populations (Hyndman and de Alwis 2003). They offer planning tools and checklists to assist in the organization and functioning of camps, but they do not generally allow gender identities or relations to *change* the assumptions of the overall planning framework in which field staff work. Historical context, regional geopolitics, cultural dynamics, and race relations are left for field workers to 'fill in' once they are on the ground. Such policies are flawed because they do not analyse the *intersection* of these multiple relations of power and the ways in which they shape economic disparities and produce differential outcomes in situations of humanitarian emergencies.

Gender has become something of a household word among both development practitioners and humanitarian aid staff. It is often treated as a portable tool of analysis and empowerment that can be carried around in the back pockets of both international humanitarian and development staff. Gender has become part of the development and humanitarian lexicon, to be employed when preparing proposals and evaluating programmes. Often there is genuine concern over those who might be excluded or marginalized in the delivery of refugee assistance, but gender has also become overly institutionalized in development and humanitarian programming. In my view, 'gender mainstreaming' is often code for integrating women and gender back into the potentially gender-blind projects of development and humanitarianism.

I want to argue here for a more fully *feminist* analytic in both IR and refugee studies, one that provides a more comprehensive approach to understanding the *production* of gender identities and of disparate power relations. The idea that gender and other social identities are generated differently across space and time, and have no essential pre-given qualities, is critical to changing them. This feminist analytic, then, is at once a tool for understanding the intersection of cultural, social, economic, and political relations, but also for changing them (Staeheli and Kofman 2004).

In earlier work, Hyndman and de Alwis (2003) defined 'feminist' as analyses and political interventions that address the unequal and often violent relationships among people based on real or perceived social, economic, political, cultural, and sexual differences. There is certainly more than one kind of feminism. The analysis and elimination of inequitable gender relations is a primary focus of feminist politics, but not the sole one. It is quite possible that one's status as a refugee is a far greater predictor of poor health outcomes than one's gender or sex. Likewise, separating one's gender from one's religious affiliation and class is impossible: what it means to be a refugee woman is shaped by historical and geographical context and conditioned by one's multiple social and cultural identities (ibid.). In short, gender analysis has fallen prey to institutionalized rigidities, limiting its analytical strength and practicality for planning. Feminist analysis and practice, on the other hand, are more analytically robust.

GENDER-BASED APPROACHES TO IR

Much 'contemporary political geography describes a "world without people" or at least a world of abstract, disembodied political subjects.... The ways in which knowledge is produced within political geography constitute a masculinist practice. It yields a kind of knowledge that is claimed to be universal (or at least all-encompassing) and impartial' (Staeheli and Kofman 2004: 5). The same can be said for IR. While a comprehensive discussion of all feminist scholarship related to IR is precluded here, the pioneering work of authors such as Cynthia Enloe (1989), Jan Jindy Pettman (1996, 1997), V. Spike Peterson (1992, 1996), Ann Tickner (1992), Eleonore Kofman and Gillian Youngs (1996), and Sandra Whitworth (1994) has been central to critical thinking around gender and international relations. From questions of 'where are the women in international politics?' (Enloe 1989; Pettman 1997), to 'security for whom?' (Peterson 1992), to probing militarized masculinities (Enloe 1994, 2000; Whitworth 1994), a sizeable literature analysing women, gender relations, and identities in IR has emerged.

In 1998, Zalewski and Parpart edited a volume entitled *The 'Man' Questions in International Relations*, in which they observed that theories and practices of international relations remained relatively untouched by feminist insights about gender and the international. Reflecting upon this tome in a new book a decade later, the editors note that

> The focus on man drew attention to the way masculinities, in their variable forms (which includes the simultaneous evisceration and inclusion of the feminine), structure the theories and practices of international politics but also—crucially—signalled quite clearly that the whole of international politics was gendered; a point more

easily, if wrongly, missed when the gender focus remains on woman. (Zalewski and Parpart 2008)

Most recent work in political theory and cultural studies has moved away from 'women' as a unified subject, instead examining how 'woman' is constructed in subordination:

Feminism, for me, is the struggle for the equality of women. But this should not be understood as a struggle for realizing the equality of a definable empirical group with a common essence and identity, women, but rather as a struggle against the multiple forms in which the category 'woman' is constructed in subordination. (Mouffe 1992: 382)

Chandra T. Mohanty (2003) has also written about 'woman' as an unstable category because it attempts to include as equivalent subjects women from disparate backgrounds whose differences from Western feminists exceed their similarities and solidarities with them. Likewise, Mohanty is critical of the production of 'Third World women', a homogenizing category that misses the nuances of class, education, caste, faith, and ethnicity.

In both IR and geopolitics, a reaction against the disembodied state-centric dominant narratives of international politics has led to a focus on bodies and embodiment. This feminist critique has emerged as a materialist corrective to free-floating scholarship, both in the realist tradition and in the poststructuralist critiques of this tradition, in IR and geography. On the one hand, this interest is epistemological: '[M]uch IR writing remains disembodied. The writers and their subjects do not have (visible) bodies' (Pettman 1997: 95). On the other, materialist feminism is also concerned with bodies as the finest scale of political space (Hyndman 2004).

Bodies emerged inscribed with differences that matter; bodies were gendered, racialised, culturalised, classed—and sexualized. Sex—as desire, danger, eroticized bodies, transgressions, violations—came through... as boundary markers or community possessions, as women warriors, as commodified cheap labour on the global assembly line, as labour migrants, 'foreign' domestic workers, and international sex workers. (Pettman 1997: 94)

In a turn toward feminist poststructuralist approaches, recent work in international relations treats 'gender as a noun, a verb and a logic that is product/productive of the performances of violence and security....' (Shepherd 2008: 3). This recursive understanding of power emphasizes the ways in which politics are an expression of particular constellations of power, rather than acts of volition. Such deconstructive impulses are vital to prying apart the now hermetically sealed tool of 'gender' in both development and humanitarian programming. However, discursive analyses of recursive power relations do not necessarily improve conditions for refugees on the ground.

Matt Hills' research (2002) on audiences argues that meaning is made or conveyed through acts of media consumption. Drawing on Judith Butler's poststructuralist understanding of how norms are produced [they are 'regulative ideals' in her words], Hills proposes the idea of 'non-volitional volition' (cited in Dittmer and Dodds 2008: 449). Laura Shepherd, also drawing on Butler (2004), puts it this way:

> I espouse a feminism that seeks to challenge conventional constructions of gender subjectivity and political community, while acknowledging the intellectual heritage of feminisms that seek to claim rights on behalf of a stable subject and maintain fidelity to a regime of truth that constitutes the universal category of 'women'. (Shepherd 2008: 3)

While critics of such an approach might argue that this leaves no subject to engage in, Butler's response has been that '[t]he deconstruction of identity is not the deconstruction of politics; rather, it establishes as political the very terms through which identity is articulated' (Butler cited in Shepherd 2008: 3).

This is what I call the Humpty Dumpty conundrum in relation to critical geopolitics. Critical geopolitics, and critical security studies, usefully decentre the nation-state and expose the power relations that produce dominant geopolitical narratives, but unless they engage more embodied ways of seeing, they will fail to put Humpty Dumpty back together again, so to speak. Nor do they necessarily question why Humpty is always falling off the wall. Without a feminist sensibility, critical geopoliticians and critical security studies scholars are left with well-interrogated categories, but no clear way forward in practice. Feminist and poststructuralist readings of geopolitics, like those of critical geopolitics, question not only the epistemological stakes but also the dominant categories of analysis, especially sovereignty and the centrality of the state as a primary political actor.

FEMINIST GEOPOLITICS

The work of feminists in political science and geography is foundational to the project of feminist geopolitics. Feminist critiques of IR and poststructuralist camp of 'critical geopolitics', or critical security studies, share a common concern about the centrality of states as the major units of analysis and action, a corollary of which is an emphasis on state security at the expense of other scales.

'Part of the task of critical geopolitics is the investigation of the (territorial) construction of political community and the exploration of the possibilities of constructing forms of political communities which are not so vulnerable to the violence of sovereignty' (Dalby 1994: 606; 2008). Feminist critiques of security have long challenged the tacit territorial assumptions of states by asking whether states actually render their populations secure (see Peterson 1992). If citizenship is asymmetrical in practice (Pateman 1989), then the security of nationals within the territorial borders of the state is also likely to be asymmetrical. What does geopolitical practice look like if their political community of concern is not the nation-state, but the security of a minority ethnic group in Georgia or of refugee women in Chad?

Geographer Eleonore Kofman (1996: 218) imagines a feminist geopolitics that would incorporate feminist analyses and gender into an extant set of geopolitical practices.

> The most successful incorporation of feminist insights and gender issues into geopolitics would dismantle and democratize geopolitics such that it no longer involved the personnel of statecraft located with the most repressive echelons of the state. Real groups would then begin to figure in the landscapes and maps of the global economy and power relations. Geopolitics would open out into a broader context which we could call global political geography, in which comparative analyses and the local, however that is defined, would also be included.

Her description of feminist geopolitics aspires to a more democratic and less punitive version of state-centric realist geopolitics. She also tacitly identifies a gap in the geographical literature: that the scale at which security is generally conceptualized precludes collective concerns, civil groups, and individual protection. I aim to extend the feminist imagination Kofman articulates by suggesting that a feminist geopolitical analytic need not only dismantle the dominant discourse of geopolitics but subvert, shift, and animate the geographically specific narratives of particular groups.

Just as critical geopolitics should not be understood as a general theory of geopolitics or an authoritative intellectual negation of it, neither is feminist geopolitics about ushering in a new order of space (Hyndman 2001). Whereas feminist critiques of IR query the primary categories of analysing difference, critical geopolitics disputes the taken-for-granted containers into which geopolitics are poured (Weber 1994). Both approaches implicitly or explicitly question the centrality of state as the principal site at which power is negotiated and inscribed. Developing a feminist geopolitical analytic is an important step towards reordering the conventions of statehood and their neo-realist assumptions.

Feminist geopolitics, I argue, is an approach to international relations and geopolitics that provides more accountable, embodied ways of seeing and understanding the intersection of power and space. I have made the case before (Hyndman 2008) and still contend that it refers to an analytic that is contingent upon context, place, and time, rather than a new theory of geopolitics or a new ordering of space. Specifically, feminist geopolitics attempts to challenge the prevailing scales and epistemologies of knowledge production in relation to international relations. They focus less on politics and more on 'the political' (Sharpe 2007) at various scales, from the macro security of states to the micro security of people, their homes, and livelihoods.

Within geography, '[c]ritical geopolitics is one of many cultures of resistance to Geography as imperial truth, state-capitalized knowledge, and military weapon. It is a small part of a much larger rainbow struggle to decolonize our inherited geographical imagination so that other geo-graphings and other worlds might be possible' (Ò Tuathail 1996: 256). This aspiration to create other possible worlds overlaps with the project of feminist geopolitics. Despite common political practice of deconstructing dominant geopolitical discourse, however, feminist geopolitics aims to expose the disembodiment inherent in non-feminist poststructuralist critique:

> Whereas postmodernist critiques are alike in exposing the domination dynamics of a binary metaphysics, feminist postmodernists expose the essentializing, instrumentalist move at the core of this metaphysics as itself a consequence of masculinist experience and standpoint. Without destabilizing the fundamental dualism of 'gender difference' (essentialized sexual identities), nonfeminist postmodernists effect a reinscription of the universal-particular (identity-difference) problematic as exclusively oppositional; they retain rather than transgress the oppressive boundary-systems of Western metaphysics. (Runyan and Peterson 1991: 76–7)

Political scientists Runyan and Peterson (1991) employ the term 'displace' in relation to realism because they present strategic interventions that expose what realism is unable to represent or deem 'real'. Feminist geopolitics builds upon this work, but also offers up the possibility of a reconstructive, potentially transformative politics that involves material engagement with people and places.

In summary, feminist geopolitics combines a materialist corrective to the poststructuralist impulses of critical geopolitics and critical security studies to challenge dominant modes of knowledge production in IR. IR often effaces certain scales and subjects, such as households, neighbourhoods, and even cities, where the politics and processes of forced migration also take place. Feminist geopolitics aims to recast war and related displacement, not as

collateral damage or even migration flows, but as a field of live human subjects with names, families, and hometowns. By representing war and forced migration this way, I have argued that feminist geopolitics offers more epistemologically embodied 'accounts' of war that more effectively convey the loss and suffering of people affected by it. People as much as states are the subjects of geopolitics. In what follows, I bring feminist geopolitics to bear on a pressing issue related to refugees.

FEMINIST GEOPOLITICS IN ACTION

One example of the way in which feminist geopolitics takes expression is in the critique and collapsing of the private–public divide around sexual violence once ensconced in international law on war crimes. The geopoliticization of rape as a tactic of war and not just a violent encounter between individuals has taken decades. Rape on the battlefield was a private act, the bad behaviour of random soldiers: 'boys will be boys'. Such acts were not considered part and parcel of conflict until the mid-1990s, specifically during the two War Crimes Tribunals for the Former Yugoslavia and Rwanda.[2] In June 1996, for the first time in history, the tribunal for Yugoslavia prosecuted rape as a weapon of war and a 'crime against humanity'. It issued indictments for the arrest of eight men, charged with sexual assault for the purposes of torture and enslavement. Ample evidence that men used rape to terrorize, humiliate, and contaminate the women of opposing ethnic groups in Bosnia-Herzegovina led to the indictments. An estimated 20,000 women endured sexual assaults in the form of torture and rape during the war in Bosnia-Herzegovina (Salzman 1998). In Rwanda, the estimated number of rapes in the context of genocide is 250,000 (Drumbl 2000). 'To rape women with impunity and to mark their bodies with the symbols of the other side is to assert domination and to symbolically assault ethnic identity in its most protected space' (Coomaraswamy 1999: 10). Men were also raped and sexually mutilated; in some cases they were forced to rape or sexually mutilate other men (Pettman 1996). People's bodies, construed as territory, become the sites of gendered, public violence on which symbolic constructions of the nation and its boundaries take place.

The ruling that rape is a weapon of war is significant because it publicizes sexual violence as a weapon of war. The tacit theatre of war was the battlefield, the public space around which the rules of war—the Geneva Conventions—have been written. But the public–private divide between the battlefield and civilian bodies has dissolved. People's bodies, homes, communities, and livelihoods have become the battlefields of contemporary conflict. Hence, notions of security must also be re-scaled, as a feminist geopolitics promulgates. By identifying rape as a strategic weapon of war, its violence is recorded as a public act and punishment for such crimes is legitimized. The safety of the body as the finest scale of geopolitical space is politicized (Hyndman 2001).

One important observation for both IR and for refugee studies is the 'geopoliticization' of human rights, resulting in human security in the mid-1990s (Hyndman 2007). Where legal covenants about minimum entitlements known as human rights were once the prevailing norm for development programming, the end of the Cold War ushered in the more politicized notion of 'human security'. Indeed, it was the United Nations Development Programme itself that defined human security in its 1994 report. The Canadian Government, as one example, adopted human security as a pillar of its foreign policy in 1996. Human security has a range of definitions and debates associated with it that I will not rehearse here, but it is a concept often applied to refugees whose dispossession implies multiple forms of insecurity: political, economic, health, and environmental.

If one takes the example of refugee health in a camp, for example, feminist geopolitics may help one to ascertain why disease affects one area and not another. To foreground gender as an automatic explanatory factor forces an approach that lacks an analysis of power. The Dadaab camps of Northeastern Kenya were established in 1992 and remain in place with more than 100,000 refugee residents living in the three camps of Ifo, Dagahaley, and Hagadera in 2009. The vast majority is from Somalia, sharing the same language, faith, and nationality. But such apparent commonalities hide other axes of difference that produce disparate outcomes. Those with relatives abroad who send money may afford to live in Nairobi and send their children to school there. Those without must live in the camps and send their children to school there. Class is critical; it is produced and transformed through transnational social relations and economic remittances (Horst 2006) and shapes how healthy refugees will be.

Likewise, discrimination against the so-called 'Bantu Somalis', descendants of slaves of ethnic Somalis who originally came to Somalia from Tanzania, remains today and has been transposed into the spatial organization of the camps. This group gets the least desirable bits of land, low and prone to flooding, and farthest from the central food stores where biweekly distributions take place. Sitting water is a health risk, and it is no surprise that the prevalence of malaria in these parts of the camp was higher than average. Gender discrimination was not the problem; racism and its spatialized effects were. They shaped the physical well-being of refugees and their 'health security'. Certainly, gender figured prominently during this same period when refugee women were assaulted while collecting firewood with which to cook near the camps (UNHCR 1993*a*, 1993*b*). This was a very difficult task in a semi-arid area where pastoralists normally moved *across* the land seasonally, rather than settled on it for long periods. Nonetheless, their vulnerability to rape and sexual violence was produced in one sense by the types of foodstuff donated and collected by the international UN agency, the World Food Programme (WFP). WFP acts as a broker for food aid given by countries with surpluses, though aims to raise cash and buy crops locally whenever possible.

In the context of the Dadaab camps, however, the vast majority of Somali refugees in the camps were pastoralists themselves, unaccustomed to eating and preparing grains and used to living off the milk and meat of their camels and cattle (Hyndman 2000). I remember one refugee telling me that 'corn-soy' blend, a flour donated by the United States to WFP, was not a popular foodstuff, and that they would only use it to feed animals. So, a feminist geopolitics in this context might question the wisdom of international 'donations' of rice and cereals if they have the unintended effect of creating unsafe spaces where women collecting firewood may be raped. This is an extremely practical example of feminist geopolitics in action, but the uncritical application of development practices into humanitarian ones warrants empirical evidence and argument.

Humanitarian needs assessments and planning tools in refugee milieux almost always include gender analyses, even if it is the simple disaggregation of population into sex-specific statistics. What they miss are more robust ways to analyse the power relations that produce marginalization, minority status, and exclusion. Refugees' lack of citizenship and its normal entitlements to mobility and employment are also not figured into their predicament. Refugee projects aimed at self-sufficiency can be short-sighted if they do not account for differentiated access to land, jobs, and credit due to refugee status. A fully feminist analysis takes stock of power relations that include gender but go beyond to analyse other axes of identity and difference that may produce disparities, exclusions, and even violence.

CONCLUSION

Feminist geopolitics in this context attempts to do two things: (*a*) challenge the prevailing scales and epistemologies of knowledge production in relation to international relations and (*b*) rework the ways in which humanitarian practice and programming is conceived. It eschews the state-centrism of dominant geopolitical commentary and the disembodiment of omniscient epistemologies. Feminist geopolitical analyses are more accountable to the safety of civilian, and, specifically, refugee bodies. Traversing scales from the macro security of states to the micro security of people, their homes, and (lack of) livelihoods, this short chapter has attempted to chart the challenges and potential for IR in refugee studies. From the disembodied space of neo-realist geopolitics, feminist geopolitics aims to recast war and displacement as a field of people whose security is differentially scored. By diversifying scales of inquiry and places of knowledge production in IR, refugee studies will have more grounds for connection with such scholarship.

NOTES

1. I worked as a field officer for UNHCR in 1993 and received no training related to gender before being dispatched to Bardera, Somalia.
2. One criticism of this talk revolved around the very 'humanist' notions of justice and politics described. While I understand the limitations of what I have called 'UN humanism', I am not simply endorsing the ways in which justice is meted out by the international war crimes tribunals. As Dianne Martin and Mark Drumbl have written, 'the increased criminalization of gendered crimes and hate crimes represents a reinforcement of retributive criminal justice model', one that may well be counter-intuitive to feminist politics (Drumbl 2000: 22). One must consider the context of such crimes and the goals of any response: is the aim reconciliation among segments of a shattered society? Is it punishment, so that by prosecuting perpetrators a local sense of justice is achieved and civil society can resume? Is the aim political, that is, to bring major war criminals to 'justice' for the satisfaction of certain allied governments on a more international scale? I thank Adrienne Burk for her insights on these geographies of justice and collective memory. Thanks also to Dan Hiebert for his insights on these issues.

BIBLIOGRAPHY

Butler, J. 2004. *Precarious life*. New York: Verso.

Coomaraswamy, R. 1999. A question of honour: women, ethnicity, and armed conflict, third minority rights lecture, Hotel Intercontinental, Geneva, Switzerland. 25 May.

Dalby, S. 1994. Gender and critical geopolitics: reading security discourse in the new world order. *Environment and Planning D: Society and Space*, 12, 595–612.

Dalby, S. 2008. Imperialism, domination, culture: the continued relevance of critical geopolitics. *Geopolitics*, 13 (3), 413–36.

Dittmer, J. and Dodds, K. 2008. Popular geopolitics past and future: fandom, identities and audiences. *Geopolitics*, 13 (3), 437–57.

Drumbl, M. 2000. Punishment goes global: international criminal law, conflict zones, and gender (in)equality. In: *Canadian Woman Studies* special issue 'Women in Conflict Zones', 19 (4), 22–7.

Enloe, C. 1989. *Bananas, beaches and bases: making feminist sense of international politics*. Berkeley, CA/LA: University of California Press.

——1994. *The morning after: sexual politics at the end of the Cold War*. Berkeley, CA/LA: University of California Press.

——2000. *Maneuvers*. Berkeley, CA/LA: University of California Press.

Hills, M. 2002. *Fan cultures*. New York and London: Routledge.

Horst, C. (2006) *Transnational Nomads: How Somalis Cope with Life in the Dadaab Refugee Camps*. Oxford/New York: Berghahn Books.

Hyndman, J. 2000. *Managing displacement: refugees and the politics of humanitarianism* Minneapolis, MN: Minnesota University Press.

——2001. Towards a feminist geopolitics, *The Canadian Geographer*, 45(2): 210–22.

——2004. Mind the gap: bridging feminist and political geography through geopolitics. *Political Geography*, 23, 307–22.

——. 2008. Whose Bodies Count? Lessons from Iraq. In: Mohanty, C. M., Riley, R. L., and Pratt, M. B. (eds.). *Feminism and war reader*. London: Zed Press.

——and de Alwis, M. 2003. Beyond gender: towards a feminist analysis of humanitarianism and development in Sri Lanka. *Women's Studies Quarterly*, 31 (3–4): 212–26.

Kofman, E. 1996. Feminism, gender relations and geopolitics: problematic closures and opening strategies. In Kofman, E. and Youngs, G. *Globalization: theory and practice*. London/New York: Pinter, pp. 209–24.

——and Youngs, G. 1996. *Globalization: theory and practice*. London/New York: Pinter.

Lind, A. 1995. *Gendered paradoxes: women's movements, state restructuring, and global development in Ecuador*, Pennsylvania State Press.

Mohanty, C. T. 2003. *Feminism without borders: decolonizing theory, practicing solidarity*. Durham/London: Duke University Press.

Moser, C. 1993. *Gender planning and development*. London: Routledge.

Mouffe, C. 1992. Feminism, citizenship, and radical democratic politics. In Butler, J. and Scott, J. *Feminists theorize the political*. New York/London: Routledge, pp. 369–84.

Ó Tuathail, G. 1996. An anti-geopolitical eye: Maggie O'Kane in Bosnia, 1992–93. *Gender, Place and Culture*, 3 (2), 171–85.

Parpart, J. 2000. Rethinking participation, empowerment, and development from a gender perspective. In: Freeman, J. (ed). *Transforming development: foreign aid for a changing world*. Toronto: University of Toronto Press: 222–234.

Pateman, Carole. 1989. *The disorder of women: democracy, feminism and political theory*. Stanford: Stanford University Press.

Peterson, V. S. 1992. Security and sovereign states: what is at stake in taking feminism seriously. In: Peterson, V. S. *Gendered states: feminist (re)visions of international relations theory.* Boulder, CO: Lynne Rienner.

——. 1996. Shifting ground(s): epistemological and territorial remapping in the context of globalization(s). In: Kofman, E. and Youngs, G. *Globalization: theory and practice* London/New York: Pinter, pp. 11–28.

Pettman, J. J. 1996. *Worlding women: a feminist international politics.* London/New York: Routledge.

Pratt, M. B. 2007. Conflict, Citizenship, and Human Security: Geographies of Protection. In: Cohen, D. and Gilbert, E. (eds.). *War, Citizenship, Territory.* New York: Routledge, pp. 241–57.

Rathgeber, E. 1990. WID, WAD, GAD: trends in research and practice. *Journal of Developing Areas* 24 (4): 489–502.

Runyan, A. Sisson, Peterson, V. S. 1991. The radical future of realism: feminist subversions of IR Theory. *Alternatives*, 16, 67–106.

Salzman, T. 1998. Rape camps as a means of ethnic cleansing: religious, cultural, and ethical responses to rape victims in the former Yugoslavia. *Human Rights Quarterly*, 20 (2): 348–78.

Sharp, J. (2007) *Geography* and gender: finding feminist political geographies. *Progress in Human Geography 2007*, 31: 381–7.

Shepherd, L. J. 2008. *Gender, violence and security.* London: Zed Press.

Staeheli, L. A. and Kofman, E. 2004. Mapping gender, making politics: toward feminist political geographies. In: Staeheli, L. A., Kofman, E. and Peake, L. J. (eds.). *Mapping women, making politics: feminist perspectives on political geography.* New York and London: Routledge, pp. 1–14.

Tickner, J. A. 1992. *Gender and international relations.* New York: Columbia University Press.

UNHCR. 1990. UNHCR policy on refugee women, Geneva, August.

——. 1991. Guidelines on the protection of refugee women, Geneva, July.

——. 1993*a*. Note on certain aspects of sexual violence against refugee women, Executive Committee, A/AC.96/822, 12 October.

——. 1993*b*. Refugee women victims of violence: a special project by UNHCR, a proposal, Nairobi, October.

Weber, C. 1994. Shoring up a sea of signs: how the Caribbean Basin Initiative framed the US invasion of Grenada. *Environment and Planning D: Society and Space*, 12 (5), 547–60.

Whitworth, S. 1994. *Feminism and international relations: towards a political economy of gender in multilateral institutions.* Houndmills, Basingstoke, Hampshire: Macmillan.

Zalewski, M and Parpart, J. L. 2008. Introduction: rethinking the man question. In: Parpart, J. L. and Zalewski, M. (eds.). *Rethinking the man question: sex, gender and violence in international relations.* London: Zed Press.

——and Parpart, J. 1998. *The 'man' question in international relations.* Boulder, CO: Westview Press, Introduction: pp. 1–13.

9

'Global' Governance of Forced Migration

Sophia Benz and Andreas Hasenclever

ABSTRACT

Even the most powerful nation-states are increasingly incapable of coping with the emergence of the new and the intensification of existing trans-sovereign problems that cannot be solved unilaterally. According to institutionalist theories, states share an interest in solving or better managing these challenges and in overcoming problems in the provision of collective goods. For this purpose they create international institutions that regulate the behaviour of actors within various policy fields. Because the growing complexities of trans-border relations challenge states' autonomous problem-solving capacity as well as the capacities of rather specialized intergovernmental agencies, more inclusive governance structures engaging private actors are also expected to emerge. Others, however, are less optimistic. They doubt the meaningful influence of non-state actors and the effectiveness of international institutions at least in certain issue areas. This chapter argues that the policy field of forced migration offers an ideal test case for these expectations. The international community indeed responded to the growing magnitude and complexity of the problem with the establishment, extension, and adjustment of the forced migration regime in general and the refugee protection regime in specific. Today, *international* governance of forced migration is a matter of fact. However, the existing approach might reach beyond international governance. We therefore ask whether *global* governance of forced migration can be observed. Herein two meanings of the attribute global are distinguished: governance of forced migration that *is* global (referring to the spatial reach of the governance approach) and governance of forced migration *in the* global (implying a multilevel, multidimensional governance approach). The subsequent empirical analysis identifies severe gaps in the protection of forced migrants. This leads to the final conclusion that global governance of forced migration rather remains a vision than a description of the actual state of affairs.

According to Josef Ackermann (2004: 9), CEO of Germany's major financial institution, nation-states are increasingly incapable of coping with the consequences of globalization. Even the most powerful states fail to unilaterally manage the dynamics of world markets, the complexities of climate change, the proliferation of weapons of mass destruction, the consequences of social disparities, or the spread of transnational terrorism. Governments need to coordinate their policies and to form international institutions to support their common efforts. But even perfectly coordinated state actions fall short as long as *international* governance does not transform into *global* governance. States have to reach out to the private sector to mobilize powerful allies and resources. Unless reliable trans-boundary networks emerge that are based on a 'partnership principle', meaning they comprise members from different sectors of society who share responsibility in the management of globalization, 'the world will fall back into a myriad of factions all pursuing their own special interests' (Ackermann 2004: 11).

Many doubt the emergence of such global governance networks, the effectiveness of international institutions, and the meaningful influence of non-state actors in world politics at least in certain issue areas where governments are unwilling to share sovereignty.[1] Others, however, are more optimistic. In academia, institutionalists of various kinds are rather sanguine that the international community will finally meet the challenge (Brühl & Rittberger 2001; Ruggie 2004; Schäferhoff, Campe, & Kaan 2009; Witte & Reinicke 2005). States as purposeful actors do share a strong interest in common institutions to manage trans-sovereign problems that they cannot address unilaterally (Hasenclever, Mayer, & Rittberger 1997; Krasner 1983: 2; Keohane 1989). Given the growing complexities of trans-border relations, governments cannot but realize the need of support from private actors. With the end of the Cold War the set-up of inclusive governance structures becomes even more feasible. Constraints and opportunities thus work hand in hand to give rise to a new 'global public domain' (Ruggie 2004).

We argue that the policy field of *forced* (or involuntary) *migration* offers an ideal test case for these optimistic expectations. In line with the aforementioned, empirical developments in the number of 'people who flee or are obliged to leave their homes or places of habitual residence because of events threatening to their lives or safety' are alarming (Martin 2004: 4). This holds for all types of forced migrants—refugees, asylum-seekers, (conflict-induced) internally displaced persons (IDPs), development-induced displaced persons (DIDPs), environmental and disaster displacees, and victims of human trafficking. With the end of the Cold War a peak of 18.2 million refugees was reached (Castles 2003: 14). Decreasing numbers since the mid-1990s recently reversed when figures went up again from an estimated 9.9 million in 2006 to 11.4 million in 2007.[2] This number even excludes 4.6 million Palestinian refugees. For the first time in four years, annual asylum applications in industrialized countries also increased to a total of 647,200 at the end of 2007 (UNHCR 2008*a*: 13–15). In addition, by the end of 2007 some 25 million were internally displaced by natural disasters (UNHCR 2008*a*: 2). The number of people compelled to move for large-scale development projects is also presumed to be high[3] while some 0.5 to 4 million people are at any given time recruited, entrapped, transported, and exploited by trafficking (UNODC 2006, 2007). Still, it is foremost the number of conflict-induced internally displaced persons that has been rising from an estimated 1.2 million in 1982 to 20–25 million in 1995.[4] During this period major increases were mostly due to conflicts following the break-up of the former Yugoslavia and the Soviet Union. By 2001, however, most internal displacement happened *outside* Europe. In 2007, over 26 million people were internally displaced in at least fifty-two (mostly African) countries (IDMC 2008: 6, 18, 23). This constitutes the highest year-end estimate since the first half of the 1990s.

This aggravation of the problem of forced migration was accompanied by a global normative change. *Internal* affairs are increasingly subject to *international* law and norms (Hasenclever & Mayer 2007: 16–17). Accordingly and although the majority of forced migrants are internally displaced, the trans-sovereign nature of the problem has been recognized. From a normative or legal perspective the international community is facing a 'Responsibility to Protect' internally displaced people where national governments are unwilling or unable to do so. From a rationalist perspective, neighbouring countries, regional and international actors fear destabilizing spillover effects (Snyder 2008). Due to these security concerns and to avoid economic or political costs, states share an interest in preventing or at least rapidly solving (internal) displacement crises as well as an interest in stopping IDPs from crossing borders and becoming refugees or asylum-seekers. This provides ground for the emergence of respective governance mechanisms.

The following shows that the international community indeed responded to the growing magnitude and complexity of the problem with the establishment, extension, and adjustment of the forced migration regime in general and the refugee protection regime in specific. Today, international governance of forced migration is a matter of fact. However, the existing approach should reach beyond *international* governance. We therefore ask whether *global* governance of forced migration can be observed. After introducing the concept of global governance, two meanings of the attribute global are distinguished:

governance of forced migration that *is* global (referring to the spatial reach of the governance approach) and governance of forced migration *in the* global (implying a multilevel, multidimensional governance approach). The subsequent analysis identifies severe gaps in the protection of forced migrants. This leads to the final conclusion that global governance of forced migration rather remains a vision than a description of the actual state of affairs.

THE EMERGENCE OF UNHCR AND THE REFUGEE PROTECTION REGIME

For centuries, nation-states' reactions to refugee crises remained entirely ad hoc. Later, mandates of intergovernmental organizations established in the 1920s and 1940s remained narrowly restricted to Russians fleeing political persecution, refugees from Germany, or those displaced by World War II. Policies and changes therein were mainly driven by economic interests and since 1945 by Cold War ideologies (Barnett 2002; Barnett & Finnemore 2004; Chimni 1999; Loescher 2001; Toft 2007). However, the fate of the so-called 'hard cases'—the unemployable, the sick, elderly, or handicapped World War II refugees—and new refugee flows from Eastern Europe, India, China, or Palestine led the international community to realize that the problem was not a temporary one. Therefore, UNHCR was established in 1950.

However, UNHCR also started as a temporal, non-operation agency that worked under the UN General Assembly. Its mandate was restricted to protect *individuals* (not entire populations) who had been displaced because of *persecution* by their *governments* (not conflict or other violent circumstances) *prior* to 1951. 'Protection' meant the provision of *legal* services only. The Soviet Union resisted the creation of the new body, pushed for repatriation rather than resettlement, and also never became a signatory to the 1951 UN Convention on the Status of Refugees, instead accusing it for protecting people associated with fascist and anti-democratic regimes. Still, the 1951 Convention finally regularized the status of refugees, set out 'some of the most widely accepted international norms', rights, and obligations, and, until today, remains the sole legally binding international instrument that provides specific protection to refugees. However, the Convention was based on an even more restrictive refugee definition than the one given in the UNHCR's statute. It only covered those displaced in *Europe* prior to *1951* and was therefore criticized for its temporal *and* geographical limitations. In addition, it emphasized the fact that a refugee resides outside his/her home country respecting the principle of sovereignty and enforcing the inability for an international organization to look within a nation's borders (Barnett 2002: 7–8; Barnett & Finnemore 2004: 81–2).

During the 1970s empirical developments forced UNHCR to expand and adjust its efforts, as increasing numbers of refugees were coming from developing countries. Again, the office did not only respond to shifting needs but was also driven by Cold War ideology. One reason for UNHCR's engagement in Africa was to block Soviet power (Barnett 2002: 9–10). Regional organizations also began to pay more attention to refugee issues. The Organization of African Unity (OAU) and the Organization of American States (OAS) developed their own policies and expanded refugee definitions in 1969 and 1984. UNHCR responded with its Protocol Relating to the Status of Refugees, waiving '(...) the temporal and geographic limitations that obstructed the expansion of the refugee definition in the post-World War period' (Barnett 2002: 9). The General Assembly extended UNHCR's mandate to protect forced migrants outside the official Convention refugee definition. For the first time, UNHCR assisted IDPs in Sudan in 1971.

However, the commitment by states to take in refugees diminished in the mid-1970s due to a decline in economic growth and increasing unemployment. Furthermore, the end of the Cold War sparked political and ethnic conflicts in developing countries, massively increasing (internal) displacement (Barnett 2002: 10; Loescher 2001: 287). Borders also became easier to cross given cheaper transportation and the disintegration of many of the rigid boundaries upheld by Cold War politics. As a result, asylum claims were on the rise. These developments reinforced the shift of the refugee regime towards a North–South rather than an East–West focus. Russia finally joined UNHCR, whose profile 'was raised during the Yugoslavia crisis in the early 1990s when the UN Secretary-General asked the agency to coordinate humanitarian action (...) significantly broadening its scope and responsibility' (Barnett 2002: 11). Hence, changes in the Security Council's actions, reflecting the UN's new emphasis on Human Security and the emerging doctrine of Responsibility to Protect, greatly affected the international refugee regime. Since the exodus of 1.8 million Kurds from Iraq in 1991, the Security Council considers the refugee problem a threat to international peace and security. According to Laura Barnett 'this was the beginning of the Security Council's move towards humanitarian intervention and is significant in that it treated refugees and IDPs as equally deserving of protection' (Barnett 2002: 13). Security Council Resolutions also declared refugee emergencies in Somalia, the Former Yugoslavia, Rwanda, or Haiti to be threats to international peace and security (Hammerstad 2000: 392).

In summary, over the decades, UNHCR shifted from a refugee protection regime to a more broadly based humanitarian agency. Today, the agency focuses on security, containment, and preemptive humanitarian action and assistance (including the strengthening of local civil society and democratic governance). In its search for more durable, long-term solutions UNHCR became more homeland-oriented and proactive (Barnett 2002; Hammerstad 2000: 396). The agency provides care for refugees on location and emphasizes international presence to encourage *potential* refugees to stay. Because refugee resettlement is no longer seen as a viable option, UNHCR's repatriation policy, rendered obsolete by the Cold War, came back into force (Chimni 1999: 4; Loescher 2001: 280; Turton 2003*a*: 13, 14). In addition, UNHCR now includes IDPs within its scope of responsibility. Since the establishment of the so-called Cluster Approach in 2005, a key aspect of the UN humanitarian reform agenda, UNHCR has even taken over the lead role in the protection of conflict-induced IDPs.

The Cluster Approach aims to address gaps in humanitarian assistance, to strengthen effectiveness through partnership-building, and to ensure predictability and accountability by clarifying the division of labour among organizations. Within this specific inter-agency initiative and beyond, UNHCR is working closely with non-governmental organizations (NGOs). While in the mid-1960s, UNHCR's NGO partners numbered less than twenty, of which half were large international NGOs, by 2007, the agency had signed 629 and 467 agreements with international and national NGOs (UNHCR 2007*a*; 2008*b*: 55). The largest increase in UNHCR's NGO partners was observed in the 1990s when UNHCR recognized that the magnitude of challenges exceeded its own capacity. The Partnership in Action Initiative was launched that later evolved into the Framework Agreement for Operational Partnership (UNHCR 2007*a*: 8, 18). Today, NGOs support UNHCR in various fields of activity and cooperation happens at all levels. UNHCR–NGO partnerships are either operational (voluntary but close coordination without financial support by UNHCR) or implementing partnerships (where UNHCR provides funds to an NGO implementing projects in the field, based on a formal project agreement subject to UNHCR's financial rules and regulations). Between 1994 and 2006, UNHCR gave US$5.4 billion mostly to international NGOs (43.4%), followed by governmental agencies (27.9%), and national NGOs (22.1%) for activities carried out mainly in Africa (45.7%) and Europe (28%) (UNHCR 2007*a*).

UNHCR also increasingly engages with the private sector. In 2005, UNHCR's Council of Business Leaders was launched to 'catalyze innovative public-private partnerships, to explore synergies among UNHCR's corporate partners, to assist in maximizing sources of financial and other support (such as knowledge, expertise, access and reach), to champion UNHCR within the corporation and in the external business community and to raise public awareness of UNHCR and its cause'. Members of the Council are the top executives of UNHCR's leading corporate partners, for example, Merck, Microsoft, Nestlé, Nike, and PricewaterhouseCoopers. These companies helped with fund and awareness raising, for example, the 'ninemillion.org' initiative for which Microsoft offered advertising and editorial space on its online properties and launched a 'Click for Cause' initiative where every internet search made by using Microsoft's Live Search facility resulted in a financial donation by the company (UNHCR 2007*b*). Microsoft also helped to develop solutions to reunite refugees, educated refugees through computer learning centres, and developed and provided refugee registration kits and software. Others are helping to improve refugee girls' access to education, to introduce mobile health libraries in refugee camps in Tanzania, to improve a major water treatment facility in Ethiopia, or to provide better information on refugee situations and humanitarian efforts on the ground.[5]

THE EMERGENCE OF THE FORCED-MIGRATION REGIME

Although UNHCR is the major player, the agency is only part of a much broader network of institutions working on forced migration. Since the beginning of the millennium, (forced) migration not only appeared on the agenda of various UN and non-UN agencies but was also linked with other policy fields, for example, (economic) development, security/peacekeeping, transnational crime or human rights (Newland 2005: 13). Increasingly, formal and informal *inter-agency* initiatives have been prompted to promote dialogue and cooperation across policy fields and to develop more coherent, comprehensive, and coordinated governance approaches. Thus, in addition to public–private partnerships, public–public networks emerged that reach far beyond refugees and UNHCR. Examples are the International Migration Policy Program (co-sponsored by UNITAR, UNFPA, ILO, and IOM), the Global Migration Group that brings together heads of ten (UN) agencies, the Inter-Agency Standing Committee (IASC) of the UN Office for the Coordination of Humanitarian Affairs (OCHA), the 2006 High Level Dialogue on Migration and Development of the UN General Assembly, or the 2007 High Commissioner's Dialogue on Protection Challenges (IASC 2009; Martin 2000: 31–3; Newland 2005: 13; UNOCHA 2008*a*). Outside the UN system, informal, voluntary, and mostly multilateral processes like the Berne Initiative, the Hague Process, the Global Forum on Migration and Development (GFMD), or the Global Commission on International Migration (GCIM) emerged (GCIM 2005; GFMD 2008; Newland 2005: 13–14).

Since the beginning of the millennium, decisive steps have also been taken in response to human trafficking. Between 2003 and 2005, the UN Convention against Transnational Organized Crime and its Trafficking Protocol came into force. Because previous instruments failed to provide a definition of human trafficking and focused mainly on the punishment of traffickers these documents constitute 'the first serious attempts' to fight human trafficking through international law (UNODC 2006: 49, 50). Already in 1999, the Global Program against Trafficking in Human Beings was launched that works with member states and regional organizations to implement the Trafficking Protocol by providing technical training and legal advice. Since 2002 and 2003, UNODC and UNESCO collect and improve data on the subject (UNESCO 2008; UNODC 2006: 48–9, 110). Finally, in 2007, the Global Initiative to Fight Human Trafficking (UN.GIFT) was launched to raise public awareness and mobilize resources (UNODC 2007). Despite these recent (international) efforts, however, the anti-human trafficking regime is only at its beginning.

The same holds for internal displacement, though since 1998, the Internal Displacement Monitoring Center (IDMC) has been gathering data at least on conflict-induced internal displacement which lead to an increase in and attention to the plights of IDPs (IDMC 2007: 12, 13). Especially the publication of the Guiding Principles on Internal Displacement paved the way for significant progress. Already in 1992, the UN Commission on Human Rights asked its Representative on IDPs to examine the extent to which existing international law provided adequate coverage for IDPs and to develop an appropriate framework. With the support of legal experts, the Guiding Principles, setting out the rights and guarantees relevant to the protection of IDPs in all phases of displacement, were presented in 1998. Since then, international bodies have welcomed and explicitly referred to these principles,[6] as did UN treaty bodies in their observations to states when monitoring the implementation of international law. The Guiding Principles have also been incorporated into policies of multiple UN agencies, of regional organizations (e.g. the African Union (AU), the Economic Community of West African States, the Inter-Governmental Authority on Development in the Horn of Africa, OAS, the Organization for Security and Cooperation in Europe (OSCE), or the Council of Europe), and of individual states such as Angola, Burundi, and Colombia among others (RSC 2008).

Very recent regional initiatives by the AU are promising, too. In October 2009, the AU approved a Convention for the Protection and Assistance of Internally Displaced Persons in Africa that will come into force within 30 days of ratification by 15 of the AU's 53 member states. Participants of the International Conference on the Great Lakes Region recently signed the Great Lakes Pact, which contains several important instruments that aim to guarantee IDPs their rights (e.g. a Protocol on the Protection and Assistance of IDPs and a Protocol on the Property Rights of Returning Populations) (IDMC 2008: 40). While these regional initiatives are only in the process of emerging in Africa, the OAS was the first regional body to endorse and apply the Guiding Principles on Internal Displacement. Already in 1992, the OAS Inter-American Commission on Human Rights established the Permanent Consultation on Internal Displacement in the Americas. Several international conferences in the 1980s and early 1990s also focused on the protection, assistance, and reintegration of uprooted populations in this region (IDMC 2008: 51). Finally, European governments continued to take responsibility for their internal displacement situations and worked to facilitate returns. Regional organizations, for example, the Council of Europe and OSCE, actively participated in these efforts (IDMC 2008: 88–9; Martin 2000: 30).

Again, cooperative institutions such as the Inter-Agency Internal Displacement Division within OCHA or the Senior Network on Internal Displacement emerged and various inter-agency tools were designed, such as the IDP Profiling Guidelines, the IDP Protection Handbook by IDMC and OCHA, and the Handbook for the Protection of IDPs by the Global Protection Cluster Working Group (PCWG) (Global Protection Cluster Group 2007; UNOCHA 2008*b*). Institutions outside the UN system also emerged—for instance, the Brookings-Bern Project on Internal Displacement (Brookings 2009).

This illustrates that the growing size and complexity of forced migration came along with a growing interest in and awareness of the issue as well as a growing demand for the international community to better understand and address this phenomenon. Especially UNHCR responded with a rapid growth in budget, staff, and mandate. In addition, many joint initiatives inside as well as outside the UN system emerged to address more or less all types of forced migration. International institutions like the very basic convention of sovereignty or UNHCR as a formally organized international organization are very relevant within this policy field. Today, the forced migration regime consists of principles (e.g. the Guiding Principles on Internal Displacement or the principle of non-refoulement), norms (e.g. codified in the UN Refugee Convention and its Protocol Relating to the Status of Refugees, the UN Convention against Transnational Organized Crime and its Trafficking Protocol), as well as rules and procedures (e.g. given in the Handbook on Refugee Status Determination Procedures or emerging from annual sessions of UNHCR's Executive Committee). Thus, *international* governance of forced migration within the established forced migration regime is a matter of fact (Stavropoulou 2008). Nevertheless, today's governance of forced migration might reach beyond the concept of *international* governance that does not adequately capture new actors, spheres of authority, and governance mechanisms above and below the state. Especially the increasing frequency and importance of public–private partnerships might support the thesis of an emerging new *global* governance approach to forced migration. Today, non-state actors are not only an increasing part of the problem (e.g. networks of organized crime involved in human trafficking or non-state actors displacing civilians in New Wars) but also part of the solutions (e.g. NGOs gathering data on IDPs and implementing projects on behalf of the UN or companies participating in UNHCR's Business Council Initiative). The governance of forced migration increasingly affects and includes non-state actors, who in the past have not been granted adequate participatory rights in policy-making (Rittberger 2008). However, neither the increasing number of non-state actors nor the pure existence of new forms of partnerships tells much about their true significance or influence within the forced migration regime.

FROM *INTERNATIONAL* TO *GLOBAL* GOVERNANCE OF FORCED MIGRATION

As a normative concept, global governance points to the growing need of coordinated responses by public and private actors to trans-sovereign challenges. Global governance, however, is also used as an analytical concept. Among others, John Ruggie (2004) and Volker Rittberger (2008) observe the emergence of new spheres of authority in world politics. Public and private actors do coordinate their policies in the absence of a world state. They create, and comply with, an ever-expanding network of rules intentionally designed to provide necessary public goods. In this perspective, global governance implies non-hierarchical, multi-actor policy-making. States and intergovernmental organizations like the UN remain active and critical in the conduct of global governance, but they are only part of the full picture (Rosenau 1995: 13; Ruggie 2004: 507). On the one hand, international bureaucracies emancipate from their masters (Barnett & Finnemore 2004). International organizations increasingly assume a life of their own, shaping the conduct of member states by their legitimacy and expertise. On the other hand, civil society actors, NGOs, the media, judicial actors, transnational corporations, or scientific communities not only deserve equal attention in the analysis of world politics, but are also equal in status when it comes to the constitution of rule systems. Accordingly, Volker Rittberger (2008) expects the decline of *Exclusive Executive Multilateralism* characterized by non-public intergovernmental negotiations and an at most informal access for non-state actors to decision-making processes. Instead, we should at least observe the rise of

Open or Advanced Executive Multilateralism that grants formal consultative status to certain (international) NGOs giving them the chance to raise their concerns and to offer expertise. At best we should observe *inclusive Multipartite Institutions* of global governance that provide not only public but also private actors with the possibility of membership even endowing them with formal participation, decision-making, and voting rights in the policy-making process of international organizations.

Global governance as an analytical concept fits nicely with neoliberal approaches to international relations. States as rational actors recognize a strong demand for new coalitions with private actors and start to set up corresponding multi-party networks to supply necessary public goods. But this is only half of the story. Global governance also supports the constructivist view that trans-border interactions are deeply affected by identities and ideas. Since the end of the Cold War traditional power resources are devalued as international bargaining chips. Instead, international bureaucracies, NGOs, and transnational corporations contribute financial resources and sound arguments. As far as governments start to listen to them as respected interlocutors, a new global public space emerges that cannot be understood in purely instrumental terms. The world changes because new actors provide new arguments that prevail in global politics. For both neoliberals and constructivists, the forced-migration regime should be an easy case. Neoliberals see a strong demand for multi-party action to cope with the potentially destabilizing effect for entire regions of millions of displaced persons. Constructivists, on the other hand, point to the deep normative change that has taken place within the global community since the end of the Cold War. The traditional understanding of sovereignty as state security has given way to a new and qualified understanding of sovereignty as decent governance to promote human security. The international community now recognizes a responsibility to protect which implies major efforts to support displaced persons and to improve their life conditions everywhere. Therefore, from both perspectives international governance should give way to global governance of forced migration. For one reason or another, governments should seek the support of private actors and form inclusive policy networks that address the misery of displaced persons.

The following two sections confront these theoretical expectations with empirical facts. For this purpose, we distinguish two dimensions of *global* governance (Dingwerth & Pattberg 2006; Latham 1999). We first ask whether governance of forced migration *is* global (in terms of spatial reach), that is, whether it (equally) covers all countries and regions or whether there remain severe gaps in geographical reach. The latter would fundamentally challenge the constructivist perspective since the *universal* concept of human security does not allow for major regional differences in the treatment of displaced

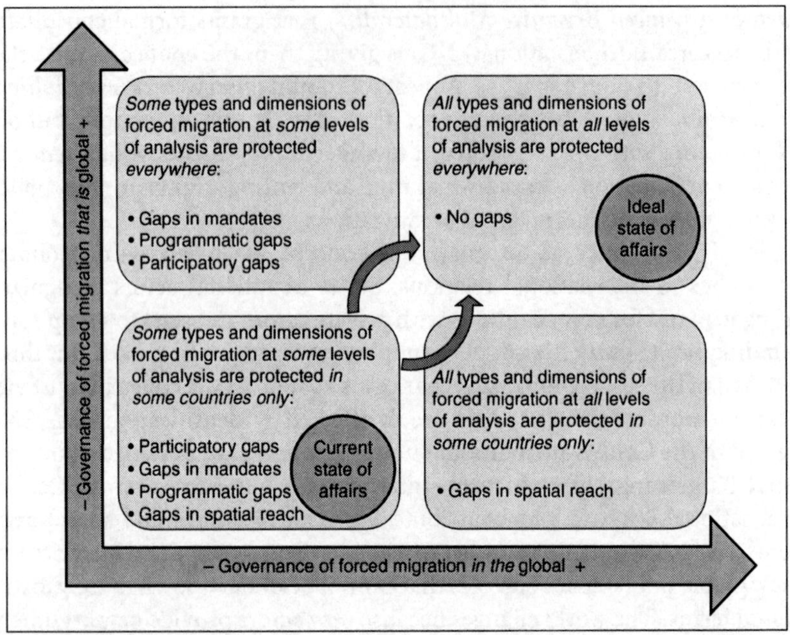

Figure 9.1 Taxonomy of the Governance of Forced Migration

persons by international and transnational institutions. Secondly, we ask whether we observe governance of forced migration *in the* global, that is, a governance approach that covers all levels of analysis and all dimensions of forced migration. On the one hand, we investigate existing instruments and ask whether they are appropriate to protect displaced persons of any kind. On the other hand, we look at the governance structure in this issue area. Do we indeed observe the emergence of 'global governance' in terms of 'inclusive multilateralism'? If not, what are the obstacles to fully integrate international bureaucracies, NGOs, and transnational corporations into core decision-making structures at the international level? Together the two dimensions produce the following fourfold taxonomy (Figure 9.1).

GOVERNANCE OF FORCED MIGRATION THAT *IS* GLOBAL?

Not surprisingly, global coverage and a high degree of homogeneity in forced migration governance are hardly found in reality. Differences in the severity of forced migration crises between countries and regions are due to the fact that causes (e.g. natural disasters or violent conflicts) hit countries or regions to a varying degree. Partly, however, these differences are also due to great variance in the extent and quality of protection, assistance, and crisis management provided at all levels of analysis.

For example, early regional initiatives in *Africa* (e.g. the two International Conferences on Assistance to Refugees in Africa of 1981 and 1984 or the Office of Emergency Operations in Africa established in 1984) 'had little lasting legacy', 'disappointed many', and remained unsuccessful (Betts 2004: 2; Martin 2000: 25–6). Only recent initiatives by the AU to protect and assist IDPs are promising. At the national level, governments' policies of obstruction and refusals to acknowledge internal displacement crises and IDPs' special needs, the denial of access to humanitarian agencies, or even the targeting of humanitarian aid workers inhibited the protection of IDPs specifically in Ethiopia, Zimbabwe, Sudan (Darfur), and Somalia. Although national authorities of other African countries (e.g. Ivory Coast) demonstrated willingness to provide better protection, their efforts remained ineffective due to lack of resources and experience (IDMC 2008: 39, 40).

Despite early and successful regional initiatives to assist displaced people in the *Americas* (e.g. the 1989 Conference on Refugees, Displaced Persons and Returnees in Central America), many countries in this region are also still struggling to adequately address the needs of their IDPs (Martin 2000: 28). IDMC reports that even where conflicts had ended with Peace Accords many years ago, 'structural and social inequalities persisted and the implementation of provisions to enable durable solutions to displacement crises was poor. It hinged on political will as well as capacity, and both were still broadly lacking in 2007' (IDMC 2008: 43). Limited political will to fund a reparation budget, to set up criteria to identify victims, and register those IDPs eligible for compensation hindered progress in Peru and Guatemala. In 2007, Colombia's National Reconciliation and Reparation Commission tasked to compensate victims of the conflict failed to decide whether IDPs were eligible and lacked funds and procedural clarity. The original causes of displacement remained unchanged. During 2007, IDPs' situation also worsened in Mexico, while El Salvador, Honduras, and Haiti not even attempted to establish the numbers of IDPs, let alone to initiate effort to compensate them for violations of their rights. Collective responses by citizens, often supported by NGOs or church-based groups, ran counter to the financial and political interests of armed groups and came under threat, for example, in Colombia or Guatemala.

In the *Middle East*, national responses to internal displacement also remained uneven and often ineffective due to lack of capacity, the absence of political will, and, most importantly, insecurity. Restricted access and threats to humanitarian aid workers remained major obstacles, for example, in Yemen or Iraq. At the regional level, the League of Arab States addressed internal displacement only indirectly because it touches upon politically sensitive issues such as the crisis in the Occupied Palestinian Territories or reconstruction in Iraq (IDMC 2008: 62, 63).

Restricted access for humanitarian aid workers (e.g. in Pakistan, Sri Lanka, and Myanmar), insufficient national responses, or even the refusal to acknowledge an IDP problem also characterize the situation in *Asia*. Most governments limited their actions to ad hoc humanitarian interventions, did little to improve their human rights record, and instead continued to be the main agent of displacement. Some countries (e.g. Timor-Leste, Indonesia, or Afghanistan) demonstrated goodwill but struggled with corruption or weak administrative capacity. This resulted in a wide gap between policy commitments and their implementation. During 2007, there were no regional IDP initiatives as the issue continued to be viewed as a strictly internal matter. UN involvement on behalf of IDPs in Asia was restricted to Nepal, Timor-Leste, Sri Lanka, Afghanistan, and (to a lesser extent) the Philippines and Indonesia. Assisting IDPs in Myanmar, Bangladesh, India, Thailand, Laos, and Uzbekistan was impossible mainly because of governments' opposition (IDMC 2008: 76–7).

These and other severe response failures at the national level, particularly in some of the most affected countries, as well as no, limited, or only recent progress at the regional level in Asia, the Middle East, and Africa stand in sharp contrast to the improving situation of IDPs in some single countries and in *Europe* (IDMC 2008: 88–9). Newland (2005) even notes that the EU has produced a comparatively high level of joint governance of migration issues in general (Newland 2005: 6).

The great variance in the extent to which IDPs receive support from their *national governments* is reflected by great variance in *national and regional norm-setting*. While some countries (Azerbaijan, Bosnia and Herzegovina, Colombia, Croatia, Georgia, and the Russian Federation) have adopted legislation providing for the creation of a 'national status' for at least certain groups of IDPs, many did not. The degree to which the process of return or local integration of IDPs meets national and international standards (e.g. in regard to informed consent to return) varies as well (IDMC 2008: 27). National and regional standards also differ for other types of forced migration, for example, victims of human trafficking. By 2006, only ninety-three countries worldwide had prohibited trafficking as a matter of law, relatively few cases are prosecuted successfully, and only 'sometimes' national jurisprudence sees trafficking as persecution (Betts 2008: 10). The latter contributes to significant cross-national differences in recognition rates of asylum-seekers (UNIFEM 2007; UNHCR 2008*a*: 17; UNODC 2006: 36, 48).

Similarly, only some countries do permit refugees to become naturalized (UNHCR 2008*a*: 11).

The degree to which national and international *non-governmental actors* are present, able and allowed to advocate on behalf of forced migrants, and to deliver assistance also differs between countries and regions. In some cases of state collapse (e.g. in DRC and Somalia), they provide vital state functions, including the provision of assistance and protection to IDPs, while in other places like India, Algeria, Pakistan, Rwanda, or Zimbabwe, governments severely restrict international involvement, insisting on the principles of state sovereignty and non-interference (IDMC 2008: 19, 21). Barriers to non-governmental activism are especially high in closed and repressive authoritarian systems like Myanmar.

Finally, protection and assistance provided by *intergovernmental organizations* also varies in coverage. Early organizations established to deal with the refugee problem focused exclusively on European and later Cold War issues. 'Refugees existed in other parts of the world, but these flows were generally ignored by a Euro-centric state system that concentrated on humanitarian action closer to home' (Barnett 2002: 15). Even UNHCR has not been truly international until the last quarter of the century. Loescher (2001: 10, 277) reminds that UNHCR only evolved into 'a truly global organization' during the decade following the agency's expansion into Africa in the 1960s. The break-up of the former Soviet Union at the beginning of the 1990s further extended the reach of the refugee regime by opening up an 'entirely new region'. Today, UNHCR at least in theory has a global mandate, encompassing all but the Palestinian refugees. However, in practice, UNHCR does not reach all those falling under its mandate. In addition, there exist differences in the treatment of refugees by the agency itself. Evaluation Reports found wide discrepancies between Middle Eastern countries in refugee status determination procedures conducted by UNHCR (Loescher 2001: 326).

Geographical bias also exists in regard to UNHCR's protection of and assistance to *IDPs*. Only in areas deemed strategically vital to the growing East–West confrontation, IDPs obtained the attention and resources of the nascent UNHCR (Toft 2007: 142). Even after the end of the Cold War, UNHCR only intervened in 'high profile IDP emergencies' like Northern Iraq and Bosnia but kept a cautious distance in other cases, for example, Chechnya. There, states avoided to directly challenge Russia, a major power and veto-wielding permanent member of the UN Security Council. Only after heavy public pressure the international community intervened in the Kosovo and East Timor crises that had no overriding geopolitical or strategic importance for Western states. The international community then focused its resources on these cases while hidden humanitarian emergencies and displacement crises in Africa were 'virtually ignored' (Loescher 2001: 295, 327, 335–6). Barnett (2002: 14–15) even speaks of 'racial discrimination in the governance of forced migration'. UNHCR itself admits wide-ranging variations in its assistance and protection provided to IDPs within comparable phases of conflicts and displacement, for example, in Rwanda (one-time relief) vs. Bosnia (around-the-clock engagement) or Sri Lanka (direct involvement) vs. Sierra Leone and Sudan (very indirect involvement) (Martin 2004: 305).

At least in terms of *membership*, today's international refugee protection regime is rather 'global'. Still, as of 1 October 2008, only 141 UN member states are also members to the 1951 UN Refugee Convention *and* its 1967 Protocol committing themselves to the protection of refugees and the principle of non-refoulement without geographical and temporal limitations (UNHCR 2008*c*). Almost all and exclusively West, South, and Southeast Asian countries have not yet acceded to the Convention or its Protocol. Other international conventions, for example, the UN and ILO Conventions on the Rights of Migrant Workers or the Trafficking Protocol of the UN Convention against Transnational Crime suffer from even lower numbers of signatories and ratifications and/or long ratification processes (Newland 2005; UNODC 2000). This reflects a 'lack of *normative consensus* on migration issues', a 'lack of basic minimum internal coherence in the current discourse of forced migration', or a lack of a 'common understanding of terms and concepts' (Newland 2005; Turton 2003*b*: 15; UNHCR 2007*c*: 4–5). Agreement on the very basic concepts of human trafficking and IDPs took decades and resulted in an IDP category that Turton (2003*a*: 15) describes as even more 'hazy and imprecise' than the category of development displacees. The fact that regional organizations came up with their own, extended definitions shows that strictly speaking there does not even exist a globally accepted definition of refugees. Without any agreement on basic concepts, not to speak of agreement on goals or strategies, it is difficult to see how a governance approach can ever be worldwide or global. Today, governance of forced migration covers the world's regions at best unevenly.

GOVERNANCE OF FORCED MIGRATION *IN THE* GLOBAL?

The above equates 'global' with 'worldwide' and refers to the restricted spatial reach of governance of forced migration. Contrary to this, governance of forced migration *in the* global refers to an all-embracing governance approach—the extreme (or ideal) case being an approach that coordinates activity at all levels of analysis while also covering all dimensions of forced migration. A truly global governance approach in this sense equally relates to all types of forced migrants, to women as well as men, to those fleeing new warfare as well as those fleeing traditional internal or interstate warfare. It covers the human rights as well as the material assistance dimension of protection. It embraces local, national, regional, as well as international actors. Obviously, this is not happening today.

While the international community has a locus standi (i.e. a sufficient legal interest entitling it to intervene on behalf of refugees), a comparatively strong body of legally binding norms, an instrument like the UN Refugee Convention and a specialized international agency like UNHCR designed to protect and assist *IDPs* do not exist (Castles 2004; Goodwin-Gill 1999: 20; Martin 2000: 18; Turton 2003*a*: 7). Although the Guiding Principles on Internal Displacement formed the framework for a number of legally binding standard-setting initiatives, the Guidelines themselves remain non-binding. Furthermore, UNHCR resisted an expansion of its mandate to fully include IDPs and is only willing to play an expanded role when the links between refugees and IDPs are strong and when serious protection problems require the Office's expertise. UNHCR's involvement with IDPs is also contingent upon a request from the General Assembly, the Secretary-General, the Economic and Social Council, or another UN organ, upon the consent of the state concerned and upon the availability of resources (Loescher 2001: 356; UNHCR 1994). Initial guidelines did not clarify the scale, scope, or duration of UNHCR's involvement on behalf of IDPs. Loescher (2001: 354) therefore identifies a lack of clarity regarding the allocation of responsibilities and a lack of predictable response as no UN agency can be counted upon to react automatically when there is an IDP crisis. Even the above-mentioned UN Cluster Approach will be implemented in cases meeting the UN criteria for complex emergencies only. Non-emergency situations with nevertheless significant numbers of IDPs and protracted displacement crises remain beyond its scope. By the end of 2007, the Cluster Approach was activated in only ten countries affected by conflict-induced displacement, hosting only nine of the 26 million conflict-induced IDPs worldwide (IDMC 2008: 20). Because UNHCR does not have a mandate to protect or assist all conflict-generated IDPs, the number of IDPs and people in IDP-like situations who directly or indirectly received protection and assistance from UNHCR stood at only 13.7 million at the end of 2007 (UNHCR 2008*a*: 18).

Development displacees constitute another group larger than official refugee populations, for whom there is no protective regime. Effective legal guidance is also comparatively sparse on *trafficked persons* and on very specific issues such as the restitution of property especially in informal ownership settings.

People fleeing new types of warfare also fall outside of the existing regime. In New Wars, deliberate violence against and displacement of civilians is committed by non-state actors. Yet, countries such as France, Germany, Italy, Sweden, Norway, and Switzerland do not recognize non-state persecution when assessing refugee applications (Barnett 2002: 13). This illustrates that today's regime neglects the protection and assistance needs of entire groups of forced migrants due to a lack in clarity or gaps in institutional mandates. Generally speaking, those whose protection needs arise from reasons other than conflict or state persecution and those who do not meet the definition of true refugees are less well protected or do not receive the same range of benefits.

In addition, programmatic gaps emerge if certain groups of forced migrants are not protected and assisted properly although the mandate to do so exists. Barnett (2002) addresses this issue for the category of *female refugees* who by the end of the 1980 had begun to form the majority of refugees due to shifting forms of persecution (Barnett 2002: 16; UNHCR 2008*a*: 12). Changes in the gender composition came along with changing demands in the provision of safeguards, physical and psychological counselling, how shelters are run, or how food is distributed. UNHCR started to institutionalize gender sensitization in the field, but there is still no legally binding instrument on the specific needs of female refugees. Refugee regime eligibility criteria typically focus on public forms of persecution, ignoring private forms, such as rape or oppression due to non-compliance with dress codes, loss of virginity, or refusal to enter into a contracted marriage. This prevents many women from receiving or even seeking refugee status (Barnett 2002: 16, 17). During the 1990s a few governments issued non-binding guidelines to govern their domestic policies. UNHCR's Executive Committee (ExCom) also published a Conclusion in 1993 allowing women to use the 'well founded fear of being persecuted' to encompass distinctly female forms of persecution such as sexual violence (Barnett 2002: 17). Yet, in 2008, the very same committee remains 'deeply preoccupied' by current and persisting protection problems and continuing sexual and gender-based violence and exploitation (UNHCR 2008*d*).

Some also see the central importance of *human rights protection* of displaced populations as being frequently neglected. Protection has been sidelined in favour of a more pragmatic and operational approach—'humanitarian emergencies came to be perceived chiefly in terms of logistics' (Loescher 2001: 363). Furthermore, during the 1990s, traditional concerns such as legal and human rights or humanitarian needs of individual refugees became subsumed within a security discourse (Hammerstad 2000: 395).

Finally, the governance of forced migration suffers from *participatory gaps*. *Affected populations* are often excluded in the planning and implementation of initiatives not to speak of decision-making processes in intergovernmental bodies (Loescher 2001: 363; Martin 2000: 17). Though perhaps the area with the greatest potential, partnerships with affected populations seem to be least developed to date. Others see *national and local actors* as largely excluded (IDMC 2008: 15). Even within the UN Cluster Approach that has been designed to close such gaps 'authorities and civil society actors are (...) not fully considered as protection partners by international protection cluster actors' (IDMC 2007: 15). A first critical assessment of this approach was published in the aftermath of the earthquake in Pakistan in October 2006. It revealed that 'local NGOs regarded cluster meetings as meetings of an elite group of foreigners, which (...) did not pay sufficient attention to the ideas and issues raised by local NGOs. The vast majority of NGOs, both local and international, felt that cluster meetings, which were always held in English, should have had an Urdu interpreter present to enable local NGOs to be involved. Even those who spoke English among the Pakistani NGOs said that they had difficulty in following all the UN acronyms (ActionAid International 2006). Within the refugee regime, the involvement of NGOs in general remains limited and tightly controlled. UNHCR thoroughly selects its NGO partners, dictates formal project agreements, and regularly monitors and reviews their work (UNHCR 2007*a*: 15). The agency determines which programme areas are open for joint initiatives while emphasizing that '(...) some aspects of protection are directly related to the performance by UNHCR of its mandate and cannot be devolved on others (UNHCR 2007*a*: 9). In addition, and although UNHCR proudly announces that around 75 per cent of its implementing partners are local or national NGOs they received only 20 per cent of UNHCR's partnership funds while over 40 per cent of the money went to international NGOs (UNHCR 2007*a*: 12).

In terms of distribution of *formal decision-making power*, it remains to be said that UNHCR's governing body (ExCom), which decides on policies and budget allocations, consists of member states only (UNHCR 2004: 2). Each year, ExCom adopts a set of conclusions and decisions which contributes to the development of international refugee law and are considered to be 'soft law'. Since 2004, NGOs are able to feed into the conclusions process through written comments and meetings held prior to the drafting meetings. Yet it is only ExCom members that participate in the actual negotiations of the text. NGOs are not even allowed to explain, elaborate, or defend the suggestions and comments put forward. In the 59th session of the ExCom only twenty-five NGO observers were present (ICVA Secretariat 2006; UNHCR 2008*d*). Thus and despite the fact that the UN and others very much and increasingly rely on the expertise and resources of NGOs, nation-states remain the gatekeepers and sole decision-makers within the decisive institutions. In their advisory and advocacy role, NGOs at best exert moral authority. These power imbalances between state and non-state actors hinder a truly global governance approach.

Similarly, the role of the *private sector* remains limited, mostly to funding and fundraising. In addition and although their absolute amount increased, private funds only constitute a very small and not significantly increasing proportion of UNHCR's total budget. Large increases in UNHCR's private funds only came in response to major crises (the Tsunami in 2005 or the Kosovo Crisis in 1999), rendering long-term planning difficult or impossible. A recent study on business-philanthropy partnerships (which looked at 20,000 companies and 550 NGOs, UN agencies, foundations, and others with which companies had partnered) also revealed that forced migration does not rank among the most popular issue areas for public–private partnership-building. Companies were asked to assess their partnerships with NGOs and UN bodies according to four criteria—accountability, adaptability, communication, and execution. UNHCR was only ranked sixteenth (though the third-highest UN agency) in terms of the extent and value of business partnerships (UNHCR 2007*d*, 2008*b*: 58). Because human trafficking has become 'big business' and many of us (mostly unwittingly) buy the products and services produced by forced migrants, this area of forced migration has great potential for anti-human-trafficking initiatives that include the private sector as well as consumers. Yet, 'the international community has [only] been discussing this (...) for ten years [and] has an idea of what should be done'.[7] Respective and inclusive initiatives such as the above-mentioned UN.GIFT have only recently been established. Similarly, the Hague Process which is praised for its inclusiveness remains 'chronically underfunded and understaffed' (Newland 2005: 13–14). Whether these and other initiatives are nevertheless the starting point of extensive public–private partnership-building on forced migration issues remains to be answered. Today, other policy areas (e.g. environmental protection, education, or public health) seem to be more attractive to the private sector. In these policy fields, states are more open to share authoritative power with non-state actors.[8]

Even a closer look at UNHCR's degree of authoritative power and autonomy within the entire regime reveals mixed results. Some accord the agency considerable moral, delegated, and expert authority, which it used to greatly expand the groups of people it assisted, and the kinds of assistance it could give, to overcome temporal and geographical restrictions in its mandate, to shape the agenda of ExCom, to obtain the capacity to independently raise funds, or to interpret and diffuse refugee law (Barnett & Finnemore 2004: 73, 77, 90, 93, 118; Loescher 2001: 1, 26). Many instances, however, also clearly demonstrate the boundaries of UNHCR's authoritative power, even a loss of authority and autonomy, or at least a strong influence of state interest and dependence from government funding.[9] For instance, after the end of the Cold War and despite the fact that states and ExCom were also exhorting UNHCR to favour repatriation, the agency 'on its own' shifted away from its 'exilic bias' towards a more favourable view of repatriation—even if circumstances in the country of origin are not ideal. Still, UNHCR refused to go as far as states wanted and insisted on balancing repatriation and refugee rights (Barnett & Finnemore 2004: 94–105, 119; Loescher 2001: 283). From another viewpoint, however, a new thinking about repatriation within UNHCR combined with state pressure for early repatriation. Some even see UNHCR 'bowing to the demands of its donor states', increasingly engaging in forced repatriation or violating the core principle of non-refoulement (Chimni 1999; Hammerstad 2000: 393–4; Loescher 2001: 17; Martin 2000: 23; Toft 2007: 154). The truth lies somewhere in between. UNHCR has been driven by both—the Office acting independently, as a purposeful actor in its own right with independent interests and capabilities, *and* by state interests (Barnett & Finnemore 2004: 90–1; Loescher 2001: 6).

In summary, governance of forced migration still fails to adequately include local and national actors, such as affected populations and (mostly national or local) NGOs. The role of the private sector also remains limited. States are the gatekeepers and decisive actors within this policy field. Thus, fundamental changes in the nature of sovereignty and authority cannot be detected. We at best observe 'Open or Advanced Executive Multilateralism'. Besides gaps in participation we identified gaps in institutional mandates, programmatic gaps, and gaps in spatial reach.

CONCLUSION

The degree and quality of protection and assistance provided to forced migrants greatly varies between countries, regions, levels of analyses, and types of forced migrants. Today, governance of forced migration cannot be regarded truly 'global', neither in terms of worldwide reach nor in terms of a multilevel, multidimensional approach. The 'current state of affairs' in the governance of forced migration therefore fits into the lower left corner of Figure 8.1.

Given constraints in resources, step-wise improvement seems reasonable: one strategy might be to first close gaps in spatial reach so that in every country and region the same but not all types and dimensions of forced migration are addressed. This lifts the current state of affairs to the upper left corner of Figure 8.1. However, gaps in mandate, programmatic gaps, and participatory gaps persist or are even reinforced by further exporting this imperfect approach. These gaps need to be eliminated in order to arrive at truly global governance. An alternative strategy first eliminates gaps in mandates, programmes, and participation in those countries that are already reached by today's governance approach. The current state of affairs then moves to the lower right corner of Figure 8.1. Because gaps in spatial reach persist, governance then needs to be spread for worldwide coverage.

Obstacles to global governance of forced migration are numerous and have only been touched upon. These include a *lack of knowledge and quality data*, particularly on certain aspects and categories of forced migration, and a *lack of (financial) resources and (local and/or national) capacity.* Finally, a truly global governance approach is perverted by states' interests. This can be referred to as a *lack of will* to agree on, implement, and comply with domestic, regional, and international norms, rules, and procedures; to intervene on behalf of forced migrants; and to share or transfer authoritative power. Especially insistence on the principles of state sovereignty and non-interference is blocking both, a worldwide as well as a multilevel, multidimensional approach. Once again, governments need to be reminded that their claims to territorial sovereignty are tied to their responsibility to protect their own citizens.

NOTES

1. For an overview of sceptical studies, see Hasenclever & Mayer (2007) and Rittberger (2008).
2. Despite large differences between and within countries and regions, refugees are overwhelmingly concentrated in poor, institutionally weak, and/or war-torn countries, mostly in Asia and Africa (Toft 2007: 146; UNHCR 2008*a*). Over 80 per cent of refugees remain within their region of origin and the majority is hosted by neighbouring states. Between 2001 and 2005, Tanzania on average provided asylum to 868 refugees per US$1 GDP (PPP) per capita. If burden-sharing is measured in this manner, the United States (US) and Great Britain only occupy the 34th and the 37th position (UNHCR 2005: 75).
3. The World Bank which funds many such projects estimates that they alone displace 10 million people per year (Castles 2004). In Asia, millions are displaced each year as a consequence of urban development projects, energy production, and natural resources extraction (IDMC 2008: 65).
4. http://www.internal-displacement.org/guidingprinciples [accessed 15 August 2009].
5. For these and other initiatives see http://www.unhcr.org/pages/49c3646c308.html, 08/13/09; UN News Centre 2005. From 2000 to 2007, the amount of

UNHCR's funds coming from the private sector was constantly increasing from US$15 to US$34.1 million (UNHCR 2001, 2008*b*).

6. The Commission on Human Rights (in 2005), the UN Security Council (Resolution 1286 on Burundi, 2000), and the UN General Assembly (Resolution 58/177, 2004) (http://www.internal-displacement.org/guidingprinciples [accessed 15 August 2009]).
7. A. M. Costa (Executive Director, UNODC) cited in UNOCD (2007).
8. For example, the Global Compact or the Global Fund to Fight HIV/AIDS, Tuberculosis and Malaria that involves multiple stakeholders within both the deliberation *and* decision-making process (Brown 2010; Rittberger 2008).
9. For example, especially in its early days, 'the denial of American financial and diplomatic support directly affected the UNHCR's ability to define an independent role and to implement its goals and programmes'. During the Cold War, the United States considered refugee policy too important to permit the UN to control it and simply created US-led organizations. The creation of specialized UN agencies to deal with refugees from strategic conflict areas undermined UNHCR's scope of mandate and authority, too (Loescher 2001: 7–8). UNHCR was also largely 'bypassed' by the European Union in the development and implementation of decisive legislation on immigration. During the Kosovo crisis, only a small amount of money was channelled through UNHCR and 'some governments and agencies simply (...) set up their own programs and camps without notifying the office' (Loescher 2001: 330, 317). Governments also earmark an increasing and large proportion of funds for programmes that are of political or strategic interest to them (Loescher, Betts, & Milner 2008: 94). The emerging problem of militarized refugee camps in the 1980s is given as another example for UNHCR's loss of autonomy. Because virtually all of UNHCR's funding came from Western states 'who had a geopolitical interest in supporting UNHCR camps, which housed anti-communist refugees' the High Commissioner found it hard to maintain an impartial and humanitarian approach. This 'cost [the agency] the relative autonomy it had developed during the Sadruddin era' (Loescher 2001: 12).

BIBLIOGRAPHY

Ackermann, J. 2004. The partnership principle. In: Stern, S. & Seligmann, E. Eds. *The partnership principle: New forms of governance in the 21st century.* London: Archetype Publications, 9–12.

ActionAid International. 2006. *The evolving UN cluster approach in the aftermath of the Pakistan earthquake: an NGO perspective.* Executive Summary and Action Points. URL: http://www.icva.ch/doc00001756.html [accessed 14 August 2009].

Barnett, L. 2002. Global governance and the evolution of the international refugee regime. *International Journal of Refugee Law* 14(2), 238–62.

—— & Finnemore, M. 2004. *Rules for the world: international organizations in global politics.* Ithaca, NY: Cornell University Press.

Betts, A. 2004. *International cooperation and the targeting of development assistance for refugee solutions: lessons from the 1980s.* New Issues in Refugee Research. Geneva: UNHCR. URL: http://www.unhcr.org/415d0d982.html [accessed 15 August 2009].

——. 2008. North-South cooperation in the refugee regime: the role of linkages. *Global Governance: a review of multilateralism and international organizations* 14(2), 157–78.

Brookings. 2009. *The Brookings-Bern project on internal displacement.* URL: http://www.brookings.edu/projects/idp.aspx [accessed 14 August 2009].

Brown, G. 2010. *Safeguarding deliberative global governance: the case of the Global Fund to Fight ADS, Tuberculosis and Malaria.* Review of Internation Studies 36(2), 511–530.

Brühl, T. & Rittberger, V. 2001. From international to global governance: actors, collective decision-making, and the United Nations in the world of the twenty-first century. In: Rittberger, V. Ed. *Global governance and the United Nations system.* Tokyo, New York, Paris: United Nations University Press, 1–47.

Castles, S. 2003. The international politics of forced migration. *Development* 46(3), 11–20.

——. 2004. *Confronting the realities of forced migration.* (Migration Information Source). URL:http://www.migrationinformation.org/Feature/display.cfm?id=222 [accessed 14 August 2009].

Chimni, B. S. 1999. *From resettlement to involuntary repatriation: towards a critical history of durable solutions to refugee problems.* New Issues in Refugee Research. Geneva: UNHCR. URL: http://www.unhcr.org/research/RESEARCH/3ae6a0c50.pdf [accessed 14 August 2009].

Dingwerth, K. and Pattberg, P. 2006. Global governance as a perspective on world politics. *Global governance: a review of multilateralism and international organizations* 12(1), 185–203.

Global Commission on International Migration (GCIM). 2005. *Migration in an interconnected world: new directions for action.* URL: http://www.gcim.org/attachements/gcim-complete report-2005.pdf [accessed 15 August 2009].

Global Forum on Migration and Development (GFMD). 2008. *Global Forum on Migration and Development.* URL: http://www.gfmd-fmmd.org/; http://www.gfmd2008.org [accessed 14 August 2009].

Global Protection Cluster Working Group (PCWG). 2007. *Handbook for the protection of the internally displaced persons.* Geneva. URL: http://www.humanitarianreform.org/Default.aspx?tabid=294 [accessed 10 November 2008].

Goodwin-Gill, G. 1999. Closing Address: Principles and protection: making it work in the modern world. In: McNamara, D. and Goodwin-Gill, G. Eds. *1999: UNHCR and international refugee protection,* Working Paper No. 2. Refugee Studies Center, University of Oxford. Oxford. URL:http://www.rsc.ox.ac.uk/PDFs/workingpaper2.pdf [accessed 06 December 2008].

Hammerstad, A. 2000. Whose security? UNHCR, refugee protection and state security after the Cold War. *Security Dialogue* 31, 391–403.

Hasenclever, A. and Mayer, P. 2007. Einleitung: Macht und Ohnmacht internationaler Institutionen. In: Hasenclever, A., Mayer, P. & Zürn, M. Eds. *Macht und Ohnmacht internationaler Institutionen*. Frankfurt/Main; New York: Campus. (Studien der Hessischen Stiftung Friedens- und Konfliktforschung, 53).

——, Mayer, P., and Rittberger, V. 1997. *Theories of international regimes*. Cambridge: Cambridge University Press.

ICVA Secretariat. 2006. *UNHCR ExCom Conclusions: update on process for NGO input to conclusions*. E-Mail to ICVA Members, NGO Participants of UNHCR's Pre-EXCOM 2005. Geneva. URL: http://www.icva.ch/doc00001739.html [accessed 14 August 2009].

Inter Agency Standing Committee (IASC). 2009. *About the Inter Agency Standing Committee*. URL: http://www.humanitarianinfo.org/iasc/pageloader.aspx?page=content-about-default [accessed 14 August 2009].

Internal Displacement Monitoring Center (IDMC). 2007. *Appeal 2008*. URL: http://www.internal-displacement.org/idmc/website/resources.nsf/(httpPublications)/9D27B2C5092B5F16C12573B70058F7A5?OpenDocument [accessed 14 August 2009].

——. 2008. *Internal displacement. global overview of trends and developments in 2007*. URL: http://www.internal-displacement.org/8025708F004BE3B1/(httpInfoFiles)/BD8316FAB5984142C125742E0033180B/$file/IDMC_Internal_Displacement_Global_Overview_2007.pdf [accessed 14 August 2009].

Keohane, R. O. 1989. Neoliberal Institutionalism: a perspective on world politics. In: Keohane, R. O. Ed. *International institutions and state power: essays in international relations theory*. Boulder, CO: Westview Press, 1–20.

Krasner, S. D. Ed. 1983. *International regimes*. Ithaca, NY: Cornell University Press.

Latham, R. 1999. Politics in a floating world: toward a critique of global governance. In: Hewson, M. and Sinclair, T. J. Eds. *Approaches to global governance theory*. Albany, NY: State University of New York Press, 23–53.

Loescher, G. 2001. *The UNHCR and world politics: a perilous path*. New York: Oxford University Press.

——, Betts, A. and Milner, J. 2008. *The United Nations High Commissioner for Refugees (UNHCR): the politics and practice of refugee protection into the twenty-first century*. New York: Routledge.

Martin, S. F. 2000. *Forced migration and the evolving humanitarian regime*. New Issues in Refugee Research. Geneva: UNHCR. URL: http://www.unhcr.org/research/RESEARCH/3ae6a0ce4.pdf [accessed 9 June 2008].

——. 2004. Making the UN Work: forced migration and institutional reform. *Journal of Refugee Studies* 17(3), 301–18.

Newland, K. 2005. *The governance of international migration: mechanisms, processes and institutions*. Paper prepared for the Policy Analysis and Research Programme of the Global Commission on International Migration. URL: http://www.gcim.org/mm/File/TS%208b.pdf [accessed 11 June 2008].

Refugee Studies Centre (RSC). University of Oxford, 2008: Ten years of the Guiding Principles on Internal Displacement. *Forced Migration Review* (Special Issue December 2008). URL: http://www.fmreview.org/FMRpdfs/GP10/GP10.pdf [accessed 15 August 2009].

Rittberger, V. 2008. *Global governance: from 'exclusive' executive multilateralism to inclusive, multipartite institutions.* (Tübinger Arbeitspapiere zur Internationalen Politik und Friedensforschung). URL: http://www.uni-tuebingen.de/ifp/taps/tap52.pdf [accessed 13 June 2008].

Rosenau, J. N. 1995. Governance in the twenty-first century. *Global governance: a review of multilateralism and international organizations* 1(1), 13–15.

Ruggie, J. G. 2004. Reconstituting the global public domain—issues, actors, and practices. *European Journal of International Relations* 10(4), 499–531.

Schäferhoff, M., Campe, S. and Kaan, C. 2009. Transnational public-private partnerships in international relations: making sense of concepts, research frameworks, and results. *International Studies Review* 11(3), 451–74.

Snyder, J. 2008. *Realism, refugees, and strategies of humanitarianism.* Paper presented at the University of Oxford, Centre for International Studies and the Refugee Studies Centre, 17 October 2008. URL: http://www.globaleconomicgovernance.org/migration/events.php [accessed 11 November 2008].

Stavropoulou, M. 2008. *Influencing state behavior for refugee protection: UNHCR and the design of the refugee protection regime.* New Issues in Refugee Research. Geneva: UNHCR. URL: http://www.unhcr.org/research/RESEARCH/481721302.pdf [accessed 9 June 2008].

Toft, M. D. 2007. The myth of the borderless world: refugees and repatriation policy. *Conflict Management and Peace Science* 24(2), 139–57.

Turton, D. 2003*a*. *Refugees and 'other forced migrants'*. Working Paper No 13, Refugee Studies Centre, University of Oxford. URL: http://www.rsc.ox.ac.uk/PDFs/workingpaper13.pdf [accessed 14 June 2010].

——. 2003*b*. *Conceptualising forced migration.* Working Paper No 12, Refugee Studies Centre, University of Oxford. URL: http://www.rsc.ox.ac.uk/PDFs/workingpaper12.pdf [accessed 14 June 2010].

UNESCO. 2008. *Trafficking statistics project.* URL: http://www.unescobkk.org/index.php?id=1022 [accessed 14 August 2009].

UNHCR. 1994. *Protection aspects of UNHCR activities on behalf of internally displaced persons*: EC/1994/SCP/CRP.2. Geneva. URL: http://www.unhcr.org/excom/EXCOM/3ae68cd11c.html [accessed 14 August 2009].

——. 2001. *UNHCR global report 2000.* URL: http://www.unhcr.org/4a0d27b66.html [accessed 14 August 2009].

——. 2004. *UNHCR global appeal 2005.* URL: http://www.unhcr.org/4a0ae8276.html [accessed 14 August 2009].

——. 2005. *2005 UNHCR statistical yearbook.* URL: http://www.unhcr.org/464049e711.pdf [accessed 14 August 2009].

——. 2007*a*. *NGO partnerships in refugee protection: questions and answers.* URL: http://www.unhcr.org.au/pdfs/UNNGOpart.pdf [accessed 14 August 2009].

——. 2007*b*. *Microsoft launches 'Click for Cause' initiative to support UNHCR web campaign.* (News Stories). Geneva. URL: http://www.unhcr.org/news/NEWS/45ae35054.html [accessed 14 August 2009].

——. 2007*c*. *Chairman's summary of the High Commissioner's dialogue on protection challenges*. Geneva. URL: http://www.unhcr.org/protect/PROTECTION/476146702.pdf [accessed 14 August 2009].

——. 2007*d*. *UNHCR ranked 16 in survey of business-philanthropy partnerships*. (News Stories). URL: http://www.unhcr.org/4694f3222.html [accessed 14 August 2009].

——. 2008*a*. *2007 global trends: refugees, asylum-seekers, returnees, internally displaced and stateless persons*. URL: http://www.unhcr.org/statistics/STATISTICS/4852366f2.pdf [accessed 14 August 2009].

——. 2008*b*. *UNHCR global report 2007*. URL: http://www.unhcr.org/gr07/index.html [accessed 14 August 2009].

——. 2008*c*. *States parties to the 1951 Convention relating to the status of refugees and the 1967 Protocol*. URL: http://www.unhcr.org/protect/PROTECTION/3b73b0d63.pdf [accessed 14 August 2009].

——. 2008*d*. *Report of the fifty-ninth session of the Executive Committee* (6–10 October 2008): Report by the Rapporteur. URL: http://www.unhcr.org/excom/EXCOM/49083d6d2.pdf [accessed 14 August 2009].

UNIFEM. 2007. *Violence against women—facts and figures*. URL: http://www.unifem.org/gender_issues/violence_against_women/facts_figures.php?page=5 [accessed 14 August 2009].

UNOCHA. 2008*a*. *Inter-Agency Standing Committee*. URL: http://ochaonline.un.org/Coordination/MandatedBodies/InterAgencyStandingCommittee/tabid/1388/language/en-US/Default.aspx [accessed 14 August 2009].

——. 2008*b*. *OCHA annual report 2006*. URL: http://ochaonline.un.org/ocha2006ar/html/part2_management.html [accessed 14 August 2009].

UNODC. 2000. *Protocol to prevent, suppress and punish trafficking in persons, especially women and children, supplementing the United Nations convention against transnational organized crime*. New York. URL: http://www.unodc.org/unodc/en/treaties/CTOC/countrylist-traffickingprotocol.html [accessed 14 August 2009].

——. 2006. *Trafficking in persons: global patterns*. URL: http://www.unodc.org/pdf/traffickinginpersons_report_2006-04.pdf [accessed 14 August 2009].

——. 2007. *UNODC launches Global Initiative to Fight Human Trafficking*. (eNewsletter, Perspectives). URL: http://www.unodc.org/newsletter/en/perspectives/no03/page009.html [accessed 14 August 2009].

Witte, J. M. and Reinicke, W. H. 2005. *Business UNusual: facilitating United Nations reform through partnerships*. New York: United Nations Global Compact Office.

10

Refugees and Military Intervention[1]

Adam Roberts

ABSTRACT

Refugees and IDPs are often seen simply as the victims of power politics. However, they are often involved in power politics, in various ways. Members of refugee communities sometimes form armed groups for self-defence or join armies that offer the prospect of liberating their homeland. Partly because refugee communities do often have a military aspect, large-scale refugee movements can be interpreted as a threat to international peace and security. International military action is sometimes seen as a necessary means of preventing or reversing refugee flows. Especially in the post-Cold War era, states and international bodies have often cited refugee issues as grounds for threatening, and embarking on, international military action, including forcible intervention within states. Similarly, as regards countries in which there are large numbers of internally displaced persons (IDPs), outside powers and international organizations have sometimes taken action aimed at preventing them from becoming refugees.

The first part of the chapter glances at five types of connection between refugee issues and power politics. The second (and main) part looks at the frequency with which, in the post-Cold War era, and especially in resolutions of the UN Security Council, refugee issues have been cited as part of the justification for military action, including interventions: nine examples from the 1990s are cited to illustrate the point. The third part explores some of the thinking about these issues at the UN. Finally the chapter draws some conclusions on the central questions: granted that considerations relating to refugees have played a significant part in the initiation of certain military actions, what are the criticisms of this trend? What are the problems that this connection with power politics poses for humanitarian organizations? And what are the challenges to be faced if the connections between refugee issues and international interventions prove to be enduring facts of world politics?

Scholars and practitioners concerned with refugee issues are often sceptical about all manifestations of war and power politics, which are seen as a significant cause of refugee flows and an obstacle to their resolution. In this perspective, refugees are first and foremost the losers in the game of power politics. This tendency to view power politics and war negatively is reflected in the UNHCR's publication *The State of the World's Refugees 2006* (2006, p. 3): 'The start of the new century has seen a decline in armed conflict when compared with the 1990s. Consequently, there have been fewer and smaller outflows of refugees.'

This chapter suggests that the negative view of power politics is too simple. It is not completely wrong, but it omits important parts of the story of refugees and refugee return. The quoted passage could easily be read as implying that armed conflicts in general are a main cause of refugee flows. The implication is doubtful not only because of the widely accepted fact that such flows can be caused by dictatorial government, social breakdown, and natural disaster but also because in some cases armed intervention may be a necessary condition for stopping and even reversing such flows. The same edition of *State of the World's Refugees* (UNHCR 2006, pp. 66–7) came close to recognizing this when it stated:

> In the late 1990s a number of UN Security Council resolutions marked the increasing attention of states to security issues arising from refugee movements. In these resolutions, states recognized that massive population displacement could constitute a threat to regional and international peace and stability, and even represent a deliberate strategy of war. More concretely, the Security Council linked population displacement to threats to international peace and security and considered such threats grounds for international action in Haiti, Iraq, Kosovo, Liberia, Rwanda and Somalia.

In the past few decades there has been a significant change in the approach and activities of the Office of the UN High Commissioner for Refugees (UNHCR). By a gradual process which began before the 1990s, UNHCR came to accept the legitimacy of discussing refugees as a source of security concerns; and at the same time it concerned itself increasingly with internally displaced persons (IDPs) as well as refugees.[2] These changes marked a departure from an earlier insistence on simply stressing the legal obligations of states towards refugees, and on sticking to an avowedly 'non-political' approach. This process was sometimes referred to as the 'securitization' of refugee issues (Hammerstad 2000). Sometimes 'securitization' has been viewed negatively as a wilful and culpable introduction of power political issues into the treatment of refugee problems. Sometimes it has been seen more positively as part of a transformation in the very idea of security, which was hitherto allegedly purely about state security, and was now being expanded to encompass human security—including that of refugees.

FIVE CONNECTIONS BETWEEN REFUGEES AND POWER POLITICS

In practice the connections between refugee issues and the conduct of power politics have always been varied and complex. Five distinct types of connection are noted here.

1. Refugees as proof of the unpopularity of certain dictatorial regimes.
2. Refugee flows as a contribution to ending the Cold War.
3. Refugee flows as an intended consequence of military actions.
4. Military dimensions of refugee communities.
5. Refugee returns as a consequence of military interventions.

Refugees as Proof of the Unpopularity of Certain Dictatorial Regimes

During the Second World War refugees from Nazi-controlled countries played an important symbolic role as legitimizers of the Allied effort. For example, the fact that many European governments in exile, based in London, supported the war effort and that many individuals from Axis-occupied Europe fought in the British armed forces contributed to the legitimacy of the British cause against Hitler. It could be seen as an international cause, not a mere pursuit of national interest.

Similarly, during the Cold War, refugees from communist countries who fled to the West helped greatly to legitimize Western positions. Although in some cases their political demands posed problems, in general these refugees were seen by Western societies as a prized asset, whose very presence exposed the faults of communist systems and the comparative merits of the West. Unlike some of today's refugees, they had considerable political and strategic value, and were thus especially deserving of help.

Refugee Flows as a Contribution to Ending the Cold War

Refugee flows were not merely a significant factor in the Cold War; they also played a major part in ending it. The events in East Germany, culminating in the decision on 9 November 1989 to open up the Berlin Wall, constituted a clear case of a very reluctant regime being forced to change and its leaders to resign by peaceful public pressure. Various manifestations of peaceful opposition, including mass emigration, had increased in

1989. From May onwards, a flood of refugees to the West via Hungary had forced many close to the regime to rethink radically the utility of the Wall and many other key policies as well. In the first eight months of 1989 there were 50,000 legal emigrations to West Germany; in addition, in August, September, and early October at least 30,000 left for West Germany through Hungary or via the West German embassies in Prague and Warsaw. The opening up of Hungary's border with Austria had started in May 1989 when the dismantling of fences on the border began. This had huge ramifications. By enabling East German refugees to escape from their country via Hungary it rendered the Berlin Wall pointless and led directly to its eventual opening. In addition, it raised hopes that the iron curtain could disappear along its entire length.

What enabled the Hungarian leadership to embark on, and maintain, so bold a step as the opening of its border with Austria? One factor was international law relating to refugees. On 17 March 1989 Hungary had become the first eastern European state formally to accede to the terms of the 1951 UN Convention on Refugees and the follow-up Protocol of 1967—an event prompted by the influx of some 13,000 ethnic Hungarian refugees from Romania. The 1951 convention was to prove a useful buttress to Hungary in the autumn in reinforcing its resolve to permit East German refugees to transit Hungarian territory en route to Austria. It provided Hungary with a good legal ground for repudiating on 10 September a secret bilateral agreement with East Germany, which had been concluded in June 1969 and which barred nationals of the other state from unauthorized travel to third states.[3]

The role that refugee flows played in ending the Cold War illustrates the extraordinary power that refugees can sometimes wield by the simple act of abandoning a country, and a political system, from which they feel deeply alienated. This power was non-violent but had major strategic consequences. Sometimes, however, refugee power has taken a more militant or even military form.

Refugee Flows as a Deliberate Consequence of Military Action

Whether or not it is publicly acknowledged by the power concerned, some military actions have as their basic purpose the eviction of inhabitants from their homes. Most such cases come under the grim heading of 'ethnic cleansing'. The fundamental purpose is not to kill all the members of a despised or feared population group, but simply to terrorize them so that they flee, whether as refugees or IDPs.

Military Dimensions of Refugee Communities

The UNHCR publication *State of the World's Refugees 2006* noted the phenomenon of refugee involvement in military matters, but identified this as primarily a problem of getting caught up in the rivalries within the host state. It referred to 'a tradition among refugee warriors of allying themselves with political factions—whether in government or opposition—in their host state' (UNHCR 2006, p. 67). This is certainly one aspect of the multifaceted problem of the involvement of refugees in, and their vulnerability to, armed activities of many kinds, but it is only one.

The idea that asylum is essentially a non-political and non-military status is an important part of the intellectual and legal underpinning of the international regime relating to refugees. Yet frequently refugees become actively involved in military matters. Moves to arm refugee communities can happen for a variety of reasons, including their need to resist cross-border attacks by their old persecutors, armed movements in their midst, or forcible repatriation by the host state. Refugees often aim to return, armed, to the country from which they had fled, in order to change the regime there which had led them to flee.

The story of Cambodian refugees in Thailand in the late 1970s and early 1980s illustrates many of these problems. The Cambodian refugees in Thailand were vulnerable to many threats; and armed elements among them, especially Khmer Rouge personnel ousted from Cambodia following the Vietnamese invasion in December 1978, benefited from the refugee camp operation on the border (Shawcross 1984, pp. 80–94, 340–61). Sometimes the modus operandi of a refugee assistance operation may contribute to the emergence of armed groups among the refugees. In Gaza, over many years, the UN had huge supplies of food and needed a partner to help distribute it. Hamas filled the gap, and did so effectively.

Refugee Returns as a Consequence of Military Interventions

Many mass returns of refugees to their countries of origin have happened after a military intervention brought about a change in the country's government. The two largest refugee returns in the past half century were both the consequences of military intervention.

- The return of some ten million of refugees from India to East Bengal after it became Bangladesh as a result of the 1971 India–Pakistan War.

- The return of almost five million refugees from Pakistan and Iran to Afghanistan following the 2001 war.

The Afghanistan return is the subject of some controversy. According to UNHCR, which played a key part in the repatriation process, between 1 January 2002 and 31 December 2007 a total of 4,997,455 refugees returned to Afghanistan. This is the largest refugee return in the world in a generation. It is striking that even in 2006 and 2007—years of considerable conflict in parts of Afghanistan—the returns continued, albeit at a reduced rate (UNHCR 2007, p. 36; 2008, pp. 8, 9; UNHCR statistical online population database).

Impressive as the figures of this return to Afghanistan are, four major qualifications have to be made. First, they have to be understood against the backdrop of the sheer numbers of Afghan refugees: at the end of 2007, Afghanistan was still the leading country of origin of refugees world-wide. Secondly, not all returns were fully voluntary. Within the countries of asylum there have been heavy pressures on these refugees to return, including the closing of some camps. Thirdly, many returning refugees have encountered the lack of employment opportunities in Afghanistan, and many have experienced dire conditions in makeshift settlements. Fourthly, displacement continues. In 2007 and 2008 unknown numbers of returnees left the country again. Also the number of IDPs within Afghanistan increased, and by the end of 2008 stood at about 235,000. Some returnees seamlessly became IDPs (Afghanistan Independent Human Rights Commission 2008, p. 49; Ellick 2008). Despite all these qualifications, and irrespective of whether refugee return was a purpose of the military operations in 2001, the US-led intervention in that year did undoubtedly provide a basis for the largest refugee return in the past thirty years.

REFUGEE ISSUES AS A JUSTIFICATION FOR MILITARY ACTION

Military action as a response to violations of human rights and humanitarian norms, including situations leading to refugee flows, has a long history. In the 1820s, it was largely as a consequence of reported Turkish atrocities that French and British governments decided to give naval support to the cause of Greek independence from Ottoman rule. The history of European colonialism is replete with cases in which a public justification for intervention was the violation of basic humanitarian norms in one or another part of the non-European world.

In the post-Cold War era there has been a developing practice of using military action to protect civilians, including refugees and IDPs. This subject is controversial. An exploration of it may challenge the long-standing and important principle that the law relating to resort to war (*jus ad bellum*) is a separate and distinct subject from the law relating to conduct in war (*jus in bello*). Likewise, any suggestion that humanitarian and human rights workers and organizations may play some part in triggering military action challenges their deep (and in some cases legally based) commitment to impartiality and neutrality.

'Military action' is a broad term. It may involve war or intervention but is not synonymous with either of them. As used here, it encompasses the use of military force, or the explicit threat of such use, for a variety of purposes that can include altering the policies of particular factions or governments; weakening or defeating certain armed forces and the infrastructure that supports them; arresting suspected violators of the law of war; providing humanitarian relief; and providing physical protection for vulnerable people, activities, and institutions. Specifically regarding refugees and IDPs, it may include not only aid to them but also attempts to prevent situations from degenerating to the point where they cause large refugee flows. Its forms can include the use of air, naval, and land forces, whether in direct combat operations, in protection, in intervention in a state, or in making threats against a particular state or group.

Military action can have several types of legal authorization. In some cases it has a legal basis in the consent of the government of the state where the action takes place. As for external authorization, this can assume three main forms.

1. UN command and control, as with enforcement operations which are approved by the Security Council and remain directly under UN.
2. Action following a UN authorization under which powers are delegated to national or alliance command and control.
3. Action without explicit UN backing, for example, under the auspices of a regional alliance or organization.

The broad subject of military action as considered here overlaps with, but is not quite the same as, humanitarian intervention. 'Humanitarian intervention' in its classical sense means military intervention in a state, without the approval of its authorities, and with the purpose of preventing widespread suffering or death among the inhabitants. Shorn of the epithet 'humanitarian', the term 'intervention' still carries an implication of forcible action against the wishes of the government of the state concerned. Many military actions with stated humanitarian purposes fit these definitions of intervention, but by no means do all. Some, indeed, may have the explicit consent of the government of the territory in which the action takes place (e.g. when such action is taken against insurgents or separatists in a civil war) and therefore do not count as interventions in the classical sense, whether humanitarian or otherwise. Equally, some actions, even if grounded in humanitarian considerations, may have other purposes (e.g. concern with international peace and security) that are not strictly speaking humanitarian, and are therefore doubtful candidates for inclusion in the category of 'humanitarian intervention'.

In a single decade—1991 to 2000—there were at least nine crises in which humanitarian issues, including actual or potential refugee flows, were referred to prominently in UN Security Council resolutions, after which military action was authorized either by the UN Security Council itself or (in the case of northern Iraq and Kosovo) by major Western states. In all but the first of these cases, relevant Security Council resolutions explicitly referred to Chapter VII of the UN Charter, indicating that the Council's powers to take action, including sanctions and enforcement, were being invoked. These nine cases are briefly outlined below. Many more examples could be added from the first decade of the present century.

Of particular importance in the nine cases is the reluctance or refusal of neighbouring countries to accept large numbers of refugees, and the consequent need to remedy the refugee-producing situation at source. The desire to avert or reverse refugee flows is not specifically mentioned in every one of the resolutions concerned, but it may be hinted at in more general references to the regionally destabilizing effects of a crisis within one country. In short, it is evident that averting refugee flows was one motive, or at least public rationale, for a wide range of military actions.

Northern Iraq, 1991

Following a failed uprising within Iraq after the end of the 1991 Gulf War there was a huge exodus of Kurds and others to neighbouring countries, especially Turkey and Iran. Turkey refused admission, leaving thousands of refugees stranded in the mountains on its border with Iraq. A UN Security Council resolution in April 1991 required that 'Iraq allow immediate access by international humanitarian organizations to all those in need of assistance in all parts of Iraq'.[4] This was not adopted explicitly under Chapter VII of the UN Charter, but it did state that Iraqi actions causing refugee flows 'threaten international peace and security in the region'. The resolution, while less than a formal authorization of intervention, was of considerable help to the United States and its coalition partners when the US-led military operation within northern Iraq began on 17 April 1991. Iraq subsequently consented to the presence of the UN Guards Contingent in Iraq (UNGCI).

Bosnia and Herzegovina, 1992–5

During this war, a principal motive for the high degree of external involvement was to reduce the risk of refugee flows. The situation was typical of many post-Cold War conflicts in that policy on refugees and IDPs was heavily influenced by the reluctance of developed Western states to take more refugees. The UNHCR, under the leadership of Mrs Sadako Ogata, took the fateful decision to be the lead agency within the former Yugoslavia for delivery of humanitarian aid—thus undertaking actions very different from the traditional UNHCR role of assisting people once they had become refugees. Protection and provision of inhabitants in situ, including in the six 'safe areas' in Bosnia, was seen as a means of warding off a feared refugee flow. This was one important rationale for the UN Protection Force (UNPROFOR)—the UN peacekeeping operation in the former Yugoslavia.

The terms of the many Security Council resolutions about Bosnia confirm that limiting the causes of refugee flows was one purpose of the involvement, and that force might be used if necessary. From as early as June 1992 onwards several UN Security Council resolutions on Bosnia suggested that if UNPROFOR and its humanitarian activities were obstructed, further measures not based on the consent of the parties might be taken to ensure delivery of humanitarian assistance.[5] The resolutions on the 'safe areas' in Bosnia approved by the Security Council in April–June 1993 all condemned violations of international humanitarian law, and referred also to other humanitarian considerations, including the Security Council's duty to prevent the crime of genocide and its condemnation of 'ethnic cleansing'.[6] Certain subsequent uses of force by NATO in Bosnia in 1993–5 were based on these resolutions.

Somalia, 1992–3

A UN Security Council resolution passed on 3 December 1992 broke new ground when it authorized military action against a state not because it had attacked other countries, but because of internal chaos. The resolution determined 'that the magnitude of the human tragedy caused by the conflict in Somalia…constitutes a threat to international peace and security'. This may well have been a reference to actual or anticipated refugee flows. It also referred to 'the urgent calls from Somalia for the international community to take measures to ensure the delivery of humanitarian assistance in Somalia', and expressed alarm at 'continuing reports of widespread violations of international humanitarian law occurring in Somalia'.[7] This resolution was the basis for the US-led invasion of 9 December 1992 by the Unified Task Force (UNITAF).

In 1993, the expanded UN peacekeeping force, UN Operation in Somalia (UNOSOM II), was established on the basis of a resolution 'deploring the acts of violence against persons engaging in humanitarian efforts' and 'expressing its appreciation for the invaluable assistance the neighbouring countries have been providing to the international community in its efforts to restore peace and security in Somalia and to host large numbers of refugees displaced by the conflict and taking note of the difficulties caused to them due to the presence of refugees in their territories'.[8] This resolution accorded UNOSOM II specific powers of enforcement, confirming that it was intended to be more than a normal peacekeeping force. It left Somalia in March 1995 following a number of disastrous incidents, mainly in Mogadishu in 1993 and 1994, which raised questions about the command structure and purposes of the international forces in Somalia and about their failures to observe fundamental humanitarian norms. Subsequently the continuing internal crisis in Somalia resulted in large refugee flows to neighbouring countries, as had been feared in 1992.

Rwanda, 1994

The UN response to the genocide in Rwanda in April–July 1994 was marked by weakness and indecision, despite the presence in the country of a small peacekeeping force, the UN Assistance Mission for Rwanda (UNAMIR). When the Security Council did begin to call for forceful action in response to the crisis, it stressed the importance of humanitarian issues as a basis for such action. For example, a resolution on these lines passed in April 1994 stated:

> *Deeply concerned* that the situation in Rwanda, which has resulted in the death of many thousands of innocent civilians, including women and children, the internal displacement of a significant percentage of the Rwandan population, and the massive exodus of refugees to neighbouring countries, constitutes a humanitarian crisis of enormous proportions,...

The resolution then decided on an expansion of UNAMIR's mandate to include these additional responsibilities:

1. To contribute to the security and protection of displaced persons, refugees, and civilians at risk in Rwanda, including through the establishment and maintenance, where feasible, of secure humanitarian areas; and

2. To provide security and support for the distribution of relief supplies and humanitarian relief operations.[9]

This mandate was repeated and reaffirmed in a resolution in early June, which referred to 'reports indicating that acts of genocide have occurred in Rwanda', and underscored that 'the internal displacement of some 1.5 million Rwandans facing starvation and disease and the massive exodus of refugees to neighbouring countries constitute a humanitarian crisis of enormous proportions'.[10] Great difficulties arose in obtaining forces to go to Rwanda to carry out the mandate.

On 22 June, in a further decision on Rwanda, the Security Council accepted an offer from France and other member states to establish a temporary operation there under French command and control. The Council authorized France to use 'all necessary means to achieve the humanitarian objectives' that had been set out in the resolutions cited above.[11] This was the prelude to the controversial French-led 'Opération Turquoise' in western Rwanda in the summer of 1994.

Haiti, 1994

Following the *coup d'état* in Haiti in September 1991, the UN Security Council eventually passed a resolution in July 1994 stating *inter alia* that it was 'gravely concerned by the significant further deterioration of the humanitarian situation in Haiti, in particular the continuing escalation by the illegal de facto regime of systematic violations of civil liberties, the desperate plight of Haitian refugees and the recent expulsion of the staff of the International Civilian Mission (MICIVH)', and authorizing the use of 'all necessary means to facilitate the departure from Haiti of the military leadership...and to establish and maintain a secure and stable environment'.[12] This resolution is remarkable for its unequivocal call for action to topple an existing regime. It was undoubtedly the refugee issue, and the admirable campaign waged by the Congressional black caucus on behalf of Haitian refugees, which got the US government, neighbouring governments, and the UN Security Council to the point of authorizing intervention within a sovereign state.

The US-led Multinational Force in Haiti (MNF) arrived in September 1994, with the last-minute consent of the military regime to its presence. In 1995 its place was taken by the UN Mission in Haiti (UNMIH)—a peacekeeping force which inherited the powers, including those under Chapter VII, which had earlier been accorded to the MNF.[13] These and subsequent outside involvements did not suddenly transform the situation in Haiti, which remained difficult, but they did significantly reduce the refugee flows.

Albania, 1997

In March 1997, during a period of widespread disorder in Albania, there was a large refugee exodus, mainly by boat, which became 'the biggest maritime exodus from a European country since the Second World War'.[14] This was a key part of the background against which the UN Security Council adopted a resolution approving the establishment of an Italian-led multinational protection force (MPF) 'to facilitate the safe and prompt delivery of humanitarian assistance, and to help create a secure environment for the missions of international organizations in Albania, including those providing humanitarian assistance'.[15] This operation had the consent of the beleaguered Albanian government. The MPF was deployed in Albania shortly after the resolution was passed, and by the time that the force was withdrawn in June it had contributed significantly to the restoration of order.

Kosovo, 1998–9

Following the outbreak of hostilities and atrocities in Kosovo from February 1998 onwards, and a worsening of the situation over the summer, the UN Security Council passed a resolution in September 1998 demanding that the parties take certain concrete steps including a cease-fire and acceptance of an effective international monitoring force in the province. In the course of repeated references to humanitarian issues, this resolution stated that a main purpose was 'to avert the impending humanitarian catastrophe', and it also demanded that the Federal Republic of Yugoslavia 'facilitate, in agreement with the UNHCR and the ICRC, the safe return of refugees and displaced persons to their homes and allow free and unimpeded access for humanitarian organizations and supplies to Kosovo'.[16] The subsequent major resolution on Kosovo, endorsing agreements concluded in Belgrade on 15–16 October, and adopted just over a week later, made similar references to humanitarian issues as a basis for action.[17]

Over Kosovo in 1998–9, as in the case of northern Iraq in 1991, the Security Council did not explicitly authorize the use of force, but did spell out demands relating *inter alia* to humanitarian issues: these resolutions were then cited by representatives of NATO member states as evidence that the military action they were taking, even though not endorsed by the Security Council, was in pursuit of goals (including humanitarian ones) that the Council had proclaimed. During the air campaign in 1999, one of the five demands repeatedly made by NATO was the return of all refugees.

The refugee problem was indeed serious. In March 1999, on the eve of the NATO air campaign, UNHCR reckoned that there were over 260,000 IDPs within Kosovo, over 100,000 IDPs or refugees in the region, and over 100,000 refugees and asylum-seekers outside the region (Morris 1999). Following the war between NATO states and Yugoslavia in March–June 1999, the Security Council passed a further resolution deciding to deploy an international civil and security presence in Kosovo, the latter with substantial NATO participation and with extensive powers. Its assigned tasks included establishing 'a secure environment in which refugees and displaced persons can return home in safety, the international civil presence can operate, a transitional administration can be established, and humanitarian aid can be delivered'.[18]

East Timor, 1999

When pro-Indonesian elements in East Timor refused to accept the outcome of the referendum of 30 August 1999, which had favoured independence for the territory, and embarked on large-scale killings and expulsions, there was a significant exodus of refugees, some of whom headed for Indonesia, some for Australia. The Security Council passed a resolution in mid-September authorizing an Australian-led multinational force to restore peace and security in East Timor, and 'to facilitate humanitarian assistance operations'. The resolution, which stressed no less than three times the requirement that refugees must be allowed to return in safety to East Timor, was passed only after considerable pressure had been applied to the Indonesian government to gain its consent to the presence of the multinational force.[19]

A resolution adopted in the following month made provision to replace the Australian-led force with the UN Transitional Administration in East Timor (UNTAET), which was authorized 'to take all necessary measures to fulfil its mandate'. Again, humanitarian considerations and organizations, and the right of refugees to return, were mentioned.[20] A major factor throughout the story of East Timor's emergence to independence was the number of refugees—and the proper insistence of states on their right to return.

Sierra Leone, 1999–2000

Faced with the difficult task of ensuring implementation of the Lomé Peace Agreement of 7 July 1999, that was intended to end the long civil war in Sierra Leone, in October 1999 the Security Council adopted a resolution establishing a new UN force there with certain limited enforcement powers.

The UN Mission in Sierra Leone (UNAMSIL), which replaced a UN observer mission with fewer powers, was authorized 'to take the necessary action to ensure the security and freedom of movement of its personnel and, within its capabilities and areas of deployment, to afford protection to civilians under imminent threat of physical violence'. The resolution also called on all parties 'to ensure that refugees and internally displaced persons are protected and enabled to return voluntarily' and 'to ensure safe and unhindered access of humanitarian assistance to those in need in Sierra Leone, to guarantee the safety and security of humanitarian personnel and to respect strictly the relevant provisions of international humanitarian and human rights law'.[21]

A subsequent resolution adopted in February 2000 strengthened UNAMSIL's mandate, giving it authority to 'take the necessary action' regarding an enlarged range of tasks that included, *inter alia*, 'to facilitate the free flow of people, goods and humanitarian assistance along specified thoroughfares'.[22]

UN CONSIDERATION OF PROTECTION OF CIVILIANS AND REFUGEES

Apart from all this case-by-case evidence that humanitarian and refugee issues have played some part in decision-making, are there also signs of systematic discussion and coherent policy on this matter? Since the early 1990s there have been extensive discussions within the UN addressing the role of the military in supporting humanitarian operations. These discussions gradually moved in the direction of concentrating not just on the legal and physical protection of aid, but also on the physical protection of civilians at risk, and gradually came to accept the validity of military action, especially in opposing systematic murder of civilians. The focus here is on the evolution of discussion in the late 1990s.

One early high-level discussion of these matters, in which serious differences of opinion were expressed, was the Security Council's day-long session on 21 May 1997 on 'Protection for humanitarian assistance to refugees and others in conflict situations', in which senior representatives from many leading international agencies as well as from states took part. This exposed a conflict between those in favour of international military support for humanitarian operations and those who are sceptical or even opposed to such support, fearing above all that it would threaten the neutrality and impartiality of humanitarian work (UN 1997).

In 1999, three UN documents addressed directly the question of how the international community should respond when civilians are at risk, whether in armed conflict or at the hands of a brutal regime. These were the Secretary-General's report on the protection of civilians in war; his report on the fall of Srebrenica; and the Independent Inquiry's report into the UN role during the 1994 genocide in Rwanda. With the publication of the reports on Srebrenica and Rwanda, opinion at the UN moved in the direction of accepting the importance of military action in certain extreme circumstances, but implementing this on the ground proved difficult. What follows is a distillation of the conclusions of the three reports as to how humanitarian and refugee issues should sometimes be a basis for the initiation of military action.

Secretary-General's Report on the Protection of Civilians in Armed Conflict

This report, issued in September 1999, was the follow-up to an open meeting of the UN Security Council on protection of civilians in armed conflict. It is the most general of the three reports. It is based on an explicit recognition that forced displacement is a major part of the problem, and that both refugees and IDPs stand in need of protection (UN Secretary-General 1999*b*, paras. 11–15).[23] The report recommended that the Security Council, '[i]n the face of massive and ongoing abuses, consider the imposition of appropriate enforcement action' (UN Secretary-General 1999*b*, recommendation 40).

Despite this apparently robust conclusion, the report has certain weaknesses that might be seen as typical of the UN's failures in handling such difficult problems. For example, it advocates arms embargoes in respect of situations where parties to the conflict target civilians, but fails to show any awareness of why particular forms of arms embargo came to be seen as deeply unsatisfactory in the former Yugoslavia in 1991–6 and in Sierra Leone from 1997 (UN Secretary-General 1999*b*, recommendation 26). Likewise the report appears to assume that any security zone should be demilitarized (UN Secretary-General 1999*b*, recommendation 39). This is open to two objections. First, it was precisely the zones in Bosnia that were subject to demilitarization agreements (albeit imperfect) that were conquered by Bosnian Serb forces in summer 1995. Secondly, there is an obvious risk in demilitarizing a zone and then putting all reliance for defence on small outside forces, especially if those forces are imbued with the mentality of the 'safe-exit option'.

The greatest omission in the report is one that is not easily remedied. It fails to discuss the capacity and will of states to act. Proposals for enforcement action depend crucially upon major regional or global powers, equipped with intervention forces, being willing to commit their military assets over a substantial period, and to accept the possibility of casualties. There is persuasive evidence from the years since 1990 that such willingness is in limited supply. Hence the protection of civilians has sometimes assumed perverse forms: empty promises to protect the 'safe areas' in Bosnia, and retaliatory bombing from a safe height as a response to ongoing killings and expulsions in Kosovo.

UN Reports on Srebrenica and Rwanda

The genocide of Tutsis in Rwanda in 1994 and the killings at Srebrenica in Bosnia in 1995 were catastrophes that reflected badly on the UN because in both cases UN peacekeeping forces were present in the area and failed to prevent mass killings. The UN Secretary-General's report on Srebrenica is a powerful account and analysis of a difficult subject, leaving the reader in little doubt about the complex causes and tragic consequences of the failure of states and the UN to take serious action to protect this UN-proclaimed 'safe area'. It suggests that the policies to protect vulnerable populations must involve elements that go well beyond the purely humanitarian. In particular, member states and the UN must on occasion be willing to use armed force, support one side in a conflict and oppose the other, and/or impose a settlement. Its central conclusion (UN Secretary-General 1999*a*, para 490) is blunt:

> The community of nations decided to respond to the war in Bosnia and Herzegovina with an arms embargo, with humanitarian aid and with the deployment of a peacekeeping force. It must be clearly stated that these measures were poor substitutes for more decisive and forceful action to prevent the unfolding horror.

In April–July 1994, between half a million and a million people were killed in massacres in Rwanda in the worst case of genocide since the Second World War. The UN report on Rwanda examines why the international response was so weak. Its focus is particularly on the response to the crisis within the UN, and says far less about the equally important subject of the responses of key national governments. The report's narrative confirms that for too long key UN personnel, especially in New York, failed to heed information about impending or actual massacres, and stuck for too long to the concept of impartial peacekeeping when stronger measures were required. A key conclusion of the report (UN Security Council 1999, pp. 50–1) consciously echoes the Srebrenica report issued the previous month when it states:

> While the presence of United Nations peacekeepers in Rwanda may have begun as a traditional peacekeeping operation to monitor the implementation of an existing peace agreement, the onslaught of the genocide should have led decision-makers in

the United Nations—from the Secretary-General and the Security Council to Secretariat officials and the leadership of UNAMIR—to realize that the original mandate, and indeed the neutral mediating role of the United Nations, was no longer adequate and required a different, more assertive response, combined with the means necessary to take such action.

CONCLUSIONS

Since the end of the Cold War there has been a strong trend towards identifying humanitarian considerations, including refugee flows, as a basis for certain military mandates and actions. This trend has been observed not only in armed conflicts, whether civil or international (e.g. Bosnia and Sierra Leone), but also in situations of tyrannical or brutal government (Rwanda and Haiti), uncontrolled violence (Somalia and Albania), and the establishment of international forces to help implement a peace agreement (Kosovo and East Timor). Some of the cases mentioned had characteristics of several of these types of situation.

This trend is particularly marked in the case of the UN Security Council. There has been no serious contestation of the proposition that its capacious powers include the authority to authorize military intervention to help deal with major forced population displacements. The UN General Assembly's formal acceptance in 2005 of the idea of Responsibility to Protect merely recognizes this fact.

Four Criticisms

It is easy to criticize this trend on four grounds. First, some extremely serious humanitarian crises causing large refugee flows did not result in military action. Crises that have led to no international military action at all, or else to notably limited action, include those in Abkhazia in the 1990s; the war in Chechnya in 1999–2000; and the long-running crisis in Darfur, Sudan, since 2003. There is inevitably a selective element in international military responses.

Secondly, there is no practical prospect of developing a coherent and agreed general international legal doctrine of humanitarian intervention by states to protect civilians, including refugees, in cases where the Security Council is unable to agree. The possibility of military action, the practical aspects thereof, and its legitimacy or lack of it, must necessarily be considered taking into account the unique aspects of each case.

Thirdly, military actions initiated on largely humanitarian grounds are sometimes too little, too late. They are often characterized by lack of clarity about strategy and aims, reluctance to accept sacrifices, nervousness about siding with one or other of the belligerent parties, and unwillingness to keep forces in a crisis area for more than a short period.

Fourthly, the fact that humanitarian issues, including those relating to refugees, were cited in so many UN Security Council resolutions does not mean that states and international bodies had experienced a sudden conversion to humanitarianism. In some crises they adopted a response in the name of humanitarianism because they were unable to formulate, or to agree, substantive policies dealing with the fundamental policy issues involved. Nor does the emphasis on humanitarian aspects mean that there were no other purposes, interests, or motives at stake. In each case there were. They included the following:

Avoiding unwelcome influx of refugees. While enabling refugees to return home, and assisting IDPs so that they do not become refugees, may appear to be humanitarian causes, they also reflect a strong interest of states faced with a sudden refugee influx or a threat thereof. In many cases states taking a significant role in military action in a crisis, or urging others to do so, were also those that faced a major influx of refugees. Thus the urge to take action on refugee issues often had a basis that was strong but hardly liberal.

International peace and security. In all the above crises, considerations of international peace and security were mentioned alongside humanitarian issues as a basis for international action. For the UN Security Council, reference to this matter is procedurally important in order to justify the Council involving itself in a crisis. In general, the crises demonstrate that humanitarian issues, including those relating to refugees, are not easily separable from more explicitly political ones.

Credibility of commitments and/or demonstration of power. If states, or the UN Security Council, have called for certain action to be taken by a party to a conflict, and their calls have been ignored, they may have an interest in taking military action in order to maintain the international credibility of their words and of their military capacity. In addition, some states may embark on military action, including in support of humanitarian causes, partly out of a concern to demonstrate a capacity for exercising power, including in cases where their material interests are not directly involved.

In many cases there may have been other interests at stake, encompassing the rescue of fellow nationals, the protection of UN personnel from attack, the security of present or future investments, and the spreading of democracy. Yet the main problem in connection with many of these crises has been the *lack* of solid interests on the part of actual and potential intervening states, and a resulting lack of willingness to take any seriously committing action. In some cases (as in Bosnia) they have acted too late; in other cases (as in Rwanda) most states failed to act at all; in still other cases (as in Somalia) those intervening were not willing to stay for the length of time, nor accept the level of casualties, nor understand the country's social structures, that completion of the tasks assigned to the mission might have required.

The cynical conclusion from these considerations would be that the references to refugee issues in so many UN resolutions and the similar statements of governments, regional bodies, and alliances were little more than mere window-dressing, a mere cover for actions that had other purposes. This view underestimates the sheer strength of the reasons impelling governments to focus on refugee issues: the concern of publics well informed by electronic media; the clear interest of some states to stop refugee influxes; and the worry that such influxes could lead to war.

Dilemmas for Humanitarian Organizations

In a number of post-Cold War crises, international humanitarian workers and organizations have themselves called for outside military intervention in a crisis. For example, in the second half of 1992 a number of agencies called for military action to protect humanitarian aid in Somalia; and in April and May 1994 the UK charity Oxfam described the killings in Rwanda as genocide and called for international action.

In certain cases, even if they do not explicitly call for military action, humanitarian workers and organizations may provide an analysis and description of the crisis in such a way as to assist building a consensus for it. A case in point may be the evidence of the situation in Kosovo presented by a representative of UNHCR to the UN Security Council meeting on 10 September 1998. This contributed something to the subsequent strongly worded resolution 1199 on Kosovo.

Even if such workers and organizations are silent, actions taken against them can have the effect of leading to calls for intervention. Today's aid workers may sometimes, involuntarily, have a role similar to Western missionaries in distant lands in the era of European colonialism: violence against them may lead to outside intervention. Such a process may have been reinforced by the 1994 Convention on the Safety of UN and Associated Personnel, especially its Article 7(3), which requires states parties to co-operate in implementation of the Convention, 'particularly in any case where the host state is unable to take the required measures'.

For humanitarian organizations it is almost inevitable that there will be a division of labour not just in their activities but also in their moral stance. Some will stress absolute impartiality and neutrality. Others may be more prepared to engage in advocacy—even, occasionally, military advocacy—and also to seek some degree of military protection for their activities. This suggests a key conclusion: while neutrality and impartiality may represent one valid moral position for humanitarian organizations, especially the ICRC, it is not the only moral position that is valid.

Despite all the problems, there are positive outcomes from the ways in which humanitarian considerations have played some part in the initiation of military actions. Many lives have been saved in many crises; international military action has helped to end some vicious wars, including in Bosnia; many threatening refugee flows have been averted; and many refugees, including those from Albania, East Timor, and Afghanistan, have been enabled to return to their countries.

Two Challenges

As to the future, refugee issues seem destined to remain intertwined with decisions about the use of force. Whether this development is condemned or celebrated, it must probably be accepted as a fact; and it poses the challenge of how to address some of the problems associated with it, and to take the matter forward.

For states and intergovernmental bodies, two main challenges need to be faced. The first is that if military force is used in support of at least partly humanitarian goals or in implementation of international humanitarian law, it is important that it should itself comply with that body of law. Experience suggests that there can be particular pressures in military operations with humanitarian purposes that make observance of the law difficult. The perception of those involved that a military action is disinterested, and in support of high moral purposes, can easily lead to an attitude of superiority over the people they are seeking to save. Whether committed for this or other reasons, the crimes by the forces intervening in Somalia in 1992–5 are evidence of the seriousness of the problem. The case of the 1999 Kosovo war suggests two further grounds for worry. One is that where a military operation has the purpose of changing the policy of a government, it may involve putting pressure on individuals and installations that are as much connected with the government as they are with the army, and may have some elements of civilian function or character. A second worry exemplified by Kosovo is that conducting low-risk war by bombing from 15,000 feet may make it difficult to attack military units or to protect vulnerable civilians. These concerns arising from the Kosovo war suggest that the clear distinction in the laws of war between civilian and military targets is at risk of being eroded.

The second challenge is how to combine humanitarian aims with the effective strategic and political management of armed force. This problem has many dimensions. In particular, there is an urgent need to develop clear concepts and procedures for a process that has recurred in an ad hoc and muddled fashion in the crises of the post-Cold War world: the metamorphosis of a peacekeeping and observer mission into an enforcement operation with, among other things, responsibilities for protecting inhabitants. For peacekeeping tasks, forces are often spread out widely within a country. For enforcement, forces must be constituted differently: they generally need to be concentrated, and an efficient system of command and control becomes more important than in peacekeeping. Until there is a clearer idea of how such forces may be deployed and used, humanitarian issues and refugee crises may remain triggers more for failure than for effective intervention to achieve the humanitarian objectives that have been so frequently proclaimed and only rarely achieved.

NOTES

1. The chapter is based on a presentation at the seminar on 'Refugees in International Relations' at Oxford on 19 Jan. 2009. I am grateful to the participants for vigorous discussion of key issues. Some parts of this chapter draw on my article 'Humanitarian Issues and Agencies as Triggers for International Military Action', *International Review of the Red Cross*, Geneva, vol. 82, no. 839 (Sep. 2000), pp. 673–98.
2. In this chapter I use the term 'refugee' mainly to refer to all those who have crossed a border to flee extreme adverse conditions (which may include persecution, war, economic meltdown, famine, and environmental despoliation). Occasionally I have used the term in its looser usage to encompass IDPs as well as refugees proper.
3. The full text of this secret protocol between Hungary and East Germany dated 20 June 1969—including the clause providing that 'this Protocol shall not be published'—was published in *United Nations Treaty Series*, vol. 986, New York, 1983, p. 46. The Hungarian foreign ministry passed this document to the UN for publication.
4. SC Res. 688 (5 Apr. 1991).
5. See, for example, SC Res. 758 (8 June 1992), SC Res. 761 (29 June 1992), and SC Res. 770 (13 Aug. 1992), this last being explicitly under Chapter VII.
6. SC Res. 819 (16 Apr. 1993); SC Res. 824 (6 May 1993); and SC Res. 836 (4 June 1993), the last two adopted explicitly under Chapter VII.

7. SC Res. 794 (3 Dec. 1992), adopted under Chapter VII.
8. SC Res. 814 (26 Mar. 1993), adopted under Chapter VII.
9. SC Res. 918 (17 May 1994), only part of which was adopted under Chapter VII.
10. SC Res. 925 (8 June 1994).
11. SC Res. 929 (22 June 1994), adopted under Chapter VII.
12. SC Res. 940 (31 July 1994), adopted under Chapter VII.
13. SC Res. 975 (30 Jan. 1995), provided for UNMIH to take over certain specific powers that had been accorded to the MNF in Haiti by SC Res. 940.
14. *Keesing's Record of World Events*, p. 41558.
15. SC Res. 1101 (28 Mar. 1997), adopted under Chapter VII. See also SC Res. 1114 (19 June 1997), deciding that the operation in Albania was to be limited to a period of 45 days from 28 June.
16. SC Res. 1199 (23 Sep. 1998), adopted under Chapter VII.
17. SC Res. 1203 (24 Oct. 1998), adopted under Chapter VII.
18. SC Res. 1244 (10 June 1999), adopted under Chapter VII.
19. SC Res. 1264 (15 Sep. 1999), adopted under Chapter VII.
20. SC Res. 1272 (25 Oct. 1999), adopted under Chapter VII.
21. SC Res. 1270 (22 Oct. 1999), adopted under Chapter VII, paras. 14, 19, and 22.
22. SC Res. 1289 (7 Feb. 2000), adopted under Chapter VII.
23. Many of the recommendations, including 33 and 35–7, relate directly to refugees and IDPs.

BIBLIOGRAPHY

Afghanistan Independent Human Rights Commission. 2008. *Economic and social rights report in Afghanistan—III*. Kabul: Afghanistan Independent Human Rights Commission.

Ellick, A. B. 2008. Afghan refugees return home, but find only a life of desperation. *New York Times*, 2 Dec. 2008.

Hammerstad, A. 2000. Whose security? UNHCR, refugee protection and state security after the Cold War. *Security dialogue* 31(4), pp. 391–403.

Morris, N. 1999. Coping with the Kosovo crisis. Informal presentation at UNHCR headquarters, 7 May 1999. Geneva.

Shawcross, W. 1984. *The quality of mercy: Cambodia, holocaust and modern conscience*. London: André Deutsch.

UN. 1997. Difficulty of providing military support for humanitarian operations while ensuring impartiality focus of Security Council debate. 21 May 1997: UN Press Release SC/6371.

UN Secretary-General. 1999*a*. *Report of the Secretary-General pursuant to General Assembly resolution 53/35: the fall of Srebrenica*. UN Doc. A/54/549 (15 Nov. 1999).

——. 1999*b*. Report of the Secretary-General to the Security Council on the protection of civilians in armed conflict. UN Doc. S/1999/957 (8 Sep. 1999).

UN Security Council. 1999. *Report of the Independent Inquiry into the actions of the United Nations during the 1994 Genocide in Rwanda.* UN Doc. S/1999/1257 (16 Dec. 1999).

UNHCR. 2006. *The state of the world's refugees 2006: human displacement in the new millennium.* Oxford: Oxford University Press.

——. 2007. *2006 UNHCR statistical yearbook.* Geneva: UNHCR.

——. 2008. *Global trends: refugees, asylum-seekers, returnees, internally displaced and stateless persons.* Geneva: UNHCR.

UNHCR statistical online population database www.unhcr.org/statistics/populationdatabase.

11

UNHCR and the Securitization of Forced Migration

Anne Hammerstad

ABSTRACT

Since the end of the Cold War, and particularly after the terror attacks of 11 September 2001 in the United States, refugee movements have increasingly been portrayed by state policy makers, the media, and even the UN High Commissioner for Refugees as a threat to security. This development is intrinsically linked to the widening of the concept of security in the post-Cold War period beyond the traditional Realist notion of national security as the military protection of state sovereignty and territorial integrity. This trend can be seen in the academic literature as well as in the discourses of states, regional organizations, and the UN. It is a phenomenon that can be observed in the industrialized North as well as in the developing South, albeit in different manifestations.

The securitization of forced migrants, whether they be mass influxes of refugees in the global South or asylum seekers in the North, has had a significant impact not only on how we talk about displacement, but also on what solutions we deem appropriate for dealing with their situation. Using the securitization approach of the Copenhagen School, this chapter will trace the process of securitization of forced migration over the past two decades. It will then discuss the consequences of this securitization for the treatment of asylum seekers in the North and mass refugee flows in the South. The links between, on the one hand, Northern attitudes and actions to deter and return asylum seekers, and on the other hand, an increased unwillingness to receive refugees in the South will also be explored.

We must attempt to reduce complex political questions in the minds of nations into simple moral and humanitarian components for the heart to answer. (Sadruddin Aga Khan, UN High Commissioner for Refugees, November 1974)

Population displacement, whether internal or international has gone beyond the humanitarian domain to become a major political, security and socio-economic issue, affecting regional and global stability, as the crises in former Yugoslavia, Somalia and Rwanda have clearly shown. (Sadako Ogata, UN High Commissioner for Refugees, October 1994)

These quotations are by the two longest-serving UN High Commissioners for Refugees: Sadruddin Aga Khan, who dominated UNHCR throughout the 1970s, and Sadako Ogata, in charge of the refugee agency for almost the entire decade of the 1990s. The quotations provide an apt snapshot of how perceptions of the refugee problem have changed over the decades. When even UNHCR, which oversees the international refugee regime and is tasked with protecting the rights of refugees, takes on a discourse of security, we can be fairly confident that the refugee problem has gone through a process of *securitization*. This process—how it started, how it has unfolded, and what are its consequences—is the concern of this chapter.

There is by now what seems to be a broad consensus among scholars that, since the end of the Cold War, and particularly after the terror attacks of 11 September 2001 (9/11) in the United States, refugee movements have increasingly been portrayed as a threat to security by state policy makers, the media, and even UNHCR. In the IR literature, scholars began studying refugees through the analytical prisms provided by Security Studies in the early 1990s (pioneers including Weiner (1993) and Loescher (1992)). This happened at the same time as the so-called 'widening debate' took off within the academic field of Security Studies at the end of the Cold War (see, e.g., Mathews 1989; Buzan 1991; Deudney 1990; Booth 1991; Baldwin 1997; Krause and Williams 1997; Paris 2001). The securitization of refugee movements is intrinsically linked to the widening of the concept of security in Security Studies, beyond the traditional Realist notion of national security as the protection of state sovereignty and territorial integrity against military threats and beyond the narrow definition of Security Studies as 'the study of the threat, use, and control of military force' (Walt 1991: 212). Refugees were as such not the only newcomers on academic and state security agendas in the early 1990s; they were in the erstwhile company of other perceived emerging global threats such as migration (in general) (Wæver et al. 1993) and the environment (Homer-Dixon 1991, 1994; Myers 1993).

The aim of this chapter is to track the securitization of refugee movements, not in academic literature, but in the discourse of political elites who are more directly responsible for maintaining the international refugee regime. *Securitization* denotes the process wherein 'an issue is presented as an existential threat, requiring emergency measures and justifying actions outside the normal bounds of political procedure' (Buzan et al. 1998: 23–4). The securitization of displacement is a phenomenon that can be observed in the industrialized North as well as in the developing South, albeit in different manifestations. I will aim to document this process by focusing on the evolution of UNHCR's official discourse.

The chapter is structured as follows: I begin by sketching UNHCR's traditional discourse, dominated by descriptions of the refugee problem as nonpolitical and humanitarian and the refugee agency's own role as purely legal and neutral. I then trace the evolution of this discourse over the decades, with particular emphasis on the adoption of a fully fledged security discourse in the 1990s. After mapping these dramatic discursive changes, I discuss the reasons *why* this shift took place.

The final section looks at the impact and implications of this securitization process on the functioning of the international refugee regime, and provides evidence suggesting that viewing forced migration through a security prism has encouraged an atmosphere where the hosting of refugees is understood by states as a zero-sum game rather than a question of solidarity (with each other and with refugees). This takes us to the question of desecuritization: 'the shifting of issues out of emergency mode and into the normal bargaining processes of the political sphere' (Buzan et al. 1998: 4). I discuss the desirability of desecuritizing forced migration, and view this against the many reasons given for securitizing the issue in the first place. I agree with Wæver's view (1995) that, in general, desecuritization is desirable. More specifically, I argue that the reasons for securitizing the refugee problem have been outweighed by the problems caused by viewing forced migrants through a security prism. I also discuss some trends that seem to suggest that such a desecuritization, or at least partial desecuritization, of forced migration is indeed currently taking place within UNHCR's discourse.

WHY UNHCR?

Before turning to the main analysis, it would be prudent to say some words about its relevance. Some may question the choice of UNHCR as the main subject of study. Why not instead investigate the discourse of more powerful actors such as the United States; of major refugee-hosting states in the South such as Thailand and Tanzania; or of major asylum destinations in the North such as Sweden and the United Kingdom? The first reason is methodological: Although it has grown to become one of the UN's largest agencies, UNHCR has a relatively narrow mandate and a unique structure where the *person* of the High Commissioner enjoys an unrivalled position as the voice of refugees on the international arena. This means that UNHCR is an unusually contained and unitary actor that lends itself well to discourse analysis.

Second, UNHCR's official discourse is worth analysing because it is linked to, and reflects, a broader securitization trend. The refugee agency would not have developed and refined a discourse of security if this did not reflect changes in the perceptions and interests of key states. UNHCR relies on states for funding,[1] and for access to refugee populations, and therefore feels keenly the need to remain relevant and responsive to their fears and needs. In the words of High Commissioner Thorvald Stoltenberg:

> If UNHCR is static and unresponsive to the political realities surrounding us, we become meaningless both to the refugees and to the internal [sic] community which have [sic] established us. If on the other hand, we are dynamic in analysing, understanding and responding to the very same political realities, we would be in a position not only to serve those who need us directly, but we will also be occupying an important and meaningful place on the world stage (…) (Stoltenberg, 17 January 1990*a*)[2]

It is unlikely that UNHCR would have taken on a security discourse without the belief that this resonated with the perceptions of core donor (in particular) and refugee host states. Having said that, it is also unlikely that the refugee agency would have adopted a security discourse unless it thought it could harness this discourse to further the cause of protecting refugees and finding solutions to their plight. This means that UNHCR's security discourse varies in its emphases and its conceptualizations of security from the discourses of states.

WHY DISCOURSE ANALYSIS?

But is securitization really that interesting? Is it not merely a matter of rhetoric? The study of refugees and security indicates that discourse does matter. How we perceive and understand an issue affects how we act on it. Changing perceptions of forced migrants, whether mass influxes of refugees in the global South or asylum seekers arriving individually in the North, have had a significant impact not only on how we talk about refugees but also on what actions we deem appropriate and acceptable for dealing with their situation. According to UNHCR, part of whose mandate it is to monitor states' adherence to the international refugee regime, the protection climate for refugees has deteriorated markedly in recent years (e.g. Feller 2008). In this chapter I argue that, due to security language's 'specific capacity for fabricating and sustaining antagonistic relations between groups of people' (Huysmans 2006: xii), the deterioration in the protection climate is linked to the securitization of the refugee problem.

However, I would exaggerate the importance of discourse if I were to imply that there is some direct and one-way causal link between the securitization of refugee movements (the cause) and a deterioration in the international protection climate (the effect). Instead, taking as a starting point the securitization approach of the Copenhagen School, this chapter attempts to analyse the process of securitization of forced migration as a form of hermeneutical spiral between discourse and practice. The way we talk about a phenomenon helps shape how we react to it. But our actions—and their consequences—in turn help shape how we discuss the phenomenon.[3] Thus, for the analysis to be complete, in addition to studying the securitization of how we talk about forced migration, the chapter will also discuss how changing realities on the ground have facilitated such a securitization process.

UNHCR'S SECURITIZATION OF FORCED MIGRATION: AN INTELLECTUAL HISTORY

An analysis of UNHCR's official discourse from its inception in 1951 until today reveals startling changes in the refugee agency's understanding and presentation of the refugee problem through the decades.[4] From a timidly legalistic and non-political discourse studiously avoiding controversy in the 1950s, UNHCR had by the mid-1990s abandoned caution for a high-profile interventionist outlook, ready to deal with the root causes of displacement, even when that meant being actively involved in humanitarian action in the midst of war. Instead of its traditional emphasis on its uniqueness as the world's only refugee protection agency, UNHCR began to routinely describe itself as a central cog in the UN's international security mechanism. In its own words, UNHCR's discourse shifted from a 'reactive, exile-oriented and refugee-specific' paradigm to a 'proactive, homeland-oriented and holistic' one (UNHCR 1995: 43).

UNHCR's discursive evolution was a gradual one. In its first decade, the 1950s, the agency stuck to a strictly legal self-definition, focusing (in dry tones and general terms) on monitoring state signatories' implementation of the 1951 Refugee Convention. In the 1970s, the agency's language became more humanitarian in its outlook, and more flamboyant in style. In this period, material *assistance* to refugees took an increasingly central place in the agency's discourse. The 1980s saw the advent of a human rights agenda and a more political approach to the refugee problem. In this period UNHCR would admonish states to deal with the 'root causes' of flight, not just leave the refugee agency to alleviate the symptoms of the underlying political ills causing displacement. Finally, a security discourse emerged in the early 1990s.

While there has been a gradual evolution of key concepts and ideas in UNHCR's discourse throughout its existence, the securitization of the refugee problem happened surprisingly swiftly. For instance, a statistical analysis of the frequency of the use of the term 'security' in UNHCR's annual *Reports to the General Assembly* shows a clear trend. From 1970 to 1986 you hardly see the term (average 3.5 times per report). From 1986 to 1987 the mention of 'security' more than trebles, and the average frequency for one *Report* in the period between 1987 and 1999 is 17.5. The trend continued upwards in the early 2000s, with a peak in 2001 of thirty-eight mentions of security in its different permutations. The average frequency in the years 2000 to 2006 is 21.7, but there is a clear downward trend from 2002 onwards, down to only ten mentions of security in the 2006 report. The word 'frequency' count thus shows a sharp growth in the use of the term 'security' from the late 1980s onwards, with a gentler but clear decline in the new millennium. A similar trend can be found when counting the term 'security' in UNHCR's annual *Notes on International Protection* over the same period.[5]

Not only was the term 'security' employed more frequently since the early 1990s but it evolved into an overarching framework within which UNHCR embedded its other core concepts and which provided a new reason for the refugee agency's very existence. This can be seen when broadening the discourse analysis beyond word frequencies to an analysis of the High Commissioners' speeches, the occasional publication *The State of the World's Refugees* (five issues over a fifteen-year period), editorial themes of *Refugees Magazine*, various funding appeals, and a range of other central UNHCR policy documents. My discourse analysis of these texts attempts to determine the core concepts of UNHCR's discourse; how these core concepts relate to each other; how their meaning is adjusted and changed over time (for instance, how the meaning of being 'non-political' changes dramatically over the years); and how new concepts emerge (especially security), while others recede in their significance and centrality.

If one were to pinpoint a 'watershed', a moment when security terminology seized centre stage in UNHCR's discourse, it would probably be High Commissioner Stoltenberg's speech in October 1990, where he describes UNHCR as a global security organization. The speech outlines three ambitions for UNHCR and relates all three to the goal of furthering global security. The first ambition, to promote voluntary repatriation, is justified as 'a concrete contribution to peace and security'. The second, safeguarding asylum, which must be done through containing economic migration through the alleviation of poverty, is a task that is both 'a moral issue and (...) a problem of our collective security'. The third ambition, 'to have the international community recognize the importance of the issues of refugees and migration and to place them firmly on the international political agenda', is necessary in order to overcome the narrowly defined, and now obsolete, security thinking of the Cold War period. Instead we must recognize 'the interdependence of states and the need to confront together the common problems and challenges to our global security' (Stoltenberg 1990*b*).

Stoltenberg's tenure was short. However, his successor Sadako Ogata intensified the process he started. With a background as a Japanese diplomat and a former professor of International Relations, she redefined UNHCR's purpose from the narrower goal of protecting the rights of refugees to the broader purpose of furthering international peace and security. She aimed to place UNHCR at the centre of the attempt in the early 1990s to create a post-Cold War 'new world order' of peace and stability. She argued that in order 'to reach a new order, the problem of displacement must be addressed effectively and humanely' (Ogata 1992*a*). Peace and security became, throughout the 1990s, a routine topic of Ogata's speeches.

The Nature of UNHCR's Discourse in the 1990s

The Ogata decade saw the consolidation and expansion of UNHCR's security discourse throughout the agency's various publications and official utterances. But *how* did UNHCR understand and employ the concept of security in the 1990s? A brief look at the publications *The State of the World's Refugees* gives a clear idea of both how central the concept of security was to UNHCR's discourse and how this concept developed over time. The 1997 edition gave the concept of security an exceptionally prominent role: The first chapter set out UNHCR's understanding of 'security' and the term was subsequently employed as a guiding concept throughout the survey. At the same time the 1997 edition exemplified how the refugee agency attempted to redefine security into a more refugee-friendly concept. This was also a theme of Ogata's speeches: in 1995 she declared that a 'major test for the coming decades (...) will be to develop a humanitarian perspective of security' (Ogata 1995).

This more humanitarian perspective took the form, in UNHCR's discourse, of the adoption of the concept of *human security* towards the end of the 1990s. UNHCR's advocacy of holistic approaches to the refugee problem led the agency also to advocate a holistic notion of security: a concept of human security that aimed to incorporate all aspects of security from the individuals to states and the international community. UNHCR, in common with many other advocates of human security, did not go into detail about how this could be achieved. The message was simply that by focusing on human rights and dignity, 'food security', and other aspects of bettering the life of individuals, the security of states and the international community will—eventually—follow. Human security was endorsed as a new humanitarian and superior notion of security, which had the potential of replacing narrow, short-sighted, and egotistical national security concerns with a broader and longer-term perspective of collective security.

The introduction of the concept of human security into UNHCR's official vocabulary made away with any dualism between the security of states and regions and that of individuals. Instead, the security of individuals and that of states and the international community became inextricably—and harmoniously—linked. Matching UNHCR's post-Cold War mantra of comprehensive and holistic approaches to solving the refugee problem, then, was the refugee agency's new comprehensive and holistic concept of security. The agency had travelled a long way from when UNHCR's discourse was framed around the concepts of being non-operational and non-political. In the 1970s, High Commissioner Aga Khan had understood his role to be to keep refugee issues *out* of the sphere of international politics and security. Ogata stressed the opposite: Population movements could no longer 'be dealt with through charity', she said: there 'must now be a clear realization that movements of people are likely to become both a major political and security issue in the near future' (Ogata 1992*b*).

WHY DID UNHCR SECURITIZE THE REFUGEE PROBLEM?

Since 2001, there has again been a considerable shift in UNHCR's discourse, this time away from the use of security language, at least to some extent. Before I turn to a more detailed analysis of how and why this partial desecuritization has occurred, this section will look at some of the political, operational, and bureaucratic reasons why UNHCR adopted a security discourse in the first place. I do this by placing UNHCR's discursive evolution in the context of

1. the agency's operations on the ground;
2. the discourse and actions of core donor and refugee host states;
3. the emergence of more people-friendly conceptualizations of security; and
4. some bureaucratic shifts within the refugee agency itself.

Changes in the Agency's Operations on the Ground

Changes in UNHCR's operational environment have had a significant impact on the agency's security language. UNHCR began as a non-operational agency, which then gradually became more involved in the field, first indirectly through 'implementing partners', and then increasingly through the field presence of its own staff. It is now one of the largest humanitarian relief agencies in the world, with most of its staff located in remote field offices rather than at the Geneva headquarters. But not only has UNHCR become increasingly operational but the nature of its operations has also changed. Traditionally UNHCR used to sit on the other side of the border waiting for refugees to flow out. This sat well with its discourse of being a non-political and humanitarian agency. In UNHCR's 1970s discourse, security is never mentioned without pairing it with politics, and both concepts are considered as negative, alien elements in the refugee discourse, as in this example:

> If a [formal refugee status determination] procedure does not exist, there is no guarantee that a bona fide asylum seeker will be treated according to accepted humanitarian standards, and that *extraneous considerations, such as those of a political, economic or security nature*, will not influence the case. (UNHCR 1971, para. 12, emphasis added)

Since UNHCR was so remote from the conflicts and crises that created refugees, it was relatively easy for it to take a stance wherein the agency would *never* comment on why refugees in its care had fled their own country:

> Since UNHCR is strictly a humanitarian and non-political organization, it is not for us to comment on the cause [of refugee flight]—which is debated in many other forums of this Organization [the UN]—but only to find rapid and durable solutions to the effect. (Sadruddin Aga Khan, UN High Commissioner for Refugees, November 1970)

While the emphasis on operational presence happened gradually over the decades, a qualitative shift took place after the end of the Cold War regarding the *nature* of the operational environment in which the agency deployed its field teams. In the early 1990s, beginning with the assistance of Iraqi Kurdish internally displaced persons (IDPs) in the so-called safe haven of Northern Iraq in 1991, the agency became increasingly involved in providing assistance and protection (to the degree protection was possible) in the midst of conflict. No longer does the agency sit on the other side of the border awaiting the arrival of refugees. It acts proactively in any situations where displacement is a threat or a reality, regardless of whether this displacement takes place across borders or not. As a result, there are for instance today more IDPs than refugees among the 'population of concern' to UNHCR.[6]

This in-conflict nature of operations has put UNHCR staff in harm's way at unprecedented levels. It has also put the refugee agency in relations of close cooperation with traditional security actors, such as the Security Council, NATO, and UN peace keeping forces. Adding these operational experiences in war zones together with these new institutional relationships with political and military actors resulted in an operational environment in which the language of security came more naturally to the agency's staff and leadership. Experiencing conflicts first-hand allowed UNHCR to see the security implications of forced migration on the ground. Thus, in the 1990s, UNHCR began to paint a franker, often quite pessimistic, picture of the refugee problem, such as in this 1997 *Note on International Protection*:

> Militarized populations in exile, particularly on a large scale, can carry domestic conflicts across borders, sustaining and exacerbating those conflicts, as well as igniting fresh violence in other States. Such flashpoints can rapidly become unmanageable if the international community remains passive even when the ground rules of asylum are ignored. (UNHCR 1997)

This frankness stands in stark contrast to the agency's discursive history: throughout most of its existence UNHCR did its utmost to refute all claims, when made by states, that refugees constituted security threats. In contrast, the *Notes* from the latter half of the 1990s routinely warned about 'the importance for refugees and asylum seekers to conform to the laws and regulations of the host country and refrain from actions that would undermine local security' (UNHCR 1999: para. 10). This message came most starkly across in High Commissioner Ogata's speeches:

> Refugee problems invariably affect key state interests. They are related to matters of national, regional and even international peace and security. Humanitarian crises in our times increasingly *are* strategic crises, although they are infrequently dealt with as such. (Ogata 1997: 4, emphasis in the original)

This less benign view of refugee populations stemmed in particular from UNHCR's experiences in the Great Lakes region of Africa, where civilians and armed perpetrators of the Rwandan genocide were mixed together in refugee camps and UNHCR had no means with which to separate militants from refugees. Part of the rationale behind UNHCR adopting such security language was to spur decisive international political and military action to demilitarize the camps by appealing to the security interests of states. However, UNHCR also highlighted the security costs of coping with mass influxes in general. The High Commissioner often argued that refugees, apart from being victims of insecurity, had 'also become a major source of instability and conflict' (Ogata 1999).[7] As seen above, even the protection and rights-oriented *Notes* warned of refugees as potential security burdens.[8]

Changes in the Discourse and Action of Core Donor and Refugee Host States

With the end of the Cold War superpower rivalries, the early post-Cold War era became a period of searching for new threats and enemies, both in the academic security studies literature and among policy makers. With the collapse of the Soviet Union, one immediate fear was that of floods of migrants from former Soviet satellites into Western Europe. This never really materialized, but the wars in the former Yugoslavia created a major refugee crisis on Western Europe's doorstep and the rise in asylum seekers in the early 1990s was comet-like. Asylum soon became securitized as a problem of societal or identity security, and all sorts of measures were put in place to deter, stem, and return the flow of asylum seekers from Europe's shores.

UNHCR cannot afford not to *remain relevant* to states—and especially to its main donor states. As refugees and asylum seekers were increasingly described in security terms by policy makers, the media, and academic experts alike, UNHCR had to relate to these asylum fears and the language of security enveloping them. It did so in two ways: First, by attempting to ensure that refugees never reach the shores of Europe at all, through getting involved in 'in-country protection' and preventive activities, often in the midst of conflict; to strengthen the capacity of refugee-hosting states in the South to cope with large refugee populations; and by advocating that the international community deal with the 'root causes' of flight (i.e. resolve conflicts) in order to prepare the ground for repatriation of refugees. For instance, in Ruud Lubbers' first speech as High Commissioner (2001), a major theme was how European states and UNHCR together could 'explore the possibilities of meaningful preventive action in countries of origin and for a serious commitment to building the capacity of refugee hosting countries'.

Second, UNHCR responded to the fears and concerns of refugee and asylum hosting states by taking on the language of security itself—for instance, as shown above, by pointing to the security implications of forced migration to refugee host and sending states alike. But to understand the particular characteristics of UNHCR's security discourse, it is necessary to turn to the opening up of the security debate in the post-Cold War period.

The Emergence of More People-friendly Conceptualizations of Security

UNHCR's mandate is to protect and assist vulnerable refugees, and to find humane and durable solutions to their plight. It would be a deeply unfair exaggeration to argue that UNHCR is so beholden to donor agendas as to unquestioningly mimic a xenophobia-tainted, knee-jerk reaction of panic and fear against asylum seekers just to please European states. A more convincing analysis is based on the power inherent in the concept of security. High Commissioner Ogata (and Stoltenberg before her) thought she could harness the power of security to *increase* refugee protection and to use the urgency of security language to garner a level of resources and attention to address the refugee problem that had never before been seen.

UNHCR thus latched onto the rise in the post-Cold War era of hopes that security could be turned into a more collaborative and people-friendly concept, away from national security and towards 'our common security' or later, human security. Indirectly and in the longer term, UNHCR suggested, by protecting, assisting, and finding humane and durable solutions for IDPs and refugees, we improve global security. And by improving global security we contribute to improving the national security of donor states themselves.

Bureaucratic Changes within UNHCR

Last, but possibly not least, some bureaucratic shifts within UNHCR itself, as well as within the UN as a whole, contributed to making the adoption of the language of security more likely. Turning to internal developments first, there was in the 1990s a clear decline in the importance of the international lawyers within the refugee agency. As UNHCR became increasingly operational and increasingly involved in conflict zones, many more staff were employed in field offices than in Geneva headquarters. As the agency expanded massively, more of the numerous new recruits came from a social science, and even International Relations, background, and fewer from a legal one. The once mighty International Protection division became less prominent in the organizational hierarchy. This bureaucratic shift helps explain the discursive shift taking place away from the emphasis on legal protection, and towards the political, social, and security implications of forced migration.

Occurring parallel with these internal changes is the humanitarian reform process within the UN family as a whole—an ongoing (possibly infinite) process aimed at strengthening communication and coordination and clarifying the division of labour and responsibilities between the UN's many specialized agencies and the head office in New York. In the 1990s, UN humanitarian reform tended to strengthen UNHCR's security discourse in that it was regularly called upon by the Secretary-General to become lead agency in some of the largest humanitarian operations of the decade, including the war in the former Yugoslavia. UNHCR cherished this new-found centrality in humanitarian politics: it relabelled itself as a humanitarian organization rather than a refugee agency, and defined its work according to the contributions it made as part of the UN family in promoting international peace and security.

CONSEQUENCES OF SECURITIZATION—AND THE PATH TO DESECURITIZATION

UNHCR's discursive journey had taken the agency from first adopting the language of security in the early 1990s to endorsing 'human security' as a new, humanitarian, and superior notion of security at the end of the decade. However, soon after the turn of the century, a return to a more cautious discourse can be discerned. Increasingly UNHCR seemed to doubt the usefulness and propriety of enmeshing problems of displacement in a security language. The use of the term security decreased in the annual *Reports to the General Assembly* and *Notes on International Protection.* Ditching almost completely the concept of human security, the refugee agency instead adopted the UN buzzword *responsibility to protect* as its new rallying cry. At the same time, the old distaste for security language displayed by Sadruddin Aga Khan, re-emerged in statements such as in this speech by Antonio Guterres, who took over as High Commissioner in 2005:

> And as we look for new ways to deliver protection it has become harder to get public opinion to recognize the need for it. Unfortunately, public opinion in many societies is increasingly led by fear and suspicion. (Guterres 2005)

Although there has been a process of desecuritization in UNHCR's discourse, and although there are similarities between the discourse we see emerging from UNHCR today and that of three decades ago, we cannot say that UNHCR has come full circle back to its 1970s non-political, non-operational self. In the 1970s, the term security was hardly uttered, and if mentioned was pronounced as if it gave a bad taste in the mouth. At the end of the first decade of the twenty-first century, UNHCR still uses the term security, but in more discrete ways, in particular to describe the operational challenges it faces in the field.

Having set out in the section above the many reasons why UNHCR adopted a security discourse in the 1990s and adapted it to its own mandate, why then did the use of the concept of security wane again in the early 2000s? The desecuritization trend certainly had something to do with Ogata leaving office—she was (and still is) a particular champion of the agency's security discourse, and especially the concept of human security. However, the retreat was gradual. Ruud Lubbers, the new High Commissioner in 2001, although adopting a lower profile than Ogata, did not abandon her security language. In addition, the desecuritization trend has also been observed among other actors, most notably by Huysmans and Buonfino (2008) in UK parliamentary debates. Thus, although individual High Commissioners certainly wield a lot of power within UNHCR, it would be too simplistic to pin the flowing and ebbing of a security discourse onto personality alone.

Instead we must seek an answer by studying the consequences of securitization—some of which became particularly visible after the terror attacks on the United States in 2001. The marked deterioration in the international protection climate taking place in the months and years after 9/11 spurred a renewed scepticism within UNHCR of what the concept of security could achieve for the work of the agency in particular and for the future of refugee protection in general. A cottage industry of academic literature on the security dimensions of refugee movements (see, e.g., Loescher 1992; Weiner 1993; Dowty and Loescher 1996; Posen 1996; Poku and Graham 1998; Suhrke 1999; Newland et al. 2002; Terry 2002; Guild 2003; Lischer 2005; Martin 2005; Guild and Van Selm 2005; Loescher and Milner 2005; Muggah 2006; Huysmans 2006); the routine invocation by states of security as a reason to curb asylum and immigration; the constant lumping of asylum seekers and illegal immigrants together in states' terminology; the conundrum of so-called 'mixed flows'; the linking of terrorism and asylum in the North, and of conflict and refugees in the South: all these factors meant it was time for UNHCR to seek out a more positive image of refugees, or at least a less scary and off-putting one. This section looks at two of the factors that led to this new discursive shift within UNHCR: First, the impact of the war on terror and, second, the fraught burden-sharing relationship between refugee hosting states in the South and donor and asylum states of the North. In the analysis I suggest that both these aspects of the deterioration of the refugee protection climate have clear links to the securitization process of forced migration that started in the 1990s.

THE WAR ON TERROR AND THE DETERIORATING PROTECTION CLIMATE

Some of the hopes for what a more comprehensive and people-friendly concept of security might achieve waned after 9/11. States resorted to a more traditional realist conception of national security, not least displaying a renewed concern with old-fashioned border security. This type of security thinking is difficult to adapt to a more refugee-friendly conception of security:

it was about keeping people out, not letting them in. British Home Secretary David Blunkett displayed the new fears of asylum seekers as terrorists in November 2001:

> This is our home—it is our country. We have a right to say that if people seek to abuse rights of asylum to be able to hide in this country and organise terrorist acts, we must take steps to deal with them. (quoted in Huysmans and Buonfino 2008: 773)

Guild (2003) argues that the link between terrorism, foreignness, and asylum was made from the outset after 9/11 by the US administration. The same was the case for many other western governments. The UN Security Council set the tone with its Resolution 1373 (28 September 2001), which mentions twice the possibility of terrorists abusing the asylum system (despite none of the 9/11 terrorists being asylum seekers or refugees). The resolution further stipulates that states should not harbour individuals who 'finance, plan, support or commit terrorist acts', but does not define the term terrorism or set out safeguards regarding individual rights, due process, and fair trial (Blake 2003). Zard (2002: 32) suggests that Resolution 1373 'generated a wave of new and restrictive laws and regulations [to curb asylum] at a national level'. Blake (2003: 445–7) argues that the use of the UN Refugee Convention's exclusion clauses and definitions of 'political crime' has in the climate after 9/11 been left more to executive discretion and less to judicial scrutiny. All in all, in the post-9/11 period, national security thinking seemed to be getting the upper hand on the legal obligations set out in the international protection regime.

It should be remembered, however, that terrorism is only one way in which forced migration has been securitized in the North. Recent literature on the topic tends to overlook the fact that the securitization drive started in the early 1990s, when it took the form of claims of societal or identity insecurity (Wæver et al. 1993). This securitization of refugees and asylum seekers took more the form of a 'politics of unease' than a 'politics of exception', except perhaps in the first few frantic months of legislation after 9/11.[9] It was these more amorphous and ill-defined fears and unease over immigration and asylum that UNHCR had tried to counter with its human and comprehensive security discourse in the 1990s.

But when such societal insecurity fears became compounded by perceived threats of international terrorists arriving through asylum channels, it became increasingly difficult for UNHCR to hold on to a belief that its own security discourse could modify states' perceptions of their security interests. Far from it, by employing the language of security itself, there was a risk that UNHCR was helping to legitimize states' use of security reasoning to limit the rights of refugees and asylum seekers to seek and receive protection outside their country of origin. This realization can be seen in the first statement made by UNHCR in the immediate aftermath of 9/11. High Commissioner Lubbers warned that '[a]s emotions run high and while Americans and the rest of the world grieve following last Tuesday's terrorist attacks, we should refrain from pointing fingers and inciting hatred against innocent groups such as refugees' (UNHCR 2001*a*). This was followed up a few days later by the Director for Protection, Erika Feller (now Assistant High Commissioner for Protection). She placed states' post-9/11 security-based efforts to restrict asylum within a broader context of the increasing criminalization of asylum seekers and refugees, and called for resolute leadership 'to de-dramatise and de-politicise the essentially humanitarian challenge of protecting refugees and to promote better understanding of refugees and their right to seek asylum' (UNHCR 2001*b*).

North–South Burden-sharing

Another aspect of the international refugee regime that has deteriorated (although it never worked smoothly) is the institution of burden-sharing. According to UNHCR's ExCom, burden-sharing is intrinsic to the proper functioning of the refugee regime, because:

> (...) respect by States for their protection responsibilities towards refugees is strengthened by international solidarity involving all members of the international community and (...) the refugee protection regime is enhanced through committed international cooperation in a spirit of solidarity and responsibility and burden sharing among all States (UNHCR 2004a).

While in theory burden-sharing is about solidarity and cooperation, in practice it has mostly boiled down to financial contributions from rich countries in the North to help host states and humanitarian organizations cope with refugee situations in poorer regions of the South (e.g. almost all of UNHCR's billion-dollar budget is provided by ten donors in the North). However, in the opinion of refugee host states, burden-sharing goes beyond the question of who pays. In addition to economic, political, and even in some cases military support, it should include sharing the burden of actually *hosting* refugees, through asylum and resettlement channels. Efforts by Northern States, particularly the European Union, to contain refugee flows within their region of origin and to negotiate agreements to return asylum seekers to 'safe' first-countries of asylum, have raised shackles in refugee host countries coping with the vast majority of the world's refugee population. Despite the rhetoric in European capitals, only 14 per cent of the global refugee population makes it out of their own region (UNHCR 2008: 27). Disagreements between the North and South became particularly visible during Ruud Lubbers' tenure (2001–5), when his *Convention Plus* initiative was viewed with suspicion by refugee-hosting states, who interpreted it as UNHCR taking on an EU agenda for burden shifting of refugees away from European soil.[10]

It seems appropriate to analyse the deterioration of the institution of burden-sharing in light of the securitization of forced migration. As discussed in the introduction to this chapter, the mindset of national security 'favours zero-sum thinking', which frames a problem 'into a highly competitive game in which a state can only gain benefits at the cost of other states' (Huysmans 2006: 23). It also tends to frame problems in black and white: other actors are either friends or enemies; they are either 'with us or against us'. This makes the task of cooperating and identifying common ground and mutual interests more difficult (Deudney 1990). Burden-sharing thus becomes harder when the problem is phrased in the zero-sum survivalist language of security. From the perspective of the South, which hosts the large majority of the world's refugees, why, if a few asylum seekers are portrayed as security threats to the North, should not the mass influxes of refugees in the South be an even worse security threat? Rather than creating a common incentive to deal with the 'root causes of flight' and find durable solutions to refugee situations, the security framing of the debate has contributed to a race to the bottom. Conditions of refuge have deteriorated not only in the North but also in the South, where the 'warehousing' in insecure camps with little chance of solutions has become a common reality for an increasing number of refugees. In 2004, around two-thirds of the world's refugee population was in 'protracted refugee situations' with no solution in sight (Loescher, Betts, and Milner 2008: 60).

UNHCR's recent response to the lack of good-will and solidarity in the burden-sharing institution is very different to its attempt at humanizing security in the 1990s. Instead of trying to reinterpret security, the refugee agency has in recent years mostly rejected the appropriateness of security language to describe the refugee problem, and has returned to a discourse focused around protection. This discursive change was accompanied by institutional changes, especially the creation of an Assistant High Commissioner for Protection. In the proposal to the UN General Assembly to create this position, UNHCR performed a discourse analysis of its own, arguing that the conflation of terrorists, criminals, and refugees/asylum seekers has led to a lack of political will among states in the North as well as the South to fulfil their protection obligations:

> The fulfilment of these protection responsibilities has become an ever more difficult task in light of significant changes in the environment in which the organization operates.

Disillusionment on the part of many governments, and at the highest levels, with the capacity of States to manage their asylum responsibilities has resulted in curtailment of protection opportunities and in asylum being offered on ever more unfavourable terms. Illegal migration, growth in people smuggling syndicates, and the post-September 11 fallout have compounded the problems by confusing refugees and asylum-seekers, in the public mind and the policies of some States, with abusers of the system, criminals and terrorists. All this is coupled with a strong sense on the part of major host States that there is no good system of burden-sharing in place and that they are too often left with a disproportionate share of responsibilities which, in light of the protracted nature of many situations, they are less and less inclined to meet. (UNHCR 2004*b*: para. 5)

BACK TO THE FUTURE: DESECURITIZATION AS UNHCR'S RAISON D'ÊTRE?

Why desecuritize refugee movements? At a general level, because human movement is natural. The movement of people has helped shape the trajectory of history for as long as human communities have existed. It is a catalyst for change, sometimes in the form of upheavals but other times in the form of improvement, enriching people's economic, social, and cultural lives. If population movements—whether forced or voluntary—is inevitable, it seems counterproductive to securitize it, since, as Jef Huysmans (2006: xii) succinctly puts it, security knowledge has 'a specific capacity for fabricating and sustaining antagonistic relations between groups of people'.

On the other hand, there are situations where particular refugee movements, or particular groups or individuals within them, do warrant a security label, as for instance did the militarized refugee camps on Rwanda's borders in 1994–6. It is also true, as High Commissioners Stoltenberg and Ogata were aware, that politicizing and securitizing the refugee problem ensures more sustained and urgent efforts to deal with it. This leads us to the question: is it possible to sustain a limited security discourse that reaps the benefits from the propensity the language of security has for keeping refugee issues at the forefront of policy makers' minds while avoiding this language's pernicious effects? Is it possible to strike the right balance between security and protection?

Looking back at UNHCR's discursive trajectory, it seems that the agency's security discourse, although it had some spectacular successes in soliciting funding and support for particular operations in the 1990s, never found that balance. This became particularly obvious in the aftermath of 9/11. As a result there is already a discernible trend towards desecuritization. And this desecuritization is not only taking place in the language of UNHCR. Huysmans and Buonfino (2008) argue that the peak of securitization of forced migration took place in the United Kingdom in the first couple of years after 9/11. In the case of UNHCR, the desecuritization trend began at the same time, but did not become pronounced until the arrival of the new High Commissioner, Antonio Guterres, in 2005.

In the period since then, UNHCR's preoccupations with security have been limited in scope to an operational issue. A major theme has been the 'shrinking of humanitarian space', where warring factions prey on the civilian population and view humanitarian staff as parties to the conflict and thus as legitimate targets rather than neutral actors. UNHCR is continually conducting an internal and external debate on how to counteract this problem. The refugee agency's response seems to be, on the one hand, a deep preoccupation with the *personal security* of staff and refugees in conflict areas, while on the other, interpreting its own role as that of depoliticizing and desecuritizing displacement through the performance of its non-political and humanitarian mandate. For instance, *The State of the World's Refugees 2006* argues that '(...) the security concerns of states as well as refugees are best met by ensuring that the multilateral and humanitarian character of refugee protection is maintained'. It promotes 'preventive and "soft" measures integrated into refugee protection and assistance' in order to 'defuse many of the security threats faced by refugees and their hosts alike'(UNHCR 2006: 63 and 64).

These last two quotes are illustrative of how UNHCR's discourse has transformed itself (again). Security language has not disappeared—after all a whole chapter of *The State of the World's Refugees 2006* is dedicated to security. UNHCR remains painfully aware that states harbour an array of security concerns over refugees, and that 'the challenge of integrating the differing security interests and strategies of the various parts of the international refugee regime has grown more complex' (UNHCR 2006: 64).

It is clear from these quotes that UNHCR takes a constructivist view on state security concerns: threats can be defused and refugee movements *desecuritized* by responding to them in a particular manner. Desecuritization can be achieved through using the terminology of the Copenhagen School, *speech-acts* of affirming the neutral, non-political, and humanitarian nature of asylum and refugee protection, committing to the international refugee regime, and giving UNHCR the necessary support to provide international, multilateral, and non-political refugee protection. Thus, in one deft move, UNHCR has both described a solution to states' security concerns (desecuritization through multilateralism) and asserted its own indispensable role in achieving this solution (as the multilateral agent responsible for refugees).

The (difficult) task ahead for UNHCR is to convince states of this particular interpretation of the security challenges posed by displacement. In the words of the Assistant High Commissioner for Protection:

> UNHCR's ability to extend protection is challenged in many regions by the absence of political will to support it and the disinclination to recognise that asylum is a non-political and humanitarian act. Asylum is viewed through the security prism in many parts of the world. (Feller 2008)

While in the 1990s UNHCR was one of the key securitizing actors in the discourse on displacement, the agency has now become a voice of desecuritization. This move is also a step back to a previous era of UNHCR's history, during the reign of Sadruddin Aga Khan. In the 1974 speech quoted in the introduction to this chapter, he admitted that refugee flows could lead to 'the most strenuous tensions' (he was loath to use the term security), but the aim was to overcome these tensions by attempting '(. . .) to reduce complex political questions in the minds of nations into simple moral and humanitarian components for the heart to answer'. The jargon and terminology is very different in 1974 from 2006, but the argument is the same: UNHCR's neutral, non-political, and humanitarian mandate to protect and assist refugees is there in order to *desecuritize* refugee issues. UNHCR's mandate thus helps increase the security of states as well as that of refugees and the humanitarian staff aiding them.

This was arguably the aim of states from the outset when they decided to create the two corner stones of the international refugee regime, the 1951 UN Refugee Convention, and UNHCR. To take forced migration out of the political and the controversial, leaving it in the hands of a non-political multilateral institution, reduces the risk of tensions between states. UNHCR had archived this part of its history in the 1990s and the first half of the 2000s, but it is now brushing the dust off the insights of its founders as the effects of securitizing population movement on community relations and human rights standards have become increasingly clear—and as Huysmans argues, increasingly pernicious.

NOTES

1. Only around 3 per cent of UNHCR's billion-dollar annual expenditure is allocated automatically from the UN's central budget. The remaining 97 per cent must be raised annually from donors. Ten Western donors, headed by the US (30 per cent), account for almost 80 per cent of UNHCR's budget (Loescher et al. 2008: 91–3).

2. Remaining relevant or useful to states has been a core theme of all High Commissioners, but particular of Stoltenberg and his successor Sadako Ogata.
3. Loosely, and simplistically, based on Gadamer (2004), who asserted that our consciousness is 'historically effected' and that learning takes place in a hermeneutic circle between the text we try to interpret and the existing prejudices (or pre-judgements) and experiences found in our own horizon. Thus our understanding of the world is coloured by the historical, social, and cultural practices in which we are embedded.
4. This analysis is based on the reading of a broad range of UNHCR official documents, speeches, and publications, only some of which are directly quoted or referenced in this chapter.
5. All the *Reports of the United Nations High Commissioner for Refugees* and *Notes on International Protection*, 1970–2006, can be found on UNHCR's research tool, RefWorld, available through its web site www.unhcr.org, with the exception of the Reports from 1995, 1996, and 1999. These three have been counted in the old-fashioned way. The *Reports* and *Notes* constitute suitable material for a quantitative study, since they are produced every year to the same audience and in similar format and style.
6. In 2007, out of a total population of concern of 31.7 million people, 11.4 were refugees, while 13.7 million were IDPs. The rest were asylum seekers, returnees, stateless persons, and 'others of concern' (UNHCR 2008: 7).
7. Statements like this, as well as UNHCR's involvement in the Rwandan refugee crisis, show that the refugee agency by the mid-1990s no longer followed the UN Refugee Convention in using the term 'refugee' solely to describe civilian, non-militarized persons. UNHCR advocated the demilitarization of refugee camps, but neither its discourse nor actions in the 1990s signalled that militarized exile populations such as the Rwandan Hutus were considered to be outside the agency's competence.
8. See the 1998 *Note* for another example (UNHCR 1998: para. 17).
9. Huysmans and Buonfino (2008: 781) show how migration and asylum questions in Parliamentary debates are framed within a 'general context of societal insecurities'.
10. For an account of the fate of Convention Plus, see Loescher, Betts, and Milner (2008: 62–6).

BIBLIOGRAPHY

Baldwin, David (1997). 'The Concept of Security', in *Review of International Studies*, vol. 23, no. 1, 5–26.

Blake, N (2003). 'Exclusion from Refugee Protection: Serious Non-political Crimes after 9/11', in *European Journal of Migration and Law*, vol. 4, no. 4, 425–47.

Booth, Ken (1991). 'Security and Emancipation', in *Review of International Studies*, vol. 17, no. 4, 313–26.

Buzan, Barry (1991). *People, states and fear: an agenda for international security studies in the post-cold war era*, 2nd ed. (Hemel Hempstead: Harvester Wheatsheaf).

Buzan, Barry, Ole Wæver, and Jaap de Wilde (1998). *Security: a new framework for analysis* (London: Lynne Rienner).

Deudney, Daniel (1990). 'The Case Against Linking Environmental Degradation and National Security', in *Millennium*, vol. 19, no. 2, 461–76.

Dowty, Alan and Gil Loescher (1996). 'Refugee Flows as Grounds for International Action', in *International Security*, vol. 21, no. 1 (Summer), 43–71.

Feller, Erika (2008). 'Fifty-ninth session of the Executive Committee of the High Commissioner's Programme, Agenda item 5(a): Statement by Ms. Erika Feller, Assistant High Commissioner—Protection' (Geneva: UNHCR, 8 October 2008).

Gadamer, Hans-Georg (2004 [1960]). *Truth and method* (London: Continuum books).

Guild, Elspeth (2003). 'Editorial of Special Issue on 9/11 and Migration', in *European Journal of Migration and Law*, vol. 4, no. 4, 395–8.

——and Joanne van Selm, eds. (2005). *international migration and security: opportunities and challenges* (Abingdon: Routledge).

Guterres, Antonio (2005). *Opening Statement by Mr. António Guterres, United Nations High Commissioner for Refugees, High Commissioner's Forum* (Geneva: UNHCR, 17 November 2005).

Homer-Dixon, Thomas (1991). 'On the Threshold: Environmental Changes as Causes for Acute Conflict', in *International Security*, vol. 16, no. 2, Fall, 76–116.

——(1994). 'Environmental Scarcities and Violent Conflict: Evidence from Cases', in *International Security*, vol. 19, no. 1, Summer, 5–40.

Huysmans, Jef (2006). *The politics of insecurity: fear, migration and asylum in the EU* (Abingdon: Routledge).

——and Alessandra Buonfino (2008). 'Politics of Exception and Unease: Immigration, Asylum and Terrorism in Parliamentary Debates in the UK', in *Political Studies*, vol. 56, no. 4, December 2008, 766–88.

Khan, Sadruddin Aga (1970). *Summary of the oral statement of the United Nations High Commissioner for Refugees to the Third Committee.* Speech by the High Commissioner (New York: 16 November 1970).

——(1974). *Statement by the High Commissioner to the Third Committee of the General Assembly (twenty-ninth session)*. Speech by the High Commissioner (New York: 25 November 1974).

Krause, Keith and Michael C Williams, eds. (1997). *Critical security studies: concepts and cases* (London, UCL Press).

Lischer, Sarah Kenyon (2005). *Dangerous sanctuaries: refugee camps, civil war and the dilemmas of humanitarian aid* (Ithaca, NY: Cornell University Press).

Loescher, Gil (1992). *Refugee movements and international security*, Adelphi Paper no. 268 (London: IISS).

——and James Milner (2005). *Protracted refugee situations: domestic and international security implications.* Adelphi Paper no. 375 (London: IISS).

——, Alexander Betts, and James Milner (2008). *The United Nations High Commissioner for Refugees (UNHCR): The politics and practice of refugee protection into the twenty-first century* (London: Routledge).

Lubbers, Ruud (2001). *Statement by Mr. Ruud Lubbers, United Nations High Commissioner for Refugees, at the Informal Meeting of the European Union Ministers for Justice and Ministers for Home Affairs (Stockholm)*. Speech by the High Commissioner (Stockholm, 8 February 2001).

Martin, Adrian (2005). 'Environmental Conflict between Refugee and Host Communities' in *Journal of Peace Research*, vol. 42, no. 3, 329–46.

Mathews, Jessica Tuchman (1989). 'Redefining Security', in *Foreign Affairs*, vol. 68, no. 2, 162–77.

Muggah, Robert, ed. (2006). *No refuge: the crisis of refugee militarization in africa* (London: Zed Books).

Myers, Norman (1993). *Ultimate security: the environmental basis of political stability* (New York: Norton).

Newland, K., E. Patrick, J. van Selm, and M Zard (2002). 'Introduction', in *Forced Migration Review*, vol. 13, June, 4–7.

Ogata, Sadako (1992*a*). *Refugees: a multilateral response to humanitarian crises. Speech by the High Commissioners* (Berkley: 1 April 1992).

——(1992*b*). *Fortress Europe? Refugees and migrants: their human rights and dignity* (Graz, Austria: Akademie Graz, 23 May 1992).

——(1994). *Preparing for the future: knowledge in action* (Geneva: Graduate Institute for International Studies, 25 October 1994).

——(1995). *Opening Statement at the Forty-sixth Session of the Executive Committee of the High Commissioner's Programme* (Geneva: 16 October 1995).

——(1997). 'Humanitarian Action at the Crossroads', in *Refugees Magazine*, vol. 3, no. 109. Accessed on 11 June 2010 at http://www.unhci.org/3b681b345.html

——(1999). *Statement to the Third Committee of the General Assembly* (New York: 12 November 1999).

Paris, Roland (2001). 'Human Security: Paradigm Shift or Hot Air?', in *International Security*, vol. 26, no. 2, Fall, 87–102.

Poku, Nana and Graham, David, eds. (1998). *Redefining security: population movements and national security* (Westport, Connecticut: Praeger).

Posen, Barry R. (1996). 'Military Responses to Refugee Disasters', in *International Security*, vol. 21, no. 1, Summer, 72–111.

Stoltenberg, Thorvald (1990*a*), *High Commissioner's Speech to the Staff* (Geneva: 17 January 1990).

——(1990*b*), *The Nansen Memorial Lecture* (Geneva: 4 October 1990).

Suhrke, Astri (1999). 'Human Security and the Interests of States', in *Security Dialogue*, vol. 30, no. 3, 265–76.

Terry, Fiona (2002). *Condemned to repeat: the paradox of humanitarian action* (Ithaca: Cornell University Press).

United Nations, *United Nations Security Council Resolution 1373* (New York: UN, 28 September 2001).

UNHCR (1971). *Note on international protection, 1971* (Geneva: UNHCR).

——(1995). *The state of the world's refugees 1995* (Oxford: Oxford University Press).

——(1997). *Note on international protection* (Geneva: UNHCR).

——(1998). *Note on international protection (Geneva: UNHCR)*.

——(1999), *Report of the United Nations High Commissioner for Refugees, 1998* (UNGA Doc. A/54/12, 1 January 1999).

——(2001*a*). 'Visiting UN refugee chief underscores humanitarian considerations'. Press release (Washington, DC: UNHCR, 18 September 2001).

——(2001*b*). 'Care urged in balancing security and refugee protection needs'. Press release (Geneva: UNHCR, 1 October 2001).

——(2004*a*). *Conclusion on international cooperation and burden and responsibility sharing in mass influx situations, 8 October 2004*. No. 100 (LV)—2004. Online. UNHCR Refworld, available at: http://www.unhcr.org/refworld/docid/41751fd82.html [accessed 10 February 2009].

——(2004*b*). *Proposal to establish an assistant high commissioner (protection) post in UNHCR* (Geneva: EXCOM 55th session, A/AC.96/992/Add.1, 2 September 2004).

——(2006). *The state of the world's refugees 2006: human displacement in the new millennium* (Oxford: Oxford University Press, 2006).

——(2008). *Statistical Yearbook 2007: Trends in displacement, protection and solutions* (Geneva: UNHCR, December 2008).

Wæver, Ole (1995). 'Securitization and Desecuritization', in Lipschutz, Ronny (ed.), *On Security* (New York: Colombia University Press).

——, Barry Buzan, Morten Kelstrup, and Pierre Lemaitree (eds.) (1993). *Identity, migration and the new security agenda in europe* (London: Pinter).

Walt, Stephen (1991). 'The Renaissance of Security Studies', in *International Studies Quarterly*, vol. 35, no. 2 (June), 211–239.

Weiner, Myron, ed. (1993) *International migration and security* (Boulder, Colorado: Westview Press).

Zard, M (2002). 'Exclusion, Terrorism and the Refugee Convention', in *Forced Migration Review*, vol. 13, June, 32–4.

12

Refugees, Peacebuilding, and the Regional Dynamics of Conflict[1]

James Milner

ABSTRACT

A striking feature of the conflict management literature in recent years has been an emerging consensus on the importance of 'peacebuilding'. As illustrated by cases as diverse as Afghanistan, Burundi, and Liberia, armed conflict has the potential to re-emerge and become more protracted if active steps are not taken to build a sustainable peace. Much of this debate has, however, focused exclusively on peacebuilding activities within the country in question, with little or no attention paid to the regional nature of conflict and the regional dynamics that should be addressed as part of a successful peacebuilding program. This is especially striking given the growing literature on the regional nature of conflict and insecurity in the global South. As argued by Ayoob, Buzan, and others, intra-state conflict in the global South has the demonstrated potential to spill-over into neighbouring and equally vulnerable states, thereby regionalizing conflict. For example, civil conflict in Liberia and Burundi affected not only those two countries but also other countries in the Mano River Union in West Africa and the Great Lakes region of Central Africa as a result of the proliferation of small arms and the movement of armed elements and refugees across borders. These aspects of conflict have the demonstrated ability to spread conflict to neighbouring countries and to undermine conflict management and peacebuilding activities in the country of origin.

This paper draws on understandings of the regional nature of conflict in the global South and case studies of the regional security implications of refugee movements from Afghanistan, Burundi, and Liberia to develop a more comprehensive understanding of peacebuilding. The paper argues that the link between peacebuilding and refugees goes beyond the repatriation of refugees. Instead, the paper argues that the presence of so-called 'spoilers' within refugee populated areas, the politicization of refugees during exile, and the potential for early and forced repatriation by the country of asylum have both proven to have the potential to undermine peacebuilding efforts, while the experience of exile may enable refugees to contribute to various stages of the peacebuilding process. These dynamics hold important lessons not only for peacebuilding policy and practice but also for the study of conflict management and international relations.

A striking feature of discussions on conflict management in recent years has been an emerging consensus on the importance of 'peacebuilding' (Ali and Matthews 2004; Stedman et al. 2002). As illustrated by cases as diverse as Afghanistan, Burundi, Liberia, and Haiti, armed conflict has the potential to re-emerge and become more protracted if active steps are not taken to build a sustainable peace. While the importance of post-conflict reconstruction has been recognized for more than fifty years, the broader notion of peacebuilding became the focus of particular interest in the early 1990s when it was highlighted in the UN Secretary-General's report *An Agenda for Peace* (UNSG 1992). Since then, there have been numerous conceptual and institutional developments, including the establishment of the UN Peacebuilding Commission (PBC) in late 2005. While debates on definitions persist, recent discussions have generally revolved around developing ways to ensure stability in countries previously affected by conflict so as to prevent a slide back into war.

Much of this debate has, however, focused exclusively on peacebuilding activities within the country in question, with little or no attention paid to the regional nature of conflict and the regional dynamics that should consequently be addressed as part of a successful peacebuilding programme. This is especially striking given the growing literature on the regional nature of conflict and insecurity in the global South. As argued by Ayoob (1995), Buzan (1992), and others, intra-state conflict in the global South has the demonstrated potential to 'spill-over' into neighbouring, and equally vulnerable, states, thereby regionalizing conflict. For example, civil conflict in Sierra Leone and Burundi not only affected these two countries but other countries in the Mano River Union in West Africa and the Great Lakes region of Central Africa as a result of the proliferation of small arms and the movement of armed elements across borders. These aspects of conflict have the demonstrated ability not only to spread conflict to neighbouring countries, but also to undermine conflict management and peacebuilding activities in the country of origin.

Refugee movements also have the demonstrated ability to regionalize conflict (Loescher 1992; Loescher and Milner 2005; and Weiner 1993). In fact, refugees are to be found in some of the world's poorest and most unstable regions, and originate from some of the world's most fragile states, including Afghanistan, Burundi, Liberia, Myanmar (Burma), Sierra Leone, Somalia, and Sudan. Just as conflicts in the countries of origin have become protracted, some two-thirds of refugees in the world today are not in emergency situations, but trapped in protracted refugee situations. Such situations—often characterized by long periods of exile, stretching to decades for some groups—constitute a growing challenge for the global refugee protection regime and the international community. Refugees trapped in these situations often face significant restrictions on a wide range of rights, while the continuation of these chronic refugee problems also frequently gives rise to a number of political and security concerns for countries of origin, host states, and states in the region. In this way, protracted refugee situations represent a significant challenge to both human rights and security.

This chapter considers the regional dynamics of peacebuilding by examining the relationship between protracted refugee situations, regional insecurity, and peacebuilding. The chapter has four sections. The first section considers the focus of recent peacebuilding policy and research, especially as it is reflected in the work of the UN Peacebuilding Commission. The second section provides an overview of the growing significance of protracted refugee situations and their links to a broader range of peace and security concerns. The chapter then argues that the link between peacebuilding and refugees goes beyond the repatriation of refugees. Instead, the presence of 'spoilers' within refugee populated areas, the potential for early and forced repatriation by the country of asylum and the politicization of refugees while in exile have all proven to have the potential to undermine peacebuilding efforts, while the experience of exile may enable refugees to contribute to various stages of the peacebuilding process. The chapter concludes by considering the importance of incorporating these broader regional dynamics into broader policy and research debates on peacebuilding.

PEACEBUILDING: INSTITUTIONAL INNOVATIONS

In his 1992 report, *An Agenda for Peace*, UN Secretary-General Boutros Boutros-Ghali argued that the end of the Cold War presented new challenges and opportunities for both the international community and international institutions mandated with the preservation of peace and security. In considering the various tools at the disposal of the United Nations in responding to the new security environment, the Secretary-General added 'peacebuilding' to the more established activities of preventive diplomacy, peacemaking, and peacekeeping. He argued that such an innovation was required as the

United Nations system needed to develop the capacity to 'stand ready to assist in peace-building in its differing contexts: rebuilding the institutions and infrastructures of nations torn by civil war and strife; and building bonds of peaceful mutual benefit among nations formerly at war' (UNSG 1992: paragraph 15).

While few of these activities were new, it became increasingly recognized that these longer-term undertakings were essential elements in preventing a return to conflict. The importance of peacebuilding was clearly illustrated by several cases through the 1990s, including Liberia, Rwanda, and Sudan (Ali and Matthews 2004); however, numerous gaps remained in the conceptual and practical understandings of peacebuilding. While there is growing empirical evidence to suggest that effective peacebuilding strategies should involve long-term activities designed to support the security, political, economic, and justice and reconciliation needs of a country emerging from conflict (Ali and Matthews 2004: 409–22), no single international organization had the mandate to undertake this full range of activities. While the UN system contained a number of specialized agencies with mandates to undertake some of these activities, and while these agencies have been involved with peacebuilding activities around the world for some time, it became increasingly clear that stronger leadership and institutional coherence were required to ensure that peacebuilding was more effectively and systematically undertaken.

The establishment of a UN Peacebuilding Commission was subsequently proposed as a means of ensuring better leadership and coordination of peacebuilding activities within the UN system. The initial proposal was included in the 2004 report of the UN Secretary-General's High-Level Panel on Threats, Challenges and Change. In his 2005 memo, 'In Larger Freedom', UN Secretary-General Kofi Annan endorsed the creation of a Peacebuilding Commission as an intergovernmental advisory body, which could ensure long-term political support and funding for post-conflict recovery programmes, in addition to advising on thematic issues and specific cases.

The UN General Assembly subsequently established the UN Peacebuilding Commission (PBC), Peacebuilding Support Office (PBSO), and the Peacebuilding Fund (PBF) in December 2005.[2] In establishing the PBC, the UNGA recognized the 'interlinked and mutually reinforcing' nature of peace and security, development, and human rights, and the benefits of 'a coordinated, coherent and integrated approach to post-conflict peacebuilding' (UNGA 2005). To this end, the PBC was established to serve three functions:

- To bring together all relevant actors to marshal resources and to advise on and propose integrated strategies for post-conflict peacebuilding and recovery.

- To focus attention on the reconstruction and institution-building efforts necessary for recovery from conflict and to support the development of integrated strategies in order to lay the foundation for sustainable development.
- To provide recommendations and information to improve the coordination of all relevant actors within and outside the United Nations, to develop best practices, to help ensure predictable financing for early recovery activities, and to extend the period of attention given by the international community to post-conflict recovery.

By mid-2008, the PBC's Organizational Committee was comprised of thirty-one Member States, including members of the Security Council, members from ECOSOC, representatives of the major donor countries, troop contributing countries, and other members of the UNGA with experience in post-conflict reconstruction (UNGA 2008*a*). Additional states directly implicated in particular peacebuilding operations were also granted membership in the country-specific configurations. Selections from the various pools of candidate Member States resulted in a diverse membership of the PBC's Organizational Committee for its second session (June 2007 to June 2008) (see Appendix 1), and additional interested parties for discussions on specific peacebuilding operations (see Appendix 2). Finally, meetings of the PBC have invited contributions from senior UN representatives in the field; representatives of other UN agencies; representatives of major development institutions, including the World Bank; and representatives of civil society. In this way, the PBC brings together a wide range of institutional stakeholders implicated in peacebuilding initiatives.

The first two sessions of the PBC were largely devoted to developing a clearer understanding of the scope and nature of the Commission's work and to country-specific work on Burundi and Sierra Leone (UNGA 2007, 2008*a*), with Guinea-Bissau being added to the agenda of the PBC in its second session. Through its country-specific work on Burundi and Sierra Leone, the PBC adopted workplans, sent several missions to both countries, and identified key priority areas for peacebuilding in both cases. In the case of Burundi, the PBC focused on promoting good governance, strengthening the rule of law, security sector reform, and ensuring community recovery. In Sierra Leone, the PBC focused on youth employment and disempowerment, justice and security sector reform, democracy consolidation and good governance, and capacity building, especially the capacity of government institutions. In addition, the engagement of the PBC coincided with important developments in both countries, including parliamentary elections in Sierra Leone and the development of a Strategic Framework for Burundi.

While these are important developments for peacebuilding in both cases, it is important to note the limited scope of the early work of the PBC.[3] Specifically, the early work of the PBC has focused exclusively on activities within the country in question, with little or no attention paid to either the regional nature of conflict or the significant refugee populations associated with these conflicts. The treatment of these and similar cases by the PBC, and the sustained political and donor interest this is hoped to generate, could provide a unique opportunity for engaging the full spectrum of stakeholders required to formulate and implement a comprehensive solution, not only for peacebuilding and post-conflict recovery in the country of origin but also to resolve the related refugee situations. The emerging approach of the PBC, however, does not appear to make this link. Instead, the members of the Commission seem to be adopting a myopic, country-specific approach. Such an approach does not allow for a full consideration of factors outside the country that could upset post-conflict recovery. The current approach of the PBC also appears to adopt a limited understanding of the links between long-term displacement and peacebuilding, incorporating the issue of refugees only insofar as the return and reintegration of refugees is taken to be a barometer of the success of peacebuilding efforts.

While this is an important dimension of the issue, such a limited approach risks not only missing an important opportunity to resolve protracted refugee situations but also excludes from the work of the PBC a range of factors that could potentially undermine peacebuilding efforts. Refugee-populated areas in neighbouring states may harbour elements that seek to undermine peacebuilding in the region, especially when underlying political tensions still exist and reconciliation has not been fully achieved, and refugee populations may be drawn into a campaign of destabilization. It would therefore be problematic to assume that refugees remain passively in neighbouring countries, awaiting the opportunity to return. Instead, there are many instances where large and protracted refugee situations, left unaddressed, have the potential to undermine the consolidation of a peace process. Likewise, the concerns of host countries and the limitations on their willingness to host refugees must be taken into account. If the concerns of host states relating to the potentially negative impact of the prolonged presence of refugees on their territory are not addressed, host states may pursue early and coerced repatriation, placing fragile institutions in the country of origin under significant strain and further undermining peacebuilding efforts.

Given these dynamics, and their potential impact on peacebuilding activities, it is important to consider the growing significance of protracted refugee situations, their causes, and their links to regional security.

THE GROWING CHALLENGE OF PROTRACTED REFUGEE SITUATIONS

In June 2004, UNHCR defined a protracted refugee situation as 'one in which refugees find themselves in a long-lasting and intractable state of limbo. Their lives may not be at risk, but their basic rights and essential economic, social and psychological needs remain unfulfilled after years in exile. A refugee in this situation is often unable to break free from enforced reliance on external assistance' (UNHCR ExCom 2004*b*: 1). In identifying the major protracted refugee situations in the world, UNHCR used the 'crude measure of refugee populations of 25,000 persons or more who have been in exile for five or more years in developing countries' (UNHCR ExCom 2004*b*: 2). These figures exclude Palestinian refugees who fall under the mandate of the UN Relief and Works Agency for Palestine Refugees in the Near East (UNRWA). Applying this definition to UNHCR refugee statistics from the end of 2004, there were thirty-three major protracted refugee situations, totalling 5,691,000 refugees.

In outlining the scope and scale of the problem, UNHCR also recognized that refugees are spending longer periods in exile and that a greater proportion of the world's refugees are now in situations of prolonged exile. It estimated that 'the average of major refugee situations, protracted or not, has increased from nine years in 1993 to 17 years at the end of 2003' (UNHCR ExCom 2004*b*: 2). With a global refugee population of over 16.3 million at the end of 1993, 48 per cent of the world's refugees were in protracted situations. More than a decade later, with a global refugee population of 9.2 million at the end of 2004, over 64 per cent of the world's refugees were in protracted refugee situations.

As illustrated by the UNHCR statistics in Table 12.1, these situations are to be found in some of the most volatile regions in the world. In fact, protracted refugee populations originate from the very states whose instability lies at the heart of chronic regional insecurity. The bulk of refugees in these regions—Somalis, Sudanese, Burundians, Liberians, Iraqis, Afghans, and Burmese—come from countries where conflict and persecution have persisted for years. In this way, the rising significance of protracted refugee situations is closely associated to the growing phenomenon of so-called 'fragile states' since the end of the Cold War (Loescher and Milner 2008*a*; Morris and Stedman 2008). While there is increasing recognition that international security planners must pay closer attention to these countries of origin, it is important to also recognize that resolving refugee situations must be a central part of any solution to long-standing regional conflicts, especially given the porous

Table 12.1 Major protracted refugee situations: 1 January 2005[4]

Country of asylum	Origin	End-2004
Algeria	Western Sahara	165,000
Armenia	Azerbaijan	235,000
Burundi	Dem. Rep. of Congo	48,000
Cameroon	Chad	39,000
China	Viet Nam	299,000
Congo	Dem. Rep. of Congo	59,000
Côte d'Ivoire	Liberia	70,000
Dem. Rep. of Congo	Angola	98,000
Dem. Rep. of Congo	Sudan	45,000
Egypt	Occupied Palestinian Territory	70,000
Ethiopia	Sudan	90,000
Guinea	Liberia	127,000
India	China	94,000
India	Sri Lanka	57,000
Islamic Rep. of Iran	Afghanistan	953,000
Islamic Rep. of Iran	Iraq	93,000
Kenya	Somalia	154,000
Kenya	Sudan	68,000
Nepal	Bhutan	105,000
Pakistan	Afghanistan (UNHCR estimate)	960,000
Rwanda	Dem. Rep. of Congo	45,000
Saudi Arabia	Occupied Palestinian Territory	240,000
Serbia and Montenegro	Bosnia and Herzegovina	95,000
Serbia and Montenegro	Croatia	180,000
Sudan	Eritrea	111,000
Thailand	Myanmar	121,000
Uganda	Sudan	215,000
United Rep. of Tanzania	Burundi	444,000
United Rep. of Tanzania	Dem. Rep. of Congo	153,000
Uzbekistan	Tajikistan	39,000
Yemen	Somalia	64,000
Zambia	Angola	89,000
Zambia	Dem. Rep. of Congo	66,000
Total		5,691,000

nature of these countries' borders and the tendency for conflict in these regions to engulf their neighbours. In this way, it is essential to recognize that protracted refugee situations are closely linked to the phenomenon of fragile states, have political causes, and therefore require more than simply humanitarian solutions.

An increasing number of host states respond to protracted refugee situations by pursuing policies of containing refugees in isolated and insecure refugee camps, typically in border regions and far from the governing regime.

Many host governments now require the vast majority of refugees to live in designated camps, and place significant restrictions on refugees seeking to leave the camps, either for employment or educational purposes. This trend, recently termed 'refugee warehousing' (Smith 2004), has significant human rights and economic implications. In particular, the prolonged encampment of refugee populations has led to the violation of a number of rights contained in the *1951 UN Convention relating to the Status of Refugees*, including freedom of movement and the right to seek wage-earning employment. Restrictions on employment and on the right to move beyond the confines of the camps deprive long-staying refugees of the freedom to pursue normal lives and to become productive members of their new societies. Faced with these restrictions, refugees in camps frequently become dependent on subsistence-level assistance, or less, and lead lives of poverty, frustration, and unrealized potential.

UNHCR has noted that 'the prolongation of refugees' dependence on external assistance also squanders precious resources of host countries, donors and refugees... limited funds and waning donor commitment lead to stop-gap solutions... spending on care and maintenance... is a recurring expense and not an investment in the future' (UNHCR ExCom 2004*b*: 3). Containing refugees in camps prevents their presence from contributing to regional development and state-building (Jacobsen 2002). In cases where refugees have been allowed to engage in the local economy, it has been found that refugees can 'have a positive impact on the [local] economy by contributing to agricultural production, providing cheap labour and increasing local vendors' income from the sale of essential foodstuffs' (UNHCR ExCom 2004*a*: 3). When prohibited from working outside the camps, refugees cannot make such contributions.

Unresolved refugee situations represent a significant political phenomenon as well as a humanitarian and human rights problem. Protracted refugee situations often lead to a number of political and security concerns for host countries, the countries of origin, regional actors, and the international community. Host states and states in regions of refugee origin frequently argue that protracted refugee situations result in a wide range of direct and indirect security concerns.[5] The direct threats faced by the host-state, posed by the spillover of conflict and the presence of 'refugee warriors', are by far the strongest link between refugees and conflict. Here, there are no intervening variables between forced migration and violence as the migrants themselves are actively engaged in armed campaigns typically, but not exclusively, against the country of origin. Such campaigns have the potential of regionalizing the conflict and dragging the host state into what was previously an intra-state conflict, most clearly demonstrated by the maelstrom of violence that gripped the Great Lakes region of Central Africa between 1994 and 1996.

The outbreak of conflict and genocide in the Great Lakes Region of Central Africa in the early 1990s serves as a clear example of the potential implications of not finding solutions for long-standing refugee populations. Tutsi refugees who fled Rwanda between 1959 and 1962 and their descendants filled the ranks of the Rwandan Patriotic Front (RPF), which invaded Rwanda from Uganda in October 1990. Many of these refugees had been living in the sub-region for over thirty years. In the aftermath of the Rwandan genocide, it was widely recognized that the failure of the international community to find a lasting solution for the Rwandan refugees from the 1960s was a key factor that put in motion the series of events that led to the genocide in 1994. According to UNHCR, 'the failure to address the problems of the Rwandan refugees in the 1960s contributed substantially to the cataclysmic violence of the 1990s' (UNHCR 2000: 49). Nearly twenty years after the 1994 genocide, it would appear as though this lesson has yet to be learned, as dozens of protracted refugee situations remain unresolved in highly volatile and conflict-prone regions.

This lesson has not, however, been lost on a number of states that host prolonged refugee populations. In the wake of events in Central Africa, many host states, especially in Africa, increasingly view long-standing refugee populations as a security concern and synonymous with the spillover of conflict and the spread of small arms. Refugee populations are increasingly being viewed by host states not as victims of persecution and conflict, but as a potential source of regional instability on a scale similar to that witnessed in Central Africa in the 1990s.

The direct causes of insecurity to both host states and regional and extra-regional actors stemming from chronic refugee populations are further understood within the context of so-called failed states, as in Somalia, and the rise of warlordism, as in the case of Liberia. In such situations, refugee camps are used as a base for guerrilla, insurgent, or terrorist activities. Armed groups may hide behind the humanitarian character of refugee camps and settlements, and use these camps as an opportunity to recruit among the disaffected displaced populations. In such situations, there is the risk that humanitarian aid, including food, medical assistance, and other support mechanisms, might be expropriated to support armed elements. Some refugees continue from camps their activities and networks that supported armed conflicts in their home country. Similar security concerns may arise within urban refugee populations where gangs and criminal networks can emerge within displaced and disenfranchised populations (Loescher and Milner 2005, 2008*a*).

The security consequences of such activities for host states and regional actors are real. They include cross-border attacks on both host states and countries of origin, attacks on humanitarian personnel, refugees, and civilian populations. Direct security concerns can also lead to serious bilateral and regional political and diplomatic tensions. Cross-border flows are perceived by host states to impede on their national sovereignty, especially given the tenuous control that many central governments in the developing world have over their border regions. Finally, the activities of armed elements among refugee populations not only violate refugee protection and human rights principles, but can also constitute threats to international peace and security.

More difficult to identify, but just as potentially destabilizing as direct threats, refugee movements may pose indirect threats to the host state. Indirect threats may arise when the presence of refugees exacerbates previously existing inter-communal tensions in the host country, shifts the balance of power between communities, or causes grievances among local populations. At the root of such security concerns is the failure of international solidarity and burden sharing with host countries. Local and national grievances are particularly heightened when refugees compete with local populations for resources, jobs and social services, including health care, education, and housing. Refugees are sometimes seen as a privileged group in terms of services and welfare provisions or as the cause of low wages in the local economy and inflation in local markets. Refugees are also frequently scapegoats for breakdowns in law and order in both rural and urban refugee populated areas.

Furthermore, it has been argued that 'in countries which are divided into antagonistic racial, ethnic, religious or other groupings, a major influx can place precariously balanced multi-ethnic societies under great strain and may even threaten the political balance of power' (Loescher 1992: 42). In this way, the presence of refugees has been demonstrated to accelerate 'existing internal conflicts in the host country' (Weiner 1993: 16). This concern was made most explicitly clear in Macedonia's reluctance to accept Kosovar Albanian refugees in March 1999, citing the concern that the mass of Kosovar Albanian refugees 'threatened to destabilise Macedonia's ethnic balance'.[6] Other examples include the arrival of Iraqi Kurds in Turkey, of Afghan Sunni Muslims in Shia-dominated Pakistan, or of Pashtun Afghans in Beluchi-dominated Beluchistan (Stepputat 2004: 4).

But not all refugees are seen as threats. The question of which refugees are seen as threats, and why, may be partially explained by understanding the perception of refugees as members of the local political community or as outsiders. Indeed, 'in the Third World, the remarkable receptivity provided to millions of Afghans in Pakistan and Iran, to ethnic kin from Bulgaria in Turkey, to Ethiopians in the Sudan, to Ogadeni Ethiopians in Somalia, to southern Sudanese in Uganda, to Issaq Somali in Djibouti and to Mozambicans in Malawi has been facilitated by the ethnic and linguistic characteristics they share with their hosts' (Loescher 1992: 42). In this sense, the importance of affinity and shared group identity cannot be overstated. If a host community perceives the incoming refugee as 'one of us', then positive and generous conceptions of distributive justice will apply.

Conversely, if the refugees are seen as members of an 'out-group', they are likely to receive a hostile reception. In cases where there is a division along ethnic, linguistic, or religious lines, 'a major population influx can place precariously balanced multi-ethnic societies under great strain and may even threaten the political balance of power' (Loescher 1992: 42). Indeed, refugees, 'as an out-group, can be blamed for all untoward activities' (Maluwa 1995: 657). While levels of crime may rise by no more than expected with a comparable rise in population, refugees increasingly are seen as the cause. As argued by Maluwa, the 'presence of massive numbers of refugees' can 'create feelings of resentment and suspicion, as the refugee population increasingly, and often wrongly, gets blamed for the economic conditions that may arise within the domestic population' (Maluwa 1995: 657). This can lead to a point where 'poverty, unemployment, scarcity of resources, and even crime and disease, are suddenly attributed to the presence of these refugees and other foreigners (Maluwa 1995: 657).

The indirect threat to security that long-staying refugees can pose to host states is a key concept that has been lacking in both the research and policy consideration of refugee movements. In these cases, refugees alone are a necessary but not a sufficient cause of host-state insecurity. It is not the refugee that is a threat to the host state, but the context within which the refugees exist that results in the securitization of the asylum question for many states. Lacking policy alternatives, many host governments now present refugee populations as security threats to justify actions that would not otherwise be permissible, especially when the state is confronted with the pressures of externally imposed democratization and economic liberalization. More generally, the presence of refugees can exacerbate previously existing tensions and can change the balance of power between groups in the country of asylum. For this reason refugees play a significant but indirect role in the causes of insecurity and violence, but with consequences potentially of the same scale as the direct threats.

This dynamic has been evident in the dramatic restrictions on asylum that have been imposed by host states in Africa since the mid-1990s (Milner 2009). Numerous reports have pointed to the significance of the absence of meaningful burden-sharing and the growing xenophobia in many African countries as the key factors motivating restrictive asylum policies (Crisp 2000; Rutinwa 1999). There is significant evidence to suggest that as international assistance to refugees is cut, refugees are forced to seek alternative means to survive. This frequently places refugees in conflict with local populations and can even lead them into illegal activities, such as theft, banditry, and prostitution, thereby reinforcing the securitization of refugees and calls for early repatriation.

REFUGEES AND THE REGIONAL DYNAMICS OF PEACEBUILDING

Given these diverse links between protracted refugee situations and state and regional instability, it is striking that the question of refugees has been largely absent from recent debates on peacebuilding. Contemporary policy and research debates on peacebuilding have generally addressed refugees as a matter of secondary concern, focusing instead on programmes in the country of origin to consolidate peace and prevent a return to conflict. Within this approach, the relationship between peacebuilding and refugees is seen to be unidirectional, with the return of refugees seen as a barometer of the extent to which peacebuilding has been successful. This relationship was recently reinforced by the UN High Commissioner for Refugees, António Guterres. In addressing the UN Security Council in January 2009, the High Commissioner argued that 'the scale of return and success of reintegration are two of the most tangible indicators of progress in any peacebuilding process' (UNHCR 2009).

This is clearly an important dynamic, and effective peacebuilding activities must address the needs of refugees by ensuring that the preconditions for successful return and reintegration are present in the refugees' home country (Chimni 2002). This is often a significant challenge, especially following a protracted conflict where physical infrastructure, homes, and social services have been destroyed (Ogata 1997). As the lessons of the past decade make clear, effective peacebuilding in such contexts should also address a wider range of issues affecting returnees, from justice and reconciliation, housing and property rights, human rights monitoring, to the provision of livelihoods in war-torn economies. In this way, the reintegration of displaced populations poses a wide range of peacebuilding challenges, many of which fall beyond the mandate of humanitarian agencies such as UNHCR.

Addressing such challenges should not, however, obscure the fact that the prolonged presence of refugees in neighbouring countries cannot be treated as an isolated factor, to be addressed at the end of the peacebuilding process. As argued by Morris and Stedman (2008: 82), 'refugee movements are all too often seen only as a by-product of conflict, with limited attention paid to the various ways they may cause conflict, prolong conflict, or frustrate efforts to resolve conflicts'. In fact, a number of the political and security challenges associated with the prolonged presence of refugees in the region have the proven ability to undermine peacebuilding efforts, including the presence of so-called 'spoilers' in refugee populations and pressures from the host country to push for early and unsustainable return. A failure to engage with such regional dynamics has the real potential to undermine peacebuilding efforts within the country of origin.

Challenges to Peacebuilding: 'Refugee Spoilers'

The most significant challenge to peacebuilding posed by protracted refugee situations is the presence of the so-called 'spoilers' in refugee camps or in refugee populated border areas. Spoilers, understood as 'groups and tactics that actively seek to hinder, delay, or undermine conflict settlement' (Newman and Richmond 2006: 1), are akin to so-called 'refugee warriors', as outlined above (Stedman 2007).

During the 1970s and 1980s, examples of refugee warrior communities could be found among Afghan *mujahidden* in Pakistan, the *Khmers Rouges* in Thailand, and the Nicaraguan *Contras* in Central America. In Africa, refugee warrior communities were the product of proxy wars in the Horn of Africa and in Southern Africa, wars of national liberation, especially in Southern Africa, and post-colonial conflicts, especially in the African Great Lakes. Similar dynamics exist in many contemporary conflicts, both in Africa and elsewhere, and constitute a serious challenge to peacebuilding activities. In fact, the presence of spoilers in the refugee populated areas of neighbouring states have frustrated peacebuilding efforts in conflicts as diverse as Burundi, Liberia, Afghanistan, Myanmar, and Sudan.

It is widely understood that the best response to the presence of armed elements within a refugee population is through their physical separation and legal exclusion from refugee status, but such an undertaking has consistently proven to be beyond the capability of humanitarian actors, such as UNHCR (LCHR 2002; O'Neill 2000). For example, in the aftermath of the Rwandan genocide and the militarization of refugee camps in the region, UNHCR called for closer cooperation with regional and international security actors to more effectively address the challenge posed by refugee warriors. More than a decade later, however, broader cooperation within the UN system to deal with the problem of refugee warriors remains problematic, and the militarization of refugee camps and settlements continues to undermine refugee protection, regional security, and peacebuilding efforts in the country of origin.

Push for Early and Unsustainable Repatriation

A second challenge to peacebuilding posed by protracted refugee situations is the potential for the large-scale repatriation of refugees before the necessary conditions of safety and sustainable return exist in the country of origin. Likewise, if the concerns of host states relating to the potentially negative impact of the prolonged presence of refugees on their territory are not addressed, host states may pursue early and coerced repatriation, placing fragile institutions in the country of origin under significant strain and further undermining peacebuilding efforts.

The potential for forced and premature return is heightened as donor interest shifts from the host country to the country of origin following the outbreak of peace. Given that many host states feel that they are unfairly burdened with the great majority of the world's refugees, failure to consider the needs and interests of host states as part of broader peacebuilding efforts could exacerbate the concerns of countries of asylum, leading to additional restrictions on asylum and a push for early forced repatriation.

Such concerns were clearly visible in the case of Tanzania in recent years. With the early signs of peace in Burundi, coupled with a significant shift in donor engagement away from the refugee programme in Tanzania in early 2002, the Tanzanian government began to push for a tripling of the number of refugees repatriating to Burundi. While UNHCR did not agree to promote repatriation, given the prevailing insecurity in many regions of Burundi, some 85,000 refugees nevertheless repatriated from Tanzania to Burundi in 2003. The scale of these returns placed a significant strain on the fragile peace in Burundi. Given that these returns coincided with sustained crime and insecurity, additional reductions in food rations, and increased restrictions on refugees' freedom of movement and economic activity in Tanzania, a number of refugee advocates questioned the voluntary nature of the repatriations, suggesting that conditions in the camps had become so unbearable that many refugees felt compelled to repatriate to Burundi, notwithstanding the continuing insecurity there.

Similar dynamics have been experienced elsewhere in Africa and Asia, where donors and host countries all see an interest in pursuing refugee repatriation at the earliest possible opportunity. In many instances, however, such repatriations do not result in a solution to protracted refugee situations, but instead result in a reoccurrence of conflict and future refugee movements as the root causes of flight are often left unaddressed and the preconditions for sustainable return are not ensured. In cases as diverse as Liberian refugees in Guinea, Rohingya refugees in Bangladesh, and Afghan refugees in Pakistan, early and unsustainable repatriation did not lead to a durable solution, but instead formed the foundation of renewed refugee movements.

While part of the solution to this dynamic is to ensure that the preconditions for repatriation are in place, as outlined above, it is also important to ensure that donor interest does not rapidly shift to peacebuilding in the country of origin at the expense of refugee assistance programmes in neighbouring countries. Instead, the interests and concerns of host countries need to be more fully considered as part of the regional dynamics of peacebuilding. Such an approach would not only ensure that host states do not pursue early and unsustainable repatriation but would also contribute to the rehabilitation of refugee populated areas in host countries. While the majority of peacebuilding activities must necessarily be focused on the country of origin, any approach to peacebuilding that is not mindful of broader regional dynamics, including the presence of refugees, risks overlooking factors that could undermine peacebuilding efforts. At the same time, it is important to consider how early engagement with refugee populations in neighbouring countries may contribute to peacebuilding in the country of origin.

Experience of Exile

While the experience of exile may contribute to the politicization of refugee populations (Malkki 1995), thereby undermining prospects for post-repatriation reconciliation, it is also increasingly recognized that refugees can make a significant contribution to peacebuilding in their country of origin. As noted by Guterres in his statement to the UN Security Council (UNHCR 2006), 'refugees return with schooling and new skills... Over and over, we see that their participation is necessary for the consolidation of both peace and post-conflict economic recovery'. Thus, refugee contributions may result from particular skills that they acquire in exile that may directly contribute to post-conflict reconstruction, from the direct involvement of refugees in the negotiation of the peace agreement, and through peace education and reconciliation activities that can occur prior to repatriation. For example, special teacher training programmes have been implemented in Kenya to train Sudanese refugees to meet the educational needs both in the Kakuma refugee camps and in South Sudan (UNHCR 2007).

In fact, a wide range of training opportunities can be extended to refugees in prolonged exile that would eventually contribute to ensuring a durable solution to their plight, either through repatriation, local integration, or resettlement in a third country. Opportunities such as language training, vocational training, professional development, peace education, and other activities could all form part of a broader solutions-oriented approach, and contribute both to peacebuilding and the self-reliance of refugees. Notwithstanding the clear benefits of such programmes, they remain difficult to fund. At the same time, host states are generally wary of such programmes and view them as a backdoor to local integration.

Given the potential benefits of such programmes to both peacebuilding and the livelihood of refugees, it is important to address donor and host country concerns and ensure that such programmes become a standing feature of programmes for protracted refugee situations. Programmes to enhance the self-reliance of refugees do not, however, constitute a solution to protracted refugee situations. These short-term interventions can only help manage the situation until a resolution can be found. In the long term, the implications of protracted refugee situations can only be fully addressed through the formulation and implementation of comprehensive solutions.

CONCLUSION: TOWARDS A MORE PREDICTABLE RESPONSE TO REFUGEES AND PEACEBUILDING

This chapter has argued that there is an important link between protracted refugee situations, regional insecurity, and peacebuilding. The chapter began by considering the focus of peacebuilding policy and research, especially as it is reflected in the work of the UN Peacebuilding Commission (UN PBC). The chapter then considered the links between protracted refugee situations and a broader range of peace and security concerns to argue that the link between peacebuilding and refugees goes beyond the repatriation of refugees. Instead, the chapter outlined how the presence of 'spoilers' within refugee populated areas, the potential for early and forced repatriation by the country of asylum, and the politicization of refugees while in exile all have the proven potential to undermine peacebuilding efforts, while the experience of exile may enable refugees to contribute to various stages of the peacebuilding process. While additional research is required to understand how these dynamics present themselves in different types of protracted refugee situations, it is clear that their significance cannot be excluded from an effective consideration of the range of factors that contribute to, or undermine, peacebuilding.

Given the links between protracted refugee situations, fragile states, and peacebuilding, it is clear that actions by humanitarian agencies, such as UNHCR, without the support of peace and security and development actors will lead to neither comprehensive solutions for protracted refugee situations nor an effective response to the peacebuilding implications of prolonged exile. So long as discussions on protracted refugee situations remain exclusively within the humanitarian community and do not engage the broader peace and security and development communities, they will be limited in their impact (Loescher and Milner 2008*b*). Likewise, the links between refugee movements and regional security suggest that refugee issues need to be more fully incorporated into peacebuilding policy and practice.

The establishment of the PBC could provide a possible institutional context for this type of cross-sectoral approach. The composition and mandate of the PBC places it in a unique position to address a number of these concerns. In fact, the UNGA specifically provided that country-specific meetings of the PBC shall include as additional members the country under consideration (i.e. the country of origin), countries in the region (i.e. host countries) and senior UN representatives in the field, and other relevant UN representatives (including UNHCR). In this way, the PBC represents a unique forum for the coordination of peace and security, development, and humanitarian activities to address both protracted refugee situations and the regional dynamics of peacebuilding.

A broader recognition of the role of refugees and the regional dynamics of peacebuilding will be an important precondition for successful peacebuilding in countries like Burundi and Sierra Leone, where conflict resulted in significant refugee movements into neighbouring countries which, in turn, played a significant role in the course of the conflict. More generally, conflict in both countries is largely tied to broader regional dynamics and neighbouring conflicts—the African Great Lakes for Burundi and the Mano River Union for Sierra Leone. Given the regional dynamics of conflict and the role that refugee populations play not only as a consequence of conflict but as a source of its perpetuation in both cases, the importance of situating peacebuilding efforts within a broader regional context would seem logical.

These cases bear important lessons not only for the work of the UN PBC, but more generally for the closer consideration of the important links between refugee issues and the study of international relations. As cases from the past half-century make clear, refugee movements are more than simply humanitarian and human rights challenges. In a range of cases, refugee movements have been central to the state of regional relations and regional stability. It is therefore important for their role to be more fully considered by the discipline of international relations as it seeks to better explain the dynamics of conflict and prospects of peacebuilding. Likewise, those who seek to better understand the preconditions of solutions for refugees could usefully draw from the lessons and tools of international relations. As this chapter has suggested, solutions for refugees often rely on the interests of actors outside the humanitarian community. A more thorough understanding of the interests of these actors could serve as a useful basis for more predictable and comprehensive solutions for the world's refugees.

Appendix 1

Membership of the UN Peacebuilding Commission's Organizational Committee (23 June 2007 to 22 June 2008)

Angola
Bangladesh
Belgium
Brazil (Chair of the Guinea-Bissau configuration)
Burundi
Chile
China
Czech Republic
Egypt
El Salvador (Vice-Chairperson)
Fiji
France
Georgia
Germany
Ghana (Vice-Chairperson)
Guinea-Bissau
India
Indonesia
Italy
Jamaica
Japan (Chairperson)
Luxembourg
Netherlands (Chair of the Sierra Leone configuration)

Nigeria
Norway (Chair of the Burundi configuration)
Pakistan
Russian Federation
South Africa
Sri Lanka
United Kingdom of Great Britain and Northern Ireland
United States of America

Participants in all meetings of the Peacebuilding Commission

International Monetary Fund
World Bank
European Community
Organization of the Islamic Conference

Appendix 2

Additional members of the country-specific configurations

Additional members of the Burundi country-specific configuration

Canada
Croatia
Democratic Republic of the Congo
Denmark
Kenya
Nepal
Rwanda
Uganda
United Republic of Tanzania
African Development Bank
African Union
East African Economic Community
Economic Commission for Africa
Economic Community of Central African States
Executive Representative of the Secretary-General
Inter-Parliamentary Union
Organisation international de la francophonie
Special Representative of the Secretary-General for the Great Lakes Region

Additional members of the Guinea-Bissau country-specific configuration

Benin
Burkina Faso
Cape Verde
Gambia
Mexico
Mozambique
Niger
Portugal
Sao Tome and Principe
Senegal
Spain
Timor-Leste
African Development Bank
African Union
Community of Portuguese-speaking Countries
Economic Community of West African States
Organisation international de la francophonie
Representative of the Secretary-General
Union économique et monétaire ouest africaine
United Nations Development Programme
United Nations Office on Drugs and Crime

Additional members of the Sierra Leone country-specific configuration

Guinea
Ireland
Liberia
Sweden
African Development Bank
African Union
Central Bank of West African States
Commonwealth
Economic Commission for Africa
Economic Community of West African States
Executive Representative of the Secretary-General
Mano River Union
Special Representative of the Secretary-General for West Africa

NOTES

1. This chapter draws on previous research undertaken by the author under the auspices of *The PRS Project: Towards Solutions to Protracted Refugee Situations*, University of Oxford (http://www.prsproject.org), and the United Nations University project 'Protracted Refugee Situations: Political, Security and Human Rights Implications'. Elements of this chapter previously appeared in Gil Loescher and James Milner (2005), *Protracted Refugee Situations: Domestic and Security Implications*, Adelphi Paper no. 375, London: Routledge; G. Loescher, J. Milner, E. Newman, and G. Troeller (2007), 'Protracted Refugee Situations and the Regional Dynamics of Peacebuilding', *Conflict, Security and Development*, Vol. 7, no. 3, 491–501; and James Milner, 'Refugees and the regional dynamics of peacebuilding' *Refugee Survey Quarterly*, Vol. 28, no. 1, 2009, 13–30. The author is especially grateful to Gil Loescher for his on-going support and encouragement.
2. See http://www.un.org/peace/peacebuilding/, accessed 10 July 2009.
3. This section is based on interviews conducted in New York in May 2006, December 2006, and March 2007.
4. This table refers to refugee situations where the number of refugees of a certain origin within a particular country of asylum has been 25,000 or more for at least five consecutive years. Industrialized countries are not included. Data does not include Palestinian refugees under the mandate of the UN Relief and Works Agency for Palestine Refugees in the Near East (UNRWA). Source: UNHCR (2006: 107).
5. For a more detailed discussion of direct and indirect security concerns related to refugee movements, see Milner (2009) and Loescher and Milner (2005).
6. Comments by the Macedonian Deputy Foreign Minister at the Emergency Meeting on the Kosovo Refugee Crisis, Geneva, 6 April 1999.

BIBLIOGRAPHY

Ali, Taisier M. and Robert O. Matthews. (eds.). 2004. *Durable peace: challenges for peacebuilding in Africa*, Toronto: University of Toronto Press.

Ayoob, Mohammed. 1995. *The third world security predicament: state making, regional conflict and the international system*, Boulder, CO: Lynne Rienner.

Buzan, Barry. 1992. 'Third World regional security in structural and historical perspective', in Brian Job (ed.), *The insecurity dilemma: national security of third world states*, Boulder, CO: Lynne Reinner.

Chimni, B. S. 2002. 'Refugees and post-conflict reconstruction: a critical perspective', *International Peacekeeping*, Vol. 9, no. 2, Summer; 163–180.

Crisp, Jeff. 2000. 'Africa's refugees: patterns, problems and policy challenges', *New issues in refugee research*, Working Paper No. 28, Geneva: UNHCR, August.

Jacobsen, Karen. 2002. 'Can refugees benefit the state? Refugee resources and African statebuilding', *Journal of Modern African Studies*, Vol. 40, no. 4, 577–596.

Lawyers Committee for Human Rights (LCHR). 2002. *Refugees, rebels and the quest for justice*, New York: LCHR.

Loescher, Gil. 1992. *Refugee movements and international security*, Adelphi Paper 268, London: Brasseys for The International Institute for Strategic Studies.

——and James Milner. 2005. *Protracted refugee situations: domestic and security implications*, Adelphi Paper 375, London: Routledge.

————. 2008*a*. 'Understanding the problem of protracted refugee situations', in G. Loescher, J. Milner, E. Newman, and Gary Troeller (eds.), *Protracted refugee situations: political, human rights and security implications*, Tokyo: United Nations University Press.

————. 2008*b*. 'A framework for responding to protracted refugee situations', in G. Loescher, J. Milner, E. Newman, and Gary Troeller (eds.), *Protracted refugee situations: political, human rights and security implications*, Tokyo: United Nations University Press.

——, J. Milner, E. Newman, and G. Troeller. 2007. 'Protracted refugee situations and the regional dynamics of peacebuilding', *Conflict, security and development*, Vol. 7, no. 3.

Malkki, Liisa. 1995. *Purity and exile: violence, memory and national cosmology among hutu refugees in tanzania*, Chicago, IL: Chicago University Press.

Maluwa, Tiyanjana. 1995. 'The refugee problem and the quest for peace and security in Southern Africa', *International Journal of Refugee Law*, Vol. 7, no. 4, 653–674.

Milner, J. 2009*a*. 'Refugees and the regional dynamics of peacebuilding', *Refugee Survey Quarterly*, Vol. 28, no. 1, 13–30, 282, n 1.

——. 2009*b*. *Refugees, the state, and the politics of asylum in Africa*, Basingstoke: Palgrave Macmillan, 272, last-line; 1, 282, n 4.

Morris, Eric and Stephen John Stedman. 2008. 'Protracted refugee situations, conflict and security: The need for better diagnosis and prescription', in G. Loescher, J. Milner, E. Newman, and Gary Troeller (eds.), *Protracted refugee situations: political, human rights and security implications*, Tokyo: United Nations University Press.

Newman, Edward and Oliver Richmond. 2006. 'The impact of spoilers on peace processes and peacebuilding', United Nations University Policy Brief, No. 2, available on-line at http://www.ciaonet.org/pbei/unup/unup005/unup005.pdf.

Ogata, Sadako. 1997. 'Introduction: refugee repatriation and peace-building', *Refugee Survey Quarterly*, Vol. 16, no. 2, vi–x.

O'Neill, William. 2000. 'Conflict in West Africa: dealing with exclusion and separation', *International Journal of Refugee Law*, Vol. 12, Special Supplementary Issue, 171–194.

Rutinwa, Bonaventure. 1999. 'The end of asylum? The changing nature of refugee policies in Africa', *New Issues in Refugee Research*, Working Paper No. 5, Geneva: UNHCR, May.

Smith, Merrill. 2004. 'Warehousing refugees: a denial of rights, a waste of humanity', *World Refugee Survey 2004*, Washington, DC: US Committee for Refugees.

Stedman, Stephen John. 1997. 'Spoiler problems in peace processes', *International Security*, Vol. 22, no. 2, Fall, 491–501.

Stedman, Donald Rothchild, and Elizabeth M. Cousens (eds.). 2002. *Ending civil wars: the implementation of peace agreements*, Boulder, CO: Lynne Rienner.

Stepputat, Finn. 2004. *Refugees, security and development. current experience and strategies of protection and assistance in 'the region of origin'*, Copenhagen: Danish Institute for International Studies, Working Paper No. 2004/11.

UN General Assembly (UNGA). 2005. Resolution 60/180, 30 December.

——. 2007. 'Report of the Peacebuilding Commission on its first session', UN Doc. A/62/137-S/2007/458, 25 July.

——. 2008*a*. 'Report of the Peacebuilding Commission on its second session', UN Doc. A/63/92-S/2008/417, 24 June.

——. 2008*b*. 'Report of the Secretary-General on the Peacebuilding Fund', UN Doc. A/63/218-S/2008/522, 4 August.

United Nations High Commissioner for Refugees (UNHCR). 2000. *The state of the world's refugees: fifty years of humanitarian action*, Oxford: Oxford University Press.

——. 2006. *The state of the world's refugees: human displacement in the new millennium*, Oxford: Oxford University Press.

——. 2007. *New Story: New refugee teachers one of the keys to development in southern Sudan*, Kenya, 29 January.

——. 2009. *Statement by Mr. António Guterres, United Nations High Commissioner for Refugees, to the United Nations Security Council*, New York, 8 January.

UNHCR, Executive Committee of the High Commissioner's Programme (ExCom). 2004*a*. 'Economic and Social Impact of Massive Refugee Populations on Host Developing Countries, as well as Other Countries', EC/54/SC/CRP.5, 18 February.

——. 2004*b*. 'Protracted Refugee Situations', Standing Committee, 30th Meeting, UN Doc. EC/54/SC/CRP.14, 10 June.

UN High-level Panel on Threats, Challenges and Change. 2004. *A more secure World: Our Shared Responsibility*, New York: United Nations.

UN Secretary-General (UNSG). 1992. *An agenda for peace: preventive diplomacy, peacemaking and peace-keeping*, Report of the Secretary-General pursuant to the statement adopted by the Summit Meeting of the Security Council on 31 January 1992, A/47/227, 17 June.

——. 2005. *In larger freedom: towards security, development and human rights for all*, Report of the Secretary-General of the United Nations for decision by Heads of State and Government in September 2005, A/59/2005, 21 March.

Weiner, Myron. 1993. 'Security, Stability and International Migration', in Myron Weiner (ed.), *International migration and security*, Boulder, CO: Westview Press.

13

Post-conflict Statebuilding and Forced Migration

Dominik Zaum

ABSTRACT

While refugees have been a politically salient issue in post-conflict environments and refugee return has been an important part of statebuilding mandates, the literature mostly fails to address the role of refugees in post-conflict statebuilding processes. This chapter maps some of the roles that refugees play in statebuilding processes and examines the impact of these efforts on their ability to return. Through the lens of the statebuilding operations in Bosnia and Kosovo, it explores three issues. The first part discusses the challenges posed by refugee situations to the institutionalization and legitimation of a political settlement, in particular through the organization and conduct of elections. The second section examines the role that refugees play in post-conflict reconstruction, especially through remittances. The third section analyses a particularly prominent returns-related policy of the statebuilding operations in Bosnia and Kosovo, namely, the efforts to establish and enforce rights of refugees to their residential properties. The chapter highlights that despite the prominence awarded to refugees in the mandate of statebuilding operations, they have rarely been given a voice and a formal role in the processes. It argues that refugees play a complex role in the politics of statebuilding, affecting both the economic and political dynamics of these efforts: refugees have been instrumentalized in conflicts over the character of the state and in attempts to change or entrench local balances of power; efforts to facilitate their return has informed major rule of law reforms, in particular the resolution of private property rights; and their remittances have contributed significantly to physical reconstruction, and in a small way also to the financial sustainability of state institutions. It also shows how the returns policies of Western donor countries have threatened to compromise their statebuilding objectives in the cases examined.

Statebuilding and state formation, in particular the creation of nation-states in twentieth-century Europe, has a complicated and often tragic association with forced migration. Throughout the twentieth century, the creation and consolidation of states has been closely associated with the creation of large refugee populations. Under the 1923 Lausanne treaty, 'Turkish nationals of the Greek Orthodox Religion established in Turkish territory, and...Greek Nationals of the Muslim Religion established in Greek territory',[1] were forcibly resettled into Greece or Turkey, respectively. Following the Second World War, more than 13 million ethnic Germans from what was now Polish territory, Czechoslovakia, Hungary, Romania, and Yugoslavia were evicted and fled to Germany (Judt 2007: 273). Following the partition of India, more than 15 million people crossed the borders to live among a majority of their co-religionists, while large-scale violence left up to 1 million people dead (Kaufmann 1998). The creation of Israel, and the successful defence and consolidation of the new state, led to the expulsion of an estimated 725,000 Palestinians from Israeli territory, a refugee population that has now grown to more than 4 million (Morris 1989).

Some of these refugee situations have remained politically salient for decades, like the plight of Palestinian refugees, which continues to have important implications for any settlement of the conflict in the occupied territories, and any effort to build a Palestinian state. Others have affected interstate relations, like the demands for recognition and restitution by the German *Vertriebenenverbaende* (Refugee Associations) that have complicated relations between Germany and its eastern neighbours. Generally, though, the displacement of these populations was seen as important for the cohesion and the stability of these young states. Traditional forms of state formation and statebuilding, in particular the building of nation-states in the aftermath of the First and Second World Wars, are thus closely intertwined with major refugee crises (Mazower 1998). As Jennifer Jackson-Preece (1998) has argued, ethnic cleansing, and thus forced migration, has been an important instrument for nation-state creation.

Since the end of the Cold War, statebuilding has taken on a different form, with large-scale international involvement in post-conflict states to (re)build political and administrative institutions, embed a broadly liberal-democratic order in post-conflict societies, with institutionalize and manage power balances between salient societal groups (Call with Wyeth 2008, Caplan 2005, Chesterman 2004, Paris 2004, Paris and Sisk 2008, Zaum 2007).[2] These statebuilding efforts have generally concerned conflicts that have given rise to major refugee crises, often displacing large parts of the population. In many conflicts, this displacement was not merely a consequence of conflict, but a deliberate strategy of the conflict parties to consolidate control over the territories they held. In Bosnia, more than half of the pre-war population of 4.3 million were displaced during the war (Cunliffe and Pugh 1997). In Kosovo, about 850,000 Albanians were forced to leave their homes in 1998–9, while more than 230,000 members of minority communities, mostly Serbs, were displaced by Kosovo Albanians after the war ended and NATO-led KFOR troops were deployed (UNHCR 2000: 345). In East Timor, an estimated 500,000 people out of a population of around a million fled from the violence unleashed by pro-Indonesian militias (UN 1999: para.19). Two decades of conflict in Afghanistan meant that by the time the United States defeated the Taliban regime in late 2001, more than 3.5 million Afghan refugees lived mostly in camps in Pakistan and Iran, many for decades, and more than one million people were internally displaced (UN 2002).

The 'liberal statebuilding' efforts of the post-Cold War period have been rooted in the understanding by the UN and the main donor countries and organizations that democratic political institutions, the protection of human rights norms and the rule of law, free markets, a reasonably effective public administration able to deliver public goods, and the representation of salient societal groups in the state's institutions are central to the legitimacy, and thus the stability of post-conflict states (Paris 2004; Zaum 2007). While the interventionist policies and the imposition of a broadly Weberian conception of the state has been decried as imperial and neocolonial by some critics (see, e.g., Chandler 1999; Chopra 2000; Jahn 2007*a*, 2007*b*), this approach has dominated international statebuilding efforts over the last two decades. Proponents of liberal statebuilding see the establishment of legitimate institutions as central to the peaceful resolution of the inevitable societal conflicts that arise in divided societies, and to the establishment of the conditions for self-sustaining peace.[3] They also see it as an important precondition for the return of refugees, and for the successful integration of refugees and IDPs into the post-conflict society.

Establishing the conditions under which refugees will be able to return to their homeland—or even their homes—and managing the return process has been a key concern of many international post-conflict statebuilding operations. It is reflected in the mandates of missions such as the international presence in Bosnia and Herzegovina, the UN Interim Administration Mission in Kosovo (UNMIK), the UN Transitional Administration Mission in East Timor (UNTAET), and the UN Assistance Mission to Afghanistan (UNAMA),[4] all of which have spent extensive resources on refugee return and return-related activities: the restoration of housing stock; the resolution of property rights; socio-economic assistance to returnees; and the provision of physical security for returnees.

Refugee return has also been politically important for statebuilding operations. Return figures provide a possible benchmark to assess the success or failure of such operations. Thus, as Christopher McDowell and Marita Eastmond (2002) have argued, the statebuilding missions in Cambodia and East

Timor have pushed for rapid refugee return before the end of their mandates despite serious concerns about the sustainability of such returns, to legitimize their operations. The Serbian government, for example, regularly emphasizes the very low figures for minority returns to Kosovo when criticizing the international community's statebuilding efforts and challenging the legitimacy of the Kosovo government. Refugees can also shape the political and economic dynamics in their post-conflict home countries. The potential return of large numbers of refugees after the end of a conflict poses obvious challenges for institution-building and the public services: it puts strains on the provision of education and healthcare, leads to greater competition for already scarce employment opportunities, and increases competition for arable land, to name just a few.

The 2001 ICISS report on the *Responsibility to Protect*, which discusses statebuilding and post-conflict reconstruction in the context of an international responsibility to rebuild, highlights the importance of statebuilding, and in particular the (re)establishment of a legal framework and the rule of law, for refugee return and for the economic and political integration of refugees into post-conflict societies (ICISS 2001: paras. 5.15–5.18).

> Unequal treatment in the provision of basic services, repatriation assistance and employment, and property laws, are often designed to send a powerful signal that returnees are not welcome.... In many cases around the world, attempts by returnees to use the courts to evict temporary occupants (often themselves refugees) from their homes and regain rightful property have ended in frustration rather than re-possession. Laws either provide inadequate protection of property rights or were framed to deter potential returnees and disadvantage those who do return.
>
> [...]
>
> Facilitating returns requires the removal of the administrative and bureaucratic obstacles to return, ending the culture of impunity vis-à-vis known or suspected war criminals and the adoption of non-discriminatory property laws.
>
> [...]
>
> Additionally, the question of return sustainability—pivotal to ensuring the long-term success of repatriation—will need to be properly treated. Return sustainability is about creating the right social and economic conditions for returnees. It also includes access to health, education and basic services, and is linked to reform in other areas—eradicating corruption, promoting good governance, and long-term economic regeneration of the country.

However, despite the prominence of refugee problems in the politics of post-conflict statebuilding, the literature on the issue has mostly ignored the role of refugees. There is no systematic analysis of the role that refugees play in statebuilding processes, and in many of the most recent contributions to the field, the term 'refugee' does not even appear in the index.[5] One explanation for this *lacuna* might be that refugee problems are often seen as a humanitarian rather than a political problem. Such an understanding seems to have informed the departure of UNHCR, which formed part of UNMIK in Kosovo, from the statebuilding mission's pillar structure after one year in June 2000 when the immediate humanitarian emergency was over, emphasizing its autonomy and non-political position (McKittrick 2008). Contrary to such an understanding, this chapter argues that refugees pose a range of deeply political issues for statebuilding operations and the international actors involved in facilitating the return and reintegration of refugees.

This chapter aims to map out both some of the roles played by refugees in post-conflict statebuilding, but also how particular statebuilding policies have affected the ability of refugees to return. It uses the term 'refugees' broadly, including all persons who have been forcibly uprooted because of violence or persecution, regardless of whether they had to leave their country of origin or not (see Loescher 1992: 6–8). As a comprehensive review of the problem of forced migration in the context of statebuilding is beyond the scope of a short chapter, this discussion is merely an attempt to more systematically examine the role of refugees in three key aspects of post-conflict statebuilding operations. To that end, it first examines the challenges posed by refugee situations to the institutionalization and legitimation of a political settlement, in particular through the organization and conduct of elections. Secondly, it discusses the role that refugees play in post-conflict reconstruction, in particular through remittances. The third section analyses a particularly prominent returns-related policy of two major statebuilding operations, in Bosnia and Kosovo, namely, efforts to establish and enforce rights of refugees to their residential properties.

The chapter draws predominantly on the cases of Bosnia and Kosovo, not least because they highlight many of the dynamics of the relationship between statebuilding and forced migration. However, as both cases have seen well-funded missions that have been deeply involved not only in assistance but also in the governance of the territories, I do not claim that one can generalize from these cases to the whole universe of post-conflict statebuilding operations. Nonetheless, they raise important conceptual questions about the role of refugees in statebuilding more generally, and offer some insights into the scope and limitations of key statebuilding policies with regard to refugee return.

INSTITUTIONALIZING AND LEGITIMATING A POLITICAL SETTLEMENT

One of the key aspects of post-conflict statebuilding is the creation or strengthening of political and administrative institutions that reflect the bargains made in a peace settlement, and complementary efforts to legitimate them locally. To that end, statebuilding operations have engaged in constitutional and institutional design, the building of administrative capacity, and the holding of elections to legitimate these new political institutions.

For some donors and international organizations, there is a perceived tension between such statebuilding efforts, on the one hand, and facilitating the return of refugees and IDPs, on the other. Not only do returning refugees compete for scarce time and resources of international agencies that could otherwise be used to consolidate political order, but their return might be considered to jeopardize stability and security. Consequently, some donors and international organizations have at times actively discouraged the return of refugees on these grounds, in particular of minority returns into areas where the majority population is hostile to their presence (Belloni 2005). Beyond concerns about the negative impact of returns on security, the involvement of refugees in statebuilding processes poses logistical and conceptual challenges to efforts to build and legitimize political institutions in post-conflict societies. Many scholars and practitioners emphasize the importance of local ownership of these practices, so that newly established institutions are more likely to reflect the values and interests of different societal groups, are considered legitimate by the local population, and can be self-sustaining in the absence of an international security presence supporting them (see, e.g., Cliffe et al. 2003; Ghani and Lockhart 2008). This raises the question as to how refugees should be involved in these processes: what are the mechanisms that can be employed to enable the participation of refugees and what role should their representatives be given in the negotiation and implementation of a political settlement?

The main logistical question this raises is what mechanisms are available at an acceptable cost to involve refugees in consultations or actual decision-making? In practice, this has mostly focused on enabling refugees to participate in post-conflict elections, and statebuilding operations have often gone to great length and expense to achieve this. The registration of refugees, voter education, security costs, and ensuring the integrity of the ballot mean that elections in post-conflict countries are five to fifteen times more expensive per voter than in an established democracy (UNDP 2005). In the case of Bosnia, enabling refugees to vote meant that voting centres were established as far as Australia for the 1996 elections.

The main political issues raised by refugees relate to the question of representation. As an important objective of many statebuilding operations is the creation of a political environment that allows refugees to return, should they be accorded a distinct identity and role in the statebuilding process and in the nascent state institutions? If so, should such an identity be permanent or merely temporary—especially if return in reality does not mean return to one's previous home, but into different locations within the community? If statebuilders consult and involve representatives of refugee groups in the development and implementation of policies, how should they be selected? To what extent does the reliance on often self-appointed spokespersons for particular refugee groups entrench power structures within this community that are the result of conflict, that represent the particular interests of a small clique within wider refugee communities, or marginalize important dissenting voices within them?

While refugees often constitute a substantial share of the political community of a post-conflict territory and can be a group with a distinct identity, needs, and interests (especially if they have been displaced for many years), they are rarely participants in the negotiations leading to a political settlement or are represented in the institutions implementing it. Refugees were not represented at the 1995 Dayton conference where the settlement for Bosnia and Herzegovina was negotiated, or at the 1999 Rambouillet conference on Kosovo. They have had no representation in the consultative councils established by UNMIK in Kosovo, or UNTAET in East Timor, and had no separate voice in the process of drafting the constitutions of these territories. While their plight was discussed, and their right to return asserted, they had no input themselves. In Kosovo, Serb refugees had no independent representation in the negotiations about Kosovo's status after 2005, a process with important economic and political implications for them. Their only representation was the Serbian government, whose interests during the negotiations were not necessarily congruent with those of displaced Serbs, and who through the financing of parallel institutions in Kosovo has discouraged the integration of displaced Serbs into Kosovar society (Crisis Group 2008; OSCE 2007). An interesting exception to this non-involvement of refugees has been the emergency Loya Jirga in Afghanistan, where 100 of the approximately 1,500 delegates represented different refugee populations: forty representing refugees from Pakistan, thirty representing refugees from Iran, and thirty representing refugees from other countries (Crisis Group 2002). While the involvement of refugees in the Loya Jirga seems to have limited impact on the priorities and outcomes of the Loya Jirga discussions, their involvement was symbolically important, recognizing refugees as an important group facing distinct economic and political challenges in Afghanistan.

The political manipulation of refugees

Local political elites have at times used returning refugees to consolidate their control over particular territories by steering return to particular cities to cement the majority of their ethnic population. In Bosnia, all three ethnic groups pursued such policies to differing degrees, aided by the desire of Western European countries to quickly repatriate them. This policy of ethnic consolidation was implicitly supported by the prioritization by the international presence of 'majority returns' (returns into areas where returnees are part of the majority group), and a lack of substantial support for minority returns. Local authorities used their control over the allocation of housing to ethnically engineer the returns process (Heimerl 2005: 378–81). Refugees were instrumentalized by local elites to consolidate wartime gains. Concerns about the security of minority returnees meant that UNHCR was at times effectively complicit with these efforts, discouraging refugees and IDPs to return to their previous homes (Belloni 2005).

In addition to manipulating refugee returns, Bosnian (especially Bosnian Serb) political leaders used the electoral system at the first elections in 1996 to boost turnout of their own ethnic group in particular contested towns. The rules and regulations for the 1996 elections allowed refugees and displaced persons to vote either in the municipality where they were registered before 1991, in the municipality where they were currently residing (if they were IDPs), or, if they were refugees, in a municipality where they intended to reside on return.[6] As the Crisis Group (1996: 50–1) reported in the aftermath of the elections:

> An estimated 37,000 Bosnian Serb refugees currently living in the Federal Republic of Yugoslavia came by bus to vote in Republika Srpska on the day. Virtually all were originally from the Federation and many were visiting for the first time the towns in which they were voting and in which they supposedly intended to live.
>
> ...Concentrations of refugees in Yugoslavia were clearly twinned with towns in Republika Srpska to ensure that the operation ran smoothly. In this way, refugees living in Novi Sad, for example, were directed to Brcko, and those living in Uzice were directed to Visegrad.... To ensure a massive turn-out, refugees were told that they had to produce confirmation of *potvrda* (voting slips) to maintain their status and their entitlement to benefits and also to get on the bus taking them back to FRY. These were being handed out by appointed foremen outside the polling stations.

Many refugees complained that they had not been given the option to vote by absentee ballot where they had been living in 1991.

Political leaders exploited the economic vulnerability of refugees to consolidate ethnic divisions through a key part of the post-conflict statebuilding process: elections. Following vociferous protests in particular from Bosniak parties—who had always wanted to limit the right of refugees to vote in municipalities where they had resided before 1991 to reverse the ethnic cleansing of the conflict—the Organization for Security and Co-operation in Europe (OSCE) changed the electoral law to make it almost impossible for refugees to vote in 'new' municipalities (Tansey 2009: 185–7).

Exploiting the economic vulnerabilities of refugees for political ends, however, can take different forms and consequences. In Kosovo, it resulted in limiting the return of the minority community in Mitrovica, which was displaced from the now Albanian-controlled southern part of the city into the Serb-controlled northern part in the wake of the 1999 war. Threatened by the discontinuation of the salaries and benefits they receive from Belgrade if they move back into the old *Roma Mahalla*,[7] most Roma have stayed in the refugee camps, while many of the houses constructed by humanitarian agencies for them remain unoccupied, undermining the Kosovo government's claims to build a multi-ethnic society (see, e.g., Human Rights Watch 2009).

Refugee populations, however, are not just passive political objects manipulated by political entrepreneurs, but through their own actions can affect the political dynamics in the new institutions. The role of 'refugee spoilers' is discussed by James Milner in his chapter in this book.[8] In the Balkans, refugees have hindered state consolidation indirectly: in several Serbian elections, the presence of Serbian refugees from Bosnia, Croatia, and Kosovo has been positively correlated with electoral success of the nationalist radical party (Stefanovic 2008), hardening Serbia's response to statebuilding in Kosovo, not merely with regard to the resolution of the status question but also by strengthening the parallel institutions in Kosovo and the clandestine presence of Serbian security institutions in parts of Kosovo.

However, refugees have also had an important positive impact on the political dynamics and on the development of political institutions especially on the local level. In Bosnia, the electoral law that was instrumentalized and abused to consolidate ethnic divisions was also used to overcome them and help to wrest control from the political extremes towards the moderate centre, as Robert Belloni highlights in his discussion of refugee return to Prijedor. Before the war, Prijedor had been a small multi-ethnic town of approximately 110,000 inhabitants, of which approximately. 50,000 were Bosniaks, and

47,000 Serbs. During the conflict, the non-Serb population was almost completely displaced, and the town turned into a stronghold of the Serb nationalist SDS, the party of Radovan Karadzic. The ability of Bosniak refugees to vote in absentia in their old municipality in the municipal elections in 1997 and 2000 helped to tip the balance against the SDS and increasingly marginalize it in the town's institutions. This in turn created an environment deemed secure enough by many refugees to return, as eventually more than half of the town's pre-war Bosniak population did (Belloni 2005). Similar developments occurred in other strongholds of radical Bosnian Serbs, such as Doboj, where more than half of the pre-war Bosniak population returned (European Stability Initiative 2007).

While the political initiative of refugees was central to creating the conditions for successful minority returns to Prijedor and Doboj, policy choices of the international community in Bosnia supported this development (European Stability Initiative 1999; Crisis Group 2000). Most importantly, the depoliticization of the property restitution process, making it a question of the rule of law (rather than ethnic politics) by introducing a legal mechanism to resolve competing property claims, and the increased efforts to implement the decisions on property rights facilitated returns as it alleviated some of the socio-economic uncertainties that returnees otherwise faced. This issue will be discussed in more detail below.

REFUGEES, REMITTANCES, AND RECONSTRUCTION

The creation and sustainability of state institutions is constrained by the available economic resources; and similarly the sustainability of refugee returns ultimately depends on sufficient economic opportunities for returnees (see, e.g., Black 2001; Chimni 2004; Harvey 2006). While economic reforms and development efforts have been essential parts of any international statebuilding effort, the economic policies of statebuilding operations have generally not been geared towards encouraging return. Focusing on macroeconomic stabilization, balanced budgets, and rapid liberalization of markets, in particular through privatization (del Castillo 2008), such policies might help to stabilize the economy and encourage growth in the longer term, but do little to directly aid the return and integration of refugees and can even lead to social unrest and instability, further undermining the conditions for refugee return (Paris 2004).

However, refugees are often an important part of the economic basis of statebuilding, as the remittance income they send back from abroad in many cases constitutes one of the major sources of income in post-conflict countries, funding in particular reconstruction and housing, and the import of consumer goods. Worldwide, remittance income has been estimated to be twice as high as official development aid (Mohapatra et al. 2006) and its importance for reconstruction and economic development has been increasingly recognized by donors (Savage and Harvey 2007).

In Kosovo, the large diaspora in Western Europe, made up of *Gastarbeiter* and from the 1990s onwards increasingly of refugees, funded a parallel clandestine state which in particular provided rudimentary healthcare and education to Albanians under Milosevic's apartheid regime (Clark 2000; Hockenos 2003). Since the end of the war, remittances have continued to contribute substantially to the alleviation (or at least mitigation) of poverty, especially in rural areas, and have fuelled the post-war reconstruction boom. Indirectly, remittances aid the development of state institutions and the provision of public services, by their substantial contribution to tax revenues. The IMF (2009) estimates that in 2007 remittances amounted to €431 million, constituting approximately 12.5 per cent of Kosovo's GDP. While remittances are not directly taxed, the way in which remittances are spent predominantly on imported consumer goods means that they make a disproportionate contribution to tax revenue, as the budget relies disproportionately on excise duties and taxes collected on imports at the border (such as VAT), which make up 65 per cent of Kosovo's tax income (Ministry of Economy and Finance 2008: 13).

While refugees have undoubtedly made an important economic contribution to statebuilding in Kosovo through their remittances, on the whole this has not left a lasting developmental legacy. Instead, their remittances have substituted for effective development policies in particular in rural areas, sustaining conservative, patriarchal family units that discourage female employment and education (European Stability Initiative 2006). Rather than kick-starting entrepreneurial activity and growth, remittances have served as a safety-blanket. Furthermore, as after many other conflicts, remittances have been steadily declining in Kosovo since the end of the war and the alleviation of the humanitarian crises. One of the key reasons for this decline in Kosovo has been the return of refugees: since 1999, more than 170,000 Kosovo Albanians refugees have been returned from Germany, for example, and as outward migration has become increasingly difficult, remittances consequently declined. Furthermore, as those that have been able to remain have often brought their families abroad, they are now less likely (and less able) to send money back. This situation has been aggravated by the global financial and economic crisis.

This has important policy implications for post-conflict statebuilding. Donors have considered remittances as a regular financial transfer that could be channelled to encourage reconstruction and to strengthen tax revenue and state capacity (see, e.g., Ratha 2005). However, not only does the case of Kosovo raise questions about the developmental impact of remittances, more importantly it highlights the limits of remittances from a diaspora made up mostly of refugees. Where a post-conflict environment becomes stable enough for refugees to return (or be returned), remittance transfers are likely to decline rapidly. As return is linked to growing stability, remittances decline at a time when a post-conflict state has started to develop the capacity to benefit from this income through more effective taxation. Remittances are therefore best seen as a very temporary and unreliable source of funding for strengthening state capacity. Changing migration policies in developed countries—many of which have ageing populations—such as the eschewing of forcible return of refugees that have found work, could help to alleviate this dilemma, if they were coupled with targeted development policies in post-conflict countries to make effective use of the remittance income.

REFUGEES AND PROPERTY RIGHTS

Establishing the rule of law has become one of the key priorities of post-conflict statebuilding operations, not least because it has come to be seen as a condition for successful economic development and for the integrity of political institutions. As Paddy Ashdown (2003) suggested in his reflections on his experience as High Representative in Bosnia:

> We should have put the establishment of the rule of law first, for everything depends on it: a functioning economy, a free and fair political system, the development of civil society, public confidence in police and the courts.

Rule of law efforts of statebuilding operations have focused on the strengthening of the legal system, on judicial reform, and in particular also on transitional justice issues. All of these have obvious implications for refugees. Probably the most important rule of law issue in the context of refugees and statebuilding, however, is the effective implementation of property rights, enabling refugees to return to and occupy their property.

Land issues and property rights have long received only limited attention in post-conflict statebuilding operations, but since the late 1990s have increasingly been identified as an important priority. The importance of clear and enforceable property rights for economic development has been emphasized by development economists (see in particular De Soto 2000), while others have highlighted their importance for the rule of law and curbing corruption, in particular in post-conflict environments (Eyre and Wittkowski 2002). As Daniel Fitzpatrick (2002: 3) has argued, 'Without that certainty, investment will be deterred, reconstruction slowed, and social and political stability put at risk.' The uncertainty of property rights in post-conflict situations and the difficulties of enforcing them can allow wartime elites to consolidate their control over economic assets, and entrench their political clout through patronage (see, e.g., Cramer 2008).

Uncertain and contested property rights have also been considered to be an important obstacle to refugee return, not least as uncertainty about the availability of a home on return reduces the incentive of refugees to go back. As the final report of the UN Human Rights Commission's Special Rapporteur on Housing and Property Restitution, Paulo Sergio Pinheiro, argues, property restitution is 'a key element of restorative justice, contributes to effectively deterring future situations of displacement and building sustainable peace'.[9] Still, establishing mechanisms to resolve competing property claims and even more importantly effectively enforcing them has proved to be very difficult, and few statebuilding operations have attempted it in a systematic fashion. In both Bosnia and Kosovo, however, where statebuilding efforts have been comparatively well funded, instruments to resolve and enforce property claims have been successfully established and offer useful insights into the impact of these processes on refugee return.

Bosnia

In Bosnia, the right to return and the right to have property returned were both enshrined in the Dayton Peace Agreement. As Article 1.1 of the annex on refugees and IDPs states,

> All refugees and displaced persons have the right freely to return to their homes of origin. They shall have the right to have restored to them property of which they were deprived in the course of the hostilities since 1991 and to be compensated for any property that cannot be restored to them.

In accordance with the Dayton Agreement, a mechanism was established to resolve such claims: the Commission on Real Property Claims of Refugees and Displaced Persons (CRPC), which had international members as well as members from the three ethnic groups. However, the enforcement of its decisions was left to the local parties. Their resistance to returns and restitution of property made minority returns almost impossible during the first two years after the war (Cox 1998).

In 1998 and 1999, under extensive international pressure, property laws across Bosnia were harmonized (and changes in part imposed by the High Representative). In addition, the international community increasingly coordinated its return efforts through the Reconstruction and Returns Task Force (RRTF), and changed its approach to return and restitution, making it a question of the rule of law rather than of political negotiation. Under the Property Law Implementation Plan (PLIP), officials who refused to implement the law were dismissed by the High Representative, and the implementation of the PLIP was monitored by international officials in regular review meetings on the municipal level (Heimerl 2005; International Crisis Group 2000). These changes led to a rapid increase in the resolution of property claims after 2000. When the CRPC was closed in 2003 and handed over its remaining cases to the local courts, it had decided and enforced over 90 per cent of the 220,000 claims that had been lodged (von Carlowitz 2005: 530). UNHCR statistics show the important impact this had on minority returns: in the Republika Srpska, for example, return of Bosniak refugees increased from 11,668 in 1999 to 25,279 in 2000, and further to 37, 628 in 2001.[10] As Heimerl (2005: 386) has pointed out, a significant number of refugees, probably around a quarter, did not return to their repossessed houses, and in a third of the cases that did, only a part of the family returned, normally older members. Similar patterns of minority return could be observed in Kosovo (Human Rights Watch 2009), and there as in Bosnia reflect the economic difficulties that many minority returnees face, as well as ongoing security concerns. Statebuilding has thus not restored the *status quo ante*, or the multi-ethnic society of the international community's statements and mandate. Whether this is an unrealistic yardstick is a matter for a different debate, and even if the 'return of property to people has not always resulted in the return of people to property' (Williams 2005: 445), the proceeds from selling or renting their properties has often given refugees the economic wherewithal to settle elsewhere. As the situations in Prijedor and Doboj (discussed earlier) highlight, even if the *status quo ante* has not been restored, the scale and scope of return enabled by the effective enforcement of property rights has still transformed many of the places that had been turned into mono-ethnic villages and towns by the war.

Kosovo

When UNMIK was established in Kosovo in June 1999, it quickly realized that serious violations of property rights during and since the end of the conflict were a continued source of tension and violence in the territory, posed obstacles to refugee return, and hindered its statebuilding efforts, in particular the establishment of democratic institutions.[11] The resolution of property issues in Kosovo was complicated by a range of factors. Following the damaging and destruction of more than 50 per cent of the housing stock in Kosovo, many Serb-owned properties in Prishtina and the South and Albanian properties in the Serb-majority northern municipalities were occupied by IDPs from the other ethnic group following the end of the conflict. Evicting them would have been politically difficult, and would have had detrimental humanitarian consequences. This situation was exacerbated by competing claims to properties arising from the Socialist Yugoslavia's system of social ownership and the legal discrimination of Albanians during the 1990s. Under socialist Yugoslavia's system of social ownership of enterprises, workers in socially owned enterprises often had rights to socially owned housing, and in the 1990s these use rights were often changed into ownership rights. After Albanian workers were systematically dismissed from these enterprises after 1989, these flats and houses were reallocated to Serbs, under discriminatory legislation. When UNMIK declared that the law in force before March 1989 should be the applicable law in Kosovo,[12] it raised the question whether any property transaction under laws passed in the decade after March 1989 was invalid, and the spectre of competing claims to ownership on the basis of different legislation. Furthermore, while sales of property from Serbs to Albanians were illegal under the discriminatory legislation of the 1990s, a number of informal transactions occurred, often without any documents, some of which were challenged by the sellers after the war.

To resolve and enforce competing property claims and regularize property rights, UNMIK established the Housing and Property Directorate (HPD) and a Housing and Property Claims Commission (HPCC).[13] Unlike in Bosnia, enforcement was the responsibility of the internationally run and financed HPD, not local authorities. Funding and administrative problems related in particular to UN Habitat, who was responsible for the HPD, delayed the collection of claims and decisions. By 2002, of the 17,785 claims that had been accepted, only 448 had been decided (Smit 2006: 67). In late 2002, UN-Habitat handed over HPD's operations to UNMIK, which made substantial administrative changes to increase HPD's effectiveness. HPD stopped accepting claims on 1 July 2003, and by 2007 it had decided on almost all of the approximately 29,000 claims it had received (Housing and Properties Claims Commission 2007).

While HPD has effectively resolved conflicting property claims, this has not led to a significant increase in returns, as it did in Bosnia. Indeed, HPD and the Claims Commission explicitly stated that they were a dispute resolution mechanism, not a return agency, and their coordination with return agencies in Kosovo was limited (Smit 2006). Numbers of refugees from Kosovo living in Serbia are contested, and range from as many as 220,000 to as few as 65,000. Still, returns have been low—at best in the low thousands in recent years, and since independence they have gone down to a trickle. Not only have the security conditions not been conducive—not least the violence in 2004 against minorities—but economic conditions also remain poor, with less than 15 per cent of Kosovars, regardless of ethnicity, with employment in the formal economy. The resolution of property rights, while an important aspect of post-conflict statebuilding in Kosovo, has had only limited effect on refugee return and more importantly on integrating refugees into the post-conflict society.

CONCLUSIONS

Statebuilding, as discussed in this chapter, entails the processes of creating the institutions of the state, the strengthening of their capacity, and their legitimation. The prominence of references to capacity building and governance in statebuilding discourses might suggest that this is a technical exercise with a single set of 'right' institutional solutions. However, it is instead a deeply political activity, involving fundamentally political choices about issues such as the access to power, representation in institutions, and the distribution and control over resources, to name just a few. In most statebuilding operations since the end of the Cold War, refugee return was an important part of the mandate, even if the actual economic and institution-building activities have given little explicit regard to this objective: the voice of refugees in these processes has often been limited, and their direct participation in institution-building practices marginal. Still, as this chapter has shown, refugees play a complex role in the politics of statebuilding, affecting both the economic and political dynamics of these efforts. In both Bosnia and Kosovo, refugees have been instrumentalized in conflicts over the character of the state, and in attempts to change or entrench local balances of power. Enabling their return has informed major rule of law reforms, in particular the resolution of private property rights; and their remittances have not only contributed significantly to physical reconstruction, but (as long as they last) also to the financial sustainability of state institutions. Taking account of their different roles enhances our understanding of the specific statebuilding efforts in different post-conflict countries.

In both Bosnia and Kosovo, refugees have been caught between the conflicting statebuilding and returns policies of major European donor countries. While these states on the one hand have invested heavily into reconstruction and economic development, and even more heavily into policing to prevent instability and violence, on the other hand they have returned refugees and exacerbated an already dire economic situation characterized by increasingly impoverished, desperate, and frustrated young populations, with a growing potential for social conflict. The desire to return refugees to Bosnia and Kosovo as quickly as possible has not only put pressure on already weak public services but has also meant fewer remittances and an increased danger of social unrest, undermining international efforts to stabilize these countries. Arguably, a more effective policy would take a comprehensive look at migration and statebuilding to maximize the impact of the resources devoted to them.

NOTES

1. Treaty of Lausanne, 1923.
2. For a conceptionalisation of the state along these lines, see Papagianni (2008: 51).
3. On the problematic relationship between statebuilding and peacebuilding, see Call (2008: 370–2).
4. For UNAMA in Afghanistan, see UN doc. S/2002/278 of 18 Mar. 2002; for Bosnia, see Dayton Agreement, Annex 7; for Kosovo, see SC Res. 1244 of 10 June 1999; for East Timor, see SC Res. 1272 of 25 Oct. 1999.
5. Exceptions include Caplan (2005), who devotes a whole chapter to the issue of refugee return.
6. OSCE, Provisional Election Commission, 'Rules and Regulations', 1996 edition.
7. Author's fieldnotes, July 2009. According to officials and NGOs working with displaced Roma in Mitrovica, they have also come under pressure from Roma refugees especially in Germany, who fear that their return to the Roma Mahalla will lead to forced repatriations of Kosovo Roma by the German government.
8. On the concept of spoilers, see Stedman (1997).
9. UN doc. E/CN.4/Sub.2/2005/17 of 28 June 2005.
10. Figures from www.unhcr.ba.
11. UN doc.S/1999/779 of 12 July 1999, paras. 77–8.
12. UNMIK Regulation 1999/24, On the Law Applicable in Kosovo, 12 Dec. 1999. UNMIK had previously declared that the applicable law should be that applicable prior to 24 March 1999 (as long as it was not in contradiction with international human rights law and UNMIK's mandate), Kosovo lawyers, judges, and officials refused to apply law that they perceived as an instrument of oppression, and instead demanded to apply the law applicable before the revocation of autonomy in March 1989.
13. UNMIK Regulation 1999/23, On the Establishment of the Housing and Property Directorate and the Housing and Property Claims Commission, 15 Nov. 1999.

BIBLIOGRAPHY

Ashdown, P. 2003. What I learned in Bosnia. *New York Times*, 28 October 2003.

Bellloni, R. 2005. Peacebuilding at the local level: refugee return to Prijedor. *International Peacekeeping*, Vol.12, 3: 434–447.

Black, R. 2001. Return and reconstruction in Bosnia-Herzegovina: missing link, or mistaken priority? *SAIS Review*, Vol.21, 2: 177–199.

Call, C. T. 2008. Building states to build peace? In: Call, C. T. with Wyeth, V. Eds. *Building states to build peace*, Boulder, Co.: Lynne Rienner. pp. 365–88.

——with Wyeth, V. Eds. 2008. *Building states to build peace*. Boulder, CO: Lynne Rienner.

Caplan, R. 2005. *International governance of war-torn territories—rule and reconstruction*. Oxford: Oxford University Press.

Chandler, D. 1999. *Empire in denial: the politics of state-building*. London: Pluto.

Chesterman, S. 2004. *You, the people: the United Nations, transitional administration, and state-building*. Oxford: Oxford University Press.

Chimni, B.S. 2004. From resettlement to involuntary repatriation: towards a history of durable solutions of refugee problems. *Refugee Survey Quarterly*, Vol. 23, 3: 55–73.

Chopra, J. 2000. The UN's kingdom in East Timor. *Survival*, Vol.42, 3: 27–40.

Clark, H. 2000. *Civil resistance in Kosovo*. London: Pluto Press.

Cliffe, S., Guggenheim, S., and Kostner, M. 2003. *Community-driven reconstruction as an instrument in war-to-peace transitions*, CPR Working Paper No.7. Washington DC: World Bank.

Cox, M. 1998. The right to return home: international intervention and ethnic cleansing in Bosnia and Herzegovina. *International Comparative Law Quarterly*, 47: 599–631.

Cramer, C. 2008. Trajectories of accumulation through war and peace. In: Paris, R. and Sisk, T. D. Eds. *The dilemmas of statebuilding: confronting the contradictions of postwar peace operations*. London: Routledge: 129–48.

Crisis Group. 1996. *Elections in Bosnia & Herzegovina*. Sarejevo: Crisis Group.

——2000. *Bosnia's refugee logjam breaks: is the international community ready?* Sarajevo/Washington/Brussels: Crisis Group.

——. 2002. *The Loya Jirga: a small step forward?* Kabul/Brussels, Crisis Group.

——. 2008. *Kosovo's Fragile Transition*. Brussels/Prishtina: Crisis Group.

Cunliffe, A. and Pugh, M. 1997. The politicisation of UNHCR in the former Yugoslavia. *Journal of Refugee Studies*. Vol. 10, 2: 134–53.

de Soto, H. 2000. *The mystery of capital: why capitalism triumphs in the west and fails everywhere else*. New York: Basic Books.

del Castillo, G. 2008. *Re-building war-torn states*. Oxford: Oxford University Press.

European Stability Initiative. 1999. *Interim evaluation of Reconstruction and Return Task Force (RRTF)*. Sarajevo: European Stability Initiative.

——. 2006. *Cutting the lifeline: migration, families, and the future of Kosovo*. Berlin/Istanbul: European Stability Initiative.

——. 2007. *A Bosnian Fortress: return, energy, and the future of Bosnia*. Berlin/ Sarajevo: European Stability Initiative.

Eyre, D. and Wittkowski, A. 2002. Privatization in Kosovo: the political economy of property rights and stability in a peace-building mission. *Sűdosteuropa Mitteilungen* Vol. 42, 4: 24–9.

Fitzpatrick, D. 2002. Land policy in post-conflict circumstances: some lessons from East Timor. *New Issues in Refugee Research*. Working Paper No. 58, Feb. 2002.

Ghani, A. and Lockhart, C. 2008. *Fixing failed states: a framework for rebuilding a fractured world*. Oxford: Oxford University Press.

Harvey, J. 2006. Return dynamics in Bosnia and Croatia: a comparative analysis. *International Migration*, Vol. 44, 3: 89–112.

Heimerl, D. 2005. The return of refugees and internally displaced persons: from coercion to sustainability. *International Peacekeeping*, Vol. 12, 3: 377–90.

Hockenos, P. 2003. *Homeland calling: exile patriotism and the Balkan wars*, Ithaca, NY: Cornell University Press.

Housing and Properties Claims Commission. 2007. *Final report of the Housing and Properties Claims Commission*. Prishtina: Housing and Property Claims Commission.

Human Rights Watch. 2009. *Kosovo: poisoned by lead—a health and human rights crisis in Mitrovica's Roma camps*. New York: Human Rights Watch.

ICISS. 2001. *The responsibility to protect: report of the international commission on intervention and state sovereignty*. Ottawa: International Development Research Centre.

IMF 2009. *Republic of Kosovo—IMF staff visit concluding statement*. Prishtina: IMF.

Jackson-Preece, J. 1998. Ethnic cleansing as an instrument of nation-state creation: changing state practices and evolving legal norms. *Human Rights Quarterly*, Vol. 20: 817–42.

Jahn, B. 2007*a*. The tragedy of liberal diplomacy: democratization, intervention, and statebuilding (part I). *Journal of Intervention and Statebuilding*. Vol. 1, 1 (2007): 87–106.

——. 2007*b*. The tragedy of liberal diplomacy: democratization, intervention, and statebuilding (part II), *Journal of Intervention and Statebuilding*, Vol. 1, 2: 211–29.

Judt, T. 2007. *Post war: a history of Europe since 1945*. London: Pimlico.

Kaufmann, C. 1998. When all else fails: ethnic population transfers and partitions in the twentieth century. *International Security*, Vol. 23, 2: 120–56.

Loescher, G. 1992. *Refugee movements and international security*, Adelphi Paper 268, International Institute for Strategic Studies, London: Brassey's.

Mazower, M. 1998. *Dark continent: Europe's twentieth century*. London: Penguin.

McDowell, C. and Eastmond, M. 2002. Transitions, state-building, and the 'residual' refugee problem: the East Timor and Cambodian repatriation experience. *Australian Journal of Human Rights*, Vol. 8, 1: 7–30.

McKittrick, A. 2008. *UNHCR as an autonomous organisation: complex operations and the case of Kosovo*. Working Paper No.50, Refugee Studies Centre, University of Oxford, Oxford, November 2008.

Ministry of Economy and Finance 2008. *Semiannual Macroeconomic Bulletin: Issue 1*, Prishtina: Ministry of Economy and Finance.

Mohapatra, S., Ratha, D. and Xu, Z. 2006. *Migration and development brief 2: remittance trends 2006*. Washington, DC: World Bank.

Morris, B. 1989. *The birth of the Palestinian refugee problem: 1947–49*. Cambridge: Cambridge University Press.

OSCE 2007. *Parallel structures in Kosovo, 2006–2007*. Prishtina: OSCE.

Paris, R. 2004. *At war's end: building peace after civil conflict*. Cambridge: Cambridge University Press.

——and Sisk, T. D. Eds. 2008. *The dilemmas of statebuilding: confronting the contradictions of postwar peace operations*. London: Routledge.

Papagianni, K. 2008. Participation and state legitimation. In: Call, C. T. with Wyeth, V. Eds. *Building states to build peace*, Boulder, CO: Lynne Rienner, 49–71.

Ratha, D. 2005. Workers' remittances: an important and stable source of development finance. In: Maimbo, S. M. and Ratha, D. Eds. *Remittances: development impact and future prospects*. Washington, DC: World Bank: 157–75.

Savage, K. and Harvey, P. Eds. 2007. *Remittances during crises: implications for humanitarian response*. London: Overseas Development Institute.

Stedman, S. J. 1997. Spoiler problems in peace processes. *International Security*, Vol. 22, 2: 5–53.

Stefanovic, D. 2008. The path to Weimar Serbia? Explaining the resurgence of the Serbian far right after the fall of Milosevic. *Ethnic and Racial Studies* Vol. 31, 7:1195–221.

Smit, A. 2006. Housing and property restitution and IDP return in Kosovo. *International Migration*, Vol. 44, 3: 63–87.

Tansey, O. 2009. *Regime-building: democratization and international administration*. Oxford: Oxford University Press.

United Nations. 1999. *Report of the Secretary General on the situation in East Timor*, UN Doc. S/1999/1024, 4 Oct. 1999.

——2002. *The situation in Afghanistan and its implications for international peace and security*. UN Doc. S/2002/278 of 18 Mar. 2008.

UNDP. 2005. *Getting to the core: a global survey on the cost of registration and elections*. Madrid and Washington: IFES/UNDP.

UNHCR. 2000. *Global Report 1999*. Geneva: UNHCR.

von Carlowitz, L. 2005. Resolution of property disputes in Bosnia and Kosovo: the contribution to peacebuilding. *International Peacekeeping*, Vol.12, 4: 547–61.

Williams, R. C. 2005. Post-conflict property restitution and refugee return in Bosnia and Herzegovina: implications for international standard-setting and practice. *International Law and Politics*, Vol. 37: 441–553.

Zaum, D. 2007. *The sovereignty paradox: the norms and politics of international statebuilding*. Oxford: Oxford University Press.

14

Forced Migration in the International Political Economy

Sarah Collinson

ABSTRACT

Explanations of forced migration typically focus on the description of the proximate triggers of flight or displacement. This chapter considers whether, using a political economy lens, it might be possible to strengthen interrogation of the deeper drivers and displacement and protection failures and so achieve a better explanatory understanding of forced migration processes in the international political economy. In both academic and policy circles, understanding of crisis situations still remains largely stove-piped into particular channels of concern with, for instance, poverty, violence, food insecurity, corruption, extremism, or displacement. A major impediment to improving understanding of forced migration is the tendency to isolate migration or displacement as a distinct phenomenon for analysis. This chapter draws attention to the diverse, complex, and 'embedded' nature of forced migration, and to the analytical challenges that this implies. Mainstream approaches within traditional international political economy are insufficient on their own: not only are they generally wedded to a particular 'grand' (usually neo-liberal or neo-Marxist) theory but they also fail to link to the local level or take sufficient account of social institutions and processes. A more 'eclectic' and locally connected political economy approach is needed which is concerned with the interaction of political, economic, and social processes in a society. Yet a question mark remains over how far one can remain agnostic as regards deeper theory: choices between competing theories may have to be made. The question of whether capitalism is inherently violent and exploitative is particularly important for understanding processes of forced displacement. Whatever the theoretical lens used, it is critically important to appreciate the centrality of processes of deep historical, social, economic, and political change. Are analysts asking not only 'what' displacement is taking place but also what processes and associated relationships and interactions of actors and institutional factors are involved? This form of analysis will lead to more satisfactory answers to the 'why' of forced migration at all levels, from global down to local. The chapter concludes with a number of observations that arise from this approach. For example, where people move as a consequence of sudden dispossession, this is generally perceived as 'forced' migration, but where these processes take place more gradually, the associated migration tends to be seen as 'voluntary' or 'economic'. In terms of underlying or 'deep' causes, the 'forced'/'voluntary' distinction may sometimes be arbitrary or misplaced.

Due in part to its historical connection to the emergence of international refugee law and the expansion of humanitarian assistance and protection for refugees, and no doubt also because of the massive human suffering involved, forced migration has tended to be approached in refugee studies as an aberration from an implied 'norm' of effective state protection and peaceful development. The formal language and legal provisions of refugee protection are concerned with finding 'solutions' to discrete cases or episodes of refugee flight, and the 'solutions' sought have been principally concerned with meeting the immediate protection and material needs of the refugees themselves, whether through local integration, resettlement, or return. Post-Cold War humanitarian interventionism has brought more robust international engagement with the 'causes' of forced migration through, for example, direct military and political action to contain mass refugee flows or facilitate large-scale returns; yet here attention has centred largely on identifying and tackling the proximate triggers of displacement and the most tangible obstacles to return. Meanwhile, the new international focus on internal displacement has meant closer scrutiny of conditions within countries affected by forced displacement, yet attention has been fixed on normative efforts to find legal and material remedies for IDPs' plight rather than on the deeper drivers of displacement and causes of failed state protection.

In most refugee studies then—and, indeed, in migration studies more generally—explanations of forced migration have been approached in mostly atomized and descriptive terms; where displacement has been analysed, this has been largely in isolation from the broader and deeper social, political, and economic processes that it is a part of. The consequence is that all manner of seemingly basic questions that would appear crucial for understanding the causes and dynamics of forced migration seem to have been left largely unaddressed and unanswered within refugee and migration studies. Can we identify any long-term structural and/or historical political or economic processes that are particularly significant as drivers of forced migration? If so, how are they connected? How do they play out in different contexts, and have they changed or varied across space and time? How can we account for changing or varying patterns and dynamics of forced migration in terms of changes and variation in underlying causative processes? How do displacement processes themselves affect these deeper causative factors or dynamics? Are diverse and varied experiences or processes of forced displacement connected at the causative level? Only by posing and seeking to answer these types of questions is it possible to build a more genuinely explanatory understanding of forced migration.

FORCED MIGRATION AND OTHER ILLS: EXCEPTIONS TO BE 'REMEDIED'?

The apparent diffidence within refugee studies about interrogating the deeper causes of forced displacement has been mirrored to a large extent in other parallel and connected areas of social science research, and in associated policy agendas. A progressive expansion of the international security agenda to encompass a variety of international threats and challenges associated with internal conflict and state fragility has triggered an explosion of interest and engagement in complex humanitarian emergencies, development failures, governance failures, and violence in many crisis- and conflict-affected 'fragile states'. This growing 'fragile states' industry has drawn new international academic and policy attention to the need to understand the drivers of crisis much more comprehensively. And yet the rhetoric that surrounds the analysis and the policies still far outstrips the reality. At the policy level, engagement on the ground remains generally piecemeal, incoherent, and insufficient to achieve substantial positive and sustained transformations in most contexts. The associated literature remains largely 'stuck' on the more proximate manifestations of particular crises, usually stove-piped into particular channels of concern with discrete problems, such as 'poverty', 'violence', 'food insecurity', 'corruption', or, indeed, 'displacement'. Much of this work rests on the implicit assumption that state fragility and the various ills associated with it are a negative and unfortunate departure from 'normal' development, and that—much like a machine that has gone wrong—can be 'fixed' with the right mix of technical, economic, and political interventions.

Where poverty has been the focus, for example, Maia Green observes how analyses 'tell us that people are hungry because of lack of access to food or that infant mortality is high because of poor health services.... [but] do not... tell us why food cannot be accessed or why health services are inadequate'; the emphasis on poverty as the problem, she argues, diverts attention from the social relations, local, national, and international, which *produce* poverty (Green 2005: 38). According to Harriss, development research 'has generally failed to address the dynamic, structural and relational factors that give rise to poverty' (Harriss 2007: 1). Similarly, Chris Cramer notes, in respect of conflict research, how explanations of violent conflict have tended to treat conflict as abnormal or perverse and largely ignored associated processes of social change. Thus, according to standard explanations 'War breaks out when development goes wrong and young men are unemployed'; this, he argues, leads to a misleading and limited understanding of violence and conflict (Cramer 2006: 137).

Meanwhile, development agencies have generally adopted a functional understanding of state fragility, often characterizing it in descriptive terms of bad governance and weak state will, capacity, and/or legitimacy, and often associating these with violent conflict and sustained poverty (McLoughlin 2009: 16). These, in turn, are often attributed to particular causal factors, such as insurgency, weak institutions, or social inequalities, which remain poorly analysed or understood. Often the response is dominated by technically or managerially oriented institution-building initiatives that fail to take on board the underlying complexity of the problems and challenges faced. Jonathan Di John notes, for example, how the World Bank's low-income countries under stress (LICUS) approach lacks clear policy advice, has 'few specifics on the nature of deep political economy analysis', and is predicated on the idea that conflict is 'development in reverse': the goal is to get countries to achieve 'good governance', which is viewed as an input into state-building and development, an idea that is problematic, ahistorical, and not supported by the evidence (Di John 2008: 7, citing Khan (2006)). Overall, the tendency to treat conflict, poverty, or displacement as exceptions to be remedied encourages a search for oversimplistic predictive or explanatory theories that emphasize one or other 'cause'—be it market failure, youth unemployment, or ethnic diversity—and fail to pay sufficient attention to the significance of complex historical processes.

Reacting against previous simplistic 'push-pull' models of migration, newer approaches in migration studies have sought to take on the complexity of human mobility and displacement more effectively, challenging any attempt to understand migration on the basis of a single level of analysis or discrete factor. They emphasize instead the interlinkages between different migration streams; the importance of agency, autonomy, perceptions, cultural, and historical factors and institutional constraints; the complex multi-level and transnational nature of migration; and the importance of social groups and relationships—including migration networks—for shaping migration dynamics and migration experiences, straddling migration 'sending', 'receiving', and 'transit' locations, and a range of actors within them (Gold 2005).

Livelihoods studies of migration among poor populations have revealed the extent of migration as a crucial, long-standing, and highly varied and dynamic livelihood strategy among many, if not most, rural communities in different parts of the world. Migration network theories emphasize that migration is embedded in political, ethnic, familial, and communal relationships, including complex social networks and relationships that strengthen collective agency among migrants and their communities. Migration systems theories emphasize the dynamic social, cultural, economic, and institutional impacts of migration at both the 'sending' and 'receiving' ends, with analyses seeking to incorporate both the causes and consequences of migration across entire migration processes and involving geographically dispersed 'transnational communities'.

But, for all this theoretical and analytical innovation, a central limitation in migration and refugee studies remains—the tendency to isolate migration or displacement as a distinct phenomenon for analysis, rather than seeking to understand it as intimately and deeply embedded within complex social, political, and economic processes, relationships, and institutions of which it is a part. As Castles has argued recently, a general theory of migration is probably 'neither possible nor desirable', yet significant progress could still be made by re-embedding migration research in a more general understanding of contemporary society; this, he states, 'requires forms of inquiry that start from a situation of very rapid and generalised changes', which may be referred to as processes of *social transformation*. The concept of social transformation, he suggests, provides a vehicle to enable interrogation and discussion of the complexity, interconnections, variability, contexuality, and 'multi-level mediations of change' associated with migration (Castles 2008).

What is needed, therefore, are new approaches with greater explanatory and analytical power, that can cope with diversity and that do not muddle cause and effects. Analysis of a particular situation of forced displacement, for example, needs to go beyond explaining displacement in terms of a group's experience of persecution or human rights abuse: we need to be asking why that group is vulnerable or persecuted or lacking basic protection, and what the implications are, what processes are involved in displacement or migration, and how these change over time. This resonates with growing demands within conflict studies, poverty research, and the fragile states literature for more subtle, nuanced, and sophisticated analytical approaches that can surpass the weak heuristic utility both of previous narrowly framed and dogmatic theories and of the overly descriptive case study approach. As Christopher Cramer notes in respect of conflict studies, case studies may not confirm any general theoretical constancy, but studies seeking theoretical constants 'lose their connection to reality by stripping away specific contexts and ignoring processes out of which war emerges' (Cramer 2006: 92–3). Tensions between the so-called 'American' and 'British' schools in international political economy trace a similar line of contention, with International Political Economy (IPE) in the United States arguably becoming overly reliant on liberal economic theory, while the British school has embraced interdisciplinary and pluralist approaches and a certain 'analytical eclecticism' (Cohen 2009; Katzenstein 2009; Wade 2009).

According to Cramer, a clear conclusion arising from a review of the leading explanations of contemporary wars 'is the simple argument that like most social phenomena wars or violent conflicts only ever have *many* causes' (Cramer 2006: 91). Very similar 'causes' and conditions can be observed to have very different implications and outcomes in different contexts; so what is needed is a different kind of theory or methodology that is concerned with seeking explanations rather than agglomerating detailed description, but is scaled back in ambition to allow for diversity and irregularities in what is observed (ibid.:94;135–136). The key to understanding wars, he argues, 'lies in accepting a great diversity of forms and origins—the causes and mechanisms of wars are not only multiple, they vary. This explains why most explanatory models of violent conflict have very limited success' (ibid.:199). Castles argues similarly in respect of migration that:

> complexity also implies *diversity*: if there are so many factors at work, the possible combinations become infinite: there is no such thing as a 'typical migratory process'. This in turn points to the crucial role of *context*—the links between migration and all the other economic, social, political and cultural relationships at work in particular places at a particular historical juncture. An historical understanding of societies and the relationships between them is crucial. For instance, no analysis of migration to Britain could be complete without understanding of the history of British colonialism and racism; no analysis of Mexican migration to the USA could be valid without consideration of the historical expansion of the USA and its past labour recruitment policies. (Castles 2008: 8).

Arguably, what is missing from much mainstream refugee and migration research—and from much related conflict, poverty, and fragile states literature—is a serious attempt to tackle this diversity head-on and to seek useful explanations and identify significant common factors and processes in the midst of it all. The trick is to find a way of doing this which avoids getting lost in endless descriptive detail that would, in aggregate, tell us little about *why* people move or are displaced, or why they fight or are poor, or why particular countries are experiencing the particular governance problems that they are. If grand theory is not up to this task, then what is? In the following section, I argue that political economy analysis can provide an entry point, but this is not the mainstream international political economy of the 'American school' wedded to narrow economic theory and largely divorced from social reality; it is rather a far more flexible and adaptable political economy approach that draws pragmatically on a mix of theories and other disciplines, and that aims for relatively straightforward heuristic framework that can help to make sense of the otherwise bewildering variety and complexity of the real world of forced migration.

TOWARDS A POLITICAL ECONOMY OF FORCED MIGRATION

In light of the limitations and problems with much mainstream migration, conflict, and international political economy analysis reviewed in the previous section, I would argue that the kind of analytical framework needed to gain a more comprehensive understanding of the drivers and dynamics of forced migration needs to meet five essential requirements. It must

1. Incorporate dynamic and varied social, economic, political, and environmental *institutions* and *processes*, with close attention to transitions or transformations in social relations and the political economy affecting the causes and dynamics of displacement.
2. Be potentially applicable to a spectrum of highly varied, dynamic, and changing forms of mobility and displacement in different contexts.
3. Situate analysis of processes of abuse, violence, and associated forced migration within the changing (historical) social, economic, political, and environmental context.
4. Allow flexibility in terms of applicable theory, not relying exclusively on a particular grand or 'macro' theory of international political economy (e.g. Marxist/World Systems, neo-liberal economics, globalization theory).
5. Incorporate processes and analysis at multiple levels, including direct linkage to the local level.

It is noteworthy that, according to these requirements, mainstream approaches within traditional international political economy are not sufficient on their own. Not only are they generally wedded to a particular 'grand' (usually neo-liberal or neo-Marxist) theory but they also fail to link directly at the local level; and by restricting analysis to the structures and processes of the economic system and the formal political realm, they cannot account for the diverse *social* mechanisms that perpetuate inequality, or support relations of exploitation (Mosse 2007: 18), or encourage particular patterns or dynamics of mobility or displacement. These approaches therefore provide limited insight into how the macro dynamics of the international capitalist system determine or affect, in complex ways, the real-life experiences of individuals, households, and communities.

A more 'eclectic' and locally connected political economy approach is needed, which, as I have described elsewhere, is concerned with the interaction of political and economic processes in a society: the distribution of power and wealth between different groups and individuals, and the processes that create, sustain, and transform these relationships over time (Collinson 2002, citing Le Billon (2000)). Indeed, in any political economy framework, the location, relationships, and flows of resources and relative power are central to every aspect of the analysis. These include financial capital, natural resources, manufactured goods, and intellectual property—the core stuff of economic livelihoods at the local level and of national, regional, and global economies at the macro level. How these resources, ownership and control over them, and the benefits associated with them are distributed among and by actors, organizations, and institutions at different levels—including state and non-state organizations, foreign governments, international institutions, markets, courts, laws, media, class, caste, family, war (economies), ethnic divisions, welfare institutions, nationalism, cultures of violence or impunity—is determined to a large extent by the dynamic interplay of competing interests, activities, and actions among them in a variety of social, political, and economic arenas—at the local and wider national and global levels.

Some actors or organizations are more powerful and/or better endowed with resources than others, and interactions between different actors and organizations are mediated by formal and informal institutions or 'rules of the game', such as laws, kinship structures, or patrimonial relationships, and this has a crucial bearing on the specific dynamics, implications, and outcomes associated with the interplay of competing interests and actions or activities in any particular situation. This reflects and produces changing power and wealth relationships and generates continuous and varied processes of political, economic, social, and environmental change and transformation, such as famine, displacement, migration, exploitation, globalization, development, economic growth or diversification, reform, impoverishment, militarization, securitization, liberalization, state collapse, privatization, reform, etc. At the local level, the impacts, outcomes, and implications of these competing interests and actions are dynamic and highly varied, affecting a wide range of institutions and processes connected directly with people's lives and livelihoods, such as relative poverty, access to social protection, displacement, migration, environmental change or shocks, food security, or

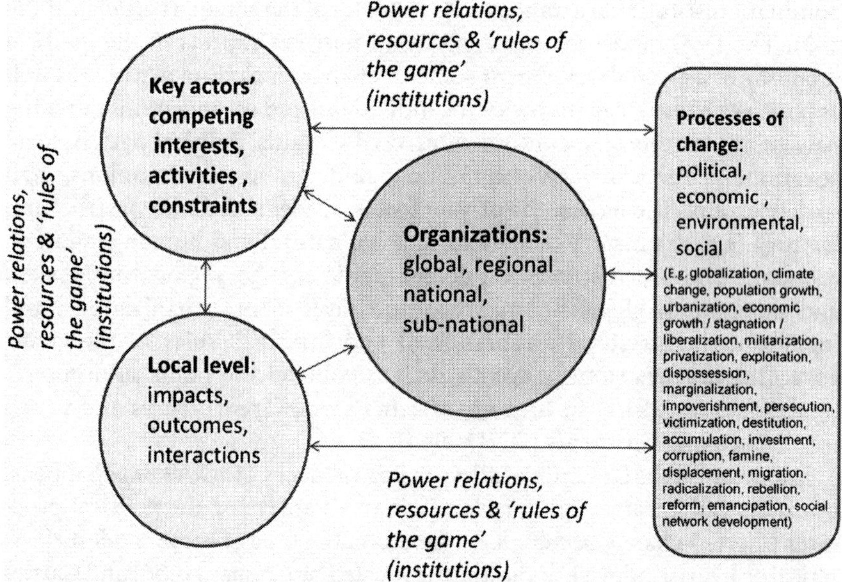

Figure 14.1 Framework for analysis of the political economy of vulnerability and forced migration

land tenure. Particularly pertinent to the analysis of forced migration is the concept of vulnerability within this approach, understood in terms of powerlessness rather than simply material need. Vulnerability and power are therefore analysed in terms of political and economic processes over time, in terms, for instance, of neglect, exclusion, or exploitation, in which a variety of groups and actors play a part (ibid.) (see Figure 14.1).

Arguably ahead of the mainstream academic curve, this type of grounded interdisciplinary approach to political economy analysis has gained considerable ground in development policy circles in recent years. Most notably, perhaps, the UK's Department for International Development's 'Drivers of Change' (DoC) initiative has been directly concerned with sharpening understanding of the 'deeper structural and institutional factors which frame the political context within which individuals and organisations act', including the analysis of the political processes which drive or restrain change and development; this, in turn, reflects a growing recognition 'that politics is fundamental, if not primary, in shaping development choices, strategies, trajectories and outcomes', since development 'is an unavoidably transformative process affecting social, economic and political relationships and institutions'. It consequently 'involves change that must inevitably challenge established interests and prevailing structures of power and hence the dominant institutional arrangements (or rules of the game)' (Leftwich 2006: 2–3). The DoC model focuses analysis on four key aspects of the political economy of a given development context: change (including negative as well as positive change); agents, including individuals and organizations pursuing particular interests (e.g. political elites, civil servants, political parties, local government, the judiciary, the military, faith groups, trade unions, civil society groups, the media, the private sector, academics, donors); structural features (e.g. the history of state formation, natural and human resources, economic and social structures, demographic change, regional influences, and integration; globalization, trade and investment, urbanization); and institutions, understood as the formal and informal 'rules of the game' governing the behaviour of agents, such as political and public administration processes, which, in turn are affected by power structures and vested interests among key agents (DFID 2004).

Importantly, the DoC model does not posit a theory of how change happens, but is instead a framework for identifying and analysing the political processes whereby change occurs. It is, therefore, the type of more modest theoretical or heuristic device of the kind advocated by Cramer (2006) and Castles (2008)—rather than supporting a grand explanatory theory, it can 'both accommodate different theories of politics and change and, when integrated with appropriate comparative and historical work, it offers the basis for classifying past, present and future paths of development in rapidly changing geo-political circumstances' (Leftwich 2006: 3).

However, particularly in respect of analysing processes of change, a big question mark hovers over how far one can remain agnostic as regards underlying theory. At certain points, choices between competing theories may have to be made, ideally on the basis of relevant empirical evidence. For instance, in conflict studies, and all within the frame of political economy analysis, several 'big ideas' relating to political economy and the primary causes of violent conflict continue to jostle for position, including: (*a*) the liberal view of war as irrational and necessarily negative; (*b*) a view of violent conflict as a ubiquitous feature of clientelist and patrimonial states that are purposefully constructed by elites to promote their interests in capital accumulation and maintenance of power; (*c*) that contemporary 'new wars' are qualitatively distinct from old wars in terms of the nature of financing, causes and methods of warfare, with war financing highly dependent on legal and illicit global networks; or (*d*) the 'resource curse' theory, which posits that abundance of natural resources can raise the risks, intensity, and duration of conflict (Di John 2008: 2–3; on this point, see also Cramer (2006)).

Cramer suggests that while theories of political economy cannot provide any kind of predictive template, it is still valid to search for substantial causal factors in the (international) political economy: 'the way in which capitalism and power are spread through the world and the variety of experiences of late development are at the heart of contemporary conflicts' (Cramer 2006: 94). Particularly important for understanding processes of forced displacement associated with malign governance and/or violent conflict is whether capitalism as a system is inherently violent and exploitative at different levels and over time. Marxist theory and neo-Marxist theories of international political economy focus attention on processes of exploitation and/or 'primitive accumulation' through which powerful actors coercively accumulate economic surplus. This is seen as a common feature of pre-, proto- and sometimes advanced capitalist societies (see, e.g., Polanyi 1944), and is typically associated with processes of intentional exclusion, marginalization, persecution, and/or dispossession of relatively poor, powerless, or vulnerable individuals or groups (see, e.g., Du Toit et al. 2005; and on famine as an consequence of intentional dispossession of vulnerable groups, see Keen (1994)). By insisting that poverty and violence—and associated displacement—are created by continual processes of exploitation and dispossession that are integral to global capitalism, this approach is fundamentally incompatible with the liberal vision of capitalism, which, according to Cramer, largely 'prettifies reality': although capitalism 'needs peace and stability', it also 'often thrives on war and instability and is typically implanted through violence' (ibid.:202–204).

Transformative processes always affect social, economic, and political relationships and institutions, and so always challenge established interests, power structures and relationships, and key institutions. Where one group is seeking to secure control or exclusive ownership of a key resource, such as land or access to a labour market, it is likely that another group is being excluded and marginalized. Personal histories of suffering, survival, social mobility, and migration within rural communities of the Eastern Cape in South Africa related by Du Toit et al. show how many of the poorest households are adversely incorporated into the broader macro political economy (including through migration) *and* within a set of highly localized and unequal socio-economic relationships; power relations are rooted in access to and claims over key resources (land, patronage, labour), and these, in turn, lead to particular households and groups being marginalized, disempowered, and trapped in long-term poverty (Du Toit et al. 2005).

Since the twin processes of forceful asset accumulation and displacement of people is precisely what is involved in primitive accumulation, Cramer suggests that the whole phenomenon of international displacement and international refugees can be understood in terms of the separation of people from their means of production (ibid.: 217). Indeed, one does not have to look hard to find contemporary examples of dispossession and displacement associated with primitive accumulation: witness, to mention only a few random examples, the forced and probably permanent displacement of Tamil communities from now designated 'Special Economic Zones' in the east of Sri Lanka; the reportedly violent evictions of rural communities by oil companies and associated private security firms in Nigeria; the association of logging concessions, violence, and large-scale displacement in Burma; and massive levels of 'development-induced' displacement in numerous countries across the world, including the forcible displacement of poor rural communities by property developers on edges of cities across China.

Whatever the theoretical lens used, what is of critical importance is to appreciate the centrality of processes of 'deep' historical social, economic, and political change, and to approach forced displacement in all its various guises as an integral and, at a general level, probably unavoidable, even 'normal', aspect of these change processes. Processes of change that are discernible in any particular context are integrally linked to the broader functioning of interacting local, sub-national, national, regional and international, or international political economies. Capitalism dominates at the global level and extends down to the local level for better (according to the liberal view), or worse (according to a neo-Marxist view), or better for some than others (e.g. according to accounts of patrimonialism, warlordism, and 'parallel states'—see, for instance, Briscoe 2008). Social change always involves competition between different individuals, groups, or actors or interest groups; it often involves conflict, sometimes this conflict is violent; sometimes it results in forms of violence or dispossession that cause particular dynamics of forced displacement; and this competition or conflict is always mediated by institutions that, in combination, are unique to that context. The key issue is whether, at every step, analysts are not only asking 'what' displacement is taking place but also what processes of change and associated relationships and interactions of actors and institutional factors are generating that displacement. This form of analysis leads to more satisfactory answers to the 'why' of forced migration.

FORCED MIGRATION VIEWED THROUGH A POLITICAL ECONOMY LENS

Conflict and violence, however, manifest at the local, inter-communal, sub-national, or at a wider level, is what drives forced displacement; and the causes of conflict and violence are arguably linked to capitalist transformation.

The precise mix of social, political, and economic processes; interests; and actors and institutions associated with particular contexts or episodes of displacement will be highly context-specific but nonetheless explicable at both broad and more intimate levels in terms of an analysis of these connected factors and their interactions over space and time. According to a neo-Marxist view of the international political economy, it is to be expected that a global capitalist system that, by its very (exploitative) nature, generates mass poverty and destitution and creates profound social, political, and economic transformations that are likely to be associated with processes of exclusion, dispossession, violence, and/or persecution. These will inevitably lead to displacement in certain places at certain times, sometimes of individuals, sometimes communities, and sometimes the mass migration of whole populations.

At the very least, examining migration and related processes and their causes and consequences within the context of local, national and international political economy, and processes of social change may reveal dynamics and implications associated with migration that might otherwise be missed or downplayed. Richard Black and Mohamed Sessay's study (1997) of Liberian and Sierra Leonean refugees and their impact on land use and deforestation in three villages in Guinea, for instance, challenged the widely held view that rapid rates of deforestation had simply resulted from the increased demand for land caused by the arrival of large numbers of refugees. Historical examination of the development of the agricultural economy of the region, and of socio-political change in local communities revealed a more complex relationship between refugee arrivals and deforestation. Local farmers—keen to establish a claim over forest land in a context where indigenous rights of access appeared under threat, and keen to invest in production of coffee and other cash crops (and encouraged to do so by government policy)—allowed refugees to clear forest land which they themselves later planted with coffee or cocoa or other cash crops. This study, they argue, 'highlights the potential role of refugee farmers as a resource that is capable of being mobilized by both the state and local communities in a developing struggle for control over the land resources of the forest region'. Hence 'the presence of refugees in an area is best viewed as a catalyst for more dynamic social relations, rather than as necessarily having one or other 'environmental' impact' (Black and Sessay 1997: 605).

At a higher or 'macro' level, a political economy approach may sensitize analysis to broad trends that are not so obvious in any specific displacement context. At the global level, for example, Mark Duffield has pointed out the stark divisions in the contemporary international political economy between the 'insured' and 'uninsured' populations of the world. The international development regime, he argues, is predicated on the widespread assumption or acceptance that non-Western populations are essentially self-reliant in terms of their general economic, social, and welfare requirements. The focus of many international development actors, therefore, is on improving self-reliance among the poor through helping to meet basic needs. When self-reliance breaks down, humanitarian assistance functions as a regime of international social protection of last resort (Duffield 2007). This means that the international 'poverty-reduction' industry has placed huge reliance on local level actors, institutions and processes, with arguably far too little attention to other key factors, including processes of exploitation or marginalization that lie at the root of much of the chronic poverty or vulnerability that they are seeking to address. The so-called 'sustainable livelihoods' approaches, for example, are notorious for ignoring the 'policies, institutions and processes' (negative as well as positive) and the broader 'vulnerability context' that affect people's livelihoods (Collinson 2003; De Haan and Zoomers 2005).

The complex, dynamic, and multi-layered nature of migration—'forced' and 'voluntary'—suggests that only a comparatively complex and multi-layered mix of policy measures could hope to achieve desired impacts on any migration process. For example, where migration includes large numbers of 'survival' or 'coping' migrants, or where it can be demonstrated that migrants' movement is determined and controlled to a significant extent by identifiable and exploitative social and economic structures, actors, and relationships—*and*, crucially, where policy is focused on the well-being of migrants and their communities, or on the protection of rural livelihoods, and/or slowing permanent rural–urban migration—the mix of relevant policy might include measures to address the underlying vulnerability of the poorest households and/or the regulatory environment in which exploitative economic and other actors operate. These same migration streams might also include large numbers of 'accumulating' migrants whose livelihoods or strategies might either be jeopardized or supported by the same policies.

What is deemed 'appropriate' policy action is, of course, a highly political and contested question, reflecting differing views as to what policy should ultimately be seeking to achieve: improved well-being of vulnerable migrants and their households and communities? Reduced rates of rural–urban or international migration? Improved 'development outcomes' (however defined) from migration streams? Maximization of remittance flows? Different policy and other actors, of course, will be seeking varied, and sometimes conflicting, policy outcomes at different levels and in different contexts. Consequently, any situation of displacement is likely to be influenced (whether intentionally or not) by highly dynamic interactions of policy objectives, measures, and impacts that will vary considerably from one context to another and over time.

Viewed through a political economy lens, migration is frequently a 'self-reliance' response by the poor to processes of exploitation, impoverishment, and dispossession. Where people move as a consequence of sudden dispossession, this is generally perceived by policy-makers and analysts as 'forced' or 'involuntary' migration (although not necessarily a refugee movement, unless in circumstances associated with violence, conflict, or severe political crisis); where these processes take place more gradually over a longer period, the associated migration tends to be perceived as 'voluntary' and usually 'economic'. In terms of underlying causes, this 'forced'/'voluntary' distinction may be arbitrary or misplaced—the defining aspect may be more one of the suddenness, or not, of the decision or trigger for migration, and relative *agency* exercised by migrants in the decision-making and strategies associated with migration, rather than on whether the migration is forced *per se*. Moreover, political processes (e.g. marginalization or exclusion) are likely to play a key role; so the label 'economic migration' is also potentially misleading.

People's relative agency at the local level, affected both by immediate and broader social relations and processes of change, always has a crucial bearing on the dynamics of displacement and subsequent mobility. Yet, despite the development industry's faith in people's own abilities to cope at the local level, there is a serious lack of attention to what 'self-reliance' means in practice in poor and vulnerable households and communities. There is a widely held assumption that in poor communities, people are mutually supportive and that supportive family and community institutions are the key to how people get by. Yet one might reflect on what really should be realistically expected among poor and highly vulnerable communities with little in the way of resources and options to fall back on, and often brutalized and traumatized by repeated cycles of violent conflict. In fact, coping and survival at the margins is just as likely to involve highly competitive, atomized, and/or destructive strategies that may benefit some but seriously harm others (Collinson 2003). Extreme, but depressingly common, examples include young men joining militias as a livelihood strategy; members of militias or army soldiers (often unpaid) expropriating resources—often violently—from poor and unprotected communities; direct or indirect participation in illicit markets, criminal networks, and war economies; and prostitution, slavery, and theft (ibid.). Many of the social, economic, and political ills that Western governments have identified as requiring responses in the interests of 'stability' are precisely those that one would expect to be prevalent as a consequence of 'self-reliance' among poor and vulnerable communities in poor and conflict- or crisis-affected 'fragile states', such as high levels of sporadic violence, criminality, economic collapse, displacement, and chronic poverty.

The arguably arbitrary nature of the 'forced'/'voluntary' distinction where large numbers of people are moving in response to conditions of severe deprivation, highly precarious livelihoods, and where 'coping' or 'self-reliance' is leading to the depletion of household or community assets, accounts for much of the analytical and policy confusion surrounding the problem of 'mixed migration flows'. One of the reasons that the phenomenon of mixed migration is so problematic for policy-makers and researchers is that the migration movements involved and associated networks are not clearly segmented according to conventional migration 'categories'. This reflects the complex institutional and political and economic dynamics at play, including, for example, the degree of power and control over people's movement that is exerted by non-state actors, including smugglers and traffickers who (unlike states' migration control institutions) are not concerned with which categories particular migrants belong to. The focus on migrants' relative agency in migration processes and the structure and dynamics of migration processes (mediated by social institutions and power relations) might help to shed light on commonalities and differences in the experiences, problems, and outcomes for different migrants caught up in 'mixed flows', despite diversity in the original causes and initial dynamics of their migration.

As highlighted by Anthony Richmond's concept of 'reactive' migration, the agency of migrants whose initial movement was compelled for whatever reason—by violence and insecurity, fear of persecution, development projects, and/or as a survival strategy in response to an economic, environmental or other shock, or due to collapsed or destroyed livelihoods—is likely to be significantly constrained in various ways (Richmond 1994). However, some refugees and internally displaced persons have a lot more control over their own destiny than others, and some certainly enjoy greater agency following their initial flight than many 'economic' migrants. Whether in the context of complex 'mixed flows' or in the context of more discrete migration processes or systems, what determines migrants' relative agency, and hence much about the circumstances, dynamics, experience, and outcomes of their migration, is how their movement and welfare is affected by the particular social, economic, political, relational, and institutional context in which it takes place, both at the micro and macro levels. For example, where movement and welfare is supported or facilitated by humanitarian agencies and permissive state policies and institutions that protect certain rights (e.g. leave to enter, free movement, right to work), 'compelled' migrants are likely to enjoy greater degrees of agency and possibly better welfare than migrants moving in circumstances where fundamental rights are denied, and where exploitative relationships (e.g. with traffickers, labour recruiters, employers) dominate the dynamics of movement. As a consequence of the specific circumstances of their movement, migrants who initially lack agency may gain more power and control over time, while others may find themselves increasingly at the mercy of other actors and other interests.

The very existence of an international humanitarian regime, representing an international welfare regime of last resort, is a direct corollary of the domination of the global economy by liberal democracies with policies of 'enlightened self-interest' and an impulse to address the most extreme situations of destitution and suffering where they arise. Thus, from a political economy perspective, the international humanitarian regime—a key global institution—arguably exists because of negative processes associated with capitalism, such as exploitation, marginalization, impoverishment, and dispossession, and in turn affects these processes through the humanitarian responses that it generates. That the international humanitarian refugee regimes and their activities are poorly coordinated and severely imbalanced across different emergencies is, in turn, a function of the competing organizational interests and donors' political, strategic, economic, and political interests and constraints; in Africa, the geopolitical and economic stakes have generally been much lower for the industrialized states, with the result that armed conflicts—and the refugee situations created by those conflicts—have been allowed to persist for years on end.

CONCLUSION

Forced displacement is always a highly complex phenomenon that is deeply embedded in the structures, relationships, and processes of micro and macro political economies and in the dynamics of people's livelihoods and relative security at the local level. Specific patterns of migration are therefore determined to a great extent by the dynamic interaction of individual or household protection and livelihood strategies with a broad range of micro, meso, and macro level relationships, processes, institutions, and structures that make up the social, economic, political, and historical contexts in which migration takes place—such as wealth distribution and access to land and other resources, kinship structures, local and wider governance institutions, labour markets, social and commercial networks, state welfare, and security regimes. The particular opportunities and constraints affecting people's options, strategies, experiences, and outcomes in the face of immediate threats or longer-term changes in their circumstances depend to a great extent on the differential distribution and changing dynamics of power, vulnerability, agency, and opportunity within households, communities, and the wider population.

A key rationale for adopting a political economy approach in the analysis of forced migration is to move beyond overly deterministic or simplistic explanations focused on proximate triggers or single causal factors, while also seeking to make some sense of the extreme diversity and complexity of displacement in the real world. While the dynamics of forced migration are highly varied, complex, and context-specific, variability and complexity need not lead to resignation as regards the prospects of developing useful theory (Castles 2008: 14). A robust political economy framework drawing on a variety of theoretical and analytical approaches, that explicitly links macro-, meso-, and micro-level processes, and that helps tease out the relational links across and between processes of change, institutions and key actors, and their interests and actions, holds a genuine prospect of providing a heuristic approach that can support explanatory insights while also handling extreme variability and complexity.

BIBLIOGRAPHY

Black, R. and Sessay, M. 1997. Forced migration, land-use change and political economy in the forest region of Guinea. *African Affairs* 96(385), October 1997, pp. 587–605.

Briscoe, I. 2008. The proliferation of the 'parallel state'. *FRIDE Working Paper 71*, October 2008. Madrid: Fundación para las Relaciones Internacionales y el Diálogo Exterior.

Castles, S. 2008. Understanding global migration: a social transformation perspective. Paper presented at the Conference on Theories of Migration and Social Change, International Migration Institute, University of Oxford, 1–3 July 2008.

Cohen, B.J. 2009. Striking a nerve. *Review of International Political Economy* 16(1), pp. 136–43.

Collinson, S. 2002. Politically informed programming: using a political economy approach. *Network Paper 41*. London: Overseas Development Institute, Humanitarian Policy Group. http://www.odihpn.org/documents/networkpaper041.pdf

——ed. 2003. *Power, livelihoods and conflict: case studies in political economy analysis for humanitarian action*. HPG Report 13. London: Overseas Development Institute.

Cramer, C. 2006. *Civil war is not a stupid thing: accounting for violence in developing countries*. London: Hurst & Company.

De Haan, L. and Zoomers, A. 2005. Exploring the frontier of livelihoods research. *Development and Change* 36(1), 27–47.

DFID 2004. *Drivers of change public information note*. London: Department for International Development.

Di John, J. 2008. Development as state-making—conceptualising the causes and consequences of failed states: a critical review of the literature. *CSRC Working Paper No.25.* January 2008. London: Crisis States Research Centre (School of Oriental and African Studies).

Du Toit, A., Skuse, A. and Cousins, T. 2005. *The political economy of social capital: chronic poverty, remoteness and gender in the rural Eastern Cape.* PLAAS and CPRC Working Paper. Manchester & Cape Town: Chronic Poverty Research Centre & Programme for Land and Agrarian Studies.

Duffield, M. 2007. *Development, security and unending war: governing the world of peoples.* Cambridge and Malden, MA: Polity.

Gold, S. J. 2005. Migrant networks: a summary and critique of relational approaches to international migration. In: Romero, M. and Margolis, E. (eds.) *The Blackwell companion to social inequalities.* Malden, MA: Blackwell.

Green, M. 2005. *Representing poverty and attacking representations: some anthropological perspectives on poverty in development.* Global Poverty Research Group Working Paper 9. Manchester and Oxford: GPRG.

Harriss, J. 2007. *Bringing politics back in to poverty analysis: why understanding of social relations matters more for policy on chronic poverty than measurement.* Q-Squared Working Paper 34 (April 2007); paper commissioned by the Chronic Poverty Research Centre and presented at the CPRC 'Workshop on Concepts and Methods for Analysing Poverty Dynamics and Chronic Poverty', Manchester 2006. Toronto: Centre for International Studies, University of Toronto.

Katzenstein, P. J. 2009. Mid-Atlantic: sitting on the knife's sharp edge. *Review of International Political Economy,* 16(1), pp. 122–35.

Keen, D. 1994. *The benefits of famine: a political economy of famine and relief in Southwestern Sudan, 1983–1989.* Princeton, NJ: Princeton University Press.

Khan, M.H. 2006. Governance, economic growth and development since the 1960s. Background paper for World Economic and Social Survey 2006.

Le Billon, P. with Macrae, J., Leader, N., and East, R. 2000. *The political economy of war: what relief agencies need to know.* Network Paper 33. London: ODI.

Leftwich, A. 2006. *From drivers of change to the politics of development: refining the analytical framework to understand the politics of the places where we work.* Part 3: Final Report. London: York: University of York.

McLoughlin, C. 2009. *Topic guide on fragile states.* London: Governance and Social Development Resource Centre (GSDRC).

Mosse, D. 2007. *Power and the durability of poverty: a critical exploration of the links between culture, marginality and chronic poverty.* Working Paper 107. Manchester: Chronic Poverty Research Centre.

Polanyi, K. 1944. *The great transformation: the political and economic origins of our time.* Boston, MA: Beacon Press.

Richmond, A. 1994. *Global apartheid.* Oxford: Oxford University Press.

Wade, R. 2009. Beware what you wish for: lessons for international political economy from the transformation of economics. *Review of International Political Economy,* 16(1), pp. 106–21.

Index

Lightning Source UK Ltd.
Milton Keynes UK
UKOW03f0010060914

238120UK00001B/1/P